WORLD OF
ATHLETICS

Edited by Ron Pickering
Compiled by Mel Watman

1979

MACDONALD AND JANE'S · LONDON

© Macdonald and Jane's Publishers Limited 1979

House Editor: *Kate Truman*

Front cover: Henry Rono and Dave Babiracki (Photo: Tony Duffy, All-Sport Photographic)
Previous page: Marita Koch (Photo: Tony Duffy)

Published by Macdonald and Jane's Publishers Limited,
Paulton House, 8 Shepherdess Walk, London, N1 7LW

Photoset, printed and bound in Great Britain by
Redwood Burn Limited, Trowbridge & Esher

Contents

Foreword from Dewhurst

What can I say about this athletic yearbook for 1979, except that its appeal is no longer merely parochial but now decidedly international. Each edition has sold out so rapidly that this year the number printed has been increased. Ron Pickering and his team have excelled themselves in producing a book which is not only packed with all the facts and records, but with eminently readable and informative comment. The book itself is like a first-rate athletics performance. Hours and hours of hard slog and painstaking preparation, meticulous checking to ensure everything is absolutely right for the starting pistol and then the final performance – according to plan, stylish and entertaining.

Even if you just pick up the book to check a fact, a date, a time, a distance or a finishing order, you will not snap it shut like a dictionary when you have found the answer you were seeking. You will linger over the text, study the action photographs and thoroughly enjoy your browse through the athletic performances of 1978.

One of the features of the past year was the growing enthusiasm for jogging. An awareness of how easy it is to become slothful and sluggish was stimulated by lively publicity and now tens of thousands of people know the great feeling of well-being following energetic activity. Once the deep relaxation which follows healthy exercise has been experienced, the shallow breathing and muscle-cramping comfort of an afternoon in an armchair by the fire seems far less attractive.

More and more people are now actively participating in athletics and sport in general. This is excellent for the health and vitality of the country so once again Dewhurst, The Master Butcher, is proud to be invited to sponsor *World of Athletics 1979*.

C. S. Cullimore

C. S. Cullimore CBE
Managing Director
J. H. Dewhurst Ltd

Metric Conversions

For the benefit of readers who might still be more familiar with measurements in feet and inches we list here key metric conversions. Note that 1 metre equals approximately 3ft 3¼in, 10 centimetres approximately 4 in.

High Jump

metres	ft	in
1.60	5	3
1.70	5	7
1.75	5	8¾
1.80	5	10¾
1.85	6	0¾
1.90	6	2¾
1.95	6	4¾
2.00	6	6¾
2.05	6	8¾
2.10	6	10¾
2.15	7	0½
2.20	7	2½
2.25	7	4½
2.30	7	6½
2.35	7	8½
2.40	7	10½

Pole Vault

3.80	12	5½
4.00	13	1½
4.20	13	9¼
4.40	14	5¼
4.60	15	1
4.80	15	9
5.00	16	4¾
5.10	16	8¾
5.20	17	0¾
5.30	17	4½
5.40	17	8½
5.50	18	0½
5.60	18	4½
5.70	18	8¼
5.80	19	0¼

Long Jump

6.00	19	8¼
6.20	20	4¼
6.40	21	0
6.60	21	8
6.80	22	3¾
7.00	22	11¾
7.25	23	9½
7.50	24	7¼
7.75	25	5¼
8.00	26	3
8.20	26	11
8.40	27	6¾
8.60	28	2¾
8.80	28	10½
9.00	29	6½

Triple Jump and Shot

14.00	45	11¼
14.50	47	7
15.00	49	2½
15.50	50	10¼
16.00	52	6
16.50	54	1¾
17.00	55	9¼
17.50	57	5
18.00	59	0¾
18.50	60	8½
19.00	62	4
20.00	65	7½
21.00	68	10¾
22.00	72	2¼
23.00	75	5½

Long Throws

40.00	131	3
45.00	147	8
50.00	164	0
55.00	180	5
60.00	196	10
65.00	213	3
67.50	221	5
70.00	229	8
75.00	246	1
77.50	254	3
80.00	262	5
85.00	278	10
90.00	295	3
95.00	311	8
100.00	328	1

In My View

Ron Pickering

In this, the sixth edition of the *World of Athletics* yearbook, we have quite deliberately set out to take a more international view of our sport. One obvious reason is that no other such publication exists and another is that ours is the most international of all sports – we are the focal point of the Olympic movement, and not only is Britain inextricably involved in world affairs but, by historical tradition, is so often in the vanguard of sports diplomacy. It sounds smug, but the International Amateur Athletic Federation is housed in Britain, the revival of the Olympic festival owes its lifeblood to that era of muscular Christianity nurtured in the English public schools by Thomas Arnold et al, quite as much as it does to Greek history and ever since that revival there has been a long line of British statesmen in the sport at international level. It may breed a certain arrogance, but never apathy. Certainly in the past Britain has never shirked the responsibilities that go with her assumed role and it might be as well to consider them now.

It is sometimes difficult to answer pointed questions on moral issues about drug testing being more stringent in Britain than elsewhere, and enquiries into 'under the counter' payments provoke cries of 'witch-hunts', and 'sacrifices' from those affected. 'It wouldn't happen in Russia or America!' Or would it? There has been increasing evidence over the past year or so that internationally agreed rules of ethics are beginning to operate in lands where the grass was always presumed greener and where breaches of rules were not only condoned by governing bodies but actually instigated by them. The banning of the Soviet athletes in particular after drug testing at the European Championships in Prague is a good case in point. Their national governing body has protested vehemently but the international ruling has been upheld by the European Athletic Association so justice has been done and seen to be done.

If that is one positive move in the right direction, it would still be absurd to attempt to give the impression that all is well at international or domestic level in our sport. We in athletics, like any other sport, are literally fighting for survival in a hostile environment, but it would seem that we are slowly beginning to accept such practices as drug-taking, illegal payments, double standards, élitism, excessive costs, and downright hypocrisy instead of seeking to abolish them. We can claim, of course, that these are more products of our society than of our sport, but looking through the newspaper headlines over the past year is a grim reminder that all is not well in the world of sport.

Quite the worst moment of the year for me personally was seeing Ilona Slupianek climb the victory rostrum in Prague as the European women's shot 'champion' having been proved guilty of, and banned for, the violation of a paramount rule – the taking of specifically banned drugs. The absurdity of the limited ban merely compounded the felony by allowing her and other banned athletes a period of 12 months or so away from international competition and thereby further scrutiny.

Having said that, rather than list all the negative aspects that occurred within athletics over the past season, let me give some examples of all not being well in other sports. When some British cricketers sought the richer rewards of the Kerry Packer circus the heartfelt cries of dismay filled the columns of *The Times* for months. It was no less startling when soccer personalities admitted taking drugs, quite apart from perjury in the High Court. Then the purist of all sports, gymnastics, came into the firing line with suggestions of drug-induced performances. The equestrian scene and the attitude there towards both the drug Butozolodin and neurectomy (severing a horse's nerve endings) is a disgrace and the absurdly excessive payments to tennis players coupled with frequent outbursts on court towards umpires and linesmen are an international scandal. One could go on but the more that one does, the more difficult it becomes to justify sport as an important and necessary part of our culture. Of course it is still vitally important but we shall go on attracting more and more critics, especially from educationalists and philosophers alike, while we allow our youngsters to grow up in such an environment.

At its best sport is a marvellous educative process where the young learn to express, to stretch and even to surpass themselves. In no other field can youth find itself fitter, faster and stronger than most adults yet he must learn the essential difference between 'aggression' and 'assertion' which is the capacity to overcome, including oneself. Sport must also provide the opportunity to lose without the loss of self-esteem. Thus it becomes a testing ground for the character and an ideal preparation for adulthood. It may sound old-fashioned, but can our schools or the average youngster's job guarantee the same variety of opportunities? I hardly dare to suggest that, even if we take our pleasures vicariously, life would be a lot duller without sport on television or in our newspapers and magazines. It is therefore worth trying to protect. It's even worth pointing out to our champions that they share that responsibility to the many hundreds who take up the sport possibly because of their very example in the first place. Many are clearly finding that responsibility difficult to live with.

To be more specific about track and field performances rather than factors affecting sport, during the year, one has first to turn to Henry Rono whose contribution to the record books has been unique. Although his times and the manner of his victories put him alongside the other Kenyan all-time greats such as Keino and Jipcho, some credit must be given to the much-maligned American college system and in particular to his coach John Chaplin at Washington State. Rono may well have inherited his aspirations and even his mighty lungs from his home environment, but it is fair to say that he was practically unknown as an athlete in Kenya and has benefitted greatly from the United States, a country which has always played 'open house' to the world's athletes. Let's hope the rewards are just as rich for the likes of Keith Connor and Colin Szwed who are just two of a dozen or so outstanding young athletes who will be missed from the British scene for a while.

Having first turned to the men, what an incredible year it was for superlative women's performances. In no particular order let me single out Marita Koch's 48.94 for 400 metres, plus 22.06 for 200 metres; Vilma Bardauskiene's long jump of 7.09m (23′ 3¼″); and Grete Waitz running an astonishing marathon in 2:32:30, which was more than two minutes faster than any other woman marathoner – and that was the first time she had run further than 10 miles! Spare a thought, too, for little Tamami Yagi of Japan who high jumped 1.90 metres (6′ 2¾″) standing only 1.64 metres (5′ 4½″) tall, giving her the best women's differential of 10¼ inches.

I shall particularly remember the superb high jumping of both Sara Simeoni and Rosemarie Ackermann, who share the world record of 2.01m (6′ 7″). Steve Ovett's lone British victory apart, theirs was *the* event of an almost unsavoury European Championships, for the manner of the competition and the relationships of the competitors contained the only real charm readily apparent in Prague. It was an astonishing comeback for Rosi Ackermann who had ankle surgery earlier in the year and, although she was down on countback to Sara Simeoni, she may yet be given the clearance at 2.01 metres since there is no evidence on film or video-tape that she touched the bar.

If the women's high jump was the ecstasy, there is no doubt about the agony for me at least – the men's 800 metres, despite the fact that British athletes finished with silver and bronze medals. Ovett and Coe are two of the greatest 800 metres runners in the world and in any other championship or on any other day the result might have been different. If Olaf Beyer's great moment was related to, dare I say it, 'periodisation' rather than inspiration then we all need to know more about it. Thank God for human frailty, and long may our sport be free of total predictability. The fact that the year produced a race in which Alberto Juantorena finished sixth, and an outstanding marathon was won by Tanzania's unknown Gidemas Shahanga gives hope to us all.

Considering British performances at home and around the world, I am not one of those who subscribe to the view that the Commonwealth Games should be gradually phased out simply because Britain is now a member of a European community. I love the atmosphere at the Commonwealth gathering, and Edmonton was no exception. It's a tremendous reunion even if it does offer richer rewards for a poorer standard of competition in some events. There are those who do not continue in athletics because they do not believe they can compete with some of their Eastern European neighbours on equal terms, but there are certainly those who will remember Edmonton for the rest of their lives. Daley Thompson may well believe that his season finished on a low note because Edmonton preceded Prague, but he set himself a tremendous set of standards and was vastly entertaining in the process. The Scots had a marvellous time thrashing the English among others in the sprint relay and Berwyn Price's gold for Wales must have given their athletic fraternity heart.

The 16 gold medals achieved by the English matched their previous best achieved in 1934 – a time when the international calendar made fewer demands and rarely led to a choice being made between the Commonwealth and the European. One particularly sobering thought from Edmonton was that there were problems in the events providing the toughest opposition, and where the best athletes were doubling up in two events and competing in both championships. There must be something wrong when Brendan Foster complains for, compared to his self-discipline and self-knowledge, most athletes are like children at a tea-party. So when he lies on his bed wondering about recovery times, the effect of high altitude on his 10,000 metres time, the boredom between events, and the lack of sound advice, then there is cause for concern. Were there enough coaches with sufficient knowledge of that environment to cover every event? What about discipline in the village? The reason why the Scots were pilloried in the national Press was apparently the order of the day in other parts of the camp, so we are again back to double standards.

Those same double standards have particularly affected British throwers for the past three or four seasons and I have never seen morale so low in any one particular area of our sport before. They have long been subjected to derision, particularly from the middle distance runners, about only being on the team for the ride and being in circus events, yet the records show that athletes such as Geoff Capes and Mike Winch have given more loyal service to the British team in the past than most of the runners. They are always in the firing line when drugs are mentioned, and it was even suggested that the shot should be dropped as an event because it is widely believed that *all* shot putters take anabolic steroids. In fact, of course, no group of athletes is free from the stigma and we now have medical evidence that suggests that so-called 'blood doping' or 'blood packing' can improve performance in endurance running by up to seven per cent! Think about that over 10,000 metres, then think about the furore that arose over how the Finns could suddenly produce an unbelievable spate of European and Olympic champions at 5000 and 10,000 metres since 1971. The purists, especially the former athletes who now write the headlines, cried that it couldn't be the Finns; not the land of Nurmi, Ritola and Kolehmainen! Whilst I share their high regard for Finnish standards of excellence, it has to be said that it was the Finns who were on the point of cancelling their match with Great Britain in 1978 if full dope-testing procedures were insisted upon. The result was that a compromise was reached to avoid the cancellation of the fixture, but does anyone imagine that a similar compromise would be reached over British athletes and in particular British throwers?

Where is the men's shot put world record holder and Olympic champion each time there is a match – he is back home with most of the other top East German throwers. He and many other top throwers simply will not come to Britain. Yet what happens when the British top throwers travel abroad and try to seek information on the drug scene as it affects other competitors? In Edmonton there were new laughs every day: urine samples were tipped down the drain at a major regional championships since the doctor involved was the man who obtained supplies of 'Dianabol' for the team. One competitor joked that his wife was a member of the testing team, and another was informed that the new retroactive testing time might catch him out and spent most of the Games running around the track drinking diuretics followed by effervescent vitamin C to affect the spectrometer test and so avoid the scrutiny of immunoassy – and it worked.

What of those teams who are now given natural testosterone for which there is no known test, and the girls who give each other vitamin B shots – or worse? This presents a totally unedifying picture of modern track and field, but evangelical crusades or sacrifices from one small country are still not the answer. The search for an internationally accepted code of ethics based on sound knowledge is essential. This is why the morale of the throwers is so low.

Their own search for positive knowledge on the dangerous side-effects of these drugs is invariably assumed to be a search for more effective drugs; and so the stigma increases, and we become blind to the other events and the other drugs. Administrators, coaches and athletes must get around the table to discuss and rationalise their approach. If the Sports Council are as seriously concerned as their offers of grants seem to suggest, let some of it be spent on the educative process as well as the testing. If any more scientists wish to help under the guise of sports medicine, let it be relevant to the problem for I have a drawerful of data concerning the results of experiments on non-athletes which mean little or nothing.

Next in line is the problem of the illegal payment of athletes, and in particular the furore over last season's Edinburgh Highland Games. Once again it looks as though British scapegoats are being sought yet it has been an almost universally adopted practice since 1896 and even appears to be condoned from the summit. The exchange between the IAAF president, Adriaan Paulen, and John Rodda of *The Guardian* on 8 November 1978 made it clear that the president knew that there were probably illegal payments; who received them; and how much. Indeed there was no way to stop them. I only raise it because I fear that the lives of people such as Allan Wells and David Jenkins could be made a misery simply because they were among the first to give an honest account of themselves.

On a more positive note there are real areas of optimism, for it can no longer be said that athletics has a terrible drop-off rate from school to club. Athletics in schools, in much the same way as gymnastics, is used to encourage physical literacy as well as provide for a post-school club activity, so one shouldn't look for a massive percentage. However, the growth in club athletics has been most encouraging over the past five years, particularly where membership has doubled. The other old chestnut about the English schools annual championships throwing up countless *unknown* 'great' athletes is acceptable no longer. The Schools Championships are still the marvellously organised spectacle they ever were but look at the impressive list of winners – most are already established club members and the others are followed up quite meticulously by the national coaches.

Last year saw the appointment of David Shaw as general secretary of the British Amateur Athletic Board. In a very short time he has already made a considerable impact on the domestic scene and has come up with some excellent ideas for future development on the international front. Hopefully someone with similar qualities will be found to fill the recently advertised post of director of coaching. The early appointment of team managers for Moscow is just as important, together with a much closer liaison with those responsible for the development of the excellent junior squads. That would provide a sound basis for professional management with real accountability.

As usual I have overrun my time, save for some random thoughts plus my very sincere thanks to our sponsors Dewhurst, The Master Butcher, and all our contributors – especially compiler Mel Watman.

☐ Allan Wells' breakthrough into world class was as delightful as it was surprising. As his tale unfolded and the coaching programme of Wilson Young was explained, that too was as refreshingly original as its undoubted results.

☐ Tipton Harriers must be congratulated on taking from Gateshead in 1978 the mantle of our outstanding cross-country and road running club.

☐ What a joy to see Ian Thompson back to winning ways in the marathon.

☐ Another victory which augurs well for our future was that of our UK juniors over West Germany.

☐ The year always sees the passing of old friends and great servants of the sport, but none will be more sadly missed than Harold Abrahams and Jack Forrester.

☐ Another very sad loss was that of Kraft sponsorship – they too will be greatly missed.

☐ I must be amongst very many in the sport to be delighted at Squire Yarrow's election as president of the AAAs.

☐ You make your own choice if you have to between Steve Ovett and Daley Thompson as the season's most outstanding athlete. I will settle for paying tribute to them both in this edition and say what a privilege it was to witness some of their finest moments.

The Master Butcher improves your selection chances.

No, we can't help you to get into the national team. But when it comes to buying meat, you'll find a great selection of prime cuts at your local Dewhurst shop. And as well as quality you'll find real Master Butcher value too. If you're shopping for meat, stop first at Dewhurst. For the best meat selections, our shops are the automatic choice.

DEWHURST
The Master Butcher

Steve Ovett - Statistically Speaking

Born at Brighton, 9 October 1955

Championship Record

1970 English Schools Cross-Country (Juniors) – 37th.
English Schools Championships (Juniors) – 1st 400m (51.8).

1971 English Schools Championships (Intermediates) – 3rd 400m (50.4).
AAA Youths Championships – 1st 400m (49.8)

1972 English Schools Cross-Country (Intermediates) – 2nd.
English Schools Championships (Intermediates) – 1st 800m (1:55.0).
AAA Youths Championships – 1st 400m (49.1).

1973 English Cross-Country Championships (Youths) – 18th.
English Schools Cross-Country (Seniors) – 2nd.
AAA Championships – 6th 800m (1:47.3).
France 'A' v UK 'A' – 3rd 800m (1:49.6).
European Junior Championships – 1st 800m (1:47.5).

1974 Poland v UK v Canada – 1st 800m (1:46.8).
AAA Championships – 1st 800m (1:46.8).
UK v Czechoslovakia – 1st 800m (1:48.8).
European Championships – 2nd 800m (1:45.8) (*European junior record*).

1975 English Cross-Country Championships (Juniors) – 1st.
GDR v UK – 3rd 800m (1:47.6).
European Cup Semi-Final – 1st 800m (1:46.7).
AAA Championships – 1st 800m (1:46.1).
European Cup Final – 1st 800m (1:46.6).

1976 UK v Poland v Canada – 1st 800m (1:46.7).
Olympic Games – 5th 800m (1:45.4); 6th.
1500m semi-final (3:40.3) (3:37.9 heat).
AAA Championships – 1st 800m (1:47.3).

1977 English Cross-Country Championships – 13th.
UK Championships – 1st 1500m (3:37.5).
European Cup Semi-Final – 1st 1500m (3:39.1).
European Cup Final – 1st 1500m (3:44.9).
World Cup – 1st 1500m (3:34.5) (*UK record*).

Steve Ovett.

Fionnbar Callanan

1978 Inter-Counties Cross-Country Championships – 1st.
English Cross-Country Championships – 4th.
UK v GDR – 1st 1500m (3:53.8).
European Championships – 2nd 800m (1:44.1) (*UK record*); 1st 1500m
(3:35.6).

Records Broken

1971: UK age-15 800m best (1:55.3).
1972: UK age-16 800m best (1:52.5).
1973: UK junior records for 1000m (2:20.0) and mile (4:00.0).
1974: European junior 800m record (1:45.8).
1977: UK records for 1500m (3:34.5) and mile (3:54.7).
1978: World outdoor 2 miles best (8:13.5);
UK records for 800m (1:44.1), mile (3:52.8) and 2000m (4:57.8).

Annual Progression

Year	400m	800m	1500m	Mile
1969	53.7	—	—	—
1970	51.6	2:00.0	4:10.7	—
1971	49.8	1:55.3	—	—
1972	48.4	1:52.5	4:02.0	—
1973	48.0	1:47.3	3:44.8	4:00.0
1974	47.5	1:45.8	3:46.2	3:59.4
1975	48.7	1:46.1	3:39.5	3:57.0
1976	48.2	1:45.4	3:37.9	—
1977	—	1:48.3	3:34.5	3:54.7
1978	48.4	1:44.1	3:35.6	3:52.8

Other events: 200 – 22.3 (1973), 2000 – 4:57.8 (1978), 3000 – 7:41.3 (1977), 2 miles – 8:13.5 (1978), 5000 – 13:25.0 (1977), half marathon – 65:38 (1977).

Five times under 1:46 (800m)

1:44.1	Prague	31.8.78
1:45.4	Montreal	25.7.76
1:45.4	Turku	27.7.78
1:45.5	Zurich	18.8.76
1:45.8	Rome	4.9.74

10 times under 3:40 (1500m)

3:34.5	Dusseldorf	3.9.77
3:35.6	Prague	3.9.78
3:35.8	Oslo	3.8.78
3:37.5	Cwmbran	12.6.77
3:37.6	Malmo	26.7.78
3:37.9	Montreal	29.7.76
3:39.1	London	16.7.77
3:39.6	London	11.6.76
3:39.8	Kingston (Jam)	13.5.77
3:39.8	Saint-Maur	1.6.77

10 times under 4:00 (mile)

3:52.8	Oslo	20.9.78
3:54.7	London	26.6.77
3:55.5	Tokyo	25.9.78
3:55.7	Dublin	11.7.78
3:56.2	Belfast	28.5.77
3:56.6	London	9.9.77
3:57.0	Stockholm	30.6.75
3:57.7	London	23.8.78
3:59.1	Cork	5.7.77
3:59.4	London	17.7.74

Steve Ovett

by Cliff Temple

Despite a year which saw him win the European 1500 metres title, the Dubai Golden Mile, and assorted other races at those distances, one question still, frustratingly, remained unanswered about Steve Ovett: Just how good is he? Usually content to do just enough to win, and normally unconcerned about records, Ovett's 1978 races before Prague always gave the impression that he was keeping something in hand. And by September, the time he *did* become a little more interested in records, the weather, the erratic pacemaking, the extensive travel, and his own feeling of anti-climax after winning the title towards which he had been pointing all year, combined to rule out the chance of getting close to the answer.

He is an enigma, capable on his day of making the destruction of a world class 1500 metres field look like a doddle, typified by his triumphant and characteristic arm-waving in the home straight. This action delights most of the Crystal Palace crowd, infuriates others, and caused one of his closest rivals to declare his own major ambition for the future as being to overtake Ovett after he has prematurely waved to the crowd.

Ovett can be temperamental, unpredictable, and in company can change within a few seconds from being the life and soul of the party with an answer for everything into a withdrawn introvert, content to gaze, preoccupied, into space. He has never deliberately courted the tag of Mr Public Relations. He shuns formal dinners, social functions, award presentations, and seldom attends post-race interviews. Even in Prague he was the only winner at the European championships who would not speak either to the official Czech 'trackside quotes' man who rushed winners' reactions back to the world's press, or appear at the traditional post-presentation conference. Personally, I feel it is a shame that he takes *abroad* his antagonism towards the British press (for that is where it started, in 1975, when he was criticised in a number of newspapers for saying that he would probably not run in the European Cup final that year; in the end he ran anyway, and won, but the memory remains). On the one occasion he did break his self-imposed rule, after his 1977 World Cup victory in Dusseldorf, he spoke articulately and graciously about his win and the unexpected demise of Olympic champion John Walker, and surprised many foreign journalists who simply could not, and still cannot, understand his reluctance to be publicly interviewed.

But, on the other hand, he does not exactly go around kicking old ladies either. He is a great club man, and infuriates promoters all over the world as they hear that on a day when this great box-office attraction has turned down the chance to run in their internationally acclaimed meeting, he has been competing instead for Brighton and Hove AC in a club relay, watched in a

Flashback to the European Junior Championships of 1973 . . . Steve (191) snatches victory in the 800 metres from Germany's Willi Wulbeck (586).   Ed Lacey

public park by eight people and a dachshund. I have seen him spend hours signing autographs for youngsters, and not so long ago he submitted to an hour of intense 'grilling' on his career and training by younger members of my own club in Folkestone.

What has happened is that over the years, as he has moved into the public spotlight, he has simply avoided being drawn into the usual web of fringe activities. The unwritten commandments of being a sports celebrity, which state that Thou Shalt Ascend to the Press Box at Crystal Palace when

Demanded, or that Thou Shalt Appear on BBC Sports Review of the Year when Summoned unto Shepherd's Bush, simply do not apply to him. He was the man who, when asked if he would care to do this, that or the other, had the courage to reply in total honesty 'No, thank you'. After all, why should he? 'I suppose I could say "I'd love to, but . . .", but that's just not me', he says of his reluctance even to offer a diplomatic excuse. 'Yet sometimes people don't seem able to accept that I just don't want to go to their functions.'

His home base, and a solid one at that, is in his native Brighton. He lives with his parents, Mick and Gay, and his younger sister and brother, Sue and Nicky. The Ovetts are a close, lively family. Living in that house, says Steve, is 'stimulating. We're totally honest with each other. We have rows, deep discussions – people get thrown out, and come back in again. You never know what's going to happen next.'

His parents are his biggest supporters. They went to Prague, and one of the reasons Steve gave for not wanting to run in the Commonwealth Games at Edmonton was that he knew his parents could not be there. During the year they provide the financial backing which gives him the independence to train as and when he wants. He has turned down thousands of pounds of sponsorship money 'because if you accept it, you find yourself running in "their" races and attending "their" functions.

'I'm completely dependent upon my parents, which could be bad, but isn't. I don't get the old "You ruddy layabout, why don't you get a job?" syndrome from them, nor the golden-boy image of "This is my son, and here he is with his medals" routine. But they are proud of me, and they recognise that I have a particular gift to run, which they don't want to share with anyone who would simply like to write out a sponsorship cheque. But we're completely open about my running. If I have a lousy race, they don't say "Never mind". They say "What a lousy race".

'My Dad works damned hard, from half past five every morning to five or six at night with his farm produce shops in the local market. We tell him to slow down. He's already been in the intensive care unit with heart trouble once. But he enjoys doing it, not just for me, but for the whole family.'

When you consider that Ovett's 800 metres silver medal in Prague – in the only race which saw him stretched all summer – was actually his second European silver at the distance, having finished second to Luciano Susanj in 1974, it is hard to realise that he only turned 23 in October 1978. But Ovett's career has not been one of a loser eventually making good. He has always been a winner. At 13 he was the fastest 400 metres runner of his age in Britain, and went on to collect a string of national junior titles. At 17, while in the sixth form at Varndean Grammar School, he became the 1973 European 800 metres junior champion, beating such names as Willi Wulbeck and Ivo van Damme. But even for that race he had been favourite, and I remember that on the way back from those championships in Duisburg, he was reflecting about the strain he had felt in being favourite for such an important competition.

Five years later, in a Prague restaurant on the night of his European 1500 metres win, he again mentioned the strain he had been under by being favourite. Everyone had tipped him to win. Even the West German Thomas Wessinghage, the European mile record holder, had said several months earlier that Ovett would be European champion and all the rest of them, himself included, were merely running for the silver medal. It had been a similar story ever since Ovett was the schoolboy who won everything on sports day. But that sort of pressure is an enormous burden to bear, because if you *do* win (and so much can go wrong), no one will be surprised, and if you lose, then everyone is shocked. Part of the normal enjoyment of victory, that of surprising people, has been constantly sliced away for Ovett by other people's positive expectation of his triumph.

Maybe that goes some way towards explaining his unorthodox attitudes towards so many things. He has never himself been an under-dog, dreaming of the day when people would finally take notice of him, the sort of motivation which drives on so many other athletes. Perhaps only at the Montreal Olympics has he ever been in danger of being thought of as 'just another athlete', and that through a lack of experience. Before the Games, he had told me, 'I'm very inexperienced as an international, but I've got a terrific ability to run. I believe that. And this ability carries me through races where most people use experience. But sometimes the experience I haven't got lets me down.'

In Montreal he was fifth in what was then his speciality event, the 800 metres, and eliminated in the semi-finals of the 1500 metres at which, he had insisted earlier, 'I'm just a joke'. In fact, his coach, Harry Wilson, feels in retrospect that Ovett should have been concentrating on the longer race in

Ovett wins the European 1500 metres title. Mike Street

Atop the victory stand in Prague, flanked by Eamonn Coghlan (left) and Dave Moorcroft.   Mike Street

Montreal. But a year later, when winning the World Cup 1500 metres with nonchalance, Ovett seemed to have found his true event. After all, he had started his career with the speed of a natural sprinter, and built onto it the strength of a long distance runner who, just a few weeks earlier, had been able to not only enter a 13-mile half-marathon in Dartford on the spur of the moment, but actually win it from a good class field.

'That Dartford half-marathon is always being thrown at me as an example of my lunacy and flexibility', says Ovett. 'I had never raced that far before, and really not intended to go the full distance. But surely athletics is concerned with finding out about yourself, not repeating yourself time and time again? I'm not trying to prove anything. I'm not attempting to be Britain's number one, or the world's number one. I'm just being *me*. But by intensifying my concentration on running, I suppose the drive to do better, to win, is greater than in other people, because in my case there's not much else to fall back on.'

His normal day begins at 7.30am when his training partner, Matt Patterson, a local schoolteacher and fellow member of Brighton and Hove AC, calls for him and they run five or six miles, discussing anything under the sun from the previous evening's television to politics. Then they run again when Patterson's school day is over. Through the winter they put in a total of around

21

100 miles a week of steady running, which forms the basis for summer success. In one particular week early in 1978 Ovett suddenly had the urge to see how many miles he could pack into seven days, and managed to clock up 168 by Saturday night: another example of his occasionally impulsive approach, and one definitely not to be copied by any of this book's younger readers!

When he left school he became a student for a while, but international athletics and exams did not mix, so something had to go. Yet he denies that everything is being sacrificed in a single-minded drive towards Olympic gold.

'I realised after Montreal how stupid it is to think that an Olympic gold medal could be the answer to everything. It's just one race on one day', he says. But it remains an unconquered peak, one potentially within his grasp and I suspect that, quite understandably, it may be one on which he is travelling on a deliberately zig-zag, scent-destroying path. Patterson, for instance, says that he feels Ovett has probably got everything worked out in his mind. If so, then Ovett himself, even sub-consciously, is perhaps throwing out a smoke-screen when he talks of the motivation which keeps him training harder and harder: 'I've thought about it a lot, and I can't find any answer, except that I enjoy discovering myself through running. That's why, when I try to explain it to anyone who is basically achievement-orientated, they can't understand me, because there is no specific goal. There is no path I follow. I feel as if I'm just drifting along, because although I can progress physically through my training, mentally and spiritually I don't know what the hell I'm doing. It's like that car sticker "don't follow me, I'm lost".

'I don't think I'm mad, but sometimes I just don't seem to bother about things that are the most important in my life. Let's face it, I don't do anything else now except run, so the World Cup race in Dusseldorf, for instance, should have been life or death for me. Yet it didn't feel like that at all. It was as though I was completely detached from what was happening, and yet taking an active part. It's a contradiction in me that I don't even know what I'm doing myself. I think that worries the people who run against me!'

1978 in Retrospect

A calendar of the major meetings and championships held in 1978

compiled by Mel Watman

ABBREVIATIONS

Alb	Albania	Ice	Iceland	StL	St Lucia
Alg	Algeria	Ind	India	StV	St Vincent
Ant	Antigua	Indo	Indonesia	Sud	Sudan
Arg	Argentina	IoM	Isle of Man	Sur	Surinam
Aus	Australia	Irn	Iran	Swa	Swaziland
Aut	Austria	Irq	Iraq	Swe	Sweden
Bah	Bahamas	Isr	Israel	Swi	Switzerland
Ban	Bangladesh	Ita	Italy	Syr	Syria
Bar	Barbados	IvC	Ivory Coast	T&C	Turks and Caicos
Bel	Belgium	Jam	Jamaica	Tai	Taiwan
Ber	Bermuda	Jap	Japan	Tan	Tanzania
Blz	Belize	Jer	Jersey	Tha	Thailand
Bol	Bolivia	Ken	Kenya	Tri	Trinidad and Tobago
Bot	Botswana	Kuw	Kuwait	Tun	Tunisia
Bra	Brazil	Leb	Lebanon	Tur	Turkey
Bul	Bulgaria	Les	Lesotho	Uga	Uganda
Bur	Burma	Lie	Liechtenstein	UK	United Kingdom
Cam	Cameroon	Lux	Luxembourg	Uru	Uruguay
Can	Canada	Mal	Malaysia	USA	United States of
CAR	Central African	Mau	Mauritius		America
	Republic	Mex	Mexico	U Volta	Upper Volta
Cay	Cayman Islands	Mgy	Malagasy Republic	Ven	Venezuela
Cha	Chad	Mli	Mali	Vir	Virgin Islands
Chi	China	Mor	Morocco	Wal	Wales
Chl	Chile	Mwi	Malawi	Yug	Yugoslavia
Col	Colombia	Nep	Nepal	Zai	Zaire (Belgian Congo)
Cub	Cuba	NI	Northern Ireland	Zam	Zambia
Cze	Czechoslovakia	Nic	Nicaragua		
Dah	Dahomey	Nig	Nigeria		
Den	Denmark	NK	North Korea		
Dom	Dominican Republic	Nor	Norway		
Egy	Egypt	NZ	New Zealand		
Eir	Republic of Ireland	Pak	Pakistan		
Eng	England	Pan	Panama		
Eth	Ethiopia	Pap	Papua, New Guinea		
Fij	Fiji	Par	Paraguay		
Fin	Finland	Per	Peru		
Fra	France	Phi	Philippines		
Gab	Gabon	Pol	Poland		
Gam	Gambia	Por	Portugal		
GDR	German Democratic	PR	Puerto Rico		
	Republic (East	Rho	Rhodesia		
	Germany)	Rom	Romania		
Ger	Germany (West)	Saf	South Africa		
Gha	Ghana	Sau	Saudi Arabia		
Gib	Gibraltar	Sen	Senegal		
Gre	Greece	Sco	Scotland		
Gren	Grenada	Sin	Singapore		
Guy	Guyana	SK	South Korea		
Hai	Haiti	SL	Sierra Leone		
Hkg	Hong Kong	Som	Somalia		
Hol	Netherlands	Sov	Soviet Union (USSR)		
Hon	Honduras	Spa	Spain		
Hun	Hungary	StK	St Kitts		

Right: *Brian Hooper on the way to a UK indoor pole vault best of 5.21 metres (17' 1").* Peter Tempest

January

27, 28 January

PHILIPS NATIONAL INDOOR CHAMPIONSHIPS

No fewer than six national bests (there are still no official records indoors) were achieved at RAF Cosford, one of them – 5:24.6 for the 2000 metres steeplechase, *sans* water jump, by Dennis Coates – even constituting a world's best for an event which appears to be contested only in Britain and the USSR.

In the triple jump and women's shot what could be termed 'absolute' UK records were established, in that Keith Connor's leap of 16.54 metres (54′ 3¼″) and Judy Oakes' put of 16.41 metres (53′ 10¼″) were both superior to anything a Briton has recorded outdoors. The other best performances fell to 17-year-old Peter Little with a 21.8 timing in his 200 metres semi-final (but he was beaten in the final by Mike McFarlane), Brian Hooper with a vault of 5.21 metres (17′ 1″) and Verona Elder with a 24.6 200 metres in a non-championship event.

Youngest champion was Jo White, born five days after Little, whose personal best 1500 metres time of 4:16.2 ranked her second on the UK indoor all-time list. She looked all set for a momentous summer but, alas, she injured her foot a few weeks later and missed the entire track season.

MEN

60m: 1 P. Little 6.84; **2** M. McFarlane 6.87; **3** D. Baptiste 6.89; **4** C. Moven 6.92; **5** R. Denham 6.93; **6** B. Green 6.97.

200m: 1 M. McFarlane 21.9; **2** P. Little 22.1 (in semi: 21.8 – *UK national best*); **3** T. Bonsor 22.1; **4** D. Thompson 22.5.

400m: 1 C. Hamilton 49.3; **2** C. O'Neill 49.3; **3** E. Tulloch 49.5; **4** N. Jackson 49.8.

800m: 1 P. Hoffmann 1:51.4; **2** J. Goodacre 1:51.8; **3** P. Browne 1:51.9; **4** M. Francis 1:52.4; **5** C. Szwed 1:52.5; **6** J. Spooner 1:55.8.

1500m: 1 T. Hutchings 3:48.4; **2** K. Newton 3:49.5; **3** M. Downes 3:51.4; **4** P. Lewis 3:52.2; **5** S. Cahill 3:52.9; **6** W. Wilkinson 3:56.2.

3000m: 1 S. Emson 8:05.4; **2** P. Shaw 8:07.8; **3** A. Weatherhead 8:07.8; **4** L. Spence 8:11.2; **5** R. Milne 8:12.2; **6** A. Mottershead 8:13.2.

2000m Steeplechase: 1 D. Coates 5:24.6 (*UK national best and world's fastest on record*); **2** P. Griffiths 5:30.5; **3** A. Bettridge 5:50.5; **4** I. Barnard 5:56.0; **5** G. Wallace 5:56.2; **6** I. Logan 5:56.6.

60m Hurdles: 1 B. Price 7.90; **2** D. Wilson 8.11; **3** I. Ratcliffe 8.22; **4** M. Kindon 8.32; **5** N. Gerrard 8.35; **6** R. Simpson 8.36.

High Jump: 1 M. Naylor 2.11m (6′ 11″); **2** M. Butterfield 2.08m; **3** A. Dainton 2.05m; **4** V. Clemmens 2.05m; **5 eq** B. Burgess and R. De Vries (Hol) 2.05m.

Pole Vault: 1 B. Hooper 5.21m (17′ 1″) (*UK national best*); **2** K. Stock 5.10m; **3** A. Williams 5.05m; **4** M. Bull 4.90m; **5** T. Gardner 4.60m; **6** R. Goodall 4.40m.

Long Jump: 1 T. Henry 7.47m (24′ 6¼″); **2** W. Kirkpatrick 7.37m; **3** C. Mitchell 7.35m; **4** K. Cocks 7.33m; **5** L. Tyson 7.22m; **6** A. Slack 7.22m.

Triple Jump: 1 K. Connor 16.54m (54′ 3¼″) (*UK all-comers and national best*); **2** D. Johnson 16.04m; **3** F. Attoh 15.85m; **4** C. Colman 15.50m; **5** E. McCalla 14.91m; **6** R. Edwards 14.81m.

Shot: 1 G. Capes 20.32m (66′ 8″); **2** M. Winch 18.39m; **3** R. Dale 18.38m; **4** S. Rodhouse 16.09m; **5** I. Mowat 15.69m; **6** N. Tabor 15.62m.

Olympic 1500 metres champion John Walker (NZ) – sadly missed for most of the year. George Herringshaw

WOMEN

60m: 1 H. Hunte 7.39; **2** E. Thomas 7.50; **3** P. Baker 7.58; **4** M. Wells 7.63; **5** B. Clarke 7.65; **6** Y. Wray 7.65.

400m: 1 E. Eddy 54.8; **2** J. Colebrook 55.2; **3** K. Williams 55.7; **4** S. Smith 56.2.

800m: 1 V. Elder 2:08.4; **2** P. Lloyd 2:10.7; **3** G. Rickard 2:13.1; **4** P. Reece 2:13.8; **5** A. Linton 2:15.2; **6** A. Hartley 2:17.6.

1500m: 1 J. White 4:16.2; **2** C. Hanson 4:19.4; **3** J. Colebrook 4:26.5; **4** J. Lawrence 4:27.2; **5** G. Dainty 4:31.2; **6** H. Fielon 4:34.6.

60m Hurdles: 1 L. Boothe 8.36; **2** B. Caines 8.46; **3** W. McDonnell 8.49; **4** T. Chipp 8.52; **5** Y. Wray 8.60; **6** M. Laing 8.80.

High Jump: 1 G. Hitchen 1.80m (5′ 10¾″); **2** L. Haysman 1.78m; **3 eq** R. Few and A. Manley 1.78m; **5 eq** B. Simmonds and M. Walls 1.75m.

Long Jump: 1 S. Reeve 6.20m (20′ 4¼″); **2** G. Regan 5.85m; **3** B. Clarke 5.83m; **4** M. Laing 5.63m; **5** M. Walls 5.52m; **6** T. Greisen 5.45m.

Shot: 1 J. Oakes 16.41m (53′ 10¼″) (*UK national best*); **2** A. Littlewood 15.75m; **3** M. Ritchie 15.65m; **4** J. Kerr 15.03m; **5** V. Redford 13.99m; **6** C. Hartnell 13.69m.

JANUARY HIGHLIGHTS

Dick Buerkle, a 30-year-old American who has been bald since he was 12, produced the first sensational result of the indoor season by registering a world indoor mile best of 3:54.9 at College Park, Maryland, on 13 January, leading all the way against a honeymooning Filbert Bayi (Tan) who finished a well-beaten second in 3:58.4. An Olympic 5000 metres runner, Buerkle had not previously been world-rated at the distance and he only got into the race as a pacemaker! The meet director confessed: 'When he entered I told him I couldn't let him run the mile – he was a two miler. Then he promised he would set a fast pace, so I finally said okay.' Buerkle was true to his word as he led through quarters of 57.2, 1:58.9 and 2:58.3.

At the same meeting, Greg Joy (Can), the Olympic high jump silver medallist, set a world indoor mark of 2.31 metres (7′ 7″) – a full five centimetres (2″) above his own Commonwealth outdoor record. In a notable contest he was pushed hard by Franklin Jacobs (USA), who jumped 2.28 metres (7′ 6″) and then declined to attempt 2.31 metres. 'It doesn't really matter', Jacobs remarked. 'I know I'm going to jump 7′ 8″ soon anyway and I'd rather do it at one of the big Madison Square Garden meets.' Just 14 days later the remarkable young Mr Jacobs – all 1.73 metres (5′ 8″) of him – scaled 2.32 metres (7′ 7¼″) in that famous New York arena, the differential between the top of his head and the height of the bar being at 59 centimetres (1′ 11¼″) easily the greatest in history. 'He's fantastic', enthused former world record holder John Thomas. 'He just utilises everything. He's not as smooth as other jumpers but when he gets on top he has this little dolphin kick that gets him over. It's like an after-burner.' Another high jump record: Debbie Brill (Can) leapt 1.92 metres (6′ 3½″) indoors in Ottawa on 28 January, a centimetre superior to her outdoor Commonwealth mark.

The advent of electrical timing at American indoor meetings resulted in a flurry of new records, including 6.54 for 60 metres at Long Beach on 7 January and 6.11 for 60 yards in New York on 27 January by Houston McTear, and 7.07 for 60 yards hurdles by teenager Renaldo Nehemiah at the latter meeting. Mike Tully vaulted 5.59 metres (18′ 4″) for new world figures at Long Beach.

Aston Moore set a UK indoor triple jump best of 16.21 metres (53′ 2¼″) at Cosford on 14 January, but it lasted only a few minutes as Keith Connor replied with efforts of 16.26 metres (53′ 4¼″) and 16.51 metres (54′ 2″) – a distance he was to increase to 16.54 metres (54′ 3¼″) a fortnight later. Allan Wells gave a foretaste of his dramatic progress during the summer by establishing a UK electrically-timed 60 metres best of 6.68 in his one and only indoor appearance. In Los Angeles on 21 January, Nick Rose clocked a UK two miles best of 8:20.3 behind Suleiman Nyambui (Tan), 8:18.0, and a certain Kenyan by the name of Henry Rono (8:18.3).

Rono served notice of his record-breaking intentions when he flew out to New Zealand and front-ran an impressive 27:48.6 for 10,000 metres in Auckland on 28 January. Olympic immortal Lasse Viren (Fin) dropped out on the seventeenth circuit when about to be lapped by Rono, and injuries continued to dog him all year. In his final race before undergoing an operation on his right calf, world mile record holder John Walker (NZ) won over that distance in 3:56.4.

Marion Fisher (Aus) equalled the Commonwealth record for 400 metres hurdles (hand timing) of 57.2 in Melbourne on 12 January.

The hilly seven and a half mile course at Derby would have been tough going even in favourable conditions, but with the route covered by snow, mud and ice it constituted a particularly searching test on the occasion of the inter-counties cross-country championship on 21 January. The winner was no grizzled cross-country specialist, though, but none other than Steve Ovett, building up for another monumental track season.

Result: 1 S. Ovett 37:49; **2** S. Jones 38:00; **3** A. Dewhirst 38:04. **Team:** Yorkshire.

February

11 February

UK v GERMANY–INDOORS

In only his fourth season at the event, Mark Naylor flopped clear at 2.18 metres (7' 1¾") to become Britain's highest-ever jumper. Placing third at Cosford in a fine contest which culminated with Wolfgang Killing attempting a European best of 2.29 metres (7' 6"), 20-year-old Naylor topped both the UK outdoor best of 2.15 metres (7' 0½") held by Brian Burgess and Mike Butterfield's indoor standard of 2.16 metres (7' 1"). Prior to the 2.18 metres jump Naylor had equalled the record of 2.16 metres, and in so doing he became only the fifth British jumper to master 7 feet (2.13 metres).

Another 'absolute' UK record came in the women's shot where Judy Oakes improved upon her own recently-established figures by over a foot. Nevertheless she expressed disappointment at reaching 'only' 16.74 metres (54' 11¼"), for her goal was 17 metres (55' 9¼"). Brian Hooper twice upped his indoor pole vault best, first to 5.22 metres (17' 1½") and then to 5.25 metres (17' 2¾").

Britain won both men's and women's matches to cancel out the double defeat sustained in Dortmund the previous winter.

MEN

60m: (A) 1 M. McFarlane (UK) 6.80; **2** P. Little (UK) 6.84; **3** U. Haupt (Ger) 6.96; **4** J. Wagner (Ger) 7.01. **(B) 1** M. McFarlane 6.81; **2** P. Little 6.87; **3** U. Haupt 6.93; **4** J. Wagner 6.96.

400m: 1 J. Rabstein (Ger) 48.9; **2** C. O'Neill (UK) 49.0; **3** C. Hamilton (UK) 49.2; **4** F–J. Lohrer (Ger) 49.6.

800m: 1 D. Reibe (Ger) 1:51.1; **2** J. Goodacre (UK) 1:51.3; **3** P. Hoffmann (UK) 1:51.4; **4** R. Aechtle (Ger) 1:52.0.

1500m: 1 K. Newton (UK) 3:48.0; **2** E. Helm (Ger) 3:48.5; **3** H. von Papen (Ger) 3:49.1; **4** T. Hutchings (UK) 3:49.3.

3000m: 1 D. Coates (UK) 8:01.5; **2** S. Emson (UK) 8:08.9; **3** I. Sensburg (Ger) 8:14.4; **4** M. Karst (Ger) 8:15.6.

60m Hurdles: (A) 1 B. Price (UK) 7.93; **2** W. Muders (Ger) 8.00; **3** I. Ratcliffe (UK) 8.11; **4** H–G. Klein (Ger) 8.14. **(B) 1** B. Price 7.93; **2** W. Muders 8.03; **3** H–G. Klein 8.07; **4** I. Ratcliffe 8.08.

High Jump: 1 W. Killing (Ger) 2.27m (7' 5¼") (*UK all-comers best*); **2** C. Thranhardt (Ger) 2.20m; **3** M. Naylor (UK) 2.18m (7' 1¾") (*UK national best*); **4** M. Butterfield (UK) 2.10m.

Pole Vault: 1 B. Hooper (UK) 5.25m (17' 2¾") (*UK national best*); **2** K. Stock (UK) 5.10m; **3** W. Mohr (Ger) 5.00m; **4** H. Gedrat (Ger) 4.80m.

Long Jump: 1 H–J. Berger (Ger) 7.63m (25' 0½"); **2** J. Knipphals (Ger) 7.59m; **3** T. Henry (UK) 7.45m; **4** W. Kirkpatrick (UK) 7.29m.

Triple Jump: 1 W. Kolmsee (Ger) 15.90m (52' 2"); **2** D. Johnson (UK) 15.88m; **3** K. Connor (UK) 15.81m; **4** R. Kick (Ger) 15.21m.

Shot: 1 G. Capes (UK) 19.89m (65' 3¼"); **2** J. Forst (Ger) 18.35m; **3** J. Krug (Ger) 18.19m; **4** R. Dale (UK) 17.57m.

4 x 400m Relay: 1 Germany 3:14.3; **2** UK 3:16.0 (N. Jackson 50.2, C. Hamilton 48.0, E. Tulloch 49.0, D. Thompson 48.8).

Match Result: UK 65½, Germany 62½.

WOMEN

60m: (A) 1 H. Hunte (UK) 7.42; **2** E. Thomas (UK) 7.52; **3** S. Kempin (Ger) 7.59; **4** R. Meurer (Ger) 7.75. **(B) 1** E. Thomas 7.46; **2** H. Hunte 7.51; **3** S. Kempin 7.59; **4** R. Meurer 7.79.

400m: 1 E. Eddy (UK) 55.0; **2** K. Williams (UK) 55.5; **3** E. Weinstein (Ger) 55.6; **4** E. Rauhut (Ger) 58.9.

800m: 1 V. Elder (UK) 2:05.8; **2** B. Theuss (Ger) 2:08.2; **3** P. Lloyd (UK) 2:09.3; **4** I. Goeser (Ger) 2:10.4.

1500m: 1 B. Kraus (Ger) 4:20.9; **2** G. Dainty (UK) 4:24.4; **3** V. Manz (Ger) 4:25.6; **4** C. Hanson (UK) 4:39.0.

60m Hurdles: (A) 1 L. Boothe (UK) 8.24; **2** S. Kempin (Ger) 8.26; **3** B. Caines (UK) 8.41; **4** U. Schaluck (Ger) 8.80. **(B) 1** L. Boothe 8.3; **2** S. Kempin 8.3; **3** B. Caines 8.5; **4** U. Schaluck 8.7.

High Jump: 1 G. Hahn (Ger) 1.84m (6' 0½"); **2** A. Harnack (Ger) 1.82m; **3** G. Hitchen (UK) 1.82m; **4** L. Haysman (UK) 1.70m.

Long Jump: 1 A. Weigt (Ger) 6.43m (21' 1¼"); **2** S. Reeve (UK) 6.34m; **3** K. Hanel (Ger) 6.32m; **4** G. Regan (UK) 6.03m.

Shot: 1 J. Oakes (UK) 16.74m (54' 11¼") (*UK national best*); **2** M. Groger (Ger) 16.05m; **3** A. Littlewood (UK) 15.80m; **4** U. Rompf (Ger) 14.79m.

4 x 200m Relay: 1 UK 1:37.7 (E. Thomas 25.0, J. MacGregor 24.4, E. Eddy 24.3, V. Elder 24.0); Germany disq.

Match Result: UK 53, Germany 40.

17 February

GDR (EAST GERMANY) v UK – INDOORS

Up one week, down the next. Just six days after beating the West Germans, the British teams crashed to their heaviest-ever defeats indoors when the East Germans walloped them 90–52 (men) and 78–32 (women) at Senftenberg. There were only two British winners in a match comprising 23 events: Keith Connor, well below par against West Germany because of 'flu, took the triple jump, and there was an upset victory by Keith Stock in the pole vault where Brian Hooper's record-breaking spree was interrupted when he failed to clear his opening height of 5.00 metres (16' 4¾"). Such was the one-sided nature of the women's match in particular that the GDR would have chalked up maximum points but for the second places gained by long jumper Sue Reeve and hurdler Lorna Boothe, who ran Johanna Klier very close when the Olympic champion lost momentum in the run-in after clouting the last hurdle.

Geoff Capes, himself absent due to illness, lost possession of the European indoor shot record when Olympic champion Udo Beyer fired the missile out to 21.10 metres (69' 2¾"), and there was a world best of sorts for Marlies Oelsner, credited with 10.41 for 100 yards. Young Peter Little clocked the fine time of 21.3 for 200 metres but it could not be considered as supplanting his own UK best of 21.8, since it was achieved around only one (admittedly sharp) bend of the 250 metres track.

MEN

60m: 1 E. Ray (GDR) 6.72; **2** E. Gernand (GDR) 6.87; **3** M. McFarlane (UK) 6.93; **4** D. Baptiste (UK) 7.03.

100y: 1 E. Ray (GDR) 9.63; **2** P. Little (UK) 9.87; **3** E. Gernand (GDR) 9.87; **4** D. Baptiste (UK) 10.15.

200m: 1 D. Kubeck (GDR) 21.0; **2** P. Little (UK) 21.3; **3** M. McFarlane (UK) 21.5; **4** J. Pfennig (GDR) 21.8.

400m: 1 M. Konow (GDR) 48.5; **2** C. Hamilton (UK) 48.6; **3** F. Richter (GDR) 48.8; **4** C. O'Neill (UK) 49.0.

800m: 1 O. Beyer (GDR) 1:49.7; **2** D. Wagenknecht (GDR) 1:50.6; **3** P. Hoffman (UK) 1:51.4; **4** J. Goodacre (UK) 1:51.5.

1500m: 1 J. Straub (GDR) 3:42.5; **2** L. Zauber (GDR) 3:43.3; **3** K. Newton (UK) 3:46.8; **4** T. Hutchings (UK) 3:47.5.

3000m: 1 J. Peter (GDR) 8:04.1; **2** P. Shaw (UK) 8:10.6; **3** K–H. Leiteritz (GDR) 8:11.6; **4** S. Emson (UK) 8:25.2.

60m Hurdles: 1 T. Munkelt (GDR) 7.72; **2** W. Becker (GDR) 7.92; **3** D. Wilson (UK) 8.20; **4** I. Ratcliffe (UK) 8.41.

High Jump: 1 R. Beilschmidt (GDR) 2.24m (7′ 4¼″); **2** M. Naylor (UK) 2.16m; **3** E. Kirst (GDR) 2.16m; **4** A. Dainton (UK) 2.00m.

Pole Vault: 1 K. Stock (UK) 5.00m (16′ 4¾″); **2** A. Weber (GDR) 5.00m; **3** J. Krumpolt (GDR) 4.90m; B. Hooper (UK) no height.

Long Jump: 1 L. Franke (GDR) 7.49m (24′ 7″); **2** D. Thompson (UK) 7.43m; **3** B. Heiland (GDR) 7.34m; **4** T. Henry (UK) 7.26m.

Triple Jump: 1 K. Connor (UK) 16.06m (52′ 8¼″); **2** K. Hufnagel (GDR) 16.00m; **3** D. Johnson (UK) 15.87m; **4** M. Bohla (GDR) 15.76m.

Shot: 1 U. Beyer (GDR) 21.10m (69′ 2¾″) (*European best*); **2** M. Schmidt (GDR) 20.13m; **3** M. Winch (UK) 18.23m; **4** R. Dale (UK) 17.93m.

Match Result: GDR 90, UK 52.

WOMEN

60m: 1 M. Oelsner (GDR) 7.24; **2** M. Koch (GDR) 7.32; **3** H. Hunte (UK) 7.41; **4** E. Thomas (UK) 7.46.

100y: 1 M. Oelsner (GDR) 10.41 (*world best*); **2** M. Koch (GDR) 10.54; **3** H. Hunte (UK) 10.67; **4** E. Thomas (UK) 10.79.

200m: 1 B. Eckert (GDR) 23.5; **2** C. Brehmer (GDR) 23.6; **3** V. Elder (UK) 24.2; **4** E. Eddy (UK) 24.5.

400m: 1 B. Popp (GDR) 54.1; **2** M. Kroning (GDR) 54.5; **3** E. Eddy (UK) 54.6; **4** K. Williams (UK) 55.6.

800m: 1 U. Bruns (GDR) 2:03.0; **2** B. Liebich (GDR) 2:04.1; **3** V. Elder (UK) 2:04.6; **4** P. Lloyd (UK) 2:15.9.

1500m: 1 G. Lehmann (GDR) 4:14.9; **2** C. Wartenberg (GDR) 4:15.9; **3** J. Lawrence (UK) 4:22.8; **4** C. Hanson (UK) 4:25.7.

60m Hurdles: 1 J. Klier (GDR) 8.22; **2** L. Boothe (UK) 8.24; **3** A. Fiedler (GDR) 8.39; **4** B. Caines (UK) 8.45.

High Jump: 1 J. Kirst (GDR) 1.84m (6′ 0½″); **2** D. Matzen (GDR) 1.81m; **3** G. Hitchen (UK) 1.78m; **4** R. Few (UK) 1.70m.

Long Jump: 1 H. Wycisk (GDR) 6.37m (20' 10¾"); **2** S. Reeve (UK) 6.19m; **3** M. Lehmann (GDR) 6.18m; **4** G. Regan (UK) 5.87m.
Shot: 1 M. Droese (GDR) 20.87m (68' 5¾"); **2** H. Knorrscheid (GDR) 18.33m; **3** A. Littlewood (UK) 16.34m; **4** J. Oakes (UK) 16.33m.

Match Result: GDR 78, UK 32.

25 February

ENGLISH WOMEN'S CROSS-COUNTRY CHAMPIONSHIPS

National junior champion in 1970 and winner of the intermediate race from 1971 to 1973, Mary Stewart celebrated her twenty-second birthday at High Wycombe by capturing the senior title at the first time of asking. An uncertain starter because of 'flu until just a few days before the race, she survived some anxious moments in the closing stages when the indestructible Joyce Smith was forcing the pace to sprint to victory over the highly-promising Wendy Smith (18), the previous year's intermediate champion, with 40-year-old Joyce finishing third . . . 22 years after her début in this event and 19 years after her first title!

Sandra Arthurton (15), the junior champion of 1977, made a successful transition to the intermediates group, running out a very commanding winner over Jo White and helping to lay the foundations for an extraordinary summer which was to see her improve at 1500 metres from 4:31.0 to 4:15.6.

SENIOR CHAMPIONSHIP

1	M. Stewart	18:32	13	J. Williamson	19:44
2	W. Smith	18:34	14	M. Coomber	19:50
3	J. Smith	18:42	15	S. Hassan	19:50
4	C. Benning	18:51			
5	P. Yule	18:57		**Team Placings**	
6	K. Binns	19:03	1	Sale Harriers	58pts
7	C. Gould	19:07	2	Feltham AC	96 pts
8	R. Smeeth	19:11	3	Stretford AC	106pts
9	M. Belk	19:22	4	Birchfield Harriers	108pts
10	J. Shepherd	19:29	5	Barnet Ladies AC	129pts
11	J. Colebrook	19:30	6	London Olympiades	146pts
12	C. Ward	19:37			

INTERMEDIATES

1	S. Arthurton	13:15		**Team Placings**	
2	J. White	13:28	1	Sale Harriers	83pts
3	R. Bowers	13:45	2	Bristol AC	90 pts
4	A. Pattison	13:52	3	Leeds City AC	192pts
5	B. Tierney	13:55			
6	J. Honeysett	13:59			

Right: *Joyce Smith (27), Mary Stewart (36) and Wendy Smith (107) battle for the English cross-country title.*
Peter Tempest

ENGLISH WOMEN'S CROSS-COUNTRY CHAMPIONSHIPS

JUNIORS

1 K. Timson	11:53	
2 J. Clarke	11:58	
3 S. Walker	12:07	
4 M. Witts	12:12	
5 S. Lonsdale	12:14	
6 P. Mathieson	12:15	

Team Placings
1 Sale Harriers	32pts
2 Blackburn Harriers	52pts
3 Cannock Chase AC	139pts

GIRLS

1 L. Silva	10:58	
2 L. MacDougall	11:14	
3 H. Brankin	11:17	
4 J. Rose	11:20	
5 T. Jones	11:25	
6 D. Hammond	11:26	

Team Placings
1 Manchester H and AC	122pts
2 Rossendale AC	202pts
3 Leeds City AC	203pts

FEBRUARY HIGHLIGHTS

The big news of the month came from Japan where, at Beppu on 5 February, Shigeru Sou (25) ran the second-fastest marathon in history. At 30 kilometres his time of 1:29:30 (that's around 4:50 miling pace) was almost one and a half minutes faster than that achieved by Derek Clayton (Aus) in his unofficial world record of 2:08:33.6 in 1969. The Japanese runner, who was twentieth in the Montreal Olympics and whose previous best was 2:14:59, was still over a minute ahead of Clayton's schedule at 35 kilometres and had 40 seconds in hand after 40 kilometres, but a head wind in the closing stages cost him the record. He finished in 2:09:05.6, with his twin brother Takeshi Sou second in 2:12:48.6.

At the other end of the distance scale, Houston McTear (USA) was responsible for an outstanding exploit when he took the AAU indoor 60 yards title in an electrically-timed world best of 6.04. 'I thought it was only a fair race', commented McTear, who first hit the headlines in 1975 when he equalled the world 100 yards record of 9.0 in a Florida high school meeting, but the fans – not to mention his easily-vanquished rivals – in New York on 24 February were impressed. Petar Petrov (Bul) tied the European 60 metres mark of 6.58 in Sofia the next day.

Britain's Nick Rose was involved in two notable indoor distance races in Toronto on 10 February and in San Diego seven days later. A twinkling final mile of 4:12.6 carried him to victory in the Toronto three miles in 13:03.0, the second-fastest in indoor history, well clear of Suleiman Nyambui (Tan), 13:09.2, with Henry Rono (Ken) fourth in 13:24.6 and world 5000 metres record holder Dick Quax (NZ) fifth in 13:35.2. Despite setting another UK best of 8:18.4, with the second mile covered in 4:04.3, Rose was beaten in San Diego by Nyambui in 8:17.9 (4:02.9 second mile) with Rono third in 8:20.0. It should be pointed out that, on 6 February, Rono had won a half marathon race in very hot weather in Puerto Rico ahead of marathon ace Bill Rodgers (USA) in 1:04:46. The night after the San Diego meet, which also featured a European indoor mile best of 3:56.0 by Ireland's Eamonn Coghlan, Rose ran Filbert Bayi (Tan) to inches in a 4:00.2 mile in San Francisco.

Among the women's indoor records established during the month, special mention must be made of a 1.95 metres (6' 4¾") high jump by Italy's Sara Simeoni in Milan on 23 February, which tied the world mark held by Rosi Ackermann (GDR), and a 1500 metres time of 4:05.0 by Natalia Marasescu of Romania in Budapest on 21 February which smashed Mary Stewart's world best of 4:08.1. Marasescu had, a month earlier, set an unofficial world record for 10,000 metres (outdoors) of 32:43.2. Debbie Brill (Can) raised the Commonwealth high jump best to 1.92 metres (6' 3¾") at Richfield, Ohio, on 11 February – or rather 12 February, as it was after midnight when she flopped over the record height! UK indoor marks for Lorna Boothe with 8.1 for 60 metres hurdles at Oviedo in Spain on 4 February and Sue Reeve, who equalled Mary Rand's 6.53 metres (21' 5¼") long jump figures in Bucharest on 25 February.

Fred Pendlebury (40), who only started to train really seriously when he was 36 years old, won the English veterans cross-country title at Sheffield on 19 February by 49 seconds from Ray Carruthers with Dick Cooper third. Bridget Cushen (37) claimed the women's over-35 championship.

March

1 March

UK v SPAIN – INDOORS

Highlights of the Philips Indoor Spectacular at Cosford, incorporating a men's match in which Britain beat Spain, appropriately were provided by the vertical jumpers. Wolfgang Killing (Ger) equalled the European high jump best of 2.28 metres (7' 5¾") and, as in the UK v Germany match, Mark Naylor was inspired by his presence to set an all-time UK best, this time of 2.19 metres (7' 2¼"). In the pole vault, Brian Hooper made up for his lapse against East Germany by clearing UK indoor record heights of 5.26 metres (17' 3") and 5.31 metres (17' 5"), losing a gripping competition on the countback to American guest Bob Pullard.

60m: 1 A. Ibanez (Spa) 6.85; **2** J. Carbonell (Spa) 6.88; **3** P. Little (UK) 6.89; **4** D. Baptiste (UK) 6.92.

800m: 1 M. Boit (Ken – guest) 1:48.1 ; **2** P. Browne (UK) 1:51.2 ; **3** J. Egea (Spa) 1:51.4 . . . **6** F. Gordillo (Spa) 1:52.3; **7** M. Francis (UK) 1:52.6.

1500m: 1 W. Waigwa (Ken – guest) 3:42.8; **2** J. Abascal (Spa) 3:44.1; **3** K. Newton (UK) 3:45.4; **4** M. Fromant (UK) 3:46.7 . . . **11** A. Cudeiro (Spa) 4:13.3.

3000m: 1 K. Lok (Hol – guest) 8:00.1; **2** S. Emson (UK) 8:01.3; **3** D. Macdonald (USA – guest) 8:02.8; **4** C. Sanjurjo (Spa) 8:08.0; **5** P. Griffiths (UK) 8:12.6; **6** R. Ortega (Spa) 8:17.8.

60m Hurdles: 1 J. Lloveras (Spa) 7.81; **2** J. Moracho (Spa) 7.90; **3** D. Wilson (UK) 8.02; **4** I. Ratcliffe (UK) 8.22.

High Jump: 1 W. Killing (Ger – guest) 2.28m (7' 5¾") (*eq European best; new UK all-comers best*); **2** M. Naylor (UK) 2.19m (7' 2¼") (*UK national best*); **3** R. Cabrejas (Spa) 2.11m; **4** M. Butterfield (UK) 2.05m; **5** J. Espejo (Spa) 2.00m.

Pole Vault: 1 R. Pullard (USA – guest) 5.31m (17' 5") (*UK all-comers best*); **2** B. Hooper (UK) 5.31m (17' 5") (*UK all-comers and national best*); **3** A. Williams (UK – guest) 5.10m; **4** K. Stock (UK) 5.00m . . . **6** S. Maranges (Spa) 4.60m; **7** E. Alonzo (Spa) 4.60m.

Triple Jump: 1 D. Johnson (UK) 16.29m (53' 5½"); **2** R. Cid (Spa) 15.50m; **3** J. Vila (Spa) 15.34m; **4** F. Attoh (UK) 15.29m.

Shot: 1 G. Capes (UK) 19.77m (64' 10½"); **2** W. Komar (Pol – guest) 19.65m; **3** M. Winch (UK) 18.11m; **4** M. Vara (Spa) 16.58m . . . **6** F. Correa (Spa) 15.80m.

4 x 200m Relay: 1 UK 1:28.3 (P. Little 22.2, C. Moven 21.9, N. Jackson 22.2, A. Hadley 22.0); **2** Spain 1:28.6.

Match Result: UK 58, Spain 48.

---

4 March

ENGLISH CROSS-COUNTRY CHAMPIONSHIPS

Bernie Ford has some fine track achievements to his name, including times of 13:26.0 for 5000 metres and 27:43.7 for 10,000 metres, but it is as a cross-country runner that his qualities of determination, doggedness and consistency have been most evident. Just look at his record in the 'National': runner-up in 1974 and 1975, winner in 1976, second again in 1977. Although

Previous page: *World cross-country champion Grete Waitz of Norway.* Fionnbar Callanan

winning the 'National' is the fulfilment of a major ambition for any British distance runner, Ford's 1976 victory didn't really satisfy him as many of the cross-country élite were absent on that occasion and he still felt the need to prove himself.

That he did in the 1978 edition of the race at Leeds when he ran out the winner over a record field (1536 starters, 1379 finishers) which included everyone of note except for the man who pipped Ford in a very close finish the previous year . . . Brendan Foster. The event developed into a monumental duel between Ford and Ian Stewart. The latter set a cracking pace and built up a substantial lead but Ford gradually pulled him back, opened up a small but vital gap on the final hill and – head down – tenaciously preserved his advantage to the end. 'That finishing straight seemed endless', he was to reflect. '"Come on, come on", I was saying to myself, expecting Ian to pull level at any moment.' The next finishers, a long way back, were Tony Simmons and Steve Ovett. Led by Ian Stewart, Tipton Harriers broke Gateshead's three-year hold on the team title.

Nick Lees (20), who had been runner-up to Scotsman Nat Muir the previous two years, finally won the junior title, with 18-year-old Mick Morton second, and there was a surprise victory in the youths race by Simon Catchpole (16).

SENIOR CHAMPIONSHIP

1	B. Ford	41:34	25	G. McCallum	43:48
2	I. Stewart	41:37	26	P. Romaine	43:51
3	A. Simmons	41:52	27	K. Steere	43:52
4	S. Ovett	42:24	28	J. Temperton	43:54
5	S. Kenyon	42:26	29	A. Catton	43:56
6	D. Black	42:29	30	R. Crabb	43:57
7	K. Newton	42:36			
8	M. McLeod	42:39	**Team Placings**		
9	D. Coates	42:41	1	Tipton Harriers	180pts
10	J. Wild	42:54	2	Gateshead Harriers	278pts
11	N. Coupland	43:04	3	Airedale and Spen Valley AC	281pts
12	T. Wright	43:07			
13	A. Dewhirst	43:15	4	Cambridge and Coleridge AC	298pts
14	Graham Tuck	43:19			
15	Grenville Tuck	43:24	5	Aldershot F and D	584pts
16	K. Dumpleton	43:25	6	Liverpool H and AC	620pts
17	J. Bicourt	43:29	7	Wolverhampton and Bilston AC	654pts
18	A. Holden	43:31			
19	P. Standing	43:37	8	Thames Valley Harriers	666pts
20	R. Brown	43:39	9	Shaftesbury Harriers	683pts
21	P. Bennett	43:42	10	Manchester H and AC	781pts
22	R. Wilde	43:44			
23	D. Bedford	43:45			
24	G. Smith	43:47			

JUNIORS

1	N. Lees	29:28	**Team Placings**		
2	M. Morton	29:55	1	Birmingham University	66pts
3	D. Clarke	29:58	2	Tipton Harriers	94pts

4 A. Milovsorov	30:03	**3** Leicester Coritanian AC	222pts
5 P. Venmore	30:15		
6 K. Tesh	30:16		

YOUTHS

1 S. Catchpole	19:16	**Team Placings**	
2 D. Lewis	19:24	**1** Birchfield Harriers	118pts
3 G. Turnbull	19:26	**2** Tipton Harriers	140pts
4 I. Stewart	19:30	**3** Rossendale AC	153pts
5 S. Wilson	19:35		
6 M. Weaver	19:36		

11, 12 March

EUROPEAN INDOOR CHAMPIONSHIPS

The 1978 winter season will forever be associated with high jumping. Greg Joy had set the ball rolling with a world indoor best of 2.31 metres (7′ 7″), and he had been superseded by the amazingly springy Franklin Jacobs at 2.32 metres (7′ 7¼″) . . . but even that was merely the prelude to the greatest performance in the annals of the event.

The setting was Milan's Palazzo dello Sport; the date 12 March. Ten thousand pairs of eyes were trained on the 19-year-old Ukrainian, Vladimir Yashchenko, as he prepared to attempt the fabulous height of 2.35 metres (7′ 8½″), two centimetres (¾″) higher than his own world record which he had achieved outdoors in 1977. Nearly four hours had elapsed since Yashchenko's faltering entry into the contest: he failed his opening attempt at 2.10 metres (6′ 10¼″) and rattled the bar while clearing at his second try – provoking derision from some sections of the crowd. But any doubts concerning the extra-special nature of his talent were swept away when he lifted himself over 2.15 metres (7′ 0½″) with a good six inches to spare, though carelessness crept back as he chalked up initial failures at 2.18 metres (7′ 1¾″) and 2.23 metres (7′ 3¾″), and needed the full quota of three attempts at 2.25 metres (7′ 4½″). He survived the crisis, however, and after making 2.27 metres (7′ 5¼″) at the second time of asking, he – along with Rolf Beilschmidt (GDR), Wolfgang Killing (Ger) and Soviet colleague Aleksandr Grigoryev – tried the European indoor record height of 2.29 metres (7′ 6″). The two floppers, Killing and Grigoryev, made their exit at this point but the straddle exponents succeeded: Beilschmidt on the first try, Yashchenko on the second.

With so many failed attempts to his name, at no time in the competition had Yashchenko actually been in the lead . . . that is, until the bar was set at 2.31 metres (7′ 7″). Second time around he cleared, Beilschmidt didn't, and he had won his first senior international title. And he hadn't finished yet, by a long chalk. After soaring over a world indoor best of 2.33 metres (7′ 7¾″) he was ready to attack the hitherto unscaled peak of 2.35 metres (7′ 8½″).

The first attempt was promising, the second less so. He had one more try and on this, his twentieth jump of the contest no less, he made it! 'What happened this evening has surpassed anything I could have imagined', gasped the 1.91 metres (6′ 3¼″) tall hero of the hour after being carried off in triumph by world shot put record holder Aleksandr Baryshnikov. Commented Beilschmidt: 'He is the greatest jumper of all time. His technique is not perfect but he has phenomenal spring. Yashchenko will certainly be the first one day to clear 2.40 metres' (7' 10½").

It was indeed a memorable weekend for high jumping, as the previous evening Italy's own Sara Simeoni had delighted the fans by retaining her title with 1.94 metres (6' 4¼"), only just failing to clear 1.96 metres (6' 5") for a world indoor mark. Despite the absence of Rosi Ackermann, recuperating after an Achilles tendon operation, the competition produced the greatest-ever mass display with no fewer than seven girls still involved with the bar up at 1.91 metres (6' 3¼"). Marlies Oelsner (GDR) was responsible for the classiest track performance as she sped to a world's best of 7.12 for 60 metres, and she had to run that fast to stay ahead of Linda Haglund (Swe) who was also inside Renate Stecher's old figures of 7.16.

Yashchenko, Simeoni and Oelsner all went on to strike gold also at the European outdoor championships some five and a half months later, as did Pietro Mennea (Ita), who in Milan scored his first important 400 metres victory, and hurdlers Thomas Munkelt and Johanna Klier (GDR). Others who were destined to triumph in Prague were not as far advanced at this time of year: Olaf Beyer (GDR) was second in the 800 metres, Vladimir Trofimenko (Sov) second in the pole vault, Venanzio Ortis (Ita) eighth in the 3000 metres, Vilma Bardauskiene (Sov) ninth in the long jump, while the Soviet Union's Lyudmila Kondratyeva (60 metres) and Tatyana Providokhina (800 metres) failed to reach the finals.

For the first time since 1972 there were no British victories but a silver medal was gained by Keith Connor, who became the first UK triple jumper ever to win a European medal; and bronze awards went to Geoff Capes (following two golds and two silvers in previous championships) and Sue Reeve, nine years after winning a silver in this meeting.

MEN

60m: 1 N. Kolesnikov (Sov) 6.64; 2 P. Petrov (Bul) 6.66; 3 A. Aksinin (Sov) 6.73; 4 M. Woronin (Pol) 6.75; 5 G. Grazioli (Ita) 6.76; 6 B. Petitbois (Fra) 6.84.

400m: 1 P. Mennea (Ita) 46.51; 2 R. Podlas (Pol) 46.55; 3 N. Chernetskiy (Sov) 46.72; 4 Z. Knapic (Yug) 47.83.

800m: 1 M. Taskinen (Fin) 1:47.4; 2 O. Beyer (GDR) 1:47.7; 3 R. Milhau (Fra) 1:47.8; 4 M. Gesicki (Pol) 1:48.1; 5 R. Gysin (Swi) 1:49.3; 6 G. Ferrero (Ita) 1:49.5.

1500m: 1 A. Loikkanen (Fin) 3:38.2; 2 T. Wessinghage (Ger) 3:38.2; 3 J. Straub (GDR) 3:40.2; 4 J. Abascal (Spa) 3:40.3; 5 A. Mamontov (Sov) 3:41.1; 6 J. Zemen (Hun) 3:43.0.

3000m: 1 M. Ryffel (Swi) 7:49.5; 2 E. Puttemans (Bel) 7:49.9; 3 J. Peter (GDR) 7:50.1; 4 D. Glans (Swe) 7:51.2; 5 K. Lok (Hol) 7:51.4; 6 K. Fleschen (Ger) 7:53.9.

60m Hurdles: 1 T. Munkelt (GDR) 7.65; 2 V. Kulebyakin (Sov) 7.72; 3 G. Buttari (Ita) 7.86; 4 B. Price (UK) 8.12; 5 J. Pusty (Pol) 8.15; 6 A. Bryggare (Fin) 9.05.

High Jump: 1 V. Yashchenko (Sov) 2.35m (7' 8¼") (world best); 2 R. Beilschmidt (GDR) 2.29m; 3 W. Killing (Ger) 2.27m; 4 A. Grigoryev (Sov) 2.25m; 5 S. Senyukov (Sov) 2.21m; 6 O. Raise (Ita) 2.21m . . . 14 M. Naylor (UK) 2.15m.

Pole Vault: 1 T. Slusarski (Pol) 5.45m (17′ 10½″); **2** V. Trofimenko (Sov) 5.40m; **3** V. Sergeyenko (Sov) 5.40m; **4** Y. Prokhorenko (Sov) 5.40m; **5** W. Kozakiewicz (Pol) 5.40m; **6** G. Lohre (Ger) 5.30m . . . **13** B. Hooper (UK) 5.00m.

Long Jump: 1 L. Szalma (Hun) 7.83m (25′ 8¼″); **2** R. Desruelles (Bel) 7.75m; **3** V. Tsepelev (Sov) 7.73m; **4** C. Arrighi (Ita) 7.71m; **5** A. Fransson (Swe) 7.68m; **6** G. Zante (Fra) 7.64m.

Triple Jump: 1 A. Piskulin (Sov) 16.82m (55′ 2¼″); **2** K. Connor (UK) 16.53m; **3** A. Yakovlyev (Sov) 16.47m; **4** C. Corbu (Rom) 16.41m; **5** P. Piapan (Ita) 16.25m; **6** R. Cid (Spa) 16.20m; **7** D. Johnson (UK) 16.13m.

Shot: 1 R. Stahlberg (Fin) 20.48m (67′ 2¼″); **2** W. Komar (Pol) 20.16m; **3** G. Capes (UK) 20.11m; **4** A. Baryshnikov (Sov) 19.95m; **5** G. Steines (Ger) 19.81m; **6** J. Brabec (Cze) 19.36m.

WOMEN

60m: 1 M. Oelsner (GDR) 7.12 (*world best*); **2** L. Haglund (Swe) 7.13; **3** L. Storoshkova (Sov) 7.27; **4** V. Anisimova (Sov) 7.30; **5** P. Sharp (Ger) 7.35; **6** C. Rega (Fra) 7.38 . . . H. Hunte (UK) 4th in semi (7.35).

400m: 1 M. Sidorova (Sov) 52.42; **2** R. Bottiglieri (Ita) 53.18; **3** K. Kafer (Aut) 53.56; **4** M. Kulchunova (Sov) 54.77.

800m: 1 U. Bruns (GDR) 2:02.3; **2** T. Petrova (Bul) 2:02.5; **3** M. Suman (Rom) 2:03.4; **4** A-M. Van Nuffel (Bel) 2:03.8; **5** H. Roock (GDR) 2:03.8; **6** V. Elder (UK) 2:09.2.

1500m: 1 I. Silai (Rom) 4:07.1; **2** N. Marasescu (Rom) 4:07.4; **3** B. Kraus (Ger) 4:07.6; **4** V. Yatzinska (Bul) 4:10.5; **5** S. Cruciata (Ita) 4:12.5; **6** C. Wartenberg (GDR) 4:14.1.

60m Hurdles: 1 J. Klier (GDR) 7.94; **2** G. Rabsztyn (Pol) 8.07; **3** S. Kempin (Ger) 8.15; **4** T. Anisimova (Sov) 8.17; **5** S. Bielczyk (Pol) 8.26; **6** L. Goucheva (Bul) 8.32 . . . L. Boothe (UK) 4th in semi (8.32).

High Jump: 1 S. Simeoni (Ita) 1.94m (6′ 4¼″); **2** B. Holzapfel (Ger) 1.91m; **3** U. Kielan (Pol) 1.88m; **4** A. Matay (Hun) 1.88m; **5** M. Van Laar (Hol) 1.88m; **6** M. Karbanova (Cze) 1.88m.

Long Jump: 1 J. Nygrynova (Cze) 6.62m (21′ 8¾″); **2** I. Erdelyi (Hun) 6.49m; **3** S. Reeve (UK) 6.48m; **4** J. Curtet (Fra) 6.44m; **5** H. Wycisk (GDR) 6.38m; **6** G. Panait (Rom) 6.34m.

Shot: 1 H. Fibingerova (Cze) 20.67m (67′ 9¾″); **2** M. Droese (GDR) 19.77m; **3** E. Wilms (Ger) 19.24m; **4** E. Stoyanova (Bul) 19.22m; **5** Z. Bartonova (Cze) 18.16m; **6** B. Philipp (Ger) 17.51m.

14 March

EUROPE v USA – INDOORS

The first-ever indoor match between Europe and the United States, staged in Milan, proved an anti-climax after all the excitement and emotion generated by the European Indoor Championships in the same arena a couple of days earlier. A travel-weary American team was outclassed by the Europe Select side which, in most events, comprised the first and second finishers at the championships, and much of the interest centred on re-matches between the European stars.

Possibly the best performance of the meeting came from the remarkable 36-year-old Romanian, Ileana Silai – a world-class runner for over a decade (she was Olympic 800 metres silver medallist in 1968) who had never won a major title until the 1500 metres in Milan. She sprinted past her countrywoman Natalia Marasescu for the second time in 48 hours, clocking 4:05.4 for the second-fastest time ever indoors.

The two British athletes involved fared well: Geoff Capes turned the tables on former Olympic champion Wladyslaw Komar (Pol) to place second, and Keith Connor – again very close to his UK indoor record – confirmed his new standing as a competitor of the highest international class.

MEN

60m: 1 P. Petrov (Bul) 6.62; **2** N. Kolesnikov (Sov) 6.66; **3** D. Merrick (USA) 6.70; **4** M. Shine (USA) 6.77.

400m: 1 H. Frazier (USA) 46.48; **2** S. Vinson (USA) 46.50; **3** R. Podlas (Pol) 47.74; **4** Z. Knapic (Yug) 48.21.

800m: 1 R. Milhau (Fra) 1:48.9; **2** O. Beyer (GDR) 1:49.0; **3** W. Martin (USA) 1:50.2; **4** R. Smelley (USA) 1:51.8.

1500m: 1 J. Straub (GDR) 3:39.1; **2** A. Loikkanen (Fin) 3:41.4; **3** B. Fischer (USA) 3:41.9; **4** S. Lacy (USA) 3:43.0.

3000m: 1 E. Puttemans (Bel) 7:49.5; **2** M. Ryffel (Swi) 7:49.7; **3** R. Melancon (USA) 7:50.9; **4** H. Lindsay (USA) 7:51.8.

60m Hurdles: 1 T. Munkelt (GDR) 7.65; **2** C. Foster (USA) 7.67; **3** V. Kulebyakin (Sov) 7.73; **4** K. Lewis (USA) 8.09.

High Jump: 1 F. Jacobs (USA) 2.26m (7' 5"); **2** R. Beilschmidt (GDR) 2.23m; **3** W. Killing (GDR) 2.20m; **4** B. Fields (USA) 2.20m.

Pole Vault: 1 V. Trofimenko (Sov) 5.52m (18' 1¼"); **2** T. Slusarski (Pol) 5.40m; **3** J. Taylor (USA) 5.00m; L. Jessee (USA) no height.

Long Jump: 1 V. Bradley (USA) 7.82m (25' 8"); **2** R. Desruelles (Bel) 7.59m; **3** L. Szalma (Hun) 7.52m; **4** A. Lanier (USA) 7.10m.

Triple Jump: 1 A. Piskulin (Sov) 16.95m (55' 7½"); **2** R. Livers (USA) 16.88m; **3** K. Connor (UK) 16.50m; **4** M. Tiff (USA) 15.90m.

Shot: 1 A. Feuerbach (USA) 20.39m (66' 10¾"); **2** G. Capes (UK) 20.01m; **3** W. Komar (Pol) 19.51m.

4 x 400m Relay: 1 USA (K. Price, M. Shine, R. Taylor, S. Vinson) 3:08.9; **2** Europe (N. Chernetskiy, Z. Knapic, V. Arkhipenko, R. Podlas) 3:09.5.

Match Result: Europe 74, USA 52.

WOMEN

60m: 1 L. Haglund (Swe) 7.19; **2** M. Oelsner (GDR) 7.25; **3** B. Morehead (USA) 7.32; **4** C. Cheeseborough (USA) 7.44.

400m: 1 M. Sidorova (Sov) 53.01; **2** S. Dabney (USA) 53.27; **3** R. Bottiglieri (Ita) 53.37; **4** K. Thomas (USA) 54.61.

800m: 1 U. Bruns (GDR) 2:05.7; **2** T. Petrova (Bul) 2:05.9; **3** D. Vetter (USA) 2:07.1; **4** K. Weston (USA) 2:10.4.

1500m: 1 I. Silai (Rom) 4:05.4; **2** N. Marasescu (Rom) 4:06.1; **3** J. Merrill (USA) 4:15.5; **4** L. Jennings (USA) 4:19.7.

60m Hurdles: 1 J. Klier (GDR) 7.94; **2** G. Rabsztyn (Pol) 7.95; **3** D. LaPlante (USA) 8.25; **4** P. Van Wolvelaere (USA) 8.33.

High Jump: 1 S. Simeoni (Ita) 1.90m (6' 2¾"); **2** U. Kielan (Pol) 1.80m; **3** P. Girven (USA) 1.80m; **4** P. Spencer (USA) 1.75m.

Long Jump: 1 J. Nygrynova (Cze) 6.40m (21' 0"); **2** J. Anderson (USA) 6.31m; **3** I. Erdelyi (Hun) 6.27m; **4** K. McMillan (USA) 6.18m.

Shot: 1 H. Fibingerova (Cze) 20.79m (68' 2½"); **2** M. Droese (GDR) 20.12m; **3** C. Van Pelt (USA) 15.15m; **4** D. Patrick (USA) 14.28m.

4 x 400m Relay: 1 Europe (K. Kafer, R. Bottiglieri, M. Kulchunova, M. Sidorova) 3:35.0; **2** USA (S. Dabney, K. Thomas, L. Hatz, P. Jiles) 3:38.6.

Match Result: Europe 67, USA 28.

25 March
IAAF CROSS-COUNTRY CHAMPIONSHIPS

Natalia Marasescu of Romania had already made quite an impression in 1978: a world's best time for 10,000 metres, a world indoor 1500 metres record, a silver medal in the European Indoor and another good run in the Europe v USA match. Here was an athlete in formidable form, yet despite placing a clearcut second in what has now become accepted as the World Cross-Country Championships she finished *half a minute* down on Grete Waitz. The Norwegian produced an absolutely stunning performance in atrociously wet conditions at Glasgow to win by such a margin in a race of less than 5000 metres. An advantage of three per cent over one's nearest opponent is equivalent to winning by three metres in a 100 metres race or over four minutes in a marathon . . . extraordinary at this level of competition.

Grete was running in the event for the first time, and so too was Ireland's John Treacy when, at the age of 20, he became the youngest-ever winner of the senior title, though he had previously competed with distinction in the junior championship by placing third in 1974 (when only 16 years of age) and 1975. The first Irishman to win the race for 47 years, Treacy – a student in the USA

Mick Morton races into an early lead in the IAAF Junior Cross-Country Championship. Mike Street

Bespattered with mud, John Treacy (Eir), left, and Aleksandr Antipov (Sov) duel for the title of World cross-country champion. Mike Street who had scored an impressive victory in the national collegiate indoor three miles championship a fortnight earlier – took the lead two kilometres from the end of the 12.3 kilometres race and grimly held at bay another outsider, Soviet champion Aleksandr Antipov.

England's big moment came in the junior event where Mick Morton romped away to a devastatingly easy victory, and led his side to the team title. Both England and Canada scored the same number of points, so the championship was decided on the position of the fourth and final scorer . . . England's came twenty-fourth, Canada's twenty-ninth. England, in fact, was the only nation to win medals in all three races – both the men (led by Tony Simmons in fourth place) and women (headed by evergreen Joyce Smith in ninth position) finished third in their team events.

Due to confusion over the identity of the runner who finished eighteenth in the senior men's race, there was a long delay in the announcing of the team result – and to everyone's surprise, themselves included, it was France who were declared the winners.

MEN'S SENIOR CHAMPIONSHIP

1	J. Treacy (Eir)	39:25	22	P. Baker (Wal)	40:36
2	A. Antipov (Sov)	39:28	23	H. Schoofs (Bel)	40:37
3	K. Lismont (Bel)	39:32	24	A. Hutton (Sco)	40:42
4	A. Simmons (Eng)	39:51	25	A. Fedotkin (Sov)	40:42
5	G. Arbogast (USA)	39:52	26	E. De Beck (Bel)	40:43
6	C. Virgin (USA)	39:54	27	S. De La Parte (Spa)	40:45
7	N. Muir (Sco)	40:00	28	N. Coupland (Eng)	40:46
8	F. Fava (Ita)	40:03	29	J. Wells (USA)	40:47
9	E. Sellik (Sov)	40:08	30	M. McLeod (Eng)	40:48
10	P. Levisse (Fra)	40:10			
11	S. Jones (Wal)	40:15		**Team Placings**	
12	A. Bougeurra (Tun)	40:16	1	France	151pts
13	L. Rault (Fra)	40:19	2	United States	156pts
14	G. Deegan (Eir)	40:22	3	England	159pts
15	J. Wild (Eng)	40:24	4	Soviet Union	169pts
16	C. Herle (Ger)	40:25	5	Belgium	175pts
17	L. Zarcone (Ita)	40:25	6	Republic of Ireland	189pts
18	R. Bouster (Fra)	40:25	7	Germany	240pts
19	A. McKean (Sco)	40:29	8	Italy	276pts
20	G. Meyer (USA)	40:33	9	Scotland	291pts
21	L. Moseyev (Sov)	40:35	10	Spain	324pts

MEN'S JUNIOR CHAMPIONSHIP

1	M. Morton (Eng)	22:57	10	R. Berry (USA)	23:24
2	R. Earl (Can)	23:10			
3	F. Alario (Spa)	23:11		**Team Placings**	
4	C. Esparcia (Spa)	23:12	1	England (1, 13, 15, 24)	53pts
5	R. Carroll (Eir)	23:14	2	Canada (2, 8, 14, 29)	53pts
6	A. Pasaryuk (Sov)	23:15	3	Spain	54pts
7	V. Zinovets (Sov)	23:20	4	Soviet Union	60pts
8	K. Dillon (Can)	23:22	5	Belgium	72pts
9	E. De Pauw (Bel)	23:23	6	Republic of Ireland	84pts

1	G. Waitz (Nor)	16:19	15	B. Webb (USA)	17:36
2	N. Marasescu (Rom)	16:49	16	P. Yule (Eng)	17:37
3	M. Puica (Rom)	16:59	17	A. Iacob (Rom)	17:37
4	J. Shea (USA)	17:12	18	M. Stewart (Eng)	17:39
5	C. Burki (Swi)	17:13	19	T. Kazankina (Sov)	17:43
6	M. Greschner (Ger)	17:14	20	C. Sokolowska (Pol)	17:44
7	J. Merrill (USA)	17:17			
8	G. Gazibara (Rom)	17:18	**Team Placings**		
9	J. Smith (Eng)	17:23	1	Romania	30pts
10	C. Valero (Spa)	17:26	2	United States	37pts
11	K. Mills (USA)	17:27	3	England	55pts
12	C. Benning (Eng)	17:28	4	Germany	85pts
13	A. Possanai (Ita)	17:32	5	Poland	122pts
14	M. Purcell (Eir)	17:35	6	Republic of Ireland	152pts

MARCH HIGHLIGHTS

Two world indoor bests were set late in the North American season: Jan Merrill (USA) became the first woman to break nine minutes for 3000 metres 'on the boards' with a time of 8:57.6 in Montreal on 5 March, and Mike Tully (USA) pole vaulted 5.62 metres (18' 5¼") in Detroit on 11 March.

Indoors in Britain, the precocious talent of pole vaulter Tim Anstiss and shot putter Tony Zaidman was in evidence at the National Under-20 Championships at Cosford on 17 and 18 March. In addition to winning youths titles, they carried off top honours in the junior category.

Results: (Junior Men) 60m/200m: M. McFarlane 6.75/22.0; **400m:** N. Jackson 49.7; **800m:** T. Young 1:52.6; **1500m:** C. Clarkson 3:55.9; **3000m:** K. Irvine 8:16.6; **60m Hurdles:** P. Johnson 8.53; **High Jump:** V. Clemmens 2.05m (6' 8¾"); **Pole Vault:** T. Anstiss 4.30m (14' 1¼"); **Long Jump:** A. Udo 7.28m (23' 10¾"); **Triple Jump:** M. Effiong 15.19m (49' 10"); **Shot:** A. Zaidman 14.30m (46' 11"). **(Youths) 60m:** M. Powell 7.04; **200m:** R. Bennett 23.1; **400m:** S. Ahamed 50.9; **800m:** N. Harper 1:57.9; **1500m:** R. Brightman 4:07.3; **60m Hurdles:** P. Whelan 8.57; **Pole Vault:** T. Anstiss 4.21m (13' 9¾"); **Long Jump:** L. White 6.37m (20' 10¾"); **Triple Jump:** N. Leech 13.71m (44' 11¾"); **Shot:** A. Zaidman 17.87m (58' 7½"). **(Intermediate Women) 60m:** P. Baker 7.57; **400m:** L. Callow 58.9; **800m:** A. Clifford 2:12.6; **1500m:** S. Arthurton 4:27.1; **60m Hurdles:** D. Baker 8.80; **High Jump:** K. Hagger 1.68m (5' 6"); **Long Jump:** A. Licorish 5.69m (18' 8"); **Shot:** E. Tinkler 11.36m (37' 3¼"). **(Junior Women) 60m:** L. MacDonald 7.82; **1500m:** A. Alford 4:47.3.

Olly Flynn notched up his third victory in four years in the RWA national '10 miles' road walk championship at Crystal Palace on 18 March; in fact the course was found to measure only about nine and a half miles.

Result: 1 O. Flynn 67:29; **2** B. Adams 68:13; **3** G. Morris 69:08; **4** A. Seddon 69:24; **5** W. Wright 69:40; **6** S. Lightman 70:02. **Team:** Ilford.

Despite very difficult weather and track conditions at West London Stadium on 25 March, fast times were recorded by Brian Adams and Carol Tyson respectively in the AAA and (inaugural) WAAA 10,000 metres walk championships. Carol's time was a British best.

Result: AAA 1 B. Adams 43:44; **2** R. Mills 45:18; **3** G. Nibre 45:40; **4** C. Lawton 45:41; **5** M. Wordsworth 45:54; **6** P. Marlow 46:20; **WAAA 1** C. Tyson 49:59; **2** M. Fawkes 50:31; **3** J. Farr 50:46; **4** V. Lovell 52:16; **5** C. Coleman 52:59; **6** I. Bateman 53:51.

Right: *It was in April that Kenya's Henry Rono achieved the first of four world records.* Peter Tempest

April

APRIL HIGHLIGHTS

It would seem logical that, as man draws closer to his physical limits, world records would be broken by ever-diminishing amounts. But every now and then an athlete comes along to make nonsense of that premise, opening up whole new vistas of what may be feasible in terms of athletic performance. Ron Clarke of Australia was such a man. The world record for 5000 metres had stood since 1957 to the exalted name of Vladimir Kuts (Sov) at 13:35.0 when Clarke began to make his impact on the sport, and people spoke in awe of the possibility that one day an athlete might break thirteen and a half minutes for the distance. In 1966, Clarke ran 13:16.6. Similarly, in the 10,000 metres, the pre-Clarke record was 28:18.2 by Pyotr Bolotnikov (Sov) and 28 minutes still seemed a long way off. Clarke clocked 27:39.4 in 1965.

The world has had to wait over a decade for Henry Rono, the next runner to push back the barriers in this way. Previously little-known internationally, even if he did rank as the fourth fastest 10,000 metres performer of all time, the short but long-striding Kenyan became in 1978 the most celebrated athlete on this planet. During a seemingly endless string of fast races he collected world records in four different events and scored gold medal doubles in both the African and Commonwealth Games.

It was on 8 April that 26-year-old Rono first achieved athletic immortality. Competing for Washington State University in a match at Berkeley, California, he reeled off 5000 metres in 13:08.4 to smash the world record set in 1977 by Dick Quax (NZ) by a full four and a half seconds. It had previously taken 11 years for the world record to be pared down 3.7 seconds since Clarke's great effort. Despite the presence of his distinguished Kenyan team-mates Josh Kimeto (who finished second, 300 metres behind, in 13:58.0) and world 10,000 metres record holder Samson Kimobwa (third in 14:03.0), there was no calculated pacing; Rono hit the front early on (the first lap, at 67.3, was the slowest of the race) and from then on it was he against the clock. He covered the first kilometre in 2:41.4 (Quax ran 2:39.2 during his record), and reached 2000 metres in 5:18.8 (5:18.4), 3000 metres in 7:55.3 (7:56.0) and 4000 metres in 10:34.7 (10:38.9). Averaging 63.1 per lap for twelve and a half laps, Rono produced his fastest split of 59.5 on the last circuit. His previous best 5000 metres time was 13:22.1.

Two days earlier, in Copenhagen, a 20-year-old Danish girl, Loa Olafsson, was responsible for a major breakthrough in women's distance running. She hacked almost a minute off the unofficial world's best for 10,000 metres with a time of 31:45.4.

Marathon history was made in the famed Boston event on 17 April when Jeff Wells (USA) recorded the fastest non-winning time ever . . . 2:10:15. In the closest finish on record for the 'Boston', Bill Rodgers (USA) won by just two seconds. For the first time in a single race, six men broke 2:12, 32 were inside 2:20, and there was a record field of 4,212 starters.

The motor racing circuit in Mexico City was the scene, on 23 April, of the most phenomenal walking performance yet. Raul Gonzales (Mex) took nearly seven minutes off the previous fastest 50 kilometres road walk time when he registered 3:45:52. En route he passed through 20 kilometres in 1:28:20 prior to increasing his pace still more to reach 30 kilometres in 2:12:17. His 10-kilometre splits were 44:09, 44:11, 43:57, 45:28, 48:07.

From the longest of the 'standard' events to the shortest: at Dallas, Texas, on 1 April an 11.18 metres per second (about 25mph) wind blew William Snoddy to the fastest 100 metres of all time . . . 9.87!

With no help from the wind in her case, Meg Ritchie opened the season in Edinburgh on 15 April with a UK discus record of 60.80 metres (199′ 6″), thus becoming the first British woman to cross the 60 metre line. That same day, at Greenville, USA, the legendary Al Oerter – still building up with an Olympic comeback in mind – produced a world best by a 41-year-old thrower of 62.06 metres (203′ 7″).

What had been anticipated as a classic confrontation between Gateshead Harriers and Tipton Harriers for the AAA national 12-stage road relay title at Sutton Coldfield on 29 April fizzled out on the third stage when Gateshead's Steve Irvine failed to finish due to a severe leg injury. Tipton went on to win by almost four minutes in a time which broke Gateshead's course record by 25 seconds.

Result: 1 Tipton 4:03:49 (R. Cytlau 26:07, R. Westwood 14:46, A. Holden 26:07, J. Wright 14:49, P. Griffiths 27:19, P. Venmore 14:50, S. Emson 25:44, B. Cole 14:41, I. Stewart 24:38, A. Milovsorov 14:09, M. Kearns 26:02, D. Fownes 14:37); **2** Aldershot Farnham and District 4:07:48; **3** Wolverhampton and Bilston 4:08:01; **4** Sheffield 4:08:11; **5** Airedale and Spen Valley 4:09:27; **6** Thames Valley Harriers 4:09:37. **Fastest laps:** *(5 miles 900 yards)* I. Stewart 24:38, B. Foster 24:42, B. Ford 24:46; *(3 miles 100 yards)* R. Smedley 13:54, K. Newton 14:02, A. Milovsorov 14:09.

Doug Fownes takes over from Mike Kearns for the last leg of the AAA Road Relay. Tim Pike

May

7 May

AAA MARATHON CHAMPIONSHIP

Tony Simmons, potentially a world beater at the event but for a tendency for his legs to cramp up in the closing stages, survived the distance at Sandbach to become AAA marathon champion in the brisk time of 2:12:33, a mark bettered by only five other Britons in history. 'No, I'm not a marathon runner yet', he commented modestly after the race, although one feels his defeated rivals – representing the cream of British marathoning – would beg to differ. The 29-year-old Welshman, who 15 years earlier was the fastest miler of his age in the world and more recently has developed into one of the finest of 10,000 metres runners (second in the 1974 European, fourth in the 1976 Olympics), had only once before completed a marathon, taking 2:23:56 in 1972. He had tried a few more since then, his most galling attempt being the 1975 AAA title race where he was struck down by cramp after holding a 200 metres lead with less than two miles to go.

At Sandbach, Simmons started off quite slowly, lagging 20 seconds behind the leaders, until he pushed forward after six miles. By 10 miles (49:01) he was about a quarter-mile clear of the pack, and he was still over a minute ahead at 20 miles (1:39:45). That lead was whittled down to 17 seconds by the finish, but that was largely due to Simmons grinding to a stop a few hundred yards from the end when a waving spectator caught him in the face. As Tony was able to joke later, 'My nose went into his fist!'

---

1 A. Simmons 2:12:33; **2** J. Norman 2:12:50; **3** T. Wright 2:13:00; **4** D. Cannon 2:13:29; **5** J. Dingwall 2:13:58; **6** S. Curran 2:14:45; **7** C. Taylor 2:15:47; **8** M. Koussis (Gre) 2:16:02; **9** L. Enquist (Swe) 2:16:55; **10** K. Penny 2:16:57; **11** M. Rowland (Swe) 2:17:21; **12** M. Hurd 2:17:24; **13** J. McLaughlin 2:17:35; **14** Greg Hannon 2:17:35; **15** R. Brown 2:17:48; **16** A. Keith 2:18:15; **17** J. Davies 2:18:20; **18** I. Beauchamp 2:19:07; **19** W. Padgett 2:19:16; **20** H. Jonsson (Swe) 2:19:34. **Team:** Duncairn Harriers (N. Ireland).

---

24 May

PHILIPS NIGHT OF ATHLETICS

What a night it was for Christine Benning (née Tranter) at the first major fixture of the season at Crystal Palace. She outshone even such luminaries as Henry Rono, Don Quarrie and Franklin Jacobs in producing the top performance of the meeting: victory over world cross-country champion Grete Waitz and European indoor gold medallist Ileana Silai in the 1500 metres. Surpassing anything she had previously achieved in the sport, Christine hung on to her more famous rivals and then proceeded – to her amazement also – to edge past them both in the final straight. As if the victory wasn't sweet enough, she could also rejoice in the time of 4:08.3, a personal best and a fifth of a second inside the UK all-comers record held by none other than Tatyana Kazankina (Sov).

Left: *Tony Simmons during his AAA marathon triumph.* Ray Martin

Fresh (or rather the opposite) from his tremendous 5000 (13:20.2)/10,000 metres (27:46.6) double 6000 miles away in Oregon a few days earlier, Henry Rono ran away from a good field in the 3000 metres, taking only about 3:44 for the second 1500 metres. Some 25 metres behind in second place was plucky Steve Ovett, running despite suffering the agonies of a septic tooth.

MEN

100m: 1 E. Obeng (Gha) 10.3w; 2 D. Quarrie (Jam) 10.4; 3 M. McFarlane 10.5.

200m: 1 D. Quarrie (Jam) 20.75w; 2 M. McFarlane 21.16; 3 J. Thomas (USA) 21.26.

400m: 1 M. Peoples (USA) 46.9; 2 R. Jenkins 47.2; 3 S. Scutt 47.2.

1000m: 1 J. Plachy (Cze) 2:19.8; 2 T. Wessinghage (Ger) 2:20.5; 3 C. Grippo (Ita) 2:21.2.

Mile: 1 W. Waigwa (Ken) 4:00.7; 2 J. Robson 4:00.7; 3 R. Dixon (NZ) 4:01.4.

3000m: 1 H. Rono (Ken) 7:43.8; 2 S. Ovett 7:48.0; 3 M. Liquori (USA) 7:48.8; 4 N. Rose 7:49.8; 5 M. McLeod 7:50.2; 6 N. Muir 7:53.3.

3000m Steeplechase: 1 D. Coates 8:33.0; 2 J. Davies 8:39.6; 3 A. Staynings 8:43.0.

400m Hurdles: 1 M. Shine (USA) 50.0; 2 D. West 51.7; 3 G. Oakes 52.1.

High Jump. 1 F. Jacobs (USA) 2.18m (7' 1¾"); 2 C. Thranhardt (Ger) 2.18m; 3 A. Dainton 2.00m.

Pole Vault: 1 W. Buciarski (Pol) 5.30m (17' 4½"); 2 B. Hooper 5.30m; 3 R. Pullard (USA) 5.30m; 4 M. Klimczyk (Pol) 5.20m; 5 J. Gutteridge 5.20m; 6 T. Slusarski (Pol) 5.20m.

Shot: 1 G. Capes 20.27m (66' 6"); 2 W. Komar (Pol) 19.53m; 3 M. Winch 18.29m.

Mile Walk: 1 R. Mills 6:11.1; 2 B. Adams 6:26.7; 3 M. Wordsworth 6:31.3.

Ernest Obeng from Ghana (left) scores an upset 100 metres victory over Don Quarrie of Jamaica (centre). Mike Street

Another surprise winner: Christine Benning (161) outsprints Grete Waitz of Norway (9) and Ileana Silai (Rom) in the 1500 metres. Mike Street

WOMEN

200m: 1 S. Lannaman 23.29w; **2** B. Goddard 23.39; **3** K. Smallwood 23.54; **4** S. Colyear 23.55; **5** I. Szewinska (Pol) 23.77.

1500m: 1 C. Benning 4:08.3 (*UK all-comers record*); **2** G. Waitz (Nor) 4:08.5; **3** I. Silai (Rom) 4:08.7.

Javelin: 1 T. Sanderson 61.14m (200' 7"); **2** E. Helmschmidt (Ger) 59.64m; **3** K. Smith (USA) 59.28m.

MAY HIGHLIGHTS

Watched by only about 200 fans, Henry Rono chalked up his second fabulous world record of the season in Seattle, Washington, on 13 May. The windy conditions (with gusts of up to eight metres per second) and lack of opposition and atmosphere did not deter the Kenyan wonder from attempting the steeplechase record of 8:08.0 set by Anders Garderud (Swe) at the 1976 Olympics, and with kilometre splits of 2:42.0, 2:42.8 and 2:40.6 he came home in 8:05.4. Rono's barrier technique, and particularly when negotiating the water jump, is fairly primitive, and Jim Johnson, the American who finished second in the race in 8:36.1, summed it up when he remarked: 'If he had any hurdles technique he'd have broken eight minutes today. His hurdling form looked ragged to me . . . but Rono has a lot of horsepower and uses it. There's certainly nothing lacking in his speed between hurdles.' Rono's best steeplechase time before 1978 was 8:29.0 in 1976, the year he made the Kenyan Olympic team in the event but was unable to race in Montreal because of the African withdrawal. He had, in April, improved to 8:14.8, less than a second outside the Commonwealth record held by his compatriot Ben Jipcho. An added distinction for Rono: he is the first man ever to hold world records in both the 5000 metres and 3000 metres steeplechase.

Another world record – or was it? – was set at Corvallis, Oregon, on 19 May when 21-year-old American, Mike Tully, pole vaulted 5.71 metres (18' 8¾") to add a centimetre (½") to the mark held by Dave Roberts (USA). Tully soared over at the first attempt, but the problems arose when officials set about remeasuring the bar as stipulated in IAAF rules concerning record applications. While moving the uprights back to the zero position for remeasurement, the bar fell off. When the bar was replaced it was found to be only 5.69 metres (18' 8"). Whether or not Tully gets official credit for the record, he is convinced he cleared 5.71 metres. 'It's mine', he claimed. 'I watched them measure it and then I jumped it.'

There was an odd world record also at Tempe, Arizona, on 27 May when a University of Southern California team of Joel Andrews (20.9), James Sanford (20.1), Billy Mullins (19.6) and Clancy Edwards (19.8) was credited with setting a 4 x 200 metres relay record of 1:20.3 . . . even though the squad finished second. Winners in 1:20.2 were the Tobias Striders foursome but they were not eligible for a world record as the team was multi-national. Guy Abrahams of Panama opened with a 20.5 leg, and he was followed by Mike Simmons of USA (20.7), Don Quarrie of Jamaica (19.7) and James Gilkes of Guyana (19.3). Oddly enough, all four of the Tobias Striders are graduates of the University of Southern California.

Marita Koch, a 21-year-old East German medical student, broke the world 200 metres record held by Irena Szewinska (Pol) at 22.21 when she sped over the distance in 22.06 at Erfurt on 28 May. The aiding wind of 1.22 metres per second was within the limit. At the same meeting, Roland Steuk set a world junior record for the hammer of 77.48 metres (254' 2"), and another East German thrower, Wolfgang Schmidt, registered a European discus record of 68.92 metres (226' 1") in Berlin on 31 May.

There are no official world records for women's races beyond 3000 metres but such events are gradually increasing in popularity. Kathy Mills (USA) produced a world's best time of 15:35.5 for 5000 metres at Knoxville on 26 May, but it lasted only four days until Loa Olafsson (Den) clocked 15:08.8, setting a national 3000 metres mark of 9:05.3 on the way.

May 1978 was a fantastic month for walking records. Pyotr Myslivsyev (Sov) was timed in 1:23:26 for a 20 kilometres road event at Kaliningrad on 12 May, the fastest-ever time for this event. Seven days later, at Forde in Norway, Mexico's Raul Gonzales followed up his earlier 50 kilometres road time of 3:45:52 with a world track record of 3:52:23.5. Passing 20 kilometres in 1:27:40.2 (over a minute inside the UK record!), he also collected world records for 30 kilometres with 2:11:53.4 and two hours with 27,247.36 metres (16 miles 1639 yards). His 10-kilometre splits were 44:07.5, 43:32.7, 44:13.2, 49:29.7 and 51:00.4. His Mexican colleague, Olympic champion Daniel Bautista, produced a world's best of 14,430 metres (8 miles 1700 yards) in the hour en route to a 1:23:37.3 20 kilometres in Madrid on 28 May, and two days later on a cinder track at Grudziadz in Poland he covered 10 kilometres in 39:39.9. The previous best for this distance had been posted at Turku on 8 May by Reima Salonen (Fin) with 40:30.7. Derek Harrison, from the Isle of Man, walked 219.5 kilometres (over 136 miles) in 24 hours at Rouen on 20 and 21 May.

Olly Flynn gained his fifth consecutive win in the RWA national 20 kilometres road walk championship at Coventry on 13 May.

Result: 1 O. Flynn 1:28:44; **2** B. Adams 1:29:47; **3** R. Mills 1:30:42; **4** A. Seddon 1:31:35; **5** S. Gower 1:31:49; **6** C. Lawton 1:32:37. **Team:** Steyning.

Meg Ritchie, already holder of the UK discus record, succeeded Mary Peters as British shot put record holder with a distance of 16.40 metres (53′ 9¾″) in the Greece v Scotland match in Athens on 14 May. In the same match, Scotland's Derek Howie, who took part in the 10,000 metres walk, became probably the first registered blind person to compete internationally.

Still only 19, Daley Thompson improved his own Commonwealth and UK decathlon record to 8238 points at Gotzis in Austria on 27 and 28 May. He held a 51-point lead over Olympic silver medallist Guido Kratschmer at the halfway mark with 4385 points, but the German produced a great second-day display to win with a score of 8410. Thompson's individual performances were: 10.77 100 metres; wind-assisted 7.95 metres (26′ 1″) long jump; 13.89 metres (45′ 7″) shot; 2.03 metres (6′ 8″) high jump; 47.76 400 metres; 14.85 110 metres hurdles; 41.40 metres (135′ 10″) discus; 4.60 metres (15′ 1″) pole vault; 56.90 metres (186′ 8″) javelin and 4:29.1 1500 metres.

The same weekend, an international decathlon and women's pentathlon match was staged at Cwmbran, featuring a UK junior record of 3987 points by Judy Livermore.

Results: Decathlon: 1 W. Roosen (Hol) 7415; **2** G. Watson (UK) 7249; **3** K. Jorgensen (Den) 7069; **4** R. Jansen (Hol) 7059; **5** P. Lewis 6942 . . . **10** P. Zeniou 6330. **Teams: 1** Netherlands 21,107; **2** Denmark 20,760; **3** UK 20,521. **Pentathlon: 1** Y. Wray (UK) 4292; **2** S. Barlag (Hol) 4281; **3** E. Stolk (Hol) 4195; **4** S. Mapstone (UK) 4013; **5** J. Livermore (UK) 3987. **Teams: 1** Netherlands 12,336; **2** UK 12,292; **3** Denmark 11,225.

The Yorkshire county championships at Cleckheaton yielded two notable performances: in the men's championships on 14 May, Sebastian Coe clocked the very fast early-season 800 metres time of 1:45.6, while in the women's events on 20 May a hand-timed Commonwealth and UK 400 metres hurdles record of 57.0 was achieved by Christine Warden. Another athlete with Yorkshire connections, Greg Colin (19), tied the UK 200 metres record of 20.66 running at 5000 feet altitude in Pretoria, South Africa, on 1 May. Colin, resident in South Africa but holder of a UK passport and a member of Leeds City AC, had in March recorded a hand-timed 10.1 for 100 metres.

The inaugural WAAA marathon title was won by Margaret Lockley (née Ashcroft), making her own marathon début. Despite hot weather and the hilly nature of the Isle of Man course she ran the fast time of 2:55:08 on 20 May, winning from Margaret Thompson (Ian Thompson's wife), 3:16:15, and Lesley Watson, 3:18:46. There were 11 runners.

June

8–10 June

AMERICAN AAU CHAMPIONSHIPS

The most prodigiously talented young high hurdler the world has ever known, Renaldo 'Skeets' Nehemiah, chalked up the first of what is likely to be many an American senior title when he zipped to a 1½-metre victory over Greg Foster at Westwood, Los Angeles. One week earlier, in the National Collegiate Championships, Foster had set an American 110 metres hurdles record of 13.22 – just one-hundredth of a second away from the world record held by Cuba's Alejandro Casanas – with 19-year-old Nehemiah a close second in 13.27 for a world junior record. But it was all Nehemiah in the re-match as he won in 13.28.

Another excellent achievement was Dwight Stones' leap of 2.30 metres (7′ 6½″) for his fifth AAU title. He had a good try at a world record 2.34 metres (7′ 8″). That might well have been the flamboyant Stones' swan-song, for later in June he – along with Kate Schmidt (the javelin world record holder), Francie Larrieu and Jane Frederick – was suspended indefinitely by the AAU for an alleged infringement of the amateur rules.

American records were registered by Brenda Morehead with 22.60 in her semi-final of the 200 metres (though she was beaten in the final) and by Jodi Anderson with a long jump of 6.90 metres (22′ 7½″); while in the 100 metres Jamaica's Lelieth Hodges broke Andrea Lynch's Commonwealth record with 11.14 in a heat in which she dead-heated with Morehead.

MEN

100m: 1 C. Edwards 10.14; **2** D. Quarrie (Jam) 10.15; **3** G. Abrahams (Pan) 10.17.

200m: 1 C. Edwards 20.25; **2** J. Gilkes (Guy) 20.46; **3** T. Darden 20.48.

400m: 1 M. Parks 45.15; **2** M. Peoples 45.22; **3** A. Rodgers 45.41.

800m: 1 J. Robinson 1:45.5; **2** M. Boit (Ken) 1:46.0; **3** M. Belger 1:46.2.

1500m: 1 S. Scott 3:38.8; **2** S. Maree (Saf) 3:38.9; **3** S. Lacy 3:39.0.

5000m: 1 M. Liquori 13:40.2; **2** G. Fredericks 13:41.0; **3** M. Centrowitz 13:41.0.

10,000m: 1 C. Virgin 28:15.0; **2** G. Bjorklund 28:35.0; **3** J. Wells 28:45.6.

3000m Steeplechase: 1 H. Marsh 8:27.3; **2** D. Brown 8:30.1; **3** G. Malley 8:30.5.

110m Hurdles: 1 R. Nehemiah 13.28; **2** G. Foster 13.43; **3** K. Bethel 13.60.

400m Hurdles: 1 J. Walker 49.03; **2** T. Andrews 49.63; **3** S. Turner 49.82.

High Jump: 1 D. Stones 2.30m (7′ 6¼″); **2 eq** B. Fields and F. Jacobs 2.24m.

Pole Vault: 1 D. Ripley 5.56m (18′ 3″); **2** M. Tully 5.48m; **3** J. Taylor 5.33m.

Long Jump: 1 A. Robinson 8.33m (27′ 4″)w; **2** J. Lofton 8.23m; **3** C. Ehizuelen (Nig) 7.94m.

Triple Jump: 1 J. Butts 16.90m (55′ 5½″); **2** R. Dupree 16.46m; **3** P. Jordan 16.46m.

Left: *Brendan Foster racing towards a European 10,000 metres record of 27:30.3.* George Herringshaw

Shot: 1 A. Feuerbach 20.46m (67' 1½"); **2** C. Anderson 20.29m; **3** D. Price 19.96m.

Discus: 1 M. Wilkins 66.98m (219' 9"); **2** K. Stadel 63.86m; **3** D. Voorhees 61.78m.

Hammer: 1 B. Djerassi 68.34m (224' 3"); **2** E. Berry 65.64m; **3** P. Galle 65.50m.

Javelin: 1 W. Schmidt 84.36m (276' 9"); **2** R. Roggy 82.94m; **3** R. Ewaliko 81.28m.

WOMEN

100m: 1 L. Hodges (Jam) 11.23; **2** B. Morehead 11.25; **3** E. Ashford 11.30.

200m: 1 E. Ashford 22.66; **2** B. Morehead 22.88; **3** C. Cheeseborough 23.55.

400m: 1 L. Forde (Bar) 51.04; **2** P. Jackson 51.11; **3** S. Dabney 51.31.

800m: 1 R. Caldwell 2:02.0; **2** E. Kelley 2:03.0; **3** M. Decker 2:03.1.

1500m: 1 J. Merrill 4:09.4; **2** D. Heald 4:10.9; **3** C. Bremser 4:11.1.

3000m: 1 J. Merrill 8:56.4; **2** K. Mills 9:03.3; **3** C. Bremser 9:11.8.

10,000m: 1 E. Goodall 33:40.2; **2** S. Kinsey 33:42.7; **3** K. Bridges 34:17.3.

100m Hurdles: 1 D. LaPlante 13.19; **2** P. van Wolvelaere 13.22; **3** M. Smith 13.50.

400m Hurdles: 1 D. Esser 57.85; **2** E. Mahal (Can) 58.60; **3** J. Smith 58.62.

High Jump: 1 L. Ritter 1.86m (6' 1¼"); **2** P. Spencer 1.86m; **3** D. Brill (Can) 1.83m.

Long Jump: 1 J. Anderson 6.90m (22' 7½"); **2** K. McMillan 6.72m; **3** J. Griffith (Guy) 6.30m.

Shot: 1 M. Seidler 18.18m (59' 8"); **2** A. Turbyne 15.96m; **3** K. Devine 15.49m.

Discus: 1 L. Winbigler 54.40m (178' 6"); **2** L. Griffin 53.70m; **3** H. Connell 52.12m.

Javelin: 1 S. Calvert 62.06m (203' 7"); **2** K. Schmidt 60.48m; **3** L. Cannon 55.30m.

10, 11 June

UK v GDR

A fighting British men's team came close to holding the East Germans, the World Cup holders, at Crystal Palace. The GDR finally squeaked home by 8 points (compared to a margin of 72 points in 1975 and 46 in 1976) but the match would have been a draw had the British management gone ahead with the steeplechase, an event for which the visitors brought no competitors. However, in deference to the two British representatives ('neither of whom wished to compete in a farcical race', explained BAAB general secretary David Shaw) and the public ('who had already been subjected to races featuring only one GDR athlete'), the decision was taken by the BAAB to cancel the race and award no points. An unopposed British one-two would have yielded 8 points to nil.

British track victories were gained by Steve Ovett (who uncorked a 51.6 last lap in a 1500 metres which, until then, looked more like a slow-motion action replay), Nick Rose, Tony Simmons and Alan Pascoe; but it was out on the field that the British lads really excelled to draw 44–44 in the eight jumping and throwing events. Brian Hooper won the pole vault, Roy Mitchell the long jump, Aston Moore the triple jump, Geoff Capes the shot and Paul Dickenson the hammer. It should be pointed out that most of the leading GDR throwers

Olaf Beyer, destined to become European champion, wins the 800 metres in the UK v GDR match. Mike Street

were absent . . . for reasons which some observers felt might not have been unconnected with the fact that the match was dope-controlled.

From the British point of view the most notable feat of all came from the high-flying Scotsman Brian Burgess (20) who flopped clear over 2.20 metres (7' 2½") for a landmark in British high jump history. A few minutes earlier on 11 June he had joined Mark Naylor in clearing 2.17 metres (7' 1½"), itself a UK record. Burgess, holder of the previous mark of 2.15 metres (7' 0½") – but, remember, Naylor jumped 2.19 metres (7' 2¼") indoors – was hastily added to Scotland's Commonwealth Games team as a result. It was a hot competition all round as Rolf Beilschmidt went on to equal Dwight Stones' UK all-comers record of 2.26 metres (7' 5") to win from Edgar Kirst. Another record fell in the non-scoring 20 kilometres track walk, Hartwig Gauder clocking 1:24:22.8 for a European mark.

The women's match was one-sided and would have been even more so had the East Germans bothered to send a full team. Nevertheless, on the second day there were a couple of home victories for the crowd to celebrate (by Sonia Lannaman and Sue Reeve), plus a UK 100 metres hurdles record of 13.08 by Lorna Boothe in a dead-heat for second place.

MEN

100m: 1 E. Ray (GDR) 10.35; **2** D. Kubeck (GDR) 10.42; **3** M. McFarlane (UK) 10.65; **4** S. Green (UK) 20.15 (*injured*).

200m: 1 O. Prenzler (GDR) 21.15; **2** K-D. Kurrat (GDR) 21.21; **3** M. McFarlane (UK) 21.35; **4** A. McMaster (UK) 21.65.

400m: 1 J. Pfennig (GDR) 47.15; **2** J. Griffiths (UK) 47.84; **3** A. Bell (UK) 47.92; **4** R. Kokot (GDR) 48.19.

800m: 1 O. Beyer (GDR) 1:46.3; **2** P. Hoffmann (UK) 1:46.6; **3** J. Straub (GDR) 1:47.0; **4** D. Warren (UK) 1:49.6.

1500m: 1 S. Ovett (UK) 3:53.8; **2** J. Straub (GDR) 3:54.1; **3** G. Ruth (GDR) 3:55.6; **4** J. Robson (UK) 3:55.9.

5000m: 1 N. Rose (UK) 13:26.6; **2** J. Goater (UK) 13:36.5; **3** A. Staynings (UK – guest) 13:40.6; **4** J. Peter (GDR) 13:47.2; **5** S. Jones (UK – guest) 13:54.6; **6** W. Cierpinski (GDR) 14:04.9.

10,000m: 1 A. Simmons (UK) 28:15.0; **2** W. Cierpinski (GDR) 28:30.8; **3** A. Hutton (UK) 28:43.9; K-H. Leiteritz (GDR) dnf.

3000m Steeplechase: Cancelled.

110m Hurdles: 1 T. Munkelt (GDR) 13.91; **2** M. Holtom (UK) 14.14; **3** B. Price (UK) 14.20; **4** T. Dittrich (GDR) 14.23.

400m Hurdles: 1 A. Pascoe (UK) 50.58; **2** M. Konow (GDR) 50.97; **3** W. Hartley (UK) 51.80; **4** K. Schonberger (GDR) 51.83.

High Jump: 1 R. Beilschmidt (GDR) 2.26m (7' 5") (*equals UK all-comers record*); **2** E. Kirst (GDR) 2.22m; **3** B. Burgess (UK) 2.20m (7' 2½") (*UK national record*); **4** M. Naylor (UK) 2.17m.

Pole Vault: 1 B. Hooper (UK) 5.20m (17' 0¾"); **2** A. Weber (GDR) 5.20m; **3** J. Gutteridge (UK) 5.10m; **4** D. Eckhardt (GDR) 4.80m.

Right: *Brian Burgess leaping for joy after setting a UK high jump record of 2.20 metres (7' 2½").*

George Herringshaw

Long Jump: 1 R. Mitchell (UK) 7.90m (25' 11")w; **2** L. Franke (GDR) 7.87m(w); **3** U. Lange (GDR) 7.66m(w); **4** D. Thompson (UK) 7.58m.

Triple Jump: 1 A. Moore (UK) 16.32m (53' 6½"); **2** D. Johnson (UK) 16.08m; **3** H. Natzmer (GDR) 16.05; **4** L. Gora (GDR) 15.47m.

Shot: 1 G. Capes (UK) 19.94m (65' 5"); **2** R. Krohn (GDR) 19.03m; **3** N. Jahl (GDR) 18.52m; **4** M. Winch (UK) 18.37m.

Discus: 1 G. Muller (GDR) 59.86m (196' 5"); **2** P. Block (GDR) 56.62m; **3** M. Winch (UK) 53.90m; **4** P. Tancred (UK) 53.46m.

Hammer: 1 P. Dickenson (UK) 70.32m (230' 8"); **2** K-H. Beilig (GDR) 70.04m; **3** T. Stopat (GDR) 68.36m; **4** J. Whitehead (UK) 68.28m.

Javelin: 1 W. Hanisch (GDR) 85.70m (281' 2"); **2** P. Yates (UK) 73.98m; **3** D. Travis (UK) 72.68m; **4** E. Kirst (GDR) 55.12m.

(non-scoring) 20km Walk: 1 H. Gauder (GDR) 1:24:22.8 (*European record*); **2** F. Sparmann (GDR) 1:27:18.6; **3** S. Gower (UK) 1:30:27.4; **4** A. Seddon (UK) 1:30:53.6; **5** C. Harvey (UK) 1:34:25.1; **6** G. Nibre (UK) 1:34:39.3.

Match Result: GDR 104, UK 96.

Invitation 400m: 1 D. Jenkins (UK) 46.99; **2** R. Ashton (UK) 47.16; **3** G. Arnold (GDR) 47.75.

WOMEN

100m: 1 M. Gohr (GDR) 11.17w; **2** M. Hamann (GDR) 11.23; **3** A. Lynch (UK) 11.42; **4** S. Lannaman (UK) 11.45.

200m: 1 S. Lannaman (UK) 23.09; **2** M. Hamann (GDR) 23.14; **3** C. Bodendorf (GDR) 23.15; **4** B. Goddard (UK) 23.41.

400m: 1 C. Brehmer (GDR) 52.27; **2** E. Streidt (GDR) 52.29; **3** D. Hartley (UK) 52.83; **4** R. Kennedy (UK – guest) 54.70; G. McCormack (UK) dnf.

800m: 1 H. Ullrich (GDR) 2:00.1; **2** U. Bruns (GDR) 2:00.4; **3** A. Creamer (UK) 2:04.2; L. Kiernan (UK) dnf.

1500m: 1 U. Bruns (GDR) 4:15.3; **2** M. Stewart (UK) 4:15.5; **3** C. Benning (UK) 4:15.7; no 4th.

3000m: 1 G. Lehmann (GDR) 9:05.7; **2** P. Yule (UK) 9:08.6; **3** R. Smeeth (UK) 9:20.7; no 4th.

100m Hurdles: 1 J. Klier (GDR) 12.89 (*UK all-comers record*); **2 eq** L. Boothe (UK) 13.08 (*UK national record*) and A. Fiedler (GDR) 13.08; **4** S. Colyear (UK) 13.39.

400m Hurdles: 1 K. Rossley (GDR) 57.23; **2** H. Ullrich (GDR) 57.68; **3** E. Sutherland (UK) 58.80; **4** S. Reed (UK) 60.96.

High Jump: 1 J. Kirst (GDR) 1.88m (6' 2"); **2** A. Reichstein (GDR) 1.85m; **3** B. Gibbs (UK) 1.79m; **4** G. Hitchen (UK) 1.76m.

Long Jump: 1 S. Reeve (UK) 6.54m (21' 5½"); **2** H. Wycisk (GDR) 6.39m; **3** J. Kirst (GDR) 6.26m; **4** R. Howell (UK) 6.11m.

Shot: 1 S. Michel (GDR) 18.62m (61' 1¼"); **2** K. Fitzner (GDR) 18.13m; **3** J. Oakes (UK) 15.78m; **4** A. Littlewood (UK) 15.60m.

Discus: 1 I. Reichenbach (GDR) 57.64m (189' 1"); **2** P. Wenlandt (GDR) 56.08m; **3** J. Thompson (UK) 50.26m; **4** A. Littlewood (UK) 45.28m.

Javelin: 1 R. Fuchs (GDR) 66.26m (217' 5") (*UK all-comers record*); **2** T. Sanderson (UK) 60.68m; **3** P. Felke (GDR) 57.72m; **4** F. Whitbread (UK) 51.80m.

Right: *Lorna Boothe, British record breaker in the 100 metres hurdles.*   Mike Street

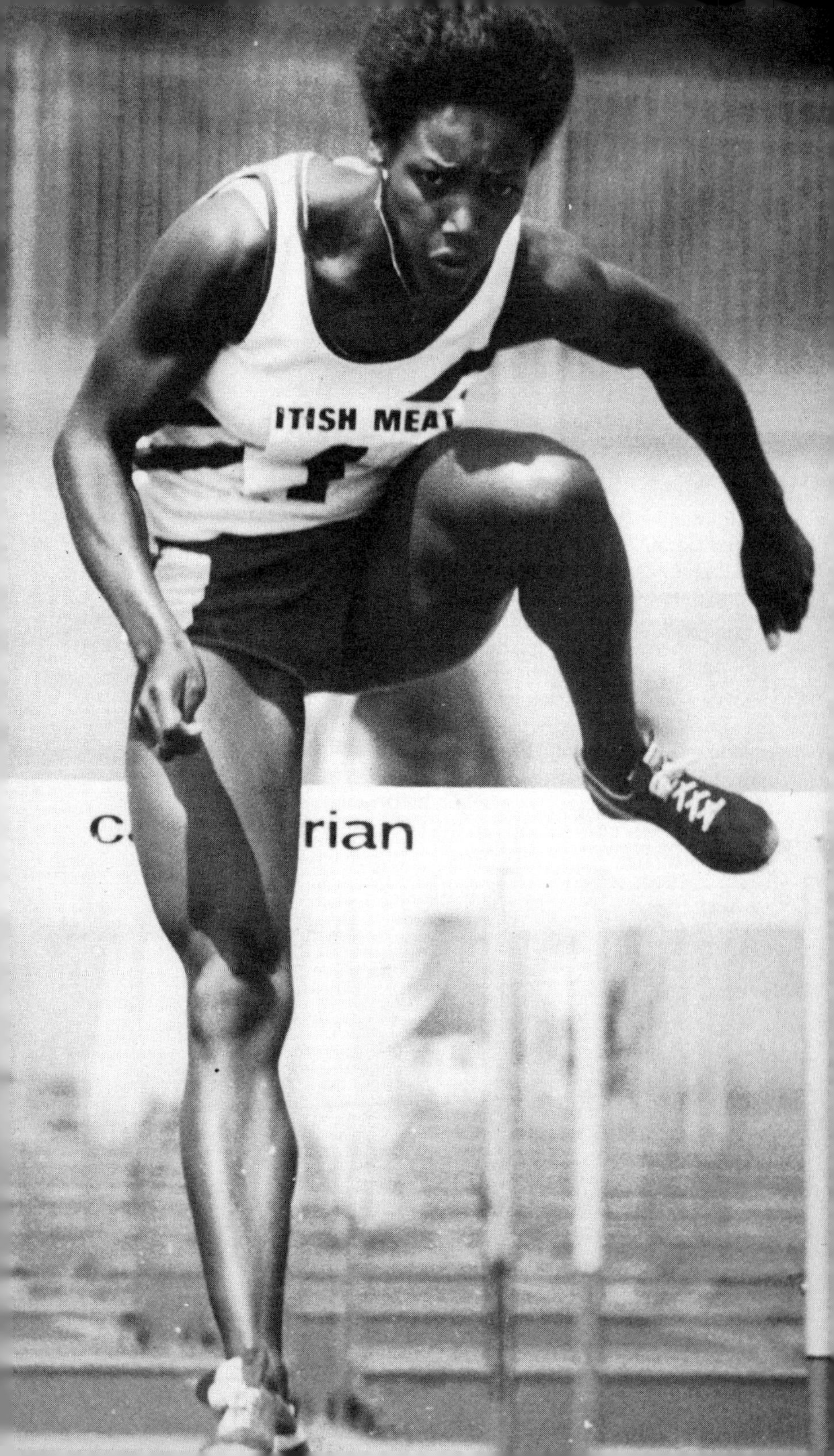
ITISH MEAT
rian

4 × 100m Relay: 1 GDR 43.54; **2** UK (B. Goddard, S. Lannaman, S. Colyear, W. Clarke) 44.25.

4 × 400m Relay: 1 GDR 3:25.9 (*UK all-comers record*); **2** UK (K. Williams, D. Hartley, R. Kennedy, J. Hoyte) 3:30.0.

Match Result: GDR 100½, UK 52½.

Invitation 100m: 1 C. Bodendorf (GDR) 11.47; **2** R. Schneider (GDR) 11.47; **3** B. Goddard (UK) 11.49.

Invitation 200m: 1 K. Smallwood (UK) 23.63; **2** R. Schneider (GDR) 23.90; **3** W. Clarke (UK) 24.16.

17 June

WAAA COMMONWEALTH GAMES TRIALS

It's an ill wind . . . The blustery conditions at Birmingham's new Alexander Stadium made life difficult for the athletes in some events, but they certainly helped Donna Hartley to break Sonia Lannaman's UK 200 metres record of 22.81. Donna improved upon her previous best electrical time by a full half-second as she sped to the spectacular clocking of 22.75 – much to her own delighted astonishment. Although the wind reading in the straight measured a legal 1.8 metres per second, there is little doubt that everyone in the race was assisted to a greater degree while rounding the bend. All eight finalists recorded personal bests, including a UK junior record of 23.16 by Kathy Smallwood (18) and a British age-15 best of 23.42 by Debbie Bunn.

Donna's joy gave way to anxiety one week later when she injured a hamstring running in the heats of the 400 metres trial at Middlesbrough. The other event held over for a week, the 1500 metres, saw both Mary Stewart and Christine Benning break the latter's UK all-comers record of 4:08.3.

100m: 1 S. Lannaman 11.43; **2** A. Lynch 11.52; **3** W. Clarke 11.61.

200m: 1 D. Hartley 22.75 (*UK all-comers and national record*); **2** B. Goddard 23.12; **3** K. Smallwood 23.16 (*UK junior record*).

400m: (24 June) **1** V. Elder 51.9; **2** J. Hoyte 53.3; **3** R. Kennedy 53.4.

800m: 1 E. Barnes 2:02.2; **2** J. Colebrook 2:03.0; **3** P. Newnham 2:03.2.

1500m: (24 June) **1** M. Stewart 4:06.0 (*UK all-comers record*); **2** C. Benning 4:07.8; **3** C. Boxer 4:10.0.

3000m: 1 A. Ford 9:03.1; **2** P. Fudge 9:03.7; **3** R. Smeeth 9:15.8 (*UK junior record*).

100m Hurdles: 1 L. Boothe 13.08w; **2** S. Colyear 13.12; **3** S. Strong 13.19.

High Jump: 1 B. Simmonds 1.79m (5' 10¼"); **2** G. Hitchen 1.77m; **3** V. Rutter 1.77m.

Long Jump: 1 S. Reeve 6.64m (21' 9¼")w; **2** S. Hearnshaw 6.42m(w); **3** A. Simmonds 6.27m(w).

Shot: 1 A. Littlewood 15.75m (51' 8¼"); **2** J. Oakes 15.48m; **3** B. Bedford 15.21m.

Discus: 1 J. Thompson 55.06m (180' 8"); **2** L. Mallin 51.04m; **3** J. Kerr 49.06m.

Javelin: 1 T. Sanderson 61.60m (202' 1"); **2** J. Rose 51.20m; **3** S. Spragg 50.84m.

Right: Donna Hartley astonished herself by setting a UK 200 metres record of 22.75.   Mike Street

23, 24 June

NATIONWIDE BUILDING SOCIETY
AAA CHAMPIONSHIPS

It was a chilly evening, the rain was teeming down and there were puddles on the Crystal Palace track. It was not, on the face of it, an occasion for record breaking, yet Brendan Foster overcame the conditions and the lack of opposition to produce arguably the greatest run of his distinguished career.

In the lead after only four of the 25 laps, Foster was 60 metres up at the half-distance in 13:45.1 and a second 5000 metres in just a fraction of a second slower carried him to the finish half a lap ahead of runner-up Mike McLeod. There was some confusion over his true time. It has been ratified as a UK record of 27:30.5, but in reality he must have run slightly faster than that. Foster was missed by the photo-timing device but the film showed that a lapped runner passed the bell in 27:30.5 and reference to the television recording indicated that Foster, as he finished, was some two metres ahead of that particular lapped competitor. It is clear, therefore, that Foster could not have run slower than 27:30.3 – the time accepted by statisticians for listing purposes.

The difference between 27:30.3 and 27:30.5 may seem trivial but actually it is very significant, for the listed world record stands at 27:30.5 by Samson Kimobwa (Ken). Henry Rono ran 27:22.5 in Vienna 12 days earlier on 11 June, but due to an irregularity there has been a delay in its ratification as a world record. Thus, Foster's time could yet go forward as a world record, either as a new mark (27:30.3) or as equal to Kimobwa. It's all academic to Foster, though. 'I don't want a world record out of this run. I know Rono has run 27:22.5 and that's a faster run than mine, as far as I'm concerned, whether they ratify his time or not.' What is certain is that he did break Dave Bedford's European and UK figures of 27:30.8.

The other British record to fall at the championships occurred also on that climatically depressing Friday evening. Until then in second place to Keith Connor, Aston Moore triple jumped 16.68 metres (54′ 8¾″) in the final round to obliterate both his own official record of 16.52 metres (54′ 2½″) and Connor's indoor mark of 16.54 metres (54′ 3¼″).

Contesting his last AAA championships, Alan Pascoe won the 400 metres hurdles to bring his title tally (including indoors) to 13 while, in the 110 metres hurdles, Berwyn Price brought his run of titles to six in a row. One more and he will equal the all-time record.

Just returned from California, Scottish discus record holder Colin Sutherland won his event but was promptly disqualified – in accordance with the rules – when he refused on principle to take a random doping test. He was later refused permission to take part in the UK Championships and did not compete again in 1978.

Left: *Tuning up for the Commonwealth Games, Dave Moorcroft triumphs in the AAA 1500 metres.*

George Herringshaw

100m: 1 J. Sanford (USA) 10.42; **2** G. Abrahams (Pan) 10.53; **3** E. Obeng (Gha) 10.67; **4** M. McFarlane 10.71; **5** T. Hoyte 10.82; **6** L. Hoyte 10.83; **7** T. Bonsor 10.84; **8** D. Baptiste 10.86.

200m: 1 D. Quarrie (Jam) 20.79; **2** J. Gilkes (Guy) 20.81; **3** J. Sanford (USA) 21.08; **4** M. McFarlane 21.52; **5** T. Bonsor 21.65; **6** G. Cohen 21.72; **7** T. Hoyte 21.81; **8** C. Monk 21.89.

400m: 1 M. Peoples (USA) 45.78; **2** D. Jenkins 46.33; **3** T. Whitehead 46.69; **4** R. Jenkins 46.93; **5** C. Hamilton 47.05; **6** M. Delaney 47.08; **7** D. Laing 47.33; **8** A. Bell 47.49.

800m: 1 T. McLean (USA) 1:48.5; **2** D. Warren 1:48.8; **3** M. Belger (USA) 1:49.0; **4** M. Cleary (USA) 1:49.3; **5** C. Szwed 1:49.4; **6** G. Cook 1:49.8; **7** P. Lewis 1:49.8.

1500m: 1 D. Moorcroft 3:42.9; **2** A. Brahmia (Alg) 3:44.3; **3** C. Masback (USA) 3:44.4; **4** S. Emson 3:44.6; **5** T. Hutchings 3:44.8; **6** R. Smedley 3:45.2; **7** P. Chimes 3:47.3; **8** G. Jones (USA) 3:47.4.

5000m: 1 H. Rono (Ken) 13:20.8; **2** W. Waigwa (Ken) 13:24.4; **3** N. Rose 13:25.4; **4** S. Nyambui (Tan) 13:29.6; **5** F. Bayi (Tan) 13:35.9; **6** M. McLeod 13:36.7; **7** D. Quax (NZ) 13:42.3; **8** M. Prince 13:43.3.

10,000m: 1 B. Foster 27:30.3 (*European, UK all-comers and UK national record*); **2** M. McLeod 28:04.2; **3** D. Black 28:06.9; **4** B. Ford 28:12.4; **5** J. Goater 28:16.7; **6** S. Kenyon 28:35.1; **7** G. Smith 28:36.5; **8** N. Coupland 28:38.6.

3000m Steeplechase: 1 D. Coates 8:34.4; **2** A. Staynings 8:35.8; **3** M. Morris 8:35.8; **4** J. Wild 8:42.2; **5** I. Gilmour 8:43.7; **6** R. Harris 8:46.9; **7** R. Hackney 8:47.6; **8** Graham Tuck 8:48.1.

110m Hurdles: 1 B. Price 14.14; **2** M. Holtom 14.49; **3** I. Ratcliffe 14.65; **4** R. Danville 14.93; **5** N. Gerrard 14.93; **6** T. Fox (USA) 14.96; **7** A. James 14.98; **8** D. Wilson 14.98.

400m Hurdles: 1 A. Pascoe 50.39; **2** R. Graybehl (USA) 50.65; **3** G. Oakes 51.08; **4** W. Hartley 51.23; **5** S. James 51.54; **6** M. Whittingham 52.03; **7** D. West 52.05; **8** R. Bell 52.82.

High Jump: 1 F. Jacobs (USA) 2.20m (7' 2½"); **2** G. Olson (USA) 2.20m; **3** B. Burgess 2.15m; **4** M. Palmer 2.10m; **5** M. Butterfield 2.10m; **6** C. Boreham 2.05m; **7** T. Foulger 2.05m; **8** A. Dainton 2.00m.

Pole Vault: 1 R. Pullard (USA) 5.40m (17' 8½"); **2** B. Hooper 5.30m; **3** A. Williams 5.00m; **4** J. Gutteridge 5.00m; **5** M. Bull 4.80m; **6 eq** R. Williamson and R. Goodall 4.40m.

Long Jump: 1 R. Mitchell 7.76m (25' 5½"); **2** K. Cocks 7.57m; **3** T. Henry 7.46m; **4** W. Kirkpatrick 7.35m; **5** A. Moore 7.34m; **6** C. Mitchell 7.33m; **7** M. Effiong 7.26m; **8** B. Garner 7.20m.

Triple Jump: 1 A. Moore 16.68m (54' 8¾") (*UK national record*); **2** K. Connor 16.39m; **3** D. Johnson 15.85m; **4** M. Effiong 15.61m; **5** C. Colman 15.44m; **6** J. Phillips 15.06m; **7** E. McCalla 15.04m; **8** N. Stoppard 15.03m.

Shot: 1 G. Capes 19.94m (65' 5"); **2** M. Winch 17.85m; **3** R. Dale 17.06m; **4** I. Lindley 16.33m; **5** S. Rodhouse 6.20m; **6** S. Francis 15.22m; **7** N. Tabor 14.96m.

Discus: 1 P. Tancred 55.78m (183' 0"); **2** J. Hillier 53.60m; **3** M. Winch 52.88m; **4** P. Gordon 52.80m; **5** G. Dirkin 51.26m; **6** M. Cushion 50.18m; **7** G. Tyler 50.00m. C. Sutherland (56.38m) disq.

Hammer: 1 P. Farmer (Aus) 70.72m (232' 0"); **2** P. Dickenson 68.24m; **3** J. Whitehead 67.70m; **4** I. Chipchase 64.10m; **5** M. Mileham 63.56m; **6** S. Egan (Eir) 60.98m; **7** P. Gordon 60.72m; **8** M. Petra 60.42m.

Javelin: 1 P. Yates 80.10m (262' 9"); **2** D. Ottley 77.60m; **3** B. Roberts 75.90m; **4** C. Clover 74.14m; **5** S. Osborne 72.94m; **6** I. Marsh 70.72m; **7** C. Harris 67.34m; **8** P. De Kremer 66.36m.

3000m Walk: 1 R. Mills 12:05.8; **2** B. Adams 12:24.7; **3** C. Lawton 12:41.1; **4** G. Seatter (NZ) 12:41.4; **5** G. Morris 12:44.4; **6** P. Fox (NZ) 12:52.0; **7** K. Carter 12:52.4; **8** J. Paul 12:54.7.

24, 25 June

FRANCE v UK (Women)

Tessa Sanderson was responsible for the top performance in a three-a-side women's match at Strasbourg, won easily by Britain. She won the javelin by the remarkable margin of 12 metres with one of the longest throws of her career: 63.80 metres (209′ 4″). The most competitive event was the long jump where just two centimetres (one inch) covered the first three. A leap of 6.58 metres (21′ 7¼″) by Jacky Curtet of France in the third round stood up as the winner, but only just, for in the fourth round 17-year-old Sue Hearnshaw jumped 6.57 metres (21′ 6¾″) and Sue Reeve 6.56 metres (21′ 6¼″), both with wind assistance.

100m: 1 C. Rega (Fra) 11.17w; **2** B. Goddard (UK) 11.44; **3** A. Lynch (UK) 11.45; **4** V. Rosset (Fra) 11.51; **5** E. Sulter (Fra) 11.58; **6** W. Clarke (UK) 11.62.

200m: 1 C. Rega (Fra) 23.54; **2** K. Smallwood (UK) 23.66; **3** V. Rosset (Fra) 24.08; **4** B. Goddard (UK) 24.08; **5** M-P. Philippe (Fra) 24.10; **6** H. Golden (UK) 24.34.

400m: 1 P. Darbonville (Fra) 53.88; **2** M-R. Cross (Fra) 54.54; **3** A. Harley (UK) 54.84; **4** A. Smyth (UK) 55.19; **5** C. Delachanal (Fra) 55.20; **6** A. Creamer (UK) 55.43.

800m: 1 J. Colebrook (UK) 2:03.3; **2** J. Prictoe (UK) 2:03.3; **3** P. Newnham (UK) 2:05.0; **4** C. Aubry (Fra) 2:06.6; **5** A-M. Jossot (Fra) 2:10.1; **6** M. Rooms (Fra) 2:19.1.

1500m: 1 H. Hollick (UK) 4:14.7; **2** V. Renties (Fra) 4:15.9; **3** M. Coomber (UK) 4:18.2; **4** C. McMeekin (UK) 4:18.3; **5** C. Icega (Fra) 4:26.5; **6** M. Ben (Fra) 4:31.0.

3000m: 1 J. DeBrouwer (Fra) 9:05.9; **2** G. Penny (UK) 9:08.1; **3** J. Smith (UK) 9:12.1; **4** J. Clarke (UK) 9:20.3; **5** M. Bouchonneau (Fra) 9:38.5; **6** V. Goreau (Fra) 9:51.4.

100m Hurdles: 1 S. Colyear (UK) 13.58; **2** S. Strong (UK) 13.75; **3** B. Caines (UK) 13.81; **4** L. Elloy (Fra) 13.86; **5** L. Lebeau (Fra) 13.90; **6** N. Prevost (Fra) 14.55.

400m Hurdles: 1 E. Sutherland (UK) 57.79; **2** S. Smith (UK) 59.02; **3** D. Lairloup (Fra) 59.07; **4** J. Roscoe (UK) 59.15; **5** F. Delavernette (Fra) 62.38; **6** G. Digiacomo (Fra) 64.01.

High Jump: 1 G. Hitchen (UK) 1.84m (6′ 0¼″); **2** S. Prenveille (Fra) 1.78m; **3** B. Simmonds (UK) 1.75m; **4** V. Dumont (Fra) 1.75m; **5** B. Gibbs (UK) 1.70m; **6** G. Garrieo (Fra) 1.70m.

Long Jump: 1 J. Curtet (Fra) 6.58m (21′ 7¼″); **2** S. Hearnshaw (UK) 6.57m(w); **3** S. Reeve (UK) 6.56m(w); **4** Y. Gacon (Fra) 6.31m(w); **5** A. Simmonds (UK) 6.03m(w); **6** O. Madkaud (Fra) 5.82.

Shot: 1 L. Bertimon (Fra) 16.13m (52′ 11″); **2** M. Ritchie (UK) 15.86m; **3** S. Creantor (Fra) 15.43m; **4** B. Bedford (UK) 14.80; **5** J. Thompson (UK) 14.33m; **6** I. Raynaud (Fra) 13.28m.

Discus: 1 M. Ritchie (UK) 57.92m (190′ 0″); **2** J. Thompson (UK) 49.68m; **3** F. Despierres (Fra) 48.30m; **4** E. Barge (Fra) 45.56m; **5** L. Mallin (UK) 45.50m; **6** B. Massart (Fra) 44.00m.

Javelin: 1 T. Sanderson (UK) 63.80m (209′ 4″); **2** A. Bocle (Fra) 51.74m; **3** F. Whitbread (UK) 49.46m; **4** N. Besso (Fra) 48.78m; **5** J. Williams (UK) 47.42m; **6** C. Glineur (Fra) 46.48m.

4 × 100m Relay: 1 UK (W. Clarke, K. Smallwood, S. Colyear, A. Lynch) 44.13; **2** France 44.18.

4 × 400m Relay: 1 France 3:35.8; **2** UK (A. Harley, A. Smyth, J. Roscoe, E. Sutherland) 3:36.1.

Match Result: UK 167½; France 132½.

30 June – 2 July

GDR (EAST GERMAN) CHAMPIONSHIPS

Marita Koch, who had already relieved Irena Szewinska of the world 200 metres record with a time of 22.06 at Erfurt on 28 May and again at Karl-Marx-Stadt on 3 June, fulfilled her destiny by succeeding the great Polish star as holder of the world 400 metres record. Competing in her national championships in Leipzig on 2 July, Marita sliced one-tenth of a second off the previous mark with 49.19. Her absence from the 200 metres left the way clear for Marlies Gohr (née Oelsner) to complete the sprint double in 11.10/22.61. Another impressive double winner was Anita Weiss who, the day after defeating world record holder Karin Rossley in the 400 metres hurdles (a new event for Anita), won the 800 metres in which five women broke two minutes. National records were posted by Rolf Beilschmidt in the high jump, Udo Beyer in the shot and Roland Steuk in the hammer, the latter's throw of 78.14 metres (256' 4") on 30 June also breaking his own world junior record of 77.82 metres (255' 4") of a fortnight earlier.

MEN

100m: 1 E. Ray 10.29; **2** A. Thieme 10.42; **3** M. Kokot 10.45.

200m: 1 O. Prenzler 20.89; **2** K. Thiele 21.15; **3** K-D. Kurrat 21.24.

400m: 1 F. Richter 45.91; **2** F. Schaffer 46.00; **3** G. Arnold 46.07.

800m: 1 D. Wagenknecht 1:45.8; **2** J. Straub 1:46.1; **3** O. Beyer 1:46.3.

1500m: 1 J. Straub 3:39.4; **2** A. Basig 3:41.1; **3** J. Peter 3:43.1.

5000m: 1 J. Peter 13:27.0; **2** M. Kuschmann 13:34.4; **3** K-P. Justus 13:43.8.

10,000m: 1 K-H. Leiteritz 28:57.2; **2** D. Knies 29:05.4; **3** J. Truppel 29:12.5.

3000m Steeplechase: 1 G. Wetzig 8:34.0; **2** Melzer 8:38.2; **3** A. Garack 8:58.5.

110m Hurdles: 1 T. Munkelt 13.68; **2** T. Dittrich 14.13; **3** A. Pannicke 14.18.

400m Hurdles: 1 M. Konow 50.65; **2** H-U. Ludwig 50.82; **3** M. Schulz 52.09.

High Jump: 1 R. Beilschmidt 2.31m (7' 7"); **2** H. Lauterbach 2.28m; **3** E. Kirst 2.19m.

Pole Vault: 1 W. Reinhardt 5.20m (17' 0¾"); **2** J. Krumpolt 5.00m; **3** D. Eckhardt 4.80m.

Long Jump: 1 F. Paschek 7.87m (25' 10"); **2** F. Wartenberg 7.83m; **3** B. Heiland 7.78m.

Triple Jump: 1 L. Gora 16.06m (52' 8¼"); **2** H-D. Haberland 16.02m; **3** H. Natzmer 15.92m.

Shot: 1 U. Beyer 21.89m (71' 10"); **2** G. Bergmann 20.30m; **3** M. Schmidt 20.22m.

Discus: 1 W. Schmidt 64.80m (212' 7"); **2** W. Warnemunde 62.06m; **3** A. Lemme 60.16m.

Hammer: 1 R. Steuk 78.14m (256' 4") (*world junior record*); **2** D. Gerstenberg 76.94m; **3** J. Sachse 73.78m.

Javelin: 1 W. Hanisch 87.16m (285' 11"); **2** D. Michel 84.32m; **3** A. Katterle 82.02m.

WOMEN

100m: 1 M. Gohr 11.10; **2** M. Hamann 11.37; **3** Pfennig 11.42.

200m: 1 M. Gohr 22.61; **2** C. Bodendorf 22.87; **3** B. Lockhoff 22.89.

400m: 1 M. Koch 49.19 (*world record*); **2** C. Brehmer 50.15; **3** B. Krug 51.36.

800m: 1 A. Weiss 1:58.6; **2** M. Kampfert 1:59.3; **3** H. Ullrich 1:59.7.

1500m: 1 U. Bruns 4:02.0; **2** W. Strotzer 4:06.1; **3** G. Lehmann 4:08.9.

3000m: 1 G. Lehmann 9:02.8; **2** U. Sauer 9:17.1; **3** H. Kleffel 9:21.4.

100m Hurdles: 1 J. Klier 12.91; **2** G. Berend 12.98; **3** A. Fiedler 13.12.

400m Hurdles: 1 A. Weiss 56.39; **2** K. Rossley 56.78; **3** M. Neumann 58.12.

High Jump: 1 J. Kirst 1.92m (6' 3½"); **2** A. Reichstein 1.84m; **3** A. Berg 1.84m.

Long Jump: 1 A. Voigt 6.61m (21' 8¼"); **2** B. Wujak 6.61m; **3** H. Wycisk 6.56m.

Shot: 1 M. Droese 20.92m (68' 7¾"); **2** H. Knorscheidt 20.49m; **3** M. Adam 19.66m.

Discus: 1 E. Jahl 66.02m (216' 7"); **2** M. Droese 63.52m; **3** S. Engel 62.88m.

Javelin: 1 R. Fuchs 65.94m (216' 4"); **2** U. Richter 63.62m; **3** P. Felke 61.66m.

JUNE HIGHLIGHTS

That indefatigable Kenyan, Henry Rono, accounted for his third and fourth world records of the year when timed at 27:22.5 for 10,000 metres in Vienna on 11 June – hacking a full eight seconds off the mark held by his countryman Samson Kimobwa – and 7:32.1 for 3000 metres in Oslo on 27 June, which cut Brendan Foster's figures by 3.1 seconds. The race in Vienna was not part of an athletics meeting, which could possibly affect recognition of the time as a record, but there are no doubts as to the authenticity of the performance. Rono reached the 5000 metres point in 13:48.2; then, running solo, he covered the second half of the race in a remarkable 13:34.3 (with a 57.0 last lap). Kilometre splits – 2:44.5, 2:44.5, 2:45.2, 2:49.8, 2:44.2, 2:47.5, 2:44.4, 2:42.1, 2:43.5, 2:37.0. Domingo Tibaduiza of Colombia finished second, half a lap behind, in a South American record of 27:53.0. Again, in Oslo, Rono ran the second part of the race faster than the first. The initial 1500 metres took 3:49.5 . . . followed by 3:42.6, which suggests that he covered the final mile in around four minutes flat! Rono was on his own once he moved to the front on the fourth lap and the enormity of his achievement was underlined by the fact that Suleiman Nyambui of Tanzania and Britain's Nick Rose became history's fifth (7:40.3) and sixth (7:40.4) fastest performers in following him home, and yet they were left over 50 metres behind. Rono, whose kilometre splits were 2:34.0, 2:30.5 and 2:27.6, thus brought the seven and a half minute 'barrier' into the realm of possibility, as he had done earlier with such landmarks as 13 minutes for 5000 m, eight minutes for the steeplechase and 27 minutes for 10,000 m.

The Oslo meeting was notable also for a great 3000 metres by Norway's own Grete Waitz, whose time of 8:32.1 (4:18.2 plus 4:13.9) could be recognised as a world record since after two years the 8:27.1 attributed to Lyudmila Bragina (Sov) in the USA had still not been forwarded for ratification, and for a distinguished mile. Wilson Waigwa (Ken) was the winner in 3:53.2, with Filbert Bayi (Tan) second in 3:53.5, Steve Scott (USA) third in 3:53.8 and

Frank Clement nipping fellow-Scot John Robson (3:54.3) for fourth in a UK record of 3:54.2.

World records fell thick and fast throughout the month. In addition to those by Rono and Marita Koch, records were claimed by Grazyna Rabsztyn (Pol) with 12.48 for the women's 100 metres hurdles at Furth on 10 June and by Vladimir Yashchenko (Sov) who in his first competition since the European Indoor Championships leapt 2.34 metres (7' 8") in Tbilisi on 16 June, one centimetre above his own official outdoor mark although still a centimetre shy of his indoor figures. Raul Gonzales (Mex) came up with the most phenomenal walking performance of all time on 11 June when winning the traditional Prague to Podebrady 50 kilometres road race in 3:41:19.2 to chop over four minutes from his already incredible world's best. Even a European road best of 3:51:39 by Reima Salonen (Fin) in Turku one week later paled by comparison. Ulrike Bruns (GDR) clocked 2:32.7 for the women's 1000 metres, best on record, at Formia on 18 June, while another world's best of sorts was accomplished by Brazil's Joao Carlos de Oliveira at Bratislava on 10 June with a triple jump of 17.44 metres (57' 2¾"). That's some way behind his official world record of 17.89 metres (58' 8½") set in Mexico City, but equals the longest achieved by Viktor Sanyeyev (Sov) away from high altitude.

More records . . . a UK 2000 metres time of 4:57.8 at Crystal Palace on 3 June by Steve Ovett, with Nick Rose (4:59.6) also well inside Brendan Foster's previous mark of 5:02.9; a Commonwealth women's shot record of 18.16 metres (59' 7") by Gael Mulhall (Aus) at Brisbane on 3 June; a world junior discus record of 63.64 metres (208' 9") by Werner Hartmann (Ger) at Strasbourg on 25 June, and European junior bests of 1:45.5 for 800 metres by Andreas Busse (GDR) at Ostrava on 7 June, 8.05 metres (26' 5") long jump by Antonio Corgos Cervantes (Spa) at Bydgoszcz on 11 June, and 85.70 metres (281' 2") javelin throw by Arto Harkonen (Fin) at Kuortane on 24 June. UK junior records were set by Wendy McDonnell with 13.65 for 100 metres hurdles at Crystal Palace on 3 June and Judy Livermore with 4028 points for the pentathlon at Hannover on 17 June.

Result of the RWA national 30 kilometres road walk championship at Sheffield on 17 June, used also as a trial for Commonwealth Games selection:

1 O. Flynn 2:21:54; 2 B. Adams 2:22:26; 3 A. Seddon 2:25:26; 4 R. Mills 2:27:11; 5 S. Lightman 2:27:37; 6 R. Dobson 2:28:54. **Team:** Sheffield.

Results of the AAA decathlon and WAAA pentathlon championships at Birmingham on 17 and 18 June:

Decathlon 1 A. Drayton 7424 pts; 2 G. Watson 7381; 3 J. Howell 7190; 4 P. Zeniou 7101; 5 M. Bull 6742; 6 P. Bredin 6721. **Pentathlon** 1 Y. Wray 4140; 2 S. Mapstone 4121; 3 G. Howell 4070; 4 R. Howell 3784; 5 S. Bull 3575; 6 V. Kelly 3493.

Britain's Fred Pendlebury won the world veterans (over-40) 10,000 metres title in 31:09.3 in West Berlin on 16 June. Next day Fritz Muller (USA) triumphed in the marathon (2:25:20), with Gordon Porteous of Britain first in the over-60 section (2:55:51) and Norma Campbell winning the women's over-50 title in 3:19:22.

Right: *The new world shot put record holder, Udo Beyer (GDR).*　　　　　George Herringshaw

July

2 July

UK v BULGARIA (Women) AND
BRITISH MEAT GAMES

Britain comfortably disposed of Bulgaria in a women's match which featured such performances as Gillian Hitchen coming close to clearing the UK record height of 1.88 metres (6' 2") and Meg Ritchie throwing the discus 60.54 metres (198' 7"), a mark which has been ratified by the BAAB as a UK record in preference to the Scottish girl's 60.80 metres (199' 6") in her club championships in April. But it was the Emsley Carr Mile for men which monopolised the headlines.

This annual race, inaugurated in 1953 when Gordon Pirie scored a famous victory over American star Wes Santee, has produced its share of miling history over the years – and the 1978 edition was one of the most notable of all. Only four days after running 3:54.3 in Oslo (inches behind Frank Clement's new UK record of 3:54.2), John Robson (21) turned in a 55.8 last quarter to win in 3:55.8. The big story, though, was the showing of Graham Williamson (who turned 18 a fortnight earlier) and 17-year-old Steve Cram. Williamson chased Robson all the way for a time of 3:56.4, which took all of three seconds from Steve Ovett's UK junior record, while Cram finished fourth in 3:57.4 – 1.6 seconds inside Jim Ryun's world best for a 17-year-old! Tim Hutchings (19) placed fifth in 3:57.8, but the race didn't belong entirely to the youngsters for third was Brendan Foster (30) in 3:57.4, his fastest for six years.

WOMEN

100m: 1 S. Lannaman (UK) 11.73; **2** A. Lynch (UK) 12.00; **3** I. Valkova (Bul) 12.16; **4** S. Polova (Bul) 12.22.

200m: 1 S. Lannaman (UK) 23.37; **2** B. Goddard (UK) 23.76; **3** L. Panayotova (Bul) 23.88; **4** M. Shishkova (Bul) 24.86.

400m: 1 J. Hoyte (UK) 53.59; **2** G. McCormack (UK) 53.68; **3** M. Andonova (Bul) 55.58; **4** V. Tsvetkova (Bul) 56.01.

800m: 1 J. Colebrook (UK) 2:03.7; **2** J. Prictoe (UK) 2:04.3; **3** I. Bonova (Bul) 2:05.6; **4** G. Atanasova (Bul) 2:06.2.

1500m: 1 T. Petrova (Bul) 4:13.0; **2** I. Silai (Rom) 4:13.0; **3** M. Stewart (UK) 4:14.3; **4** G. Waitz (Nor) 4:15.0; **5** V. Yatsinska (Bul) 4:15.8; **6** C. Boxer (UK – guest) 4:16.2; **7** C. Benning (UK) 4:18.0.

3000m: 1 R. Chavdarova (Bul) 9:08.0; **2** G. Penny (UK) 9:08.2; **3** N. Shtereva (Bul) 9:20.2; **4** J. Clarke (UK) 9:22.0.

100m Hurdles: 1 G. Rabsztyn (Pol) 13.21; **2** Z. Bielczyk (Pol) 13.69; **3** S. Colyear (UK) 13.75; **4** E. Rabsztyn (Pol) 13.86; **5** L. Gusheva (Bul) 14.27; **6** E. Kunova (Bul) 14.48; **7** F. Whitbread (UK) 19.63.

400m Hurdles: 1 K. Kacperczyk (Pol) 57.29; **2** E. Sutherland (UK) 58.22; **3** S. Smith (UK) 59.35; **4** T. Nakova (Bul) 62.06; **5** M. Kostova (Bul) 63.28.

High Jump: 1 G. Hitchen (UK) 1.84m (6' 0½"); **2** V. Rutter (UK) 1.78m; **3** M. Dimitrova (Bul) 1.75m; **4** M. Kostova (Bul) 1.55m.

John Robson wins the Emsley Carr Mile in 3:55.8 ahead of Graham Williamson, Brendan Foster (8), Steve Cram (6) and Tim Hutchings (10). Mike Street

Long Jump: 1 S. Reeve (UK) 6.35m (20′ 10″); **2** L. Gusheva (Bul) 6.27m; **3** S. Hearnshaw (UK) 6.11m; **4** E. Kunova (Bul) 5.66m.

Shot: 1 E. Stoyanova (Bul) 19.60m (64′ 3¾″); **2** V. Veselinova (Bul) 17.47m; **3** A. Littlewood (UK) 16.08m; **4** J. Oakes (UK) 15.69m.

Discus: 1 S. Bozhkova (Bul) 66.94m (219′ 7″); **2** D. Khristova (Bul) 62.88m; **3** M. Ritchie (UK) 60.54m (198′ 7″) (*UK national record*); **4** J. Thompson (UK) 51.10m.

Javelin: 1 T. Sanderson (UK) 64.00m (210′ 0″); **2** T. Mikhaylova (Bul) 56.70m; **3** I. Vancheva (Bul) 53.44m; **4** F. Whitbread (UK) 53.34m.

4 × 100m Relay: 1 UK (B. Goddard, K. Smallwood, S. Colyear, S. Lannaman) 43.59; **2** Bulgaria 44.74.

4 × 400m Relay: 1 UK (K. Williams, J. Hoyte, G. McCormack, V. Elder) 3:35.3; **2** Bulgaria 3:44.4.

Match Result: UK 91; Bulgaria 66.

MEN'S INVITATION EVENTS

400m: 1 G. Cohen 47.00; **2** D. Laing 47.05; **3** R. Jenkins 47.26.

Emsley Carr Mile: 1 J. Robson 3:55.8; **2** G. Williamson 3:56.4 (*UK Junior record*); **3** B. Foster 3:57.4; **4** S. Cram 3:57.4; **5** T. Hutchings 3:57.8; **6** C. Masback (USA) 3:58.0.

3000m: 1 N. Muir 7:52.1; **2** D. Coates 7:54.2; **3** D. Black 7:54.3.

400m Hurdles: 1 W. Hartley 51.27; **2** G. Oakes 51.69; **3** M. Whittingham 52.50.

Pole Vault: 1 R. Pullard (USA) 5.30m (17′ 4½″); **2** P. Abada (Fra) 5.30m; **3** K. Stock 5.20m.

Triple Jump: 1 D. Johnson 16.02m (52′ 6¾″); **2** C. Colman 15.77m; **3** M. Effiong 15.61m.

7, 8 July

ENGLISH SCHOOLS CHAMPIONSHIPS

Just six days after his fantastic 3:57.4 mile at Crystal Palace, Steve Cram lined up on a sub-standard cinder track at Chesterfield for the final of the English Schools 1500 metres. On paper it should have been a doddle but the reaction of that dazzling mile and its swift aftermath (selection for England's Commonwealth Games team) had taken its toll of Cram's nervous energy and he was hard put to win in 4:03.6 – equivalent to a mile in about 4:22. Another Edmonton-bound athlete at these Esso-sponsored championships, Sue Hearnshaw, achieved the outstanding performance in the girls' events. Helped by the wind she long jumped the exceptional distance of 6.59 metres (21' 7½"), backed up by two leaps of 6.58 metres (21' 7¼").

In the results which follow, * signifies a championship best performance. Sprints, hurdles and jumps were wind-assisted. The cross-country championships were held at Lincoln on 4 March (girls) and Maidstone on 18 March (boys); the road walking championships at South Croydon on 29 April.

SENIOR BOYS

100m: 1 I. Loftman 10.4*; 2 D. Trick 10.5; 3 J. Marsden 10.6.

200m: 1 P. Cooke 21.7; 2 C. Gore 21.7; 3 B. Hughes 21.8.

400m: 1 W. Armstrong 50.3; 2 N. Jackson 50.9; 3 C. Jones 51.1.

800m: 1 I. Warsama 1:56.1; 2 D. Eglen 1:57.3; 3 S. Bennet 1:57.5.

1500m: 1 S. Cram 4:03.6; 2 G. Nurse 4:03.9; 3 R. Wood 4:04.8.

5000m: 1 M. Scrutton 14:55.4; 2 D. Ellis 15:03.8; 3 C. Moore 15:07.4.

2000m Steeplechase: 1 K. Capper 5:56.0; 2 E. Wedderburn 6:01.2; 3 S. Willmott 6:04.9.

110m Hurdles: 1 N. Alexander 14.5; 2 R. Willard 14.5; 3 H. Bridgeman 14.7.

400m Hurdles: 1 M. Garmston 56.4; 2 D. Hall 56.8; 3 M. Underwood 57.1.

High Jump: 1 L. Shakes 2.02m (6' 7½")*; 2 V. Clemmens 2.02m*; 3 D. Knox 1.97m.

Pole Vault: 1 N. Barnes 4.00m (13' 1½"); 2 R. Betts 3.50m; 3 P. Nickson 3.50m.

Long Jump: 1 A. Udo 7.58m (24' 10½")*; 2 E. Starrs 7.40m; 3 R. McKenzie 7.35m.

Triple Jump: 1 D. Greene 15.52m (50' 11"); 2 S. Metcalfe 15.20m; 3 D. Corless 15.08m.

Shot: 1 D. Smedley 15.17m (49' 9¼"); 2 P. Millbourne 14.10m; 3 G. Burbridge-James 13.95m.

Discus: 1 A. Garforth 47.94m (157' 3"); 2 R. Weir 47.64m; 3 C. Dinsdale 47.02m.

Hammer: 1 M. Girvan 61.70m (202' 5")*; 2 K. McNab 51.26m; 3 A. Carruthers 47.52m.

Javelin: 1 C. Johnson 60.88m (199' 9"); 2 N. Stainton 58.88m; 3 I. Marsh 58.74.

4 x 100m Relay: 1 S. Yorks 43.8; 2 Staffs 44.0; 3 Cumbria 44.0.

Cross-country: 1 M. Scrutton 25:22; 2 A. Salter 25:39; 3 D. Ellis 25:43.

Road Walk: 1 M. Wordsworth 47:09; 2 M. Miley 48:38; 3 I. McCombie 48:58.

INTERMEDIATE BOYS

100m: 1 P. Moxam 10.8; **2** M. Powell 10.8; **3** J. Blake 10.9.

200m: 1 P. Brown 21.5*; **2** S. Lawrenson 22.0; **3** P. Edwards 22.5.

400m: 1 S. Ahamed 51.0; **2** M. Fabes 51.0; **3** P. Crule 51.6.

800m: 1 G. McGeorge 1:55.5; **2** P. Elliott 1:57.5; **3** T. Brennan 1:59.7.

1500m: 1 P. Black 4:05.8; **2** D. Hughes 4:05.9; **3** I. Jones 4:05.9.

3000m: 1 C. Bloor 8:47.4; **2** A. Bristow 8:47.4; **3** D. Jackson 8:47.4.

1500m Steeplechase: 1 D. Lewis 4:23.7; **2** D. Bennett 4:24.8; **3** D. Swain 4:27.5.

100m Hurdles: 1 A. Ash 13.5; **2** W. Barker 13.5; **3** P. Johnson 13.6.

400m Hurdles: 1 K. Lidlow 57.6; **2** A. Dammant 57.9; **3** B. Rodger 59.6.

High Jump: 1 P. Byrne 1.92m (6' 3½")*; **2** A. Bedford 1.92m*; **3 eq** R. Atun and M. O'Neill 1.92m*.

Pole Vault: 1 T. Anstiss 4.33m (14' 2½")*; **2** D. Hooper 4.00m; **3** I. McIsaac 3.80m.

Long Jump: 1 P. Hanson 7.22m (23' 8¼")*; **2** R. Dennis 7.06m; **3** G. Pullen 6.94m.

Triple Jump: 1 N. Leech 14.84m (48' 8¼")*; **2** I. Anderson 14.40m; **3** A. Bloomfield 14.25m.

Shot: 1 A. Zaidman 17.54m (57' 6½")*; **2** G. Brocklebank 14.92m; **3** E. Phillips 14.44m.

Discus: 1 F. O'Donnell 44.42m (145' 9"); **2** R. Ellis 43.46m; **3** P. Todd 43.08.

Hammer: 1 S. Pickering 57.26m (187' 10"); **2** C. Varley 57.04; **3** A. James 56.98.

Javelin: 1 C. Mackenzie 58.96m (193' 5"); **2** M. Humphries 58.30m; **3** C. Glossop 54.84m.

4 × 100m Relay: 1 West Midlands 43.9; **2** London 44.5; **3** S. Yorks 44.8.

Cross-country: 1 D. Lewis 20:38; **2** P. Gurr 20:46; **3** M. Weaver 20:48.

Road Walk: 1 G. Vale 22:32; **2** D. Jones 24:01; **3** J. Ball 24:17.

JUNIOR BOYS

100m: 1 I. George 11.3; **2** I. Richardson 11.3; **3** S. Swaffile 11.3.

200m: 1 A. Martin 23.1; **2** J. McKee 23.5; **3** G. Williams 23.6.

400m: 1 A. Leonard 54.0; **2** J. Weston 55.2; **3** P. Donner 55.5.

800m: 1 T. Varman 2:01.9; **2** P. Squires 2:03.7; **3** C. Wills 2:06.0.

1500m: 1 P. Wynn 4:24.6; **2** D. Brockwell 4:25.0; **3** M. Coleman 4:26.2.

80m Hurdles: 1 T. Leeson 11.3; **2** K. Moore 11.3; **3** N. Evan 11.6.

High Jump: 1 N. York 1.79m (5' 10½"); **2** K. Doyle 1.79m; **3** S. Chant 1.79m.

Pole Vault: 1 P. Mascoll 3.50m (11' 5¾"); **2** W. Davey 3.32; **3** S. Lyons 3.32m.

Long Jump: 1 D. Conway 6.54m (21' 5½"½); *; **2** A. Boutom 6.52m; **3** M. Gillingham 6.45m.

Triple Jump: 1 E. Hechevarria 13.92m (45' 8")*; **2** K. O'Shaughnessy 13.92m*; **3** A. Ajose 13.47m.

Shot: 1 M. Tubbs 14.57m (47' 9¾"); **2** C. Harrison 13.66m; **3** C. Gubbins 13.58m.

Discus: 1 A. Ward 39.62m (130' 0"); **2** P. Weir 39.10m; **3** I. Smith 38.54m.

Hammer: 1 A. Kenneally 59.30m (194' 7")*; **2** A. Simkins 52.16m; **3** A. Bewley 45.22m.

Javelin: 1 S. Barnett 51.00m (167' 4"); **2** J. Pickering 50.14m; **3** P. Hill 47.98m.

WORLD OF ATHLETICS 1979

4 × 100m Relay: 1 Herts 46.8; **2** London 47.6; **3** Middx 47.9.

Cross-country: 1 J. Richards 16:41; **2** A. Rayworth 16:55; **3** S. Robson 17:01.

Road Walk: 1 S. Mortimer 14:55; **2** I. Lewis 15:00; **3** C. Blundell 15:24.

SENIOR GIRLS

100m: 1 L. Stewart 11.6*; **2** S. Clark 11.7; **3** K. Sait 11.9.

200m: 1 K. Smallwood 23.4; **2** A. Foster 24.0; **3** W. Barnes 25.0.

400m: 1 J. MacGregor 57.3; **2** H. Waterhouse 59.6; **3** A. Dunn 59.6.

800m: 1 S. Ludlam 2:15.3; **2** S. Parker 2:17.0; **3** A. Scar 2:17.6.

1500m: 1 D. Kiernan 4:29.9; **2** C. Brace 4:34.3; **3** B. Madigan 4:39.9.

100m Hurdles: 1 W. McDonnell 13.8; **2** J. Livermore 13.9; **3** T. Chipp 14.1.

High Jump: 1 S. Southern 1.74m (5' 8½"); **2** V. Kelly 1.71m; **3** D. Friar 1.68m.

Long Jump: 1 S. Hearnshaw 6.59m (21' 7½")*; **2** J. Frank-Lynch 6.34m; **3** J. Davies 6.34m.

Shot: 1 S. Tudor 12.96m (42' 6¼"); **2** J. Jackson 12.23m; **3** H. Clarke 12.15m.

Discus: 1 F. Condon 44.48m (145' 11")*; **2** D. Sturman 44.16m; **3** J. Curtis 38.80m.

Javelin: 1 M. Jervis 44.06m (144' 7"); **2** J. Rose 43.32m; **3** J. Cross 39.38m.

4 × 100m Relay: 1 Cleveland 48.8; **2** Hants 49.1; **3** Devon 50.3.

Cross-country: 1 J. White 16:14; **2** J. Honeysett 17:01; **3** E. Harding 17:03.

Road Walk: 1 J. Wickham 25:56; **2** E. Cox 26:32; **3** M. De Giovanni 27:17.

INTERMEDIATE GIRLS

100m: 1 P. Baker 11.7; **2** V. Mullings 11.8; **3** D. Walker 11.8.

200m: 1 D. Bunn 24.1; **2** R. Richards 24.4; **3** C. Kelly 24.6.

400m: 1 L. Callow 59.8; **2** P. Mullins 60.3; **3** C. Pendleton 60.8.

800m: 1 A. Clifford 2:16.5; **2** J. Croasdale 2:19.0; **3** K. Almond 2:19.6.

1500m: 1 S. Arthurton 4:41.5; **2** K. Timson 4:42.4; **3** S. Jones 4:42.9.

80m Hurdles: 1 H. Ross 11.2; **2** C. St John 11.4; **3** D. Church 11.5.

High Jump: 1 B. Simmonds 1.68m (5' 6"); **2 eq** L. Matthews and S. Grady 1.63m.

Long Jump: 1 C. Henley 5.86m (19' 2¾"); **2** K. Hagger 5.82m; **3** M. Smallwood 5.64m.

Shot: 1 B. Wright 12.33m (40' 5½"); **2** S. Bracey 11.24m; **3** E. Bernard 11.23m.

Discus: 1 J. Picton 41.74m (136' 11"); **2** A. Franks 38.42m; **3** J. Wilderspin 37.06m.

Javelin: 1 S. Fry 47.70m (156' 6")*; **2** J. Bolham 38.64m; **3** C. Jenkins 36.34m.

4 × 100m Relay: 1 West Midlands 49.1; **2** Avon 49.2; **3** Derbyshire 49.3.

Cross-country: 1 S. Arthurton 14:31; **2** J. Clarke 14:39; **3** K. Timson 14:47.

Road Walk: 1 K. Eden 15:13; **2** J. Lewis 16:04; **3** M. Way 16:15.

Right: *Precocious Jane Parry storms to victory in the Junior 200 metres.*   Sportsview

JUNIOR GIRLS

100m: **1** C. Haslam 12.0; **2** P. Walsh 12.0; **3** K. Barraclough 12.0.

200m: **1** J. Parry 24.2; **2** J. Boggert 25.2; **3** H. Thorpe 25.6.

800m: **1** L. Baker 2:20.9; **2** C. Wells 2:21.2; **3** J. Windgrove 2:21.7.

1500m: **1** P. Matheson 4:46.2; **2** A. Alford 4:57.0; **3** B. Sanderson 5:00.1.

75m Hurdles: **1** L. Playel 11.0*; **2** M. Lewis 11.3; **3** D. Lake 11.4.

High Jump: **1** E. Hickley 1.73m (5′ 8″);*; **2** G. Blount 1.67m; **3** C. Summerfield 1.64m.

Long Jump: **1** S. French 5.99m (19′ 8″)*; **2** K. Glen 5.85m; **3** K. Martin 5.50m.

Shot: **1** C. Gregory 12.95m (42′ 6″)*; **2** P. Webber 12.05m; **3** S. King 11.21m.

Discus: **1** A. Roat 30.14m (98′ 11″); **2** K. Allday 30.10m; **3** A. Holleborn 28.88m.

Javelin: **1** K. Miller 33.56m (110′ 1″); **2** H. Johnstone 32.20m; **3** A. Hempstead 29.72m.

4 × 100m Relay: **1** South Yorks 51.0; **2** Staffs 51.1; **3** Oxon 51.1.

Cross-country: **1** A. Alford 13:12; **2** T. Davison 13:19; **3** P. Matheson 13:26.

Road Walk: **1** J. Harvey 12:24; **2** J. Barrett 13:44, **3** J. Mullins 13:05.

9 July

PHILIPS GATESHEAD GAMES

The writing was on the wall that Allan Wells was due for a breakthrough in his sprint times; he had notched up a personal best of 10.50 for 100 metres into a two metres per second wind and had given the two best sprinters in the Commonwealth, James Gilkes of Guyana and Don Quarrie of Jamaica, a good run for their money over 200 metres. Nonetheless, it came as something of a shock to his prestigious rivals, the 14,000 capacity crowd at Gateshead, and not least to Wells himself when he sped to victory over Gilkes, American star James Sanford, and Quarrie in 10.29 to equal Peter Radford's ancient (1958) UK record. 'I can't believe it', said the 26-year-old Scot who only began sprinting seriously in 1976 after having previously been a 7.32 metres (24′ 0¼″) long jumper. 'It didn't feel that fast. I would have been happy with 10.39.' Wells, who does not use starting blocks, led all the way and ignored a twinge in his strapped-up left thigh. He had slightly torn a hamstring five days earlier and wasn't sure of competing. To complete a memorable day, Allan's wife Margot produced a personal best in her 100 metres race, too . . . 11.68.

Other records fell in the 400 metres hurdles where Olympic champion Ed Moses (USA), making his first appearance in Britain, set an all-comers mark of 48.55 some 15 metres ahead of Alan Pascoe, and in the women's mile where that frequent and popular visitor Grete Waitz (Nor) ran the fastest mile (4:26.9) ever seen in this country. In the men's mile, local hero Brendan Foster recorded the second-fastest time of his long career (3:57.0) a stride or two behind Dave Moorcroft's lifetime-best of 3:56.6, with UK record holder Frank Clement a well-beaten third.

Olympic champion Ed Moses (USA) draws away from Alan Pascoe (5) and Bill Hartley at Gateshead.

W. Macgregor

MEN

100m: 1 A. Wells 10.29 (*equals UK national record*); **2** J. Gilkes (Guy) 10.37; **3** J. Sanford (USA) 10.39; **4** D. Quarrie (Jam) 10.39.

200m: 1 J. Gilkes (Guy) 20.74; **2** D. Quarrie (Jam) 20.90; J. Sanford (USA) 20.93.

400m: 1 M. Peoples (USA) 46.21; **2** G. Cohen 46.57; **3** D. Jenkins 46.94.

800m: 1 S. Coe 1:46.8; **2** T. McLean (USA) 1:47.1; **3** D. Paige (USA) 1:47.6.

Mile: 1 D. Moorcroft 3:56.6; **2** B. Foster 3:57.0; **3** F. Clement 3:58.7.

3000m: 1 R. Dixon (NZ) 7:47.2; **2** M. McLeod 7:48.2; **3** R. Smedley 7:49.7.

5000m: 1 D. Black 13:48.2; **2** D. Coates 13:53.5; **3** S. Kenyon 13:55.1.

400m Hurdles: 1 E. Moses (USA) 48.55 (*UK all-comers record*); **2** A. Pascoe 50.45; **3** J. King (USA) 50.99.

High Jump: 1 R. Kotinek (USA) 2.24m (7' 4¼"); **2** M. Naylor 2.15m; **3** B. Burgess 2.15m.

Pole Vault: 1 D. Ripley (USA) 5.20m (17' 0¾"); **2** E. Bell (USA) 5.20m; **3** R. Pullard (USA) 5.10m.

Shot: 1 G. Capes 19.97m (65' 6¼"); **2** P. Shmock (USA) 19.74m; **3** R. Dale 17.76m.

WOMEN

100m: 1 S. Lannaman 11.48; **2** S. Colyear 11.62; **3** M. Wells 11.68.

200m: 1 S. Lannaman 23.37; **2** S. Colyear 23.58; **3** M. Wells 24.12.

Mile: 1 G. Waitz (Nor) 4:26.9 (*UK all-comers record*); **2** M. Purcell (Eir) 4:30.5; **3** A. Wright (NZ) 4:40.4.

Javelin: 1 T. Sanderson 60.64m (198' 11"); **2** S. O'Toole 46.62m; **3** D. Williams 46.48m.

Allan Wells (6) shoots to fame by equalling the UK 100 metres record of 10.29 at Gateshead, defeating a top-class field. George Herringshaw

11 July

GERMANY v UK v USA (Juniors)

Despite wearisome travel arrangements, the British teams fought valiantly against Germany and the USA in a 'junior' match at Lubeck, which was for male athletes born in 1958 or later and girls born in 1959 or later – an extension of one year over the normal age limits for junior internationals.

The girls excelled themselves, failing to win their match by a mere two points and providing individual event winners in Heather Hunte, Kathy Smallwood, Janine MacGregor, Angela Mason and Wendy McDonnell, as well as both relay teams. On the boys' side, victories were gained by Graham Williamson, Tim Hutchings and Graham Morris, while in second place Colin Reitz accounted for a UK junior 2000 metres steeplechase record of 5:34.7 and Mick Morton a UK junior 3000 metres mark of 8:00.1.

MEN

100m: 1 M. Lattany (USA) 10.47; **2** W. Zaske (Ger) 10.64; **3** C. Young (USA) 10.65; **4** M. McFarlane (UK) 10.66; **5** C. Sharp (UK) 10.81; **6** P. Klein (Ger) 10.82.

200m: 1 M. Lattany (USA) 20.91; **2** M. McFarlane (UK) 21.06; **3** K-D. Stierhoff (Ger) 21.45; **4** E. Brown (USA) 21.52; **5** D. Daniel (Ger) 21.79; **6** D. Baptiste (UK) 21.88. Non-scoring: C. Sharp (UK) 21.52.

400m: 1 L. Goldston (USA) 46.78; **2** A. Pesch (Ger) 47.42; **3** U. Wegner (Ger) 47.73; **4** B. Denman (USA) 47.82; **5** N. Jackson (UK) 48.76; **6** S. Wymark (UK) 49.14.

800m: 1 W. Frommbold (Ger) 1:50.2; **2** C. Szwed (UK) 1:50.2; **3** A. Tufariello (USA) 1:50.3; **4** C. Aragon (USA) 1:50.4; **5** G. Henning (Ger) 1:51.4; **6** G. Cook (UK) 1:51.4.

1500m: 1 G. Williamson (UK) 3:44.9; **2** T. Harbour (USA) 3:47.8; **3** S. Cram (UK) 3:48.3; **4** A. Baranski (Ger) 3:49.4; **5** J. Grothe (Ger) 3:50.2; **6** R. Donaghue (USA) 3:54.5.

3000m: 1 T. Hutchings (UK) 7:57.7; **2** M. Morton (UK) 8:00.1 (*UK junior record*); **3** T. Koch (Ger) 8:06.3; **4** S. Ortiz (USA) 8:09.4; **5** L. Mangan (USA) 8:15.3; **6** B. Gatzke (Ger) 8:16.2.

5000m: 1 W. McChesney (USA) 13:59.6; **2** P. Nothacker (Ger) 14:10.3; **3** S. Anders (UK) 14:12.1; **4** M. Hedtkamp (Ger) 14:12.3; **5** A. Leek (UK) 14:13.3; **6** C. Assumma (USA) 14:19.9.

2000m Steeplechase: 1 M. Langler (Ger) 5:34.5; **2** C. Reitz (UK) 5:34.7 (*UK junior record*); **3** M. Hoffmann (Ger) 5:39.0; **4** G. Fell (UK) 5:39.3; **5** J. Hess (USA) 5:47.0; **6** J. Gregorek (USA) 5:47.1.

10,000m Walk: 1 G. Morris (UK) 45:43.6; **2** M. Wordsworth (UK) 46:16.5; **3** R. Sharp (USA) 46:53.7; **4** K. Schafer (Ger) 47:02.1; **5** F. Helms (Ger) 48:03.8.

110m Hurdles: 1 S. Parker (USA) 14.05; **2** R. Wilson (USA) 14.15; **3** M. Holtom (UK) 14.40; **4** M. Krause (Ger) 14.49; **5** P. Barthropp (UK) 14.71; **6** J. Rechner (Ger) 14.76.

400m Hurdles: 1 C. Person (USA) 51.12; **2** A. Phillips (USA) 51.24; **3** G. Oakes (UK) 51.24; **4** H. Weber (Ger) 51.52; **5** U. Meyer (Ger) 53.42; **6** C. Preston (UK) 53.92.

High Jump: 1 J. Frazier (USA) 2.14m (7' 0¼"); **2** D. Mogenburg (Ger) 2.11m; **3** H. Burchard (Ger) 2.08m; **4** M. Palmer (UK) 2.05m; **5** G. Robertson (UK) 1.95m; **6** R. Flowers (USA) 1.95m.

Pole Vault: 1 J. Winkler (Ger) 5.15m (16' 10¾"); **2** R. Hall (USA) 4.90m; **3** D. de Raad (Ger) 4.60m; **4** A. Jackson (UK) 4.20m; **5** A. Leiper (UK) 4.20m; J. Buckingham (USA) no height.

Long Jump: 1 L. King (USA) 7.86m (25' 9½"); **2** W. Walker (USA) 7.63m; **3** C. Mitchell (UK) 7.62m; **4** M. Spiegelhoff (Ger) 7.48m; **5** A. Udo (UK) 7.25m; **6** K. Koppenhofer (Ger) 7.19m.

Triple Jump: 1 S. Owolabi (USA) 15.75m (51' 8½"); **2** E. McCalla (UK) 15.59m; **3** K. Kubler (Ger) 15.30m; **4** G. Tyler (USA) 15.24m; **5** M. Effiong (UK) 14.71m; **6** A. Huber (Ger) 14.28m.

Shot: 1 V. Goldsmith (USA) 17.72m (58' 1¾"); **2** M. Carter (USA) 17.60m; **3** W. Hartmann (Ger) 16.86m; **4** P. Kassubeck (Ger) 15.28m; **5** A. Vince (UK) 15.28m; **6** M. Atkinson (UK) 14.50m.

Discus: 1 W. Hartmann (Ger) 58.96m (193' 5"); **2** B. Fischer (Ger) 54.98m; **3** S. Lofquist (USA) 52.00m; **4** N. Serafenas (USA) 50.82m; **5** A. Lithgow (UK) 45.68m; **6** A. Vince (UK) 45.06m.

Hammer: 1 K.-H. Muller (Ger) 64.74m (212' 5"); **2** W. Heinrich (Ger) 61.54m; **3** M. Girvan (UK) 59.42m; **4** R. James (UK) 56.02m; **5** W. Borden (USA) 50.46m; **6** D. Thomson (USA) 50.42m.

Javelin: 1 W. Kalb (Ger) 72.80m (238' 10"); **2** T. Meyer (USA) 70.02m; **3** R. Schemminger (Ger) 68.32m; **4** J. Bramlage (USA) 68.00m; **5** I. Marsh (UK) 67.36m; **6** T. Smith (UK) 62.20m.

4 × 100m Relay: 1 USA 40.23; **2** Germany 40.42; **3** UK (I. Loftman, C. Sharp, D. Baptiste, M. McFarlane) 40.51.

4 × 400m Relay: 1 USA 3:08.5; **2** Germany 3:09.2; **3** UK (J. Houston, N. Kitchen, N. Jackson, S. Wymark) 3:14.7.

Match Result: USA 167; Germany 152; UK 123.

WOMEN

100m: 1 H. Hunte (UK) 11.60; **2** K. Smallwood (UK) 11.67; **3** E. Vollmer (Ger) 11.85; **4** D. Carney (USA) 12.05; **5** A. Brown (USA) 12.09; **6** B. Knickenberg (Ger) 12.21.

200m: 1 K. Smallwood (UK) 23.30; **2** B. Vocking (Ger) 24.07; **3** F. Cobbs (USA) 24.45; **4** M. Wagner (Ger) 24.56; **5** D. Bunn (UK) 24.70; **6** P. Dunlap (USA) 25.46. Non-scoring: M. Probert (UK) 23.98.

400m: 1 J. MacGregor (UK) 53.59; **2** M. Klinger (Ger) 54.34; **3** S. Anlauf (Ger) 54.85; **4** G. Gardner (USA) 54.94; **5** E. Beton (UK) 55.40; **6** A. Emerson (USA) 55.48.

800m: 1 D. Beckford (USA) 2:06.0; **2** D. Kiernan (UK) 2:06.4; **3** B. Theuss (Ger) 2:08.0; **4** S. Bungener (Ger) 2:08.3; **5** S. Ludlam (UK) 2:10.0; **6** A. Regan (USA) 2:14.1.

1500m: 1 A. Mason (UK) 4:18.0; **2** R. Smeeth (UK) 4:21.0; **3** C. Williams (USA) 4:22.9; **4** T. Wells (USA) 4:27.0; **5** G. Schulz (Ger) 4:27.0; **6** J. Jooss (Ger) 4:33.5.

100m Hurdles: 1 W. McDonnell (UK) 13.87; **2** C. Young (USA) 13.88; **3** B. Fitzgerald (USA) 14.08; **4** J. Livermore (UK) 14.18; **5** I. Kustner (Ger) 14.21; **6** E. Oker (Ger) 14.42.

High Jump: 1 B. Dressel (Ger) 1.81m (5' 11¼"); **2** S. Serk (Ger) 1.81m; **3** D. Elliott (UK) 1.78m; **4** A-M. Devally (UK) 1.75m; **5** M. Metcalf (USA) 1.70m; **6** C. Rienstra (USA) 1.70m.

Long Jump: 1 E. Oker (Ger) 6.41m (21' 0½"); **2** A. Beirsdorf (Ger) 6.41m; **3** S. Hearnshaw (UK) 6.27m; **4** J. Davies (UK) 6.17m; **5** G. Loud (USA) 6.09m; **6** R. Keating (USA) 5.82m.

Shot: 1 A. Peter (Ger) 14.24m (46' 8¾"); **2** E. Majors (USA) 14.12m; **3** C. Losch (Ger) 13.89m; **4** E. Sobansky (USA) 13.71m; **5** S. Tudor (UK) 13.00m; **6** C. Dyer (UK) 12.41m.

Discus: 1 D. Galler (Ger) 52.04m (170' 9"); **2** B. Beuge (Ger) 50.80m; **3** C. Pyle (USA) 46.52m; **4** F. Condon (UK) 45.56m; **5** D. Sturman (UK) 45.04m; **6** L. Deniz (USA) 43.98m.

Javelin: 1 H. Repser (Ger) 53.48m (175' 5"); **2** H. Adametz (Ger) 53.12m; **3** J. Nelson (USA) 48.20m; **4** D. Williams (USA) 45.02m; **5** J. Rose (UK) 44.76m; **6** S. Flack (UK) 43.18m.

4 × 100m Relay: 1 UK (H. Hunte, K. Smallwood, M. Probert, D. Bunn) 45.03; **2** Germany 45.60; **3** USA 47.22.

4 × 400m Relay: 1 UK (C. Dawkins, K. Bissell, E. Beton, J. MacGregor) 3:37.5; **2** USA 3:38.0; **3** Germany 3:42.3.

Match Result: Germany 100; UK 98; USA 70.

14–16 July

UK NATIONAL CHAMPIONSHIPS

Allan Wells' UK record-equalling 100 metres in 10.29 at Gateshead brought him to the foothills of world-class sprinting; his 10.15 timing on his home track at Meadowbank, Edinburgh, on 15 July elevated him very close to the summit. He was controlled aggression personified as he powered down the straight to win by a full four metres in a time which was a UK all-comers record as well as a national one. The assisting wind was well inside the limit at 1.3 metres per second. Unfortunately the wind changed next day for the 200 metres and Wells had to contend with a strong head wind measured in the straight at four metres per second. That, in such conditions, he should register 20.70 (just four-hundredths of a second outside the UK record) was remarkable – as was his seven-metre winning margin over David Jenkins, the co-holder of that record.

The most dramatic event in the Kraft-sponsored championships which, unlike the AAA and WAAA meetings, are open only to UK athletes was the 5000 metres. Brendan Foster had turned up expecting a fast solo run; instead

Mike McLeod (7) and Brendan Foster waged a dramatic duel for the UK 5000 metres championship.

George Herringshaw

he found his intensely ambitious rival from Gateshead, Mike McLeod, lining up to do battle. Except for one lap, McLeod sat in as Foster set the pace and the two men were level as the bell sounded for the last lap. Foster made his effort with 200 metres to go, baulking McLeod in the process. But McLeod wasn't finished; he recovered, tracked Foster around the bend and then swung past him in the straight. Covering the final 200 metres in a spectacular 25.2, McLeod sprinted to victory in 13:25.2 to equal his personal best. Foster, who finished one-fifth of a second back, sustained his first defeat at the distance by a British runner. There was drama too in the 800 metres when Sebastian Coe, after leading from gun to tape in the 800 metres, was disqualified for breaking too early from his lane. He was, however, reinstated after the jury of appeal watched a video recording of the race.

The 1500 metres was robbed of much potential excitement through the non-appearance of Steve Ovett and Dave Moorcroft. In their absence the crowd were able to cheer home a Scots 1–2–3 as John Robson won from Frank Clement and young Graham Williamson, the latter having been most unlucky to be passed over by the Scottish Commonwealth Games selectors. Other youthful prospects showed up well in the meeting: UK junior records were set by Graham Fell (19) in the steeplechase, Ruth Smeeth (18) in the 1500 metres – where Sandra Arthurton, only 15, finished third – and Sue Hearnshaw (17) in the long jump. Jane Parry reached the 200 metres final after setting a UK age-13 best of 24.05 in her heat.

MEN

100m: 1 A. Wells 10.15 (*UK all-comers and national record*); **2** A. McMaster 10.55; **3** S. Green 10.57; **4** D. Baptiste 10.66; **5** L. Hoyte 10.69; **6** D. Thompson 10.70; **7** T. Hoyte 10.70; **8** M. Morris 10.84.

200m: 1 A. Wells 20.70; **2** D. Jenkins 21.43; **3** A. McMaster 21.56; **4** S. Green 21.57; **5** T. Hoyte 21.69; **6** C. Sharp 21.70; **7** T. Whitehead 21.75; **8** C. Monk 21.89.

400m: 1 R. Ashton 46.35; **2** D. Laing 46.97; **3** G. Cohen 47.09; **4** C. Hamilton 47.20; **5** R. Jenkins 47.26; **6** A. Bell 47.35; **7** W. Taylor 47.90; **8** N. Jackson 48.67.

800m: 1 S. Coe 1:47.1; **2** P. Hoffmann 1:48.3; **3** P. Forbes 1:49.1; **4** P. Browne 1:49.1; **5** R. Harrison 1:49.5; **6** J. Goodacre 1:49.8; **7** L. Nicholson 1:51.5; **8** D. Rafferty 1:56.0.

1500m: 1 J. Robson 3:43.9; **2** F. Clement 3:44.4; **3** G. Williamson 3:44.9; **4** N. Rose 3:45.2; **5** G. Grant 3:45.7; **6** A. Mottershead 3:46.1; **7** R. Smedley 3:46.1; **8** N. Black 3:46.4.

5000m: 1 M. McLeod 13:25.2; **2** B. Foster 13:25.4; **3** M. Prince 13:36.6; **4** C. Spedding 13:37.5; **5** K. Penny 13:37.8; **6** A. Hutton 13:41.6; **7** J. Goater 13:44.1; **8** S. Jones 13:59.9.

10,000m: 1 D. Black 28:34.8; **2** G. Smith 28:37.3; **3** B. Ford 28:40.5; **4** J. Dingwall 28:45.3; **5** Grenville Tuck 28:46.6; **6** P. Standing 28:48.0; **7** J. Wigley 28:53.8; **8** J. Odlin 28:56.3.

3000m Steeplechase: 1 D. Coates 8:26.0; **2** J. Davies 8:26.6; **3** I. Gilmour 8:31.1; **4** A. Staynings 8:38.5; **5** J. Graham 8:39.3; **6** M. Morris 8:47.5; **7** G. Fell 8:48.4 (*UK junior record*); **8** R. Harris 8:48.8.

110m Hurdles: 1 B. Price 13.93w; **2** M. Holtom 14.10; **3** D. Wilson 14.43; **4** I. Ratcliffe 14.84; **5** A. Sumner 14.90; **6** R. Simpson 15.01; **7** M. Morgan 15.17; T. Clifton (dnf).

400m Hurdles: 1 W. Hartley 51.03; **2** G. Oakes 51.09; **3** S. James 51.83; **4** D. West 52.09; **5** M. Whittingham 52.71; **6** C. Beattie 53.30; **7** R. Danville 53.46; **8** A. Tarquini 54.82.

High Jump: 1 M. Naylor 2.15m (7' 0½"); **2** B. Burgess 2.15m; **3** V. Clemmens 2.10m; **4** T. Foulger 2.05m; **5** C. Harris 2.05m; **6** A. Dainton 2.05m; **7** R. Hepburn 2.00m; **8** M. Palmer 2.00m.

You'll find our entry in your local High Street.

You won't have to do a 20 kilometre walk to buy your weekly meat from the Master Butcher, because he's in almost every high street in the land. There are 1500 Dewhurst shops, from the tip of Cornwall to the top of Scotland. For the best in British meat come to the Master Butcher in <u>your</u> local high street.

DEWHURST
The Master Butcher

Pole Vault: 1 K. Stock 5.25m (17' 2¾"); **2** J. Gutteridge 5.20m; **3** A. Williams 5.10m; **4** R. Goodall 4.60m; **5** T. Gardner 4.60m; **6** R. Williamson 4.60m.

Long Jump: 1 K. Cocks 7.56m (24' 9¾"); **2** T. Henry 7.47m; **3** C. Mitchell 7.30m; **4** P. Brugnani 7.21m; **5** J. Gloag 7.12m.

Triple Jump: 1 K. Connor 16.66m (54' 8"); **2** A. Moore 16.48m(w); **3** C. Colman 16.17m(w); **4** D. Johnson 16.16m(w); **5** F. Attoh 15.87m; **6** M. Effiong 15.58m; **7** E. McCalla 15.19m; **8** N. Stoppard 14.69m.

Shot: 1 G. Capes 19.80m (64' 11½"); **2** M. Winch 16.93m; **3** R. Dale 16.93m; **4** A. Satchwell 16.60m; **5** I. Lindley 16.07m; **6** S. Rodhouse 15.98m.

Discus: 1 P. Gordon 54.66m (179' 4"); **2** R. Slaney 54.24m; **3** G. Capes 54.20m; **4** M. Winch 53.64m; **5** D. Roscoe 52.72m; **6** A. Satchwell 49.22m.

Hammer: 1 C. Black 69.10m (226' 8"); **2** P. Dickenson 68.28m; **3** J. Whitehead 65.30m; **4** I. Chipchase 63.96m; **5** M. Mileham 62.04; **6** A. Woods 56.86m.

Javelin: 1 D. Ottley 76.62m (251' 4"); **2** J. Trower 69.16m; **3** G. Brooks 66.66m; **4** S. Osborne 61.20m.

WOMEN

100m: 1 S. Lannaman 11.24w; **2** B. Goddard 11.30; **3** W. Clarke 11.38; **4** E. Thomas 11.50; **5** M. Wells 11.53; **6** K. Smallwood 11.61; **7** H. Golden 11.68; **8** H. Hunte 12.82 (injured).

200m: 1 S. Lannaman 23.16; **2** B. Goddard 23.27; **3** K. Smallwood 23.36; **4** E. Thomas 23.51; **5** W. Clarke 23.92; **6** H. Golden 24.02; **7** J. MacGregor 24.08; **8** J. Parry 24.34.

400m: 1 J. Colebrook 53.80; **2** J. Hoyte 54.03; **3** E. Eddy 54.10; **4** G. McCormack 54.39; **5** C. Dawkins 54.49; **6** E. Beton 54.78; **7** A. Smyth 55.08; **8** A. Harley 55.48.

800m: 1 J. Colebrook 2:03.3; **2** J. Prictoe 2:04.8; **3** L. Kiernan 2:05.1; **4** M. Stewart 2:05.2; **5** D. Kiernan 2:05.2; **6** A. Creamer 2:06.0; **7** C. Boxer 2:06.3; **8** A. Linton 2:06.8.

1500m: 1 H. Hollick 4:14.1; **2** R. Smeeth 4:14.6 (*UK junior record*); **3** S. Arthurton 4.17.1; **4** S. Harvey 4:18.3; **5** G. Dainty 4:19.2; **6** A. Mason 4:25.1; **7** C. Hanson 4:29.3 (fell); W. Smith (dnf). finish (fell).

3000m: 1 P. Fudge 8:53.6; **2** G. Penny 9:06.4; **3** K. Binns 9:15.9; **4** M. Joyce 9:20.7; **5** P. Yule 9:20.9; **6** C. Gould 9:23.0; **7** T. Bateman 9:23.8; **8** A. Roberts 9:26.8.

100m Hurdles: 1 S. Colyear 13.67; **2** S. Strong 13.97; **3** B. Caines 14.00; **4** W. McDonnell 14.33; **5** A. Simmonds 14.54; **6** J. Livermore 14.67; **7** V. Douglas 14.90; **8** F. Macaulay 14.97.

400m Hurdles: 1 E. Sutherland 58.52; **2** S. Smith 59.32; **3** D. Heath 59.64; **4** L. Brady 60.86; **5** S. Reed 61.28; **6** G. Mather 61.34; **7** V. Douglas 61.78; **8** S. Dalgoutte 62.46.

High Jump: 1 G. Hitchen 1.85m (6' 0¾"); **2** T. Philpotts 1.75m; **3** V. Rutter 1.75m; **4 eq** C. Mathers and D. Brown 1.70m; **6 eq** J. Pinkerton, G. Howell and W. Phillips 1.70m.

Long Jump: 1 S. Reeve 6.43m (21' 1¼") w; **2** S. Hearnshaw 6.39m (20' 11¾") (*equals UK junior record*); **3** B. Clarke 6.22m; **4** R. Howell 6.19m; **5** A. Simmonds 6.12m; **6** S. Colyear 6.06m; **7** G. Howell 5.99m(w); **8** A. Manley 5.79m.

Shot: 1 J. Oakes 15.96m (52' 4½"); **2** A. Littlewood 15.71m; **3** V. Redford 14.81m.

Discus: 1 M. Ritchie 57.20m (187' 8"); **2** J. Thompson 52.38m; **3** L. Mallin 50.28m; **4** V. Redford 47.76m; **5** A. Littlewood 46.24m; **6** F. Condon 42.58m; **7** J. Robertson 42.18m.

Javelin: 1 T. Sanderson 59.52m (195' 3"); **2** F. Whitbread 52.52m; **3** A. Farquhar 49.48m; **4** S. O'Toole 48.76m; **5** Y. Fountain 46.88m; **6** J. Williams 44.40m.

20–27 July

AFRICAN GAMES

Without forcing his talent to the limit in the hot weather prevailing at the third African Games in Algiers, Henry Rono (Ken) ambled to a double victory, taking the 10,000 metres in 27:58.9 and the steeplechase, five days later, in 8:15.8. There were other world class performances: Hassan El Kashief, Sudan's first great athlete, won the 400 metres in 45.23 and returned to capture the 200 metres in 20.77; Filbert Bayi (Tan), who made his name at the previous Games in 1973 when defeating Kenya's Kip Keino in the 1500 metres, retained that title in 3:36.2 after a torrid duel with Wilson Waigwa (Ken); Daniel Kimaiyo (Ken) won the 400 metres hurdles in 49.48 just ahead of 1972 Olympic champion John Akii-Bua (Uga) who was making his farewell international appearance; and Nigeria's 4 × 400 metres relay team – coached by USA's world 400 metres record holder Lee Evans – averaged 45.8 per leg. Stars of the women's events, in which every single Games record was smashed, were double champions Hannah Afriyie of Ghana and Modupe Oshikoya of Nigeria. Kenya was the most successful nation in the men's events on the basis of medals, Nigeria was top in the women's events and on overall standings.

MEN

100m: 1 A. Meite (IvC) 10.35; **2** P. Okodogbe (Nig) 10.45; **3** O. Karikari (Gha) 10.46.

200m: 1 H. El Kashief (Sud) 20.77; **2** P. Oure (IvC) 20.90; **3** J. Siai Siai (Nig) 20.98.

400m: 1 H. El Kashief (Sud) 45.23; **2** D. Udo (Nig) 45.65; **3** C. Etoori (Uga) 45.65.

800m: 1 J. Maina (Ken) 1:47.1; **2** A. Brahmia (Alg) 1:47.5; **3** P. Lemashon (Ken) 1:47.8.

1500m: 1 F. Bayi (Tan) 3:36.2; **2** W. Waigwa (Ken) 3:36.5; **3** A. Brahmia (Alg) 3:37.3.

5000m: 1 Y. Mohamed (Eth) 13:44.4; **2** M. Musyoki (Ken) 13:44.8; **3** S. Nyambui (Tan) 13:49.6.

10,000m: 1 H. Rono (Ken) 27:58.9; **2** M. Musyoki (Ken) 28:05.2; **3** M. Kedir (Eth) 28:42.0.

Marathon: 1 R. Mabuza (Swa) 2:21:53; **2** D. Mede (Eth) 2:23:08; **3** G. Guermu (Eth) 2:27:35.

3000m Steeplechase: 1 H. Rono (Ken) 8:15.8; **2** J. Munyala (Ken) 8:25.7; **3** K. Rono (Ken) 8:26.4.

110m Hurdles: 1 F. Kimaiyo (Ken) 13.89; **2** P. Sang (Ken) 14.02; **3** T. Nnakwe (Nig) 14.35.

400m Hurdles: 1 D. Kimaiyo (Ken) 49.48; **2** J. Akii-Bua (Uga) 49.55; **3** P. Rwamuhanda (Uga) 50.18.

High Jump: 1 N'Gadjadoum (Chad) 2.16m (7' 1"); **2** H. Sahil (Alg) 2.14m; **3** Elhadj (Sen) 2.08m.

Pole Vault: 1 L. Rahal (Alg) 5.00m (16' 4¾"); **2** B. Rezki (Alg) 4.80m; **3** M. Bensaad (Alg) 4.80m.

Long Jump: 1 C. Ehizuelen (Nig) 7.92m (26' 0"); **2** F. Ndyanbangye (Uga) 7.75m; **3** E. Mifetu (Gha) 7.57m.

Triple Jump: 1 C. Ehizuelen (Nig) 16.51m (54' 2"); **2** S. Diallo (Sen) 16.29m; **3** S. Saad (Alg) 15.93m.

Shot: 1 J. Assad (Egy) 18.88m (61' 11½"); **2** N. Niare (Mali) 17.16m; **3** A. Fayez (Egy) 16.93m.

Discus: 1 N. Niare (Mali) 58.02m (190' 4"); **2** A. Belhassine (Tun) 55.74m; **3** T. Somete (IvC) 51.86m.

Hammer: 1 J. Benabid (Tun) 54.90m (180' 1"); 2 A. Boubekeur (Alg) 54.74m; 3 N. Bendifallah (Alg) 52.20m.

Javelin: 1 J. Arop (Uga) 76.94m (252' 5"); 2 A. Memmi (Tun) 71.28m; 3 J. Mayaka (Ken) 70.76m.

Decathlon: 1 M. Bensaad (Alg) 7338; 2 B. Ebewele (Nig) 6876; 3 A. Smail (Alg) 6822.

20km Walk: 1 B. Kachkouche (Alg) 1:39:21; 2 H. Tore (Eth) 1:39:51; 3 E. Kasuka (Ken) 1:43:21.

4 × 100m Relay: 1 Ghana 39.24; 2 Nigeria 39.39; 3 Congo 39.79.

4 × 400m Relay: 1 Nigeria 3:03.2; 2 Uganda 3:04.2; 3 Kenya 3:05.9.

WOMEN

100m: 1 H. Afriyie (Gha) 11.50; 2 U. Uko (Nig) 11.55; 3 K. Sandgodeyi (Nig) 11.92.

200m: 1 H. Afriyie (Gha) 23.01; 2 K. Vaughan (Nig) 23.70; 3 R. Waithera (Ken) 23.91.

400m: 1 K. Vaughan (Nig) 53.86; 2 R. Kyalisima (Uga) 54.49; 3 G. Aidou (Gha) 54.84.

800m: 1 T. Chemambwai (Ken) 2:04.8; 2 S. Boutamine (Alg) 2:05.6; 3 C. N'drin (IvC) 2:06.1.

1500m: 1 S. Boutamine (Alg) 4:16.4; 2 A. Kiprop (Ken) 4:19.6; 3 R. Thomson (Ken) 4:20.1.

100m Hurdles: 1 J. Bell-Gam (Nig) 13.67; 2 R. Kyalisima (Uga) 13.92; 3 B. Bell-Gam (Nig) 13.99.

High Jump: 1 M. Oshikoya (Nig) 1.77m (5' 9¾"); 2 K. Akrmi (Tun) 1.73m; 3 E. Biavo (Gha) 1.68m.

Long Jump: 1 M. Oshikoya (Nig) 6.32m (20' 9"); 2 J. Yawson (Gha) 6.29m; 3 B. Bell-Gam (Nig) 6.12m.

Shot: 1 J. Aciro (Uga) 14.47m (47' 5¾"); 2 V. Baawah (Gha) 12.88m; 3 H. Malit (Ken) 12.70m.

Discus: 1 F. Jerbi (Tun) 46.56m (152' 9"); 2 H. Alyek (Uga) 45.90m; 3 M. Jugah (Nig) 45.02m.

Javelin: 1 E. Nekesa (Ken) 51.58m (169' 3"); 2 A. Tschuinte (Cam) 49.16m; 3 C. Rwabiryaye (Uga) 45.52m.

Pentathlon: 1 B. Bell-Gam (Nig) 3709; 2 M. Bisseriko (Uga) 3488; 3 M. Bonzi (U. Volta) 3427.

4 × 100m Relay: 1 Nigeria 44.63; 2 Ghana 45 19; 3 Uganda 46.77.

4 × 400m Relay: 1 Ghana 3:35.6; 2 Kenya 3:39.3; 3 Uganda 3:39.9.

22, 23 July

AAA JUNIOR AND YOUTH CHAMPIONSHIPS

While his performances merited his flying out with the Scottish team to Edmonton, Graham Williamson instead had to content himself with winning the AAA under-20 1500 metres title at Cwmbran. He produced an exhilarating run, in the manner of an embryonic Filbert Bayi. Leading throughout, and eventually winning by 30 metres, he rocketed through the first lap in 55.0, reached 800 metres in 1:55.1 and covered the last lap in 60.4 for a magnificent UK junior record of 3:39.7 . . . and he has all of 1979 in the junior ranks!

Tim Anstiss, winner of both the AAA Junior and Youth pole vault titles.   Tim Pike

JUNIORS

100m: 1 E. Cutting 10.92; **2** D. Baptiste 10.94; **3** H. King 11.07.

200m: 1 P. Cooke 22.24; **2** E. Cutting 22.27; **3** J. Stark 22.58.

400m: 1 S. Wymark 48.19; **2** W. Armstrong 48.29; **3** R. Dickens 48.79.

800m: 1 J. Spooner 1:51.0; **2** R. Harrison 1:51.0; **3** D. Kirk 1:53.2.

1500m: 1 G. Williamson 3:39.7 (*UK junior record*) **2** N. Black 3:44.6; **3** A. Royle 3:45.3.

5000m: 1 M. Morton 14:03.9; **2** S. Anders 14:07.1; **3** E. White 14:17.2.

2000m Steeplechase: 1 C. Reitz 5:35.6; **2** D. Parish 5:47.2; **3** E. Wedderburn 5:47.2.

10,000m Walk: 1 M. Miley 47:44.8; **2** R. Sheppard 48:02.9; **3** P. Blagg 48:33.2.

110m Hurdles: 1 P. Barthropp 15.32; **2** N. Alexander 15.35; **3** A. Sumner 15.55.

400m Hurdles: 1 C. Preston 53.68; **2** D. Hall 53.87; **3** S. Sole 54.20.

High Jump: 1 T. Foulger 2.05m (6′ 8¾″); **2** V. Clemmens 2.00m; **3** S. Watts 2.00m.

Pole Vault: 1 T. Anstiss 4.40m (14′ 5¼″); **2** J. Leiper 4.20m; **3** T. Green 3.70m.

Long Jump: 1 C. Mitchell 7.14m (23′ 5¼″)w; **2** R. Palmer 6.99m; **3** T. Sinclair 6.97m.

Triple Jump: 1 M. Effiong 15.05m (49′ 4½″); **2** E. McCalla 14.37m; **3** S. Metcalfe 14.35m.

Shot: 1 A. Vince 15.42m (50′ 7¼″); **2** D. Smedley 14.15m; **3** A. Zaidman 13.75m.

Discus: 1 C. Dinsdale 43.90m (144′ 0″); **2** R. Weir 41.28m; **3** A. Garforth 40.80m.

Hammer: 1 R. James 54.34m (178′ 3″); **2** R. Earle 47.16m; **3** K. McNab 46.62m.

Javelin: 1 I. Marsh 70.14m (230′ 1″); **2** S. Pearson 69.76m; **3** C. Hodder 62.68m.

3000m (at Crystal Palace, 24 June); **1** M. Morton 8:10.2; **2** A. Royle 8:12.4; **3** N. Black 8:12.5.

Decathlon (at Crystal Palace, 12 and 13 August): **1** F. Obikwu 6471; **2** P. Edwards 6183; **3** L. Shakes 6057.

YOUTHS

100m: 1 M. Powell 10.94; **2** P. Brown 11.03; **3** P. Moxham 11.13.

200m: 1 P. Brown 22.61; **2** M. Powell 22.93; **3** P. Moxham 23.06.

400m: 1 A. Morgan 49.91; **2** J. Fernee 50.08; **3** P. Harvey 50.58.

800m: 1 G. McGeorge 1:51.7; **2** P. Elliott 1:52.1; **3** T. Brennan 1:54.6.

1500m: 1 N. Harper 3:56.2; **2** P. Dodds 3:56.5; **3** D. Hughes 3:56.7.

1500m Steeplechase: 1 D. Lewis 4:15.0; **2** D. Swain 4:19.6; **3** D. Bennett 4:19.8.

100m Hurdles: 1 D. Finnerty 14.12; **2** J. Segal 14.23; **3** S. McAslan 14.28.

400m Hurdles: 1 D. Jones 56.01; **2** K. Wilson 56.65; **3** J. Segal 57.32.

3000m Walk: 1 N. Troy 13:10.6; **2** G. Vale 13:26.0; **3** K. Walsh 14:20.0.

High Jump: 1 E. Moore 1.85m (6′ 0¾″); **2** P. Byrne 1.85m; **3** R. Hepburn 1.85m.

Pole Vault: 1 T. Anstiss 4.21m (13′ 9¾″); **2** J. Ball 3.80m; **3** M. Howells 3.30m.

Long Jump: 1 L. White 6.81m (22′ 4¼″)w; **2** I. Strange 6.59m(w); **3** P. Flanders 6.52m(w).

Triple Jump: 1 N. Leech 13.85m (45′ 5¼″); **2** A. Bloomfield 13.23m; **3** E. Hechavarria 13.21m.

Shot: 1 A. Zaidman 17.61m (57′ 9½″); **2** P. Quirke 15.93m; **3** M. Hewer 15.83m.

Discus: 1 P. Mardle 46.00m (150′ 11″); **2** R. Ellis 43.20m; **3** F. Bacon 42.92m.

Hammer: 1 L. Hickey 59.70m (195′ 10″); **2** S. Pickering 57.78m; **3** S. Rogerson 57.58m.

Javelin: 1 M. Humphries 62.54m (205′ 2″); **2** A. Bradstock 58.74m; **3** C. Glossop 57.68m.

3000m (at Crystal Palace, 23 June): **1** G. Taylor 8:34.2; **2** K. Newton 8:35.0; **3** A. Bristow 8:36.5.

JULY HIGHLIGHTS

Olympic shot put champion Udo Beyer (GDR) felt a twinge of conscience about being away in Sweden on the occasion of his wedding anniversary. As compensation he promised his wife that he would mark the day, 6 July, by breaking the world record . . . and he did just that! Competing in Gothenburg, he opened with a put of 21.33 metres (69′ 11¾″) and then fired the 16-pound missile out to the resounding distance of 22.15 metres (72′ 8″), well clear of the world record of 22.00 metres (72′ 2¼″) held by Aleksandr Baryshnikov (Sov). It was, he declared, 'a perfect put', but he feels he can improve further to around 22.50 metres (73′ 10″).

Three days later, in Moscow, the era of 80-metre hammer throwing was ushered in by Boris Zaichuk (Sov), a 30-year-old former boxer whose first faltering effort some 15 years earlier resulted in a throw of less than 26 metres – around 85 feet! He obliterated the world record of 79.30 metres (260' 2") standing to the name of Walter Schmidt (Ger) with the historic distance of 80.14 metres (262' 11"). The throw came in the third round. Like Beyer, Zaichuk feels there is still plenty of scope for improvement; he has even talked of 85 metres (278' 10") as a possibility!

West German hammer star Karl-Hans Riehm was thus frustrated in his bid to become the world's first 80-metre thrower, although he was to make his own mark in August, but three other German athletes set important records during July. Birgit Friedmann (18) accounted for a world junior mark of 4:06.0 for the women's 1500 metres in Dortmund on 1 July; Dr Thomas Wessinghage created a European mile record of 3:52.5 in Stockholm on 3 July in a great competitive race which saw Josef Plachy (Cze) clock 3:52.6 and Steve Scott (USA) 3:52.9; and at Bernhausen on 29 and 30 July Olympic silver medallist Guido Kratschmer ran up the second-greatest total in decathlon history. His score of 8498 points, a European record, comprised 10.60 for 100 metres, 7.84 metres (25' 8¾") long jump, 16.56 metres (54' 4") shot, 1.91 metres (6' 3¼") high jump, 47.64 for 400 metres, 14.01 for the hurdles, 45.46 metres (149' 2") discus, 4.50 metres (14' 9") pole vault, 58.80 metres (192' 11") javelin and 4:28.3 for 1500 metres.

Don Ritchie recorded the world's best time of six hours 18 minutes for 100 kilometres (running past 50 kilometres in 2:51:38) at Hartola in Finland on 1 July. Fellow-Scot Liz Sutherland produced a UK 400 metres hurdles record – electrically timed – of 57.43 in Dusseldorf on 6 July; Carol Tyson equalled her UK 3000 metres walk figures of 13:40.0 at Kirkby on 23 July; and Donna Hartley was timed at 51.2, a British best on hand timing, for 400 metres at a Commonwealth Games warm-up meeting in Edmonton on 28 July.

What must have been the closest mass sprint finish in international athletics history occurred in Milan on 1 July when Don Quarrie (Jam) won the 100 metres in 10.22 a whisker ahead of Steve Williams (USA) 10.22, Clancy Edwards (USA) 10.22, Houston McTear (USA) 10.23, Pietro Mennea (Ita) 10.23 – with Harvey Glance (USA) a relatively outdistanced sixth in 10.26! At sprinting speed, one-hundredth of a second represents roughly four inches in distance. Some fancy sprinting too at the Central American and Caribbean Games staged at Medellin (Colombia) from 15 to 20 July. Helped by the 5000 feet – plus altitude, the Cubans Silvio Leonard and Osvaldo Lara sped to 10.10 and 10.11 timings, while Alberto Juantorena missed his 400 metres personal best by one-hundredth with 44.27. Not to be outdone, 1972 Olympian Eddie Hart (USA) climaxed a fine comeback by clocking 10.07, also at altitude, at Colorado Springs on 30 July.

The USA men's team beat the USSR 119–102 and the women's squad lost narrowly 71–75 at Berkeley on 7 and 8 July. The titbit was the high jump where Vladimir Yashchenko cleared 2.27 metres (7' 5¼") and failed narrowly at 2.31 metres (7' 7") . . . but so did pint-sized Franklin Jacobs. Victory went to the world record holder on the basis of fewer failures. In a junior match between the two nations at Donetsk on 8 July, the USA sprint relay team achieved a world junior record of 39.51, with the USSR setting a European mark of 39.67.

Competing over the distance for only the second time, Dave Cotton (21) won the RWA national 50 kilometres road walk title at Stretford on 15 July.

Result: 1 D. Cotton 4:14:25; **2** I. Richards 4:18:32; **3** B. Adams 4:19:22; **4** A. James 4:20:24; **5** R. Dobson 4:24:57; **6** S. Lightman 4:25:24. **Team:** Sheffield.

Among several record-breaking performances in the UK Veterans Championships at Wolverhampton on 15 and 16 July was a British steeplechase best of 9:15.6 by Telwyn Davies (40) and a world's best for his age-group by 64-year-old Dr Konstantin Maksimczyk, who threw the 1kg discus 52.90 metres (173′ 7″).

Winners in the 40–44 age group: 100m/200m: R. Taylor 11.3/23.0; **400m/800m:** R. Anderson 51.2/1:56.6; **1500m:** A. Kimber 4:07.8; **5000m:** R. Fowler 14:48.8; **3000m Steeplechase:** T. Davies 9:15.6; **110m Hurdles:** C. Shafto 16.5; **400m Hurdles:** K. Robinson 69.5 (K. Whitaker 62.5 in 45–49 group); **High Jump:** J. Darlington 1.70m (5′ 7″); **Pole Vault:** R. Wilson 3.60m (11′ 9¾″) (R. Brown 3.80m (12′ 5½″) in 45–49 group); **Long Jump:** D. Gale 6.01m (19′ 8¾″); **Triple Jump:** M. Burrell 12.40m (40′ 8¼″); **Shot:** K. Madden 11.26m (36′ 11½″); **Discus:** H. Richardson 34.62m (113′ 7″) (O. Feldmanis 42.78m (140′ 4″) in 50–54 group); **Hammer:** N. McDonald 52.64m (172′ 8″); **Javelin:** P. Hable 55.22m (181′ 2″); **Pentathlon:** H. Harding 2092; **5000m Walk:** G. Smyth 25:49.2 (T. Challis 25:13.6 in 45–49 group); **10,000m Walk:** P. Markham 51:34.8; **Women: 35 and over: 100m/100m Hurdles/Long Jump:** P. McNab 12.9/14.9/5.49m (18′ 0¼″); **200m:** V. Surety 27.7; **400m:** S. Fitzmaurice 63.9; **800m:** B. Brookes 2:26.8; **1500m:** V. Howe 4:29.2; **High Jump/Discus:** R. Payne (45–49 group) 1.43m (4′ 8¼″) and 44.26m (145′ 2″); **Shot:** J. Atack 12.55m (41′ 2¼″); **Javelin:** A. Williams (40–44 group) 38.46m (126′ 2″); **3000m Walk:** J. Farr 15:27.4.

August

6–12 August

COMMONWEALTH GAMES

In 1978, for the first time in 12 years, British athletes were faced with the problem of tackling two major international championships – the Commonwealth Games and European Championships – in very close proximity. Two of the UK's brightest stars, Steve Ovett and Sebastian Coe, decided well in advance to channel all their concentration and energy towards success in the European Championships in Prague, but everyone else of prominence elected to do battle first in Edmonton, Alberta. And how well they did! No fewer than half of the 38 events were won by athletes drawn from the UK: 16 gold medals went to England (equalling the record haul dating way back to 1934), two to Scotland and one to Wales. Next in terms of gold medals came Australia and Canada with six apiece, Kenya gained five victories, Jamaica and Tanzania one each.

The African nations having boycotted the 1976 Olympics in Montreal, these Commonwealth Games were of particular significance in enabling their athletes' progress to be assessed. Unhappily, both Nigeria and Uganda declined to take part, which cost Nigeria's Dele Udo (400 metres), Joe Siai Siai (110 metres hurdles), Charlton Ehizuelen (long and triple jump), men's relay teams and Modupe Oshikoya (pentathlon), and Uganda's Cyril Etoori (400 metres) and John Akii-Bua (400 metres hurdles) their chance for medals. Deprived of all this talent in the explosive events, Africa gained most of its successes in the middle and long distance running department.

Despite the disqualification in the semi-finals of their African champion James Maina for breaking from his lane too soon, Kenya still supplied the winner of the 800 metres as Mike Boit, so often the gallant runner-up, finally captured a major title. In the 1500 metres Filbert Bayi (Tan), whose time of 3:32.2 when winning in Christchurch four years earlier is still the world record, tried his utmost to hang on to his laurels with a brave display of front running. He went through 400 metres in 57.7, 800 metres in 1:55.2 and 1200 metres in 2:53.9, which isn't hanging about, but still he couldn't shake off John Robson of Scotland and Dave Moorcroft of England. The thrilling battle continued along the finishing straight with Moorcroft prevailing in the fine time of 3:35.5, fastest in the world for 1978. Bayi took the silver in 3:35.6, just one-hundredth of a second ahead of Robson (also 3:35.6). Both Moorcroft and Robson improved on their previous best by over three seconds, while fast-finishing Frank Clement (Sco) found his personal best of 3:35.7 insufficient for a medal in this pulsating race.

It seemed mathematically appropriate that Brendan Foster (Eng), a bronze medallist in the 1500 metres at the 1970 Games and a silver medallist in the 5000 metres four years later, should finally strike gold in the 10,000 metres at Edmonton. The winning time of 28:13.7, the slowest of Foster's career, may not have looked special at face value but in fact it represented remarkable running in a temperature of 28°C and at an altitude of 2500 feet. Foster struck with three and a half laps to go to win from Kenya's Mike Musyoki. The latter's compatriot, Henry Rono, gave the 10,000 metres a miss to concentrate

Left: *Canada's golden girl of the Commonwealth Games, pentathlon winner Diane Jones-Konihowski.*

Tony Duffy

97

on the steeple chase/5000 metres double first achieved in Christchurch by another Kenyan, Ben Jipcho. Rono succeeded, virtually toying with some formidable opposition without in either race approaching Jipcho's times (8:20.8/13:14.4) let alone his own pending world records of 8:05.4 and 13:08.4.

Hampered by very blustery conditions, he was slowed to 8:26.5 in the steeplechase final, followed home by team-mates James Munyala and Kip Rono (no relation) for the first 'clean sweep' in a Commonwealth track final since Herb Elliott led an Australian 1–2–3 in the mile at Cardiff in 1958. The eagerly-anticipated 5000 metres was, frankly, a disappointment. For a start, Dick Quax of New Zealand (Rono's predecessor as world record holder) scratched from his heat after a disastrous run in the 10,000 metres, a stomach upset caused Dave Fitzsimons (Aus) to withdraw from the final, and Rod Dixon (NZ) – the man considered most likely to give Rono a run for his money – underwent the traumatic experience of having his specially-made running shoes stolen just before the final. The race was delayed for several minutes while a fruitless search was carried out and in the end a totally deflated Dixon lined up in borrowed spikes and, understandably, merely went through the motions. The strong English trio were unable to do themselves full justice either. Fairly shattered after their 10,000 metres exertions, Brendan Foster and Mike McLeod did well in the circumstances to finish third and fourth, but Nick Rose withered after a snappy start to finish twelfth. Rono romped home untroubled in 13:23.0, with Musyoki collecting his second silver medal.

Africa's other victory in the distance events came in the marathon, and it was the shock result of the Games. It would be fair to say that, outside his native Tanzania (inside too, probably!), Gidemas Shahanga was utterly unknown prior to Edmonton. Only 15 days earlier he had finished an unnoticed seventh (2:32:50) in the African Games, but a miraculous transformation occurred in the Edmonton race. Shahanga, somewhere between 19 and 21 years old (he doesn't know when he was born, and there are no records) ran with shrewd judgment which belied his limited experience. He was fifteenth at 10km, eighth at 20km, fifth at 30km (400 metres behind the leader, Scottish-born Paul Bannon here representing Canada), second at 40km (only 70 metres behind the Canadian favourite, Jerome Drayton), and in the lead just outside the stadium. Finishing astonishingly full of running, he zipped through the final half-lap of the track in 33 seconds to win in 2:15:39.8 – seven minutes inside his previous best!

There were other East African triumphs in the 400 metres hurdles where Daniel Kimaiyo (Ken) ran out a convincing winner in 49.48, and in the 4 × 400 metres relay in which Kenya retained the title in 3:03.5 even though a sizzling anchor leg of 44.5 by Richard Ashton had enabled England to finish one-hundredth of a second ahead. What marred what was otherwise a stunning final day for British athletes (seven victories out of the other eight events contested on 12 August) was the England team's disqualification for alleged impeding of the Kenyan runner, William Koskei, on the third stage by Glen Cohen.

The other men's relay title, the 4 × 100 metres, went to Scotland – a result which could not have been realistically anticipated unless one had been under the influence of that country's most famous export. But the Scottish quartet of

David Jenkins, Allan Wells, Cameron Sharp and Drew McMaster confounded everyone by clocking a UK record of 39.24 on a rainsoaked track. Admittedly, the absence through injury of Don Quarrie from the Jamaican team opened the door for them but all credit to the Scots for seizing their chance. Similarly, Allan Wells in the 200 metres. When a mid-race attack of cramp led to Olympic champion Quarrie being eliminated in the semis, Wells' prospects of victory were greatly enhanced, but he still had two very strong opponents to overcome in James Gilkes (Guy) and Olympic finalist Colin Bradford (Jam). Wells gave it everything, building up a three-metre lead around the turn and holding on for grim death along the straight as Gilkes drew relentlessly closer. The Scot still had a good half-metre in hand at the finish, though, and his time – even if it was considerably wind-assisted – was a glorious 20.12, or almost half a second inside the UK record of 20.61 he set in a heat. It was a great Games for Wells, for earlier he had picked up the silver medal in the 100 metres (in a windy 10.07), ahead of Olympic champion Hasely Crawford (Tri) no less, with 18-year-old Mike McFarlane of England also excelling by placing fifth in 10.29. The winner, for the third Commonwealth Games running, was the popular Quarrie.

Jamaican Don Quarrie, 100 metres champion for the third successive Games.   Fionnbar Callanan

The 100 metres was close, only six-hundredths of a second separating first from third; the 110 metres hurdles was even closer as five-hundredths covered the first four – Berwyn Price, the 1974 runner-up, snatching Wales' first track victory in these Games for 40 years. At the other end of the scale, Olly Flynn (Eng) dominated the 30 kilometres walk to finish nearly a minute clear. Quarrie apart, shot-putter Geoff Capes was the only champion from Christchurch to defend successfully. Another English field event victory came in the triple jump, where Keith Connor produced one of the finest performances of the entire Games when leaping a wind-assisted 17.21 metres (56' 5¾") backed up by another windy effort of 17.17 metres (56' 4") and a legal 16.76 metres (55' 0"). That latter mark, which also obliterated his previous best of 16.54 metres (54' 3¼"), broke Aston Moore's UK record – Moore himself improving to 16.69 metres (54' 9¼") for third place. Roy Mitchell (Eng) also had the benefit of wind assistance when leaping 8.06 metres (26' 5½") to win the long jump, a mark which would have equalled Lynn Davies' Games record had Mitchell not been pre-empted by team-mate Daley Thompson during the decathlon.

Thompson's all-round display of virtuosity constituted for many the supreme highlight of the Games, his final score of 8467 points being the third-highest in history behind Bruce Jenner's world record of 8618 and Guido Kratschmer's European figures of 8498 set just a few days earlier. Thompson, only just turned 20, got away to a dream start. He clocked a personal best of 10.50 (wind assisted) for 100 metres and then practically did 'a Beamon' in the long jump where a tail wind of 6.29 metres per second helped him to the prodigious distance of 8.11 metres (26' 7¼"), the best-ever recorded in a decathlon and a world class performance in its own right. However, that friendly gust had the side-effect of nullifying Thompson's two-day labours for record purposes. Decathletes are allowed a special tolerance of four metres per second instead of the normal two metres per second in the 100 metres, hurdles and long jump before records are disallowed, but from this point onward Thompson knew he could not officially break any records – although that did not inhibit him from going all out to better Jenner's fabled score. His longest shot-put in a decathlon, a personal best-equalling high jump and a superb 400 metres time in blustery conditions enabled him to pile up the highest first-day total (with electric timing) in history: 4550 points! After coming close to his personal bests in the hurdles, discus and pole vault, Thompson still had an outside chance of challenging Jenner's score but a mediocre javelin throw ruined his ambitions on this occasion . . . time and talent are on his side, though.

It was another great all-rounder, Edmonton's own Diane Konihowski (née Jones), who was the star of the women's programme. In many events, performances well short of world class sufficed for victory, yet despite a complete lack of opposition (as in Thompson's case) the Canadian was sufficiently motivated by the adoring crowds to achieve a scintillating pentathlon score of 4768 points, a Commonwealth record which ranks her third on the world all-time list. A second Commonwealth record fell as Katrina Gibbs (Aus), who has made meteoric progress during her two years as a high jumper, flopped over 1.93 metres (6' 4") to upset Canadian favourite Debbie Brill.

The English girls reaped a bumper harvest of medals, led by a clean sweep (England's first in any women's event since 1934) in the hurdles which was won by Lorna Boothe in a windy 12.98, fastest ever by a British athlete. Other golds were collected by Sonia Lannaman (100 metres), Donna Hartley (400 metres), Mary Stewart (1500 metres), Paula Fudge in the 3000 metres with twin sister Ann Ford third, Sue Reeve (long jump), Tessa Sanderson (javelin) and by both relay teams. The youngest gold medallist at the Games was Kathy Smallwood (18) in the 4 x 100 metres; earlier she had caused quite a stir in the 200 metres with a windy 22.73, easing up in the heats, and a legal 22.99 for a UK junior record in the semis. Sue Hearnshaw (17) long jumped 6.40 metres (21′0″) for another national junior record, missing out on a medal only in the final round.

Finally, back to Africa. For some years now one has been awaiting an East African woman middle distance runner who would make the sort of impact created by her male colleagues. It nearly happened in Edmonton . . . Kenya's Teckla Chemabwai was leading with just 10 metres to go in the 800 metres, before being pipped by Judy Peckham of Australia. Perhaps the first track title to be won by an African girl will be witnessed at the next Commonwealth Games, in Brisbane in 1982. It would be good for the world-wide development of the sport.

Scotland's victorious sprint relay squad: left to right – David Jenkins, Allan Wells, Cameron Sharp, Drew McMaster.
Tony Duffy

MEN'S EVENTS

100 METRES

First round (*1st 5 and 2 fastest losers to 2nd round*) **Heat 1:** (wind: −0.3m) **1** D. Quarrie (Jam) 10.43; **2** M. Nash (Can) 10.59; **3** O. Karikari (Gha) 10.60; **4** D. Roberts (Wal) 10.88; **5** R. Gnanasekharan (Ind) 10.94; **6** J. Charlotte (Mau) 11.26; **7** G. Osborne (StK) 11.62. **Heat 2:** (−0.55m) **1** J. Gilkes (Guy) 10.65; **2** G. Simons (Ber) 10.78; **3** E. Serrette (Tri) 10.87; **4** G. French (NZ) 10.94; **5** D. Lukuba (Tan) 10.96; **6** M. Bambatha (Les) 11.27; **7** F. Williams (StV) 11.28. **Heat 3:** (nil) **1** C. Brathwaite (Tri) 10.57; **2** R. Clarke (Bar) 10.66; **3** O. Heywood (Jam) 10.66; **4** D. Trott (Ber) 10.70; **5** C. Sharp (Sco) 10.78; **6** G. Nestor (StL) 11.34; **7** O. N'Dure (Gam) 11.49. **Heat 4:** (−1.21m) **1** E. Obeng (Gha) 10.47; **2** P. Narracott (Aus) 10.71; **3** A. McMaster (Sco) 10.79; **4** B. Green (Eng) 10.80; **5** J. Mwebi (Ken) 10.83; **6** M. Shamim (Ban) 11.34; **7** B. N'Jie (Gam) 11.51. **Heat 5:** (−0.9m) **1** H. Crawford (Tri) 10.55; **2** M. McFarlane (Eng) 10.57; **3** D. Williams (Can) 10.64; **4** C. Dill (Ber) 10.86; **5** E. Quarrie (Jam) 10.87; **6** P. Mwita (Tan) 11.06; **7** L. Nchee (Les) 11.46. **Heat 6:** (−0.12m) **1** A. Wells (Sco) 10.55; **2** H. Fraser (Can) 10.62; **3** G. Enchill (Gha) 10.68; **4** R. Moxey (Bah) 10.69; **5** L. Hoyte (Eng) 10.86; **6** B. Jarju (Gam) 10.98; **7** L. Ambrose (StL) 11.11.

Second Round (*1st 3 and 4 fastest losers to semis*) **Heat 1:** (+0.86m) **1** Gilkes 10.38; **2** Karikari 10.51; **3** Heywood 10.58; **4** Dill 10.63; **5** Sharp 10.65; **6** Green 10.68; **7** Mwebi 10.76; **8** Lukuba 10.80. **Heat 2:** (+1.47m) **1** McFarlane 10.32; **2** Crawford 10.33; **3** Narracott 10.35; **4** Trott 10.53; **5** Nash 10.54; **6** Moxey 10.60; **7** McMaster 10.65; **8** E. Quarrie 10.73. **Heat 3:** (+1.32m) **1** Wells 10.32; **2** Fraser 10.48; **3** Enchill 10.57; **4** Serrette 10.64; **5** Simons 10.69; **6** L. Hoyte 10.85; **7** Gnanasekharan 10.86; **8** Mwita 11.02. **Heat 4:** (−1.31m) **1** D. Quarrie 10.36; **2** Obeng 10.44; **3** Brathwaite 10.63; **4** Clarke 10.73; **5** Williams 10.76; **6** Roberts 10.84; **7** Jarju 10.91; **8** French 10.98.

Semi-finals (*1st 4 to final*) **Heat 1:** (−0.25m) **1** Wells 10.31; **2** McFarlane 10.43; **3** Narracott 10.46; **4** Brathwaite 10.54; **5** Fraser 10.55; **6** Trott 10.56; **7** Karikari 10.56; **8** Heywood 10.69. **Heat 2:** (+4.51m) **1** Quarrie 10.19 (*equals Games record*); **2** Crawford 10.24; **3** Gilkes 10.31; **4** Obeng 10.32; **5** Enchill 10.53; **6** Moxey 10.55; **7** Dill 10.72; Nash scratched.

Final: (+7.51m) **1** Don Quarrie (Jam) 10.03 (*Games record*); **2** Allan Wells (Sco) 10.07; **3** Hasely Crawford (Tri) 10.09; **4** James Gilkes (Guy) 10.15; **5** Mike McFarlane (Eng) 10.29; **6** Paul Narracott (Aus) 10.31; **7** Chris Brathwaite (Tri) 10.32; **8** Ernest Obeng (Gha) 10.34.

200 METRES

First round (*1st 5 and 2 fastest losers to 2nd round*) **Heat 1:** (+1.86m) **1** D. Bowen (Can) 21.15; **2** F. Brown (Jam) 21.30; **3** P. Narracott (Aus) 21.35; **4** T. Mochache (Ken) 21.40; **5** D. Lukuba (Tan) 21.86; **6** B. Jarju (Gam) 22.01; **7** F. Williams (StV) 22.30. **Heat 2:** (+0.2m) **1** A. Lomotey (Gha) 21.25; **2** R. Hopkins (Aus) 21.25; **3** T. Bonsor (Eng) 21.59; **4** B. Smith (NZ) 21.62; **5** D. Roberts (Wal) 21.70; **6** P. Mwita (Tan) 22.08; **7** K. Rocque (StV) 22.32; **8** M. Bambatha (Les) 22.80. **Heat 3:** (+1.07m) **1** J. Gilkes (Guy) 21.00; **2** D. Biocchi (Can) 21.33; **3** R. Gnanasekharan (Ind) 21.60; **4** C. Jacobs (Ant) 21.61; **5** A. Mutunga (Ken) 21.74; **6** L. Ambrose (StL) 22.00. **Heat 4:** (+1.9m) **1** D. Quarrie (Jam) 20.97; **2** M. McFarlane (Eng) 21.28; **3** E. Noel (Tri) 21.33; **4** C. Sharp (Sco) 21.52; **5** P. Kipkirong (Ken) 21.69; **6** V. Harvey (Ber) 22.10; **7** G. Nestor (StL) 22.45; **8** B. N'Jie (Gam) 23.04. **Heat 5:** (+3.32m) **1** C. Bradford (Jam) 20.87; **2** C. Brathwaite (Tri) 21.14; **3** R. Moxey (Bah) 21.29; **4** C. Dill (Ber) 21.34; **5** A. McMaster (Sco) 21.53; **6** R. Clarke (Bar) 21.53; **7** J. Griffiths (Wal) 21.56; **8** O. N'Dure (Gam) 22.73. **Heat 6:** (+3.2m) **1** A. Wells (Sco) 21.35; **2** T. Hoyte (Eng) 21.39; **3** C. Doty (Can) 21.42; **4** E. Ntiforo (Gha) 21.55; **5** C. Edwards (Bar) 21.69; **6** L. Nchee (Les) 22.17; **7** K. Wade (Ber) 22.17; **8** J. Charlotte (Mau) 22.67.

Second round (*1st 3 and 4 fastest losers to semis*) **Heat 1:** (+1.07m) **1** Quarrie 20.66; **2** Narracott 21.37; **3** Bonsor 21.48; **4** Biocchi 21.50; **5** Sharp 21.54; **6** Noel 21.66; **7** Ntiforo 21.81; **8** Edwards 21.85. **Heat 2:** (+2.07m) **1** Gilkes 20.97; **2** McFarlane 21.31; **3** Hopkins 21.35; **4** Brown 21.37; **5** Bowen 21.48; **6** Roberts 21.91; **7** Mochache 21.94; **8** Gnanasekharan 21.96. **Heat 3:** (+1.92m) **1**

Lomotey 21.38; **2** Clarke 21.51; **3** Dill 21.53; **4** McMaster 21.54; **5** Jacobs 21.63; **6** Moxey 21.66; **7** Mutunga 22.16; Lukuba scratched. **Heat 4:** (+1.82m) **1** Wells 20.61 (*UK national record*); **2** Bradford 20.89; **3** T. Hoyte 21.16; **4** Brathwaite 22.22; **5** Doty 21.44; **6** Smith 21.60; **7** Kipkirong 21.64; **8** Griffiths 21.65.

Semi-finals (*1st 4 to final*) **Heat 1:** (−0.47m) **1** Bradford 21.15; **2** T. Hoyte 21.31; **3** Hopkins 21.42; **4** Dill 21.46; **5** Quarrie 21.49; **6** Lomotey 21.58; **7** Bowen 21.61; **8** Clarke 22.14. **Heat 2:** (+3.54m) **1** Wells 20.68; **2** Narracott 20.71; **3** Brown 20.72; **4** Gilkes 20.75; **5** Bonsor 20.89; **6** Brathwaite 21.10; **7** Doty 21.25; McFarlane scratched.

Final: (+4.31m) **1** Allan Wells (Sco) 20.12 (*Games record*); **2** James Gilkes (Guy) 20.18; **3** Colin Bradford (Jam) 20.43; **4** Paul Narracott (Aus) 20.74; **5** Floyd Brown (Jam) 20.79; **6** Rick Hopkins (Aus) 20.88; **7** Trevor Hoyte (Eng) 20.90; **8** Calvin Dill (Ber) 21.07.

400 METRES

First round (*1st 5 and 2 fastest losers to 2nd round*) **Heat 1:** **1** D. Jenkins (Sco) 47.78; **2** F. Sowerby (Ant) 47.82; **3** M. Paul (Tri) 47.87; **4** J. Griffiths (Wal) 47.97; **5** B. Cameron (Jam) 48.49; **6** V. Harvey (Ber) 48.86; **7** G. Nestor (StL) 51.39. **Heat 2:** **1** R. Ashton (Eng) 47.50; **2** J. Coombs (Tri) 47.53; **3** M. Ongwae (Ken) 47.61; **4** B. Saunders (Can) 48.26; **5** E. Turner (Ant) 48.46; **6** R. Swan (Ber) 48.78; **7** K. Rocque (StV) 50.15. **Heat 3:** **1** T. Whitehead (Eng) 47.52; **2** R. Beaton (Guy) 47.77; **3** J. Higham (Aus) 48.27; **4** Z. Stankovic (Can) 48.31; **5** B. Sglo (Gha) 48.53; **6** D. Anderson (IoM) 48.80; **7** M. Ollivierre (StV) 51.15. **Heat 4:** **1** R. Mitchell (Aus) 46.74; **2** W. Njiri (Ken) 47.20; **3** M. Delaney (Wal) 47.56; **4** C. Beattie (NI) 47.83; **5** M. Solomon (Tri) 48.14; **6** L. Flax (Ant) 49.42; **7** H. Carver (Mau) 50.76. **Heat 5:** **1** G. Bogue (Can) 46.77; **2** C. Edwards (Bar) 46.78; **3** C. Darvall (Aus) 47.42; **4** R. Jenkins (Sco) 47.93; **5** D. Pierre (Gren) 49.19; **6** M. Calderon (StL) 50.04; **7** B. Fatty (Gam) 50.98. **Heat 6:** **1** J. Ngetich (Ken) 46.50; **2** G. Cohen (Eng) 47.15; **3** J. Bandu (Gha) 47.42; **4** B. Smith (NZ) 48.02; **5** A. Premachandra (Sri) 48.30; **6** C. Philip (Ber) 48.77; **7** N. Bailey (Blz) 49.64.

Second round (*1st 3 and 4 fastest losers to semis*) **Heat 1:** **1** Edwards 46.38; **2** Whitehead 46.52; **3** Saunders 46.59; **4** Smith 46.77; **5** Beaton 47.07; **6** Cameron 47.20; **7** Delaney 47.41; Premachandra scratched. **Heat 2:** **1** Ashton 46.27; **2** Coombs 46.40; **3** Njiri 46.46; **4** D. Jenkins 46.66; **5** Darvall 46.71; **6** Turner 48.35; **7** Swan 48.77; **8** Pierre 50.45. **Heat 3:** **1** Bogue 46.06; **2** Ngetich 46.43; **3** Cohen 46.45; **4** Bandu 47.21; **5** R. Jenkins 47.44; **6** Paul 47.83; **7** Higham 47.84; **8** Philip 48.99. **Heat 4:** **1** Mitchell 46.36; **2** Sowerby 46.80; **3** Solomon 46.89; **4** Ongwae 47.31; **5** Griffiths 47.41; **6** Beattie 47.77; **7** Stankovic 48.20; **8** Sglo 48.29.

Semi-finals (*1st 4 to final*) **Heat 1:** **1** Sowerby 46.86; **2** Coombs 46.87; **3** Ashton 46.88; **4** Saunders 47.32; **5** D. Jenkins 47.37; **6** Darvall 47.41; **7** Edwards 47.62; **8** Njiri 48.55. **Heat 2:** **1** Mitchell 46.88; **2** Cohen 47.00; **3** Bogue 47.32; **4** Solomon 47.61; **5** Ngetich 47.64; **6** Whitehead 47.85; **7** Beaton 48.05; **8** Smith 48.25.

Final: **1** Rick Mitchell (Aus) 46.34; **2** Joe Coombs (Tri) 46.54; **3** Glenn Bogue (Can) 46.63; **4** Mike Solomon (Tri) 46.97; **5** Glen Cohen (Eng) 46.99; **6** Richard Ashton (Eng) 47.32; **7** Fred Sowerby (Ant) 47.51; **8** Bryan Saunders (Can) 48.01.

800 METRES

Heats (*1st 3 and 4 fastest losers to semis*) **Heat 1:** **1** C. Darvall (Aus) 1:51.5; **2** P. Lemashon (Ken) 1:51.6; **3** S. Newman (Jam) 1:51.6; **4** J. McGuinness (NI) 1:51.7; **5** C. Philip (Ber) 1:52.8; **6** D. Hill (Can) 1:53.8; **7** T. Small (Bar) 1:55.2. **Heat 2:** **1** J. Higham (Aus) 1:48.9; **2** C. Szwed (Eng) 1:49.1; **3** P. Hoffmann (Sco) 1:49.1; **4** G. Grant (Wal) 1:49.3; **5** H. Zinentah (Gha) 1:50.2; **6** D. Wournell (Can) 1:50.4; **7** H. Carver (Mau) 1:54.8; **8** M. Calderon (StL) 2:01.1. **Heat 3:** **1** J. Maina (Ken) 1:49.5; **2** G. Cook (Eng) 1:49.9; **3** P. Forbes (Sco) 1:50.0; **4** R. Beaton (Guy) 1:50.3; **5** C. Francis (Gren) 1:52.2; **6** W. Amakye (Gha) 1:54.9; **7** J. Erysthee (StL) 1:58.4; M. Watson (Ber) disqualified. **Heat 4:** **1** M. Boit (Ken) 1:50.6; **2** D. Warren (Eng) 1:51.4; **3** D. Norris (NZ) 1:51.5; **4** P. Favell (Can) 1:51.6; **5** D. Pierre (Gren) 1:52.6; **6** E. Wilson (StK) 1:52.7.

Semi-finals (*1st 4 to final*) **Heat 1: 1** Newman 1:48.8; **2** Grant 1:49.3; **3** Darvall 1:49.3; **4** Lemashon 1:49.9; **5** Hoffmann 1:50.1; **6** Szwed 1:50.9; **7** Wournell 1:51.2; Maina disqualified. **Heat 2: 1** Boit 1:49.9; **2** Zinentah 1:50.6; **3** Cook 1:50.7; **4** Higham 1:50.8; **5** Norris 1:50.8; **6** Beaton 1:51.9; **7** Warren 1:52.0; **8** Forbes 1:56.8.

Final: 1 Mike Boit (Ken) 1:46.4; **2** Seymour Newman (Jam) 1:47.3; **3** Peter Lemashon (Ken) 1:47.6; **4** Chum Darvall (Aus) 1:47.7; **5** Garry Cook (Eng) 1:48.1; **6** Halidu Zinentah (Gha) 1:48.2; **7** John Higham (Aus) 1:48.9; **8** Glen Grant (Wal) 1:49.3.

1500 METRES

Heats (*1st 5 and 2 fastest losers to final*) **Heat 1: 1** W. Waigwa (Ken) 3:41.4; **2** R. Tuwei (Ken) 3:41.4; **3** D. Moorcroft (Eng) 3:41.5; **4** G. Grant (Wal) 3:41.6; **5** F. Clement (Sco) 3:41.6; **6** J. Craig (Can) 3:42.7; **7** P. Lawther (NI) 3:44.4; **8** D. Norris (NZ) 3:46.0; **9** J. Charvetto (Gib) 3:52.4; **10** J. Davies (Wal) 3:53.5; **11** M. Mopeli (Les) 4:00.3; **12** J. Erysthee (StL) 4:13.9; **13** T. Swann (T&C) 4:34.5. **Heat 2: 1** F. Bayi (Tan) 3:38.8; **2** J. Robson (Sco) 3:38.8; **3** R. Dixon (NZ) 3:39.0; **4** K. Koskei (Ken) 3:39.2; **5** J. McGuinness (NI) 3:39.7; **6** P. Craig (Can) 3:39.8; **7** T. Hutchings (Eng) 3:40.6; **8** D. Childs (Can) 3:44.3; **9** S. Cram (Eng) 3:44.8; **10** S. Jones (Wal) 3:49.4; **11** M. Watson (Ber) 3:50.4; **12** H. Zinentah (Gha) 3:54.0; **13** C. Francis (Gren) 4:07.1; **14** N. Akers (Cay) 4:10.3; **15** R. Ingham (T&C) 4:45.4.

Final: 1 Dave Moorcroft (Eng) 3:35.5; **2** Filbert Bayi (Tan) 3:35.6; **3** John Robson (Sco) 3:35.6; **4** Frank Clement (Sco) 3:35.7; **5** Wilson Waigwa (Ken) 3:37.5; **6** Glen Grant (Wal) 3:38.1; **7** Richard Tuwei (Ken) 3:40.5; **8** Rod Dixon (NZ) 3:41.3; **9** J. McGuinness (NI) 3:42.6; **10** T. Hutchings (Eng) 3:43.1; **11** P. Craig (Can) 3:43.4; **12** K. Koskei (Ken) 3:45.5.

The 1500 metres medal winners in Edmonton: from the left – John Robson (bronze), Dave Moorcroft (gold), Filbert Bayi (silver).   Tony Duffy

5000 METRES

Heats (*1st 6 and 3 fastest losers to final*) **Heat 1: 1** S. Nyambui (Tan) 13:51.2; **2** K. Koskei (Ken) 13:51.5; **3** M. Musyoki (Ken) 13:53.2; **4** D. Fitzsimons (Aus) 13:55.8; **5** N. Rose (Eng) 13:57.8; **6** A. Simmons (Wal) 13:57.8; **7** A. Hutton (Sco) 14:09.2; **8** A. Thurlow (NZ) 14:27.2; **9** J. Charvetto (Gib) 14:33.8; **10** P. Hendry (Can) 14:40.9; **11** N. Akers (Cay) 15:45.4. **Heat 2: 1** H. Rono (Ken) 14:02.0; **2** R. Dixon (NZ) 14:08.0; **3** M. McLeod (Eng) 14:08.5; **4** L. Spence (Sco) 14:09.6; **5** B. Foster (Eng) 14:10.3; **6** N. Muir (Sco) 14:10.4; **7** S. Jones (Wal) 14:10.8; **8** A. Falero (Gib) 14:56.3; **9** N. Musonda (Zam) 15:00.5; **10** M. Mphafi (Les) 15:25.6; **11** P. Butler (Can) 15:43.9; **12** T. Swann (T&C) 18:37.9.

Final: 1 Henry Rono (Ken) 13:23.0; **2** Mike Musyoki (Ken) 13:29.9; **3** Brendan Foster (Eng) 13:31.4; **4** Mike McLeod (Eng) 13:33.2; **5** Suleiman Nyambui (Tan) 13:34.1; **6** Nat Muir (Sco) 13:34.9; **7** Tony Simmons (Wal) 13:39.8; **8** Rod Dixon (NZ) 13:43.7; **9** A. Hutton (Sco) 13:50.1; **10** K. Koskei (Ken) 13:52.5; **11** S. Jones (Wal) 13:54.6; **12** N. Rose (Eng) 13:55.2; **13** L. Spence (Sco) 14:28.1; A. Thurlow (NZ) did not finish; D. Fitzsimons (Aus) scratched.

10,000 METRES

1 Brendan Foster (Eng) 28:13.7; **2** Mike Musyoki (Ken) 28:19.1; **3** Mike McLeod (Eng) 28:34.3; **4** Dave Black (Eng) 28:37.9; **5** Suleiman Nyambui (Tan) 28:56.7; **6** Tony Simmons (Wal) 29:01.2; **7** Joel Cheruiyot (Ken) 29:20.2; **8** Allister Hutton (Sco) 29:30.7; **9** D. Quax (NZ) 29:58.0; **10** A. Thurlow (NZ) 30:05.2; **11** S. Kimobwa (Ken) 30:13.4; **12** Shivnath Singh (Ind) 30:26.7; **13** P. Butler (Can) 31:17.2; **14** A. Falero (Gib) 31:31.4; **15** N. Musonda (Zam) 31:59.5; **16** V. Rakabaele (Les) 32:08.4; **17** P. Chiwala (Zam) 32:14.9; **18** N. Akers (Cay) 33:29.0; **19** M. Thabana (Les) 35:32.2; **20** H. Baptiste (StL) 35:57.4.

MARATHON

1 Gidemas Shahanga (Tan) 2:15:39.8; **2** Jerome Drayton (Can) 2:16:13.5; **3** Paul Bannon (Can) 2:16:51.6; **4** Kevin Ryan (NZ) 2:17:15.3; **5** Greg Hannon (NI) 2:17:25.0; **6** Paul Ballinger (NZ) 2:17:45.9; **7** Richard Mabuza (Swa) 2:19:48.6; **8** Mike Critchley (Wal) 2:19:50.9; **9** T. Wright (Eng) 2:20:14.6; **10** S. Curran (Eng) 2:21:17.6; **11** B. Maxwell (Can) 2:21:46.3; **12** J. Norman (Eng) 2:22:22.7; **13** T. Manners (NZ) 2:22:59.7; **14** E. Ndiemandai (Tan) 2:24:54.2; **15** D. Chettle (Aus) 2:25:14.5; **16** S. Kelly (IoM) 2:27:35.3; **17** J. Butterfield (Ber) 2:30:16.7; **18** J. Dingwall (Sco) 2:32:53.8; **19** D. Newton (IoM) 2:33:05.1; **20** T. Ruto (Ken) 2:36:43.8; **21** G. Wilkinson (Ber) 2:37:30.3; **22** P. Chiwala (Zam) 2:37:59.7; **23** H. Romero (Gib) 2:42:24.8; **24** R. Swan (Ber) 2:42:34.3; **25** M. Rowlands (Wal) 2:48:10.0; **26** K. Hlasa (Les) 2:52:34.8; **27** F. Mohlomanyane (Les) 2:52:57.8; **28** S. Keita (SL) 2:56:07.1; **29** B. James (StV) 3:03:04.6; **30** H. Baptiste (StL) 3:11:08.1; Shivnath Singh (Ind), J. Kirimiti (Ken), R. Juma (Ken) and J. McLaughlin (NI) did not finish.

3000 METRES STEEPLECHASE

Heats (*1st 5 and 2 fastest losers to final*) **Heat 1: 1** K. Rono (Ken) 8:31.8; **2** J. Davies (Wal) 8:48.1; **3** D. Coates (Eng) 8:48.4; **4** H. Healey (NZ) 8:48.4; **5** J. Munyala (Ken) 8:57.9; **6** J. Sax (Can) 8:59.2. **Heat 2: 1** H. Rono (Ken) 8:26.3; **2** A. Staynings (Eng) 8:50.8; **3** E. Robertson (NZ) 8:53.1; **4** I. Gilmour (Sco) 8:56.5; **5** J. Wild (Eng) 8:59.9; **6** R. Evans (Can) 9:05.3; **7** D. Childs (Can) 9:09.8; **8** P. Lawther (NI) 9:19.2.

Final: 1 Henry Rono (Ken) 8:26.5; **2** James Munyala (Ken) 8:32.2; **3** Kip Rono (Ken) 8:34.1; **4** Euan Robertson (NZ) 8:41.3; **5** Howard Healey (NZ) 8:43.8; **6** Dennis Coates (Eng) 8:47.4; **7** Tony Staynings (Eng) 8:48.9; **8** Ian Gilmour (Sco) 8:49.7; **9** J. Wild (Eng) 8:57.9; **10** J. Davies (Wal) 9:02.0; **11** R. Evans (Can) 9:06.4; **12** J. Sax (Can) 9:15.3.

110 METRES HURDLES

Semis (*1st 3 and 2 fastest losers to final*) **Heat 1:** (−1.05m) **1** M. Binnington (Aus) 14.28; **2** F. Kimaiyo (Ken) 14.29; **3** R. Pownall (NZ) 14.36; **4** D. Wright (Aus) 14.64; **5** M. Holtom (Eng) 14.85; **6** J. Jatha (Mau) 15.04; **7** B. Henschel (Can) 15.40; **8** S. Hassan (Tan) 15.88. **Heat 2:** (−2.3m) **1** W. Parr (Aus) 14.02; **2** P. Sang (Ken) 14.03; **3** B. Price (Wal) 14.20; **4** P. Mills (NZ) 14.32; **5** H. Gretzinger (Can) 14.64; **6** I. Mobarak (Mal) 14.89; **7** I. Lutama (Tan) 15.06; **8** Satveer Singh (Ind) 15.33.

Final: (+6.15m) **1** Berwyn Price (Wal) 13.70; **2** Max Binnington (Aus) 13.73; **3** Warren Parr (Aus) 13.73; **4** Fatwell Kimaiyo (Ken) 13.75; **5** Philip Sang (Ken) 13.97; **6** Phil Mills (NZ) 14.09; **7** Ross Pownall (NZ) 14.18; **8** Don Wright (Aus) 14.31.

400 METRES HURDLES

Heats (*1st 4 and 4 fastest losers to semis*) **Heat 1: 1** P. Kipchumba (Ken) 50.81; **2** G. Williams (Can) 51.17; **3** A. Pascoe (Eng) 51.39; **4** S. James (Wal) 51.42; **5** C. Beattie (NI) 51.45; **6** S. Bolkiak (Mal) 54.36. **Heat 2: 1** C. Barriffe (Jam) 50.91; **2** W. Koskei (Ken) 51.41; **3** W. Hartley (Eng) 51.89; **4** M. Forgrave (Can) 53.48; J. Appiagyei (Gha) disqualified. **Heat 3: 1** D. Kimaiyo (Ken) 51.25; **2** G. Brown (Aus) 52.91; **3** G. Oakes (Eng) 53.36; **4** D. Anderson (IoM) 53.75; **5** P. Mills (NZ) 53.78; **6** D. Taillon (Can) 54.12.

Semi-finals (*1st 4 to final*) **Heat 1: 1** D. Kimaiyo 49.20; **2** Brown 50.31; **3** Pascoe 50.83; **4** Mills 50.92; **5** Forgrave 51.98; **6** James 53.00; **7** Anderson 53.27; **8** Taillon 53.81. **Heat 2: 1** Kipchumba 50.25; **2** Koskei 50.30; **3** Barriffe 50.80; **4** Oakes 50.96; **5** Williams 51.27; **6** Hartley 51.57; **7** Beattie 52.85; Bolkiak scratched.

Final: 1 Daniel Kimaiyo (Ken) 49.48; **2** Garry Brown (Aus) 50.04; **3** Alan Pascoe (Eng) 50.09; **4** Peter Kipchumba (Ken) 50.50; **5** William Koskei (Ken) 50.69; **6** Clive Barriffe (Jam) 51.50; **7** Gary Oakes (Eng) 51.60; **8** Phil Mills (NZ) 52.01.

HIGH JUMP

1 Claude Ferragne (Can) 2.20m (7′ 2½″) (*Games record*; 2.10 − 1, 2.15 − 1, 2.18 − 3, 2.20 − 1, 2.27 − fail); **2** Greg Joy (Can) 2.18m (2.10 − 1, 2.15 − 2, 2.18 − 3, 2.20/2.23 − fail); **3 eq** Brian Burgess (Sco) and Dean Bauck (Can) 2.15m (2.05 − 1, 2.10 − 1, 2.15 − 1, 2.18 − fail); **5** Gordon Windeyer (Aus) 2.15m; **6** Mark Naylor (Eng) 2.10m; **7** Baljit Singh Sidhu (Mal) 2.05m; **8** Winston Strachan (Bah) 2.00m; **9** B. Rault (Mau) 2.00m; M. Twawakal (Tan) no height.

POLE VAULT

1 Bruce Simpson (Can) 5.10m (16′ 8¾″) (*equals Games record;* 5.10 − 1, 5.25 − fail); **2** Don Baird (Aus) 5.10m (*equals Games record;* 5.10 − 2, 5.30 − fail); **3** Brian Hooper (Eng) 5.00m (5.00 − 1, 5.20 − fail); **4** Jeff Gutteridge (Eng) 5.00m; **5** Harold Heer (Can) 4.80m; **6** Glenn Colivas (Can) 4.80m; A. Williams (Eng) and M. Bull (NI) no height.

LONG JUMP

1 Roy Mitchell (Eng) 8.06m (26′ 5½″)w (−, 7.72, 8.06w, 7.88w, −, −); **2** Chris Commons (Aus) 8.04m(w) (7.79w, 8.04w, 7.72, −, −, 8.04w); **3** Suresh Babu (Ind) 7.94m(w) (7.39, 7.77w, 7.88, 7.94w, 7.71w, −); **4** Dennis Trott (Ber) 7.89m; **5** Rick Rock (Can) 7.85m(w); **6** Emmanuel Mifetu (Gha) 7.82m(w); **7** Bogger Mushanga (Zam) 7.68m(w); **8** Ken Lorraway (Aus) 7.57m(w); **9** W. Kirkpatrick (NI) 7.53m(w); 7.66m(w) in qualifying; **10** J. MacAndrew (Can) 7.48m(w); 7.53m(w) qual; **11** R. Kumar (Ind) 7.41m; E. Mbaabu (Ken) scratched; 7.25m qual. *Non-qualifiers:* S. Hanna (Bah) 7.22m; B. Boyd (Can) 7.17m; R. Chambers (Jam) 6.86m; E. Mobogo (Tan) 6.85m; J. Wadda (Gam) 6.54m.

Right: *Roy Mitchell leaps to a Commonwealth gold medal.* Tony Duffy

Keith Connor (left) won the triple jump with a phenomenal 17.21 metres (56' 5¾"), team-mate Aston Moore finishing third.   Brian Marshall

TRIPLE JUMP

1 Keith Connor (Eng) 17.21m (56' 5¾")w (*Games record; –*, 16.76 [*equals UK national record*], 16.47, 17.21w, pass, 17.17w); **2** Ian Campbell (Aus) 16.93m(w) (16.23, 16.58, 16.54, 16.93w, 14.95, 16.32); **3** Aston Moore (Eng) 16.69m (16.17, 16.37, 16.44w, 16.69, –, –); **4** Ken Lorraway (Aus) 16.27m; **5** Michael Nipinak (Can) 16.24m; **6** Phil Wood (NZ) 16.05m; **7** Steve Hanna (Bah) 15.97m; **8** Dave Johnson (Eng) 15.84m; 16.11m in qualifying; **9** J. Phillips (Wal) 15.59m; **10** D. Watt (Can) 15.29m; 15.52m qual; **11** G. Cheruiyot (Ken) 15.28m; 15.64m qual; **12** G. Swan (Ber) 15.06m; 15.62m qual; **13** M. Peters (Ant) 15.06m(w); 15.67m qual. *Non-qualifiers:* B. Mushanga (Zam) 15.45m; R. Chambers (Jam) 15.44m.

SHOT

1 Geoff Capes (Eng) 19.77m (64' 10½") (–, 18.65, –, 19.77, 19.72, 19.51); **2** Bruno Pauletto (Can) 19.33m (18.65, 18.86, 19.32, 19.33, 19.10, 19.24); **3** Bishop Dolegiewicz (Can) 18.45m (17.97, –, –, 17.72, 18.45, 18.31); **4** Mike Mercer (Can) 17.83m; **5** Mike Winch (Eng) 16.93m; **6** Bob Dale (Eng) 16.89m; **7** Bahadur Singh (Ind) 16.57m; **8** Jagraj Singh (Ind) 16.50m; **9** Gurdip Singh (Ind) 15.74m; **10** W. Martin (Aus) 15.54m; **11** K. Falle (Jer) 15.32m; **12** B. Cooper (Bah) 14.92m; **13** M. Obange (Ken) 13.68m.

DISCUS

1 Borys Chambul (Can) 59.70m (195' 10") (59.48, –, 59.70, –, 57.22, 58.30); **2** Brad Cooper (Bah) 57.30 (–, 55.30, 57.30, 57.24, 53.60, 50.94); **3** Robert Gray (Can) 55.48m (52.22, 53.56, 54.26, –, 55.48, 54.72); **4** Robin Tait (NZ) 55.22m; **5** Wayne Martin (Aus) 54.98m; **6** Peter Tancred (Eng) 54.78m; **7** John Hillier (Eng) 52.26m; **8** Richard Priman (Aus) 50.42m; **9** M. Winch (Eng) 50.22m; **10** P. Kumar (Ind) 49.42m; **11** J. Ruto (Ken) 43.14m; M. Obange (Ken) 3 fouls.

HAMMER

1 Peter Farmer (Aus) 71.10m (233' 3") (*Games record*; 71.10, 70.32, 70.88, –, –, –); **2** Scott Neilson (Can) 69.92m (69.92, 69.64, 67.94, –, –, –); **3** Chris Black (Sco) 68.14m (67.88, 65.64, 66.04, –, 68.14, 66.14); **4** Paul Dickenson (Eng) 66.42m; **5** Jim Whitehead (Eng) 65.48m; **6** Ian Chipchase (Eng) 64.80m; **7** Martin Girvan (NI) 60.86m; **8** Gus Puopolo (Aus) 59.74m; **9** A. Simiti (Ken) 43.38m; H. Willers (Can) 3 fouls.

JAVELIN

1 Phil Olsen (Can) 84.00m (275' 7") (74.04, 81.16, 84.00, 80.90, pass, 71.36); **2** Mike O'Rourke (NZ) 83.18m (75.30, –, –, –, –, 83.18); **3** Peter Yates (Eng) 78.58m (70.64, –, 75.82, 78.58, 75.42, –); **4** Brian Roberts (Eng) 75.10m; **5** Dave Ottley (Eng) 74.28m; **6** Luc Lapierre (Can) 73.44m; **7** Manfred Rohkamper (Aus); **8** John Mayaka (Ken) 70.00m; **9** R. Moulder (Ber) 69.64m; **10** J. Corazza (Can) 69.14m; **11** Z. Marekwa (Tan) 64.12m; **12** A. Taylor (T&C) 43.96m.

DECATHLON

1 Daley Thompson (Eng) 8467 pts (*Games record*; 10.50w, 8.11w [*Games record*], 14.43, 2.07, 47.85, 14.92, 41.68, 4.80, 56.60, 4:25.8); **2** Peter Hadfield (Aus) 7623 pts (10.98w, 7.28, 13.48, 1.92, 49.24, 15.59, 46.52, 4.00, 60.80, 4:54.5); **3** Alan Drayton (Eng) 7484 pts (11.03w, 7.15, 11.85, 1.95, 50.17, 14.86, 40.60, 4.40, 57.22, 4:54.1); **4** Graeme Watson (Eng) 7261 pts (10.77w, 7.31w, 13.29, 1.89, 49.73, 16.97, 38.04, 3.80, 54.90, 4:44.7); **5** Pan Zeniou (Cyp) 7201 pts; **6** Rob Town (Can) 7138 pts; **7** Robert Sadler (NZ) 7117; **8** Charles Kokoyo (Ken) 6775 pts; **9** M. Bull (NI) 6610 pts; **10** T. Verhoeven (Can) 6453 pts; **11** Z. Smiechowski (Can) 5807 pts; **12** D. Campbell (Gren) 5515 pts; C. Considine (Aus) retired.

30 KILOMETRES ROAD WALK

1 Olly Flynn (Eng) 2:22:03.7 (*inaugural Games record*); **2** Willi Sawall (Aus) 2:22:58.6; **3** Tim Erickson (Aus) 2:26:34.0; **4** Brian Adams (Eng) 2:29:41.5; **5** Amos Seddon (Eng) 2:29:57.5; **6** Helmut Boeck (Can) 2:31:20.9; **7** Graham Seatter (NZ) 2:31:48.9; **8** Graham Young (IoM) 2:33:14.9; **9** M. Jobin (Can) 2:35:01.3; **10** E. Kasuku (Ken) 2:43:25.2; **11** R. Chege (Ken) 2:45:12.5; **12** V. Subramaniam (Mal) 2:56:07.1; M. Parker (NZ), D. Munyao (Ken), A. Callow (IoM) and R. Lambie (IoM) did not finish.

4 × 100 METRES RELAY

Heats (*1st 3 and 2 fastest losers to final*) **Heat 1: 1** Canada 39.83; **2** Trinidad 39.92; **3** Scotland 39.96; **4** England 40.36; **5** New Zealand 41.40; **6** Gambia 43.17. **Heat 2: 1** Ghana 39.92; **2** Jamaica 40.03; **3** Australia 40.61; **4** Bermuda 40.74; **5** Kenya 41.17.

Final: 1 Scotland (David Jenkins, Allan Wells, Cameron Sharp, Drew McMaster) 39.24 (*Games and UK national record*); **2** Trinidad (Eldwin Noel, Hasely Crawford, Chris Brathwaite, Ephraim Serrette) 39.29; **3** Jamaica (Errol Quarrie, Colin Bradford, Oliver Heywood, Floyd Brown) 39.33; **4** Canada (D. Williams, M. Nash, H. Fraser, C Doty) 39.60; **5** Ghana (E. Obeng, A. Lomotey, G. Enchill, O. Karikari) 39.73; **6** England (B. Green, T. Bonsor, L. Hoyte, T. Hoyte) 40.05; **7** Australia (D. Wright, P. Narracott, M. Binnington, R. Hopkins) 40.24; **8** Bermuda (K. Wade, D. Trott, C. Dill, G. Simons) 40.33.

4 × 400 METRES RELAY

Heats (*1st 3 and 2 fastest losers to final*) **Heat 1: 1** Jamaica 3:09.2; **2** Trinidad 3:09.3; **3** Australia 3:09.3; **4** Antigua 3:11.7; **5** Wales 3:11.9; **6** St Lucia 3:23.0. **Heat 2: 1** Canada 3:06.8; **2** Kenya 3:06.8; **3** England 3:06.9; **4** Scotland 3:06.9.

Final: 1 Kenya (Washington Njiri, Daniel Kimaiyo, William Koskei, Joel Ngetich) 3:03.5; **2** Jamaica (Clive Barriffe, Bertrand Cameron, Colin Bradford, Floyd Brown) 3:04.0; **3** Australia (John Higham, Chum Darvall, Garry Brown, Rick Mitchell) 3:04.2; **4** Canada (F. Van Doorn, D. Bowen, B. Saunders, G. Bogue) 3:05.9; **5** Trinidad (M. Paul, M. Solomon, R. Astor, J. Coombs) 3:06.7; **6** Scotland (R. Jenkins, P. Hoffmann, P. Forbes, D. Jenkins) 3:07.7; **7** Antigua (E. Turner, C. Jacobs, L. Flax, F. Sowerby) 3:10.5. England (T. Whitehead, A. Pascoe, G. Cohen, R. Ashton) finished 1st in 3:03.5 but disqualified.

WOMEN'S EVENTS

100 METRES

Heats (*1st 3 and fastest loser to semis*) **Heat 1:** (−2.45m) **1** D. Boyd (Aus) 11.58; **2** W. Clarke (Eng) 11.73; **3** M. Bailey (Can) 11.75; **4** D. Scott (Jam) 11.99; **5** B. Wilson (Ber) 12.36; **6** J. Gardner (Tri) 12.36; **7** G. Freemans (Gam) 12.64; **8** T. David (Mau) 13.06. **Heat 2:** (+0.5m) **1** L. Hodges (Jam) 11.52; **2** K. Robertson (NZ) 11.67; **3** M. Wells (Sco) 11.69; **4** E. Hope (Tri) 11.74; **5** V. Hancox (NI) 12.23; **6** C. Delancy (T&C) 12.37; **7** M. Mamedy (Mau) 12.61. **Heat 3:** (−1.52m) **1** B. Goddard (Eng) 11.51; **2** P. Loverock (Can) 11.57; **3** C. Beazley (Aus) 11.60; **4** J. Caddle (Bar) 12.09; **5** J. Yawson (Gha) 12.12; **6** C. Drummond (Jam) 12.26; **7** C. Briggs (Gam) 12.53. **Heat 4:** (−0.01m) **1** R. Boyle (Aus) 11.53; **2** H. Afriyie (Gha) 11.61; **3** D. Jones (Ber) 11.66; **4** J. Bernard (Tri) 11.78; **5** E. Otieno (Ken) 12.15; **6** J. Jawo (Gam) 12.94; **7** J. John (SL) 13.12. **Heat 5:** (−0.11m) **1** S. Lannaman (Eng) 11.75; **2** A. Bailey (Can) 11.79; **3** H. Golden (Sco) 11.83; **4** W. Brown (NZ) 11.84; **5** C. Ford (Ber) 12.29; **6** K. Nzael (Tan) 12.35; **7** M. Chin (Mal) 12.85.

Semi-finals (1st 4 to final) **Heat 1:** (nil) **1** Boyd 11.37; **2** Loverock 11.47; **3** Lannaman 11.49; **4** Clarke 11.56; **5** Jones 11.62; **6** A. Bailey 11.63; **7** Wells 11.73; **8** Hope 11.82. **Heat 2:** (−0.76m) **1** Boyle 11.47; **2** Goddard 11.52; **3** Afriyie 11.56; **4** Hodges 11.58; **5** Robertson 11.63; **6** Beazley 11.66; **7** M. Bailey 11.67; **8** Golden 11.71.

Final: (* +2.81m) **1** Sonia Lannaman (Eng) 11.27; **2** Raelene Boyle (Aus) 11.35; **3** Denise Boyd (Aus) 11.37; **4** Hannah Afriyie (Gha) 11.38; **5** Bev Goddard (Eng) 11.40; **6** Patty Loverock (Can) 11.40; **7** Lelieth Hodges (Jam) 11.47; **8** Wendy Clarke (Eng) 11.48.

200 METRES

Heats (*1st 3 and fastest loser to semis*) **Heat 1:** (+3.23m) **1** D. Boyd (Aus) 23.03; **2** P. Loverock (Can) 23.43; **3** M. Wells (Sco) 23.81; **4** J. Bernard (Tri) 23.96; **5** F. Nicholls (Bar) 24.07; **6** E. Otieno (Ken) 24.43; **7** C. Delancy (T & C) 25.02. **Heat 2:** (+4.33m) **1** K. Smallwood (Eng) 22.73; **2** J. Griffith (Guy) 23.02; **3** K. Robertson (NZ) 23.38; **4** M. Gottshalk (Jam) 23.69; **5** A. Taylor (Can) 23.81; **6** E. Hope (Tri) 24.19; **7** G. Freemans (Gam) 24.52; **8** M. Mamedy (Mau) 25.08. **Heat 3:** (+2.67m) **1** H. Afriyie (Gha) 23.35; **2** C. Beazley (Aus) 23.50; **3** W. Brown (NZ) 23.77; **4** A. Bailey (Can) 23.91; **5** C. Drummond (Jam) 24.94; **6** J. Jawo (Gam) 26.38; D. Burgess (Ber) did not finish. **Heat 4:** (+5.41m) **1** H. Golden (Sco) 23.17; **2** S. Lannaman (Eng) 23.36; **3** R. Boyle (Aus) 23.66; **4** P. Hunt (NZ) 24.25; **5** N. Murray (Jam) 24.53; **6** C. Ford (Ber) 24.86; **7** J. John (SL) 26.44. **Heat 5:** (+4.71m) **1** B. Goddard (Eng) 23.85; **2** R. Waithera (Ken) 23.88; **3** L. McCurry (NI) 24.24; **4** N. Koyomo (Tan) 24.75; **5** M. Bradley (Tri) 25.71; **6** A. N'Dow (Gam) 26.56.

Semi-finals (*1st 4 to final*) **Heat 1:** (+0.96m) **1** Smallwood 22.99 (*UK junior record*); **2** Lannaman 23.43; **3** Loverock 23.58; **4** McCurry 23.62; **5** Brown 23.64; **6** Wells 24.29; Afriyie and Boyle scratched. **Heat 2:** (+2.01m) **1** Boyd 23.03; **2** Goddard 23.17; **3** Golden 23.37; **4** Beazley 23.42; **5** Griffith 23.44; **6** Robertson 23.59; **7** Waithera 23.93; **8** Gottshalk 24.62.

Left: *Daley Thompson completes the 1500 metres – and a momentous decathlon.*   Tony Duffy

Final: (+5.01m) **1** Denise Boyd (Aus) 22.82; **2** Sonia Lannaman (Eng) 22.89; **3** Colleen Beazley (Aus) 22.93; **4** Bev Goddard (Eng) 22.95; **5** Kathy Smallwood (Eng) 22.96; **6** Helen Golden (Sco) 23.28; **7** Patty Loverock (Can) 23.47; **8** Linda McCurry (NI) 23.71.

400 METRES

Heats (*1st 5 and fastest loser to semis*) **Heat 1: 1** V. Elder (Eng) 53.84; **2** M. Corcoran (Aus) 54.06; **3** K. Williams (Sco) 54.28; **4** R. Williams (Jam) 54.77; **5** L. McCurry (NI) 54.83; **6** F. Nicholls (Bar) 54.93; **7** C. Muhuhe (Ken) 56.75; **8** V. Molobeka (Zam) 57.04. **Heat 2: 1** D. Hartley (Eng) 52.86; **2** B. Nail (Aus) 53.27; **3** R. Waithera (Ken) 53.36; **4** D. Byfield (Jam) 53.77; **5** M. Stride (Can) 53.81; **6** A. Smyth (NI) 53.96; **7** G. Bakari (Gha) 54.17; **8** H. N'Jie (Gam) 66.43. **Heat 3: 1** J. Griffith (Guy) 52.71; **2** J. Hoyte (Eng) 53.00; **3** H. Blake (Jam) 53.14; **4** P. Hunt (NZ) 54.53; **5** A. Harley (Sco) 54.95; **6** R. Campbell (Can) 54.98; **7** G. Aidoo (Gha) 55.16; **8** J. Boca (Gren) 56.27.

Semi-finals (*1st 4 to final*) **Heat 1: 1** Griffith 51.40; **2** Elder 52.49; **3** Nail 52.51; **4** Hoyte 52.79; **5** Waithera 53.30; **6** Smyth 54.40; **7** Harley 55.32; **8** R. Williams 57.03. **Heat 2: 1** Hartley 52.26; **2** Blake 52.63; **3** Corcoran 52.79; **4** K. Williams 52.98; **5** Stride 53.68; **6** Byfield 54.09; **7** Hunt 54.26; **8** McCurry 54.98.

Final: 1 Donna Hartley (Eng) 51.69; **2** Verona Elder (Eng) 52.94; **3** Beth Nail (Aus) 53.06; **4** Joslyn Hoyte (Eng) 53.22; **5** June Griffith (Guy) 53.25; **6** Karen Williams (Sco) 53.66; **7** Helen Blake (Jam) 54.15; **8** Maxine Corcoran (Aus) 54.46.

Above: *Donna Hartley (80) wins the 400 metres, with Verona Elder (76) second.*   Tony Duffy

Right: *Commonwealth 100 metres champion Sonia Lannaman. She won another gold in the relay and a silver in the 200 metres.*   Tony Duffy

800 METRES

Heats (*1st 4 and 4 fastest losers to semis*) **Heat 1:** 1 E. Barnes (Eng) 2:03.9; 2 T. Chemabwai (Ken) 2:05.1; 3 C. Campton (Aus) 2:07.6; 4 D. Campbell (Can) 2:08.4; 5 H. Opoku (Gha) 2:10.3; 6 P. Reece (NI) 2:11.0; 7 T. Corea (StV) 2:22.2. **Heat 2:** 1 A. Smyth (NI) 2:07.5; 2 A. Wright (NZ) 2:07.7; 3 C. Rendina (Aus) 2:07.9; 4 A. Mackie (Can) 2:08.2; 5 P. Newnham (Eng) 2:09.7; 6 G. Konadu (Gha) 2:12.9; 7 V. Molobeka (Zam) 2:15.0. **Heat 3:** 1 E. McMeekin (Sco) 2:06.1; 2 F. Gendron (Can) 2:06.5; 3 J. Colebrook (Eng) 2:06.7; 4 J. Peckham (Aus) 2:06.8; 5 R. Tata (Ken) 2:08.4; 6 H. Blake (Jam) 2:20.8; 7 J. Boca (Gren) 2:22.6; 8 H. Bantamoi (SL) 2:52.6.

Semi-finals (*1st 4 to final*) **Heat 1:** 1 McMeekin 2:03.0; 2 Rendina 2:04.8; 3 Colebrook 2:04.9; 4 Mackie 2:05.1; 5 Campbell 2:05.5; 6 Newnham 2:07.7; 7 Tata 2:13.7; 8 Reece 2:20.1. **Heat 2:** 1 Peckham 2:05.2; 2 Barnes 2:05.4; 3 Gendron 2:05.7; 4 Chemabwai 2:05.7; 5 Smyth 2:06.7; 6 Wright 2:06.7; 7 Campton 2:08.3; 8 Opoku 2:18-8.

Final: 1 Judy Peckham (Aus) 2:02.8; 2 Teckla Chemabwai (Ken) 2:02.9; 3 Jane Colebrook (Eng) 2:03.1; 4 Liz Barnes (Eng) 2:03.4; 5 Francine Gendron (Can) 2:04.0; 6 Evelyn McMeekin (Sco) 2:04.1; 7 Anne Mackie (Can) 2:04.2; 8 Charlene Rendina (Aus) 2:04.8.

1500 METRES

Heats (*1st 5 and 2 fastest losers to final*) **Heat 1:** 1 C. McMeekin (Sco) 4:17.0; 2 A. Wright (NZ) 4:17.0; 3 W. Kiteti (Ken) 4:17.1; 4 C. Benning (Eng) 4:17.2; 5 F. Gendron (Can) 4:17.6; 6 C. Boxer (Eng) 4:17.9; 7 M. Mwanjala (Tan) 4:21.4; 8 C. Campton (Aus) 4:22.6; 9 D. Scott (Can) 4:24.4; 10 G. Konadu (Gha) 4:43.1; 11 T. Corea (StV) 4:53.7; 12 B. Delancy (T&C) 5:06.6. **Heat 2:** 1 M. Stewart (Eng) 4:15.9; 2 P. Werthner (Can) 4:16.4; 3 A. Cook (Aus) 4:17.5; 4 A. Kiprop (Ken) 4:17.5; 5 H. Hollick (Wal) 4:18.4; 6 M. Coomber (Sco) 4:19.0; 7 R. Thomson (Ken) 4:21.0; 8 R. Issack (Tan) 4:21.0; 9 P. Reece (NI) 4:41.5; 10 J. Kandasamy (Sin) 4:58.5.

Final: 1 Mary Stewart (Eng) 4:06.3 (*Games record*); 2 Chris Benning (Eng) 4:07.5; 3 Penny Werthner (Can) 4:08.1; 4 Chris McMeekin (Sco) 4:12.4; 5 Hilary Hollick (Wal) 4:12.7; 6 Alison Wright (NZ) 4:12.9; 7 Francine Gendron (Can) 4:16.9; 8 Angela Cook (Aus) 4:17.3; 9 K. Kiteti (Ken) 4:18.7; 10 A. Kiprop (Ken) 4:23.2; 11 C. Boxer (Eng) 4:26.1; 12 M. Coomber (Sco) 4:26.3.

3000 METRES

1 Paula Fudge (Eng) 9:13.0 (*inaugural Games record*); 2 Heather Thomson (NZ) 9:20.7; 3 Ann Ford (Eng) 9:24.1; 4 Shauna Miller (Can) 9:30.8; 5 Nancy Rooks (Can) 9:34.1; 6 Angela Cook (Aus) 9:43.6; 7 Mwinga Mwanjala (Tan) 9:50.0; 8 Rose Thomson (Ken) 10:00.5; 9 D. Scott (Can) 10:02.6; 10 W. Kiteti (Ken) 10:12.6; 11 D. Chepyator (Ken) 10:18.5; 12 M. Masaka (Tan) 10:45.8; 13 J. Kandasamy (Sin) 11:13.0; 14 B. Delancy (T&C) 11:20.9; P. Yule (Eng) and T. Corea (StV) did not finish.

100 METRES HURDLES

Heats (*1st 4 to final*) **Heat 1:** (−0.14m) 1 L. Boothe (Eng) 13.49; 2 S. Lane (Can) 13.89; 3 E. Davidson (Sco) 14.03; 4 G. Wooten (NZ) 14.14; 5 V. Hancox (NI) 15.12. **Heat 2:** (−0.15m) 1 S. Colyear (Eng) 13.34; 2 S. Strong (Eng) 13.41; 3 D. Konihowski (Can) 14.00; 4 J. Caddle (Bar) 14.22; 5 R. Gelle (Aus) 14.23; 6 M. Chin (Malay) 14.77; 7 T. David (Mau) 16.13.

Final: (+3.56m) 1 Lorna Boothe (Eng) 12.98 (*Games record*); 2 Shirley Strong (Eng) 13.08; 3 Sharon Colyear (Eng) 13.17; 4 Elaine Davidson (Sco) 13.76; 5 Gail Wooten (NZ) 13.77; 6 Sharon Lane (Can) 13.88; 7 Diane Konihowski (Can) 14.11; 8 June Caddle (Bar) 4.13.

HIGH JUMP

1 Katrina Gibbs (Aus) 1.93m (6' 4") (*Commonwealth and Games record*; 1.75–1, 1.83–1, 1.88–1, 1.90–3, 1.93–2, 1.95–fail); **2** Debbie Brill (Can) 1.90m (1.75–1, 1.80–1, 1.85–1, 1.88–2, 1.90–1, 1.93–fail); **3** Julie White (Can) 1.83m (1.65–1, 1.70–1, 1.75–1, 1.78–2, 1.80–1, 1.83–1, 1.85–fail); **4** Gillian Hitchen (Eng) 1.80m; **5** Barbara Simmonds (Eng) 1.78m; **6** Maggie Woods (Can) 1.78m; **7** Val Rutter (Eng) 1.75m; **8** Wendy Phillips (NI) 1.70m; **9** A. Mutakyawa (Tan) 1.60m.

LONG JUMP

1 Sue Reeve (Eng) 6.59m (21' 7½") (6.28, 6.53, 6.44, 6.59, 6.52, –); **2** Erica Hooker (Aus) 6.58m (6.14, 6.29, –, –, 6.24, 6.58); **3** June Griffith (Guy) 6.52m (5.89, 6.29, 6.19, 6.52, 6.40, 6.13); **4** Sue Hearnshaw (Eng) 6.40m (21' 0") (*UK junior record*); **5** Shonell Ferguson (Bah) 6.24m(w); **6** Janet Yawson (Gha) 6.19m(w); **7** Ruth Howell (Wal) 6.17m; **8** Lyn Jacenko (Aus) 6.14m; **9** J. Ross (Can) 6.07m(w); **10** D. Konihowski (Can) 6.05m; 6.07m in qualifying; **11** N. Hodgins (NZ) 5.86m; **12** E. Otieno (Ken) 5.84m; 5.91m qual. *Non-qualifier:* J. Swanston (Bar) 5.52m.

SHOT

1 Gael Mulhall (Aus) 17.31m (56' 9¼") (*Games record*; 16.67, 16.63, 16.87, 16.82, 16.79, 17.31); **2** Carmen Ionesco (Can) 16.45m (16.45, 16.14, –, 16.43, –, –); **3** Judy Oakes (Eng) 16.14m (–, 15.15, 15.75, 16.06, 16.14, 15.32); **4** Angela Littlewood (Eng) 15.71m; **5** Bev Francis (Aus) 15.66m; **6** Venissa Head (Wal) 15.52m; **7** Luigina Torso (Aus) 15.09m; **8** Meg Ritchie (Sco) 14.99m; **9** L. Moreau (Can) 14.92m; **10** H. Malit (Ken) 12.04m; **11** B. Smith (Ber) 11.80m.

DISCUS

1 Carmen Ionesco (Can) 62.16m (203' 11") (*Games record*; 62.16, 61.18, –, 59.34, –, 58.50); **2** Gael Mulhall (Aus) 57.60m (51.44, 53.66, 57.04, –, 55.70, 57.60); **3** Lucette Moreau (Can) 56.64m (52.10, –, 50.64, 51.94, 56.64, –); **4** Meg Ritchie (Sco) 55.66m; **5** Janet Thompson (Eng) 53.70m; **6** Lesley Mallin (Eng) 50.56m; **7** Luigina Torso (Aus) 47.10m; **8** Venissa Head (Wal) 45.72m; **9** B. Bethell (Bah) 43.50m; **10** L. Cherotich (Ken) 40.72m.

JAVELIN

1 Tessa Sanderson (Eng) 61.34m (201' 3") (*Games record*; 61.34, –, 54.60, 58.12, –, 53.98); **2** Alison Hayward (Can) 54.52m (54.52, 48.62, –, –, 45.52, 43.42); **3** Laurie Kern (Can) 53.60m (50.80, 53.60, 52.10, 45.68, –, 49.02); **4** Eunice Nekesa (Ken) 51.46m; **5** Margaret Philpott (Aus) 50.08m; **6** Fatima Whitbread (Eng) 49.16m; **7** Shara Spragg (Eng) 49.02m; **8** Diane Williams (Sco) 46.02m; **9** B. Francis (Aus) 45.52m; **10** J. Zaslona (Wal) 41.08m; **11** S. Smith (Ber) 39.34m; **12** E. Twyford (StL) 29.62m; J. Kieboom (Aus) 3 fouls.

PENTATHLON

1 Diane Konihowski (Can) 4768 pts (*Commonwealth and Games record*; 13.85, 14.87, 1.88, 6.41, 2:12.1); **2** Sue Mapstone (Eng) 4222 pts (14.17, 11.32, 1.75, 6.06, 2:19.3); **3** Yvette Wray (Eng) 4211 pts (14.16, 12.15, 1.64, 6.04w, 2:15.6); **4** Jill Ross (Can) 4205 pts; **5** Karen Page (NZ) 4099 pts; **6** Ruth Howell (Wal) 4022 pts; **7** Barbara Beable (NZ) 3989 pts; **8** Julie White (Can) 3940 pts; **9** W. Phillips (NI) 3594 pts; **10** J. Swanston (Bar) 3517 pts; G. Saunders (Aus) retired.

Tessa Sanderson was in a class of her own in the javelin.

Tony Duffy

4 × 100 METRES RELAY

1 England (Bev Goddard, Kathy Smallwood, Sharon Colyear, Sonia Lannaman) 43.70; **2** Canada (Angela Bailey, Patty Loverock, Margaret Howe, Marjorie Bailey) 44.26; **3** Australia (Roxanne Gelle, Denise Boyd, Colleen Beazley, Lyn Jacenko) 44.78; **4** New Zealand (W. Brown, P. Hunt, G. Wooten, K. Robertson) 45.06; **5** Jamaica (N. Murray, D. Scott, M. Gottshalk, C. Drummond) 45.75; **6** Trinidad (M. Bradley, J. Gardner, J. Bernard, E. Hope) 45.80; **7** Scotland (E. Davidson, M. Wells, H. Golden, K. Williams) 45.91.

4 × 400 METRES RELAY

1 England (Ruth Kennedy, Joslyn Hoyte, Verona Elder, Donna Hartley) 3:27.2 (*Games record*); **2** Australia (Judy Peckham, Denise Boyd, Maxine Corcoran, Beth Nail) 3:28.7; **3** Canada (Margaret Stride, Debbie Campbell, Anne Mackie, Rachelle Campbell) 3:35.8; **4** Scotland (A. Harley, E. McMeekin, H. Golden, K. Williams) 3:36.5; **5** Ghana (H. Opoku, G. Bakari, G. Aidoo, H. Afriyie) 3:37.1; **6** Jamaica (D. Byfield, M. Gottshalk, N. Murray, H. Blake) 3:37.9.

18, 19 August

SUNSILK WOMEN'S AAA CHAMPIONSHIPS

Only just recovered from jet-lag on returning from Edmonton where she gained a silver medal in the 1500 metres, Chris Benning somewhat tentatively moved up to the unfamiliar distance of 3000 metres in the WAAA Championships at Crystal Palace – and promptly broke the Commonwealth record with 8:52.3. She had raced the distance only three times in her life prior to the championships, with a best of 9:19.5. Tracking Ann Ford until just before the finishing straight, Chris sprinted away easily and later confessed to feeling 'quite selfish sitting in' as she is by nature a front runner.

SENIORS

100m: 1 K. Smallwood 11.66; **2** H. Hunte 11.79; **3** S. Colyear 11.79; **4** E. Thomas 11.81; **5** M. Walsh (Eir) 11.87; **6** S. Ratcliffe 12.04; **7** J. MacGregor 12.11; **8** A. Foster 12.22.

200m: 1 K. Smallwood 23.24; **2** D. Hartley 23.42; **3** E. Thomas 23.79; **4** M. Probert 23.92; **5** M. Walsh (Eir) 23.95; **6** A. Foster 24.12; **7** S. Ratcliffe 24.17; **8** J. MacGregor 24.37.

400m: 1 J. Hoyte 52.66; **2** V. Elder 53.40; **3** L. McCurry 54.01; **4** C. Dawkins 54.15; **5** L. Burnett 54.80; **6** A. Dunn 55.36; **7** R. Livingston 56.15; **8** J. Saunders 56.74.

800m: 1 C. Boxer 2:03.1; **2** J. Prictoe 2:03.1; **3** D. Kiernan 2:06.9; **4** G. Rickard 2:08.6; **5** S. Parker 2:08.8; **6** K. Lock 2:09.9; **7** C. Wood 2:11.9.

1500m: 1 C. Hanson 4:11.6; **2** G. Penny 4:12.5; **3** W. Smith 4:13.4; **4** G. Dainty 4:16.3; **5** H. Hollick 4:16.8; **6** B. Madigan 4:17.0; **7** L. Harvey 4:18.4; **8** M. Joyce 4:19.6.

3000m: 1 C. Benning 8:52.3 (*Commonwealth and UK national record*); **2** A. Ford 8:53.8; **3** A. Wright (NZ) 9:14.7; **4** R. Smeeth 9:18.1; **5** A. Roberts 9:21.2; **6** S. Simpkin 9:34.1; **7** B. Green 9:42.4; **8** D. Nagle (Eir) 9:48.3.

100m Hurdles: 1 S. Colyear 13.51; **2** S. Strong 13.68; **3** Y. Wray 14.03; **4** J. Vernon 14.18; **5** W. McDonnell 14.22; **6** S. Mapstone 14.22; **7** T. Chipp 14.60; **8** V. Douglas 14.69.

400m Hurdles: 1 M. Appleby (Eir) 57.46; **2** E. Sutherland 58.36; **3** S. Smith 59.14; **4** V. Langley 60.49; **5** S. Reed 60.69; **6** S. Dalgoutte 60.92; **7** J. Roscoe 61.23; C. Warden scratched.

High Jump: 1 C. Mathers 1.76m (5' 9¼"); **2** D. Elliott 1.76m; **3 eq** K. Chaytors, L. Miller, T. Phillpots, A–M. Devalley, D. Grant and A. Thompson 1.71m.

Long Jump: 1 J. Davies 6.19m (20' 3¾"); **2** R. Howell 6.18m; **3** C. Earlington 6.17m; **4** J. Frank-Lynch 6.07m; **5** M. Chitty 5.83m; **6** D. Gray 5.60m; **7** K. Donovan 5.52m; **8** N. McGee 5.52m.

Shot: 1 A. Littlewood 15.97m (52' 4¾"); **2** V. Redford 14.56m; **3** J. Thompson 14.54m; **4** M. Walton (Eir) 14.05m; **5** S. Tudor 12.94m; **6** Y. Wray 12.53m; **7** J. Jackson 12.29m; **8** C. Pryce 11.70m.

Discus: 1 J. Thompson 49.80m (163' 5"); **2** P. Walsh (Eir) 47.28m; **3** A. Littlewood 46.22m; **4** V. Redford 45.92m; **5** F. Condon 45.36m; **6** D. Sturman 44.40m; **7** J. Frampton 42.14m; **8** S. Allday 41.34m.

Javelin: 1 A. Farquhar 49.20m (161' 5"); **2** J. Rose 48.30m; **3** F. Whitbread 47.54m; **4** S. O'Toole 46.54m; **5** Y. Fountain 45.18m; **6** M. Jervis 42.60m.

5000m Walk: (*at Birmingham, 5 August*) **1** C. Tyson 24:08.2; **2** V. Lovell 25:06.4; **3** K. Eden 25:46.6; **4** E. Cox 27:44.8.

INTERMEDIATES

100m: **1** P. Amond (Eir) 12.09; **2** P. Baker 12.09; **3** D. Walker 12.29.

200m: **1** D. Bunn 24.12; **2** P. Amond (Eir) 24.36; **3** P. Baker 24.51.

400m: **1** C. Pendleton 55.3; **2** A. Clifford 56.1; **3** L. Callow 56.6.

800m: **1** K. McDermott 2:07.7; **2** L. Parker 2:08.9; **3** J. Croasdale 2:10.8.

1500m: **1** C. Meagan (Eir) 4:21.0; **2** S. Arthurton 4:21.8; **3** K. Timson 4:29.4.

80m Hurdles: *(for Intermediates and Juniors)* **1** S. Brennan 11.48; **2** C. St John 11.55; **3** D. Baker 11.70.

100m Hurdles: **1** C. St John 14.43; **2** P. Licorish 14.68; **3** E. Little 14.70.

200m Hurdles: **1** A. Mills 28.51; **2** D. Baker 28.63; **3** P. Licorish 29.09.

High Jump: **1** H. Spencer 1.78m (5' 10"); **2** K. Hagger 1.73m; **3 eq** S. McPeake and K. Robinson 1.70m.

Long Jump: **1** K. Hagger 5.73m (18' 9¾"); **2** C. Henley 5.70m; **3** C. Neal 5.64m.

Shot: **1** S. Bracey 11.85m (38' 10½"); **2** E. Bernard 11.67m; **3** D. Jones 11.53m.

Discus: **1** J. Picton 42.40m (139' 1"); **2** J. Wilderspin 38.48m; **3** V. Simpson 35.90m.

Javelin: **1** S. Fry 45.18m (148' 3"); **2** S. Gibson 42.06m; **3** V. Price 41.42m.

Pentathlon: *(at Birmingham, 5 August)* **1** K. Hagger 3770; **2** C. Henley 3331; **3** H. Smiddy 3287.

3000m Walk: *(at Birmingham, 5 August)* **1** C. Brooke 16:43.8; **2** L. Nicholls 16:56.2; **3** A. Jones 17:14.6.

JUNIORS

100m: **1** J. Parry 12.10; **2** L. MacDonald 12.43; **3** C. Haslam 12.48.

200m: **1** J. Parry 24.57; **2** L. MacDonald 24.78; **3** J. Boggett 25.47.

800m: **1** L. Baker 2:09.8; **2** C. Wells 2:10.8; **3** S. Baxter 2:11.5.

1500m: **1** A. Alford 4:39.1; **2** T. Davidson 4:41.4; **3** B. Lovett 4:43.9.

75m Hurdles: **1** L. Playel 11.22; **2** N. Morrissey (Eir) 11.43; **3** L. Roper 11.67.

High Jump: **1** C. Summerfield 1.73m (5' 8"); **2** B. Corrigan (Eir) 1.73m; **3** K. Bachtiger 1.70m.

Long Jump: **1** S. French 5.81m (19' 0¾"); **2** B. Hart 5.27m; **3** L. Ghent 5.20m.

Shot: **1** C. Gregory 12.69m (41' 7¾"); **2** P. Webber 12.51m; **3** S. McDonald 12.28m.

Discus: **1** S. McDonald 38.46m (126' 2"); **2** D. Bushnell 35.78m; **3** M. Kavanagh (Eir) 32.52m.

Javelin: **1** K. Miller 35.92m (117' 10"); **2** A. Lockton 34.48m; **3** J. Harding 33.40m.

Pentathlon: *(at Birmingham, 5 August)* **1** S. French 3389; **2** J. Taylor 3136; **3** T. Donaldson 3092.

2500m Walk: *(at Birmingham, 5 August)* **1** J. Mullins 13:07.6; **2** F. Rider 13:19.8; **3** C. Irving 13:34.4.

Right: *Kathy Smallwood – a double sprint winner in the WAAA Championships.* Mark Shearman

118

23 August

ROTARY WATCHES INTERNATIONAL GAMES

Steve Ovett only emphasised what everyone knew already: he is the owner of the deadliest kick of any miler running today. He launched it, as usual, halfway around the last lap and such was the pace he generated when accelerating away from his rivals that despite slackening off in the straight to indulge in a frenzy of crowd-waving he still covered the last 200 metres of the Crystal Palace track in a remarkably swift 24.4. His final time was 3:57.7, with Mike McLeod delightedly edging John Robson for second in 3:59.4 for his first sub-four minute mark. Another outstanding finish came from Dave Moorcroft, who took only a shade outside four minutes for the last mile in the 3000 metres, which he won in a personal best of 7:43.5.

MEN

100m: 1 S. Leonard (Cub) 10.26; **2** H. Crawford (Tri) 10.26; **3** E. Obeng (Gha) 10.29; **4** A. Wells 10.33; **5** S. Green 10.49; **6** O. Lara (Cub) 10.58.

200m: 1 S. Leonard (Cub) 20.38; **2** A. Wells 20.63; **3** S. Green 21.05; **4** O. Lara (Cub) 21.14; **5** T. Hoyte 21.15; **6** T. Whitehead 21.51.

400m: 1 A. Juantorena (Cub) 45.64; **2** A. Rodgers (USA) 45.91; **3** D. Jenkins 45.97; **4** E. DeLeeuw (Bel) 46.40; **5** R. Ashton 46.41; **6** R. Jenkins 47.21.

800m: 1 D. Joseph 1:47.9; **2** D. Warren 1:48.1; **3** A. Brahmia (Alg) 1:48.3; **4** P. Browne 1:48.8; **5** F. Clement 1:49.1; **6** J. Spooner 1:49.5.

Mile: 1 S. Ovett 3:57.7; **2** M. McLeod 3:59.4; **3** J. Robson 3:59.4; **4** G. Williamson 4:00.9; **5** W. Wilkinson 4:01.2; **6** C. Sly 4:01.5.

3000m: 1 D. Moorcroft 7:43.5; **2** R. Dixon (NZ) 7:44.9; **3** N. Rose 7:46.8; **4** D. Black 7:49.9; **5** A. Simmons 7:51.5; **6** G. Barrett (Aus) 7:53.8.

110m Hurdles: 1 K. Bethel (USA) 13.66; **2** B. Price 13.74; **3** M. Holtom 14.21.

400m Hurdles: 1 A. Pascoe 50.12; **2** J. King (USA) 50.18; **3** G. Oakes 51.24; **4** W. Hartley 51.27; **5** C. Beattie 51.89; **6** M. Whittingham 52.21.

Pole Vault: 1 J. Taylor (USA) 5.51m (18' 1") *(UK all-comers record)*; **2** L. Jessee (USA) 5.40m; **3** R. Pullard (USA) 5.30m; **4** B. Hooper 5.20m; **5** J. Gutteridge 5.10m; **6** K. Stock 5.10m.

Shot: 1 G. Capes 19.74m (64' 9¼"); **2** G. McEvoy (Eir) 18.12m; **3** R. Dale 16.72m.

Mile Walk: 1 R. Mills 6:21.7; **2** B. Adams 6:25.7; **3** C. Lawton 6:31.8.

WOMEN

200m: 1 K. Smallwood 23.05; **2** E. Ashford (USA) 23.39; **3** B. Goddard 23.58; **4** E. Thomas 23.65; **5** S. Chivas (Cub) 23.73; **6** W. Clarke 24.06.

400m: 1 D. Hartley 51.43; **2** A. Penton (Cub) 51.47; **3** J. MacGregor 53.74; **4** L. Forde (USA) 53.87; **5** A. Smyth 54.28; **6** E. Barnes 54.37.

1000m: 1 I. Lipcsei (Hun) 2:37.9; **2** E. McMeekin 2:38.4 *(UK national best)*; **3** M. Lazar (Hun) 2:38.6; **4** P. Fudge 2:41.0; **5** A. Creamer 2:41.0; **6** C. Boxer 2:41.3.

100m Hurdles: 1 L. Boothe 13.35; **2** Y. Wray 13.77; **3** J. Vernon 13.96.

Javelin: 1 T. Sanderson 62.98m (206' 7"); **2** A. Farquhar 50.80m; **3** S. O'Toole 49.16m.

27 August

UK v GERMANY (Juniors)

British junior athletics enjoyed one of its happiest days when, at Crystal Palace in a meeting sponsored by British Meat, the West German team was defeated in both the men's and women's matches. The age limit for this encounter was one year lower than normal and thus all the athletes competing, except for some guests, are eligible to compete in the 1979 European Junior Championships. Among a wealth of impressive performances which speak well for the future of Britain's international team were a UK junior 2000 metres steeplechase record of 5:32.6 by Colin Reitz, a UK age-17 1500 metres best of 3:40.1 by Steve Cram in defeating a leg-weary Graham Williamson, a timely five-metre improvement by Maxine Jervis in the javelin, and a 200 metres victory in her international début by Jane Parry – at 13 the youngest athlete ever to wear British colours.

MEN

100m: 1 W. Zaske (Ger) 10.47w; **2** J. Stark (UK) 10.70; **3** M. Powell (UK) 10.79; **4** D. Daniels (Ger) 10.84.

200m: 1 P. Cooke (UK) 21.30; **2** H. Weber (Ger) 21.38; **3** K-H. Keth (Ger) 21.67; **4** P. Brown (UK) 21.73.

400m: 1 R. Dickens (UK) 47.88; **2** N. Jackson (UK) 48.18; **3** M. Reimers (Ger) 48.54; **4** W. Armstrong (UK – guest) 48.85; **5** B. Wudtke (Ger) 48.94.

800m: 1 K-P. Nabein (Ger) 1:51.6; **2** J. Spooner (UK) 1:51.6; **3** I. Warsama (UK) 1:52.2; **4** J. Grothe (Ger) 1:52.3.

1500m: 1 S. Cram (UK) 3:40.1; **2** G. Williamson (UK) 3:40.9; **3** A. Baranski (Ger) 3:41.3; **4** T. Koch (Ger) 3:49.3.

3000m: 1 A. Salter (UK) 8:27.8; **2** S. Cahill (UK) 8:28.2; **3** H. Renz (Ger) 8:33.1; **4** J. Ehl (Ger) 8:46.7.

5000m: 1 S. Binns (UK) 14:21.5; **2** J. Doherty (UK) 14:27.0; **3** U. Renz (Ger) 14:33.4; **4** P. Horak (Ger) 14:36.2.

2000m Steeplechase: 1 C. Reitz (UK) 5:32.6 (*UK junior record*); **2** M. Langler (Ger) 5:40.2; **3** D. Parish (UK) 5:49.1; **4** B. Ammann (Ger) 5:53.6.

110m Hurdles: 1 N. Alexander (UK) 14.91w; **2** B. Pfluger (Ger) 15.08; **3** H. Metzler (Ger) 15.13; **4** A. Sumner (UK – guest) 15.18; **5** K. Lobb (UK) 15.35.

400m Hurdles: 1 H. Weber (Ger) 52.36; **2** S. Bareuther (Ger) 53.10; **3** C. Richardson (UK – guest) 53.99; **4** T. Carrington (UK) 55.53; **5** G. Davies (UK) 56.64.

10,000m Walk: 1 M. Miley (UK) 47:41.9; **2** K. Schafer (Ger) 48:08.7; **3** F. Helms (Ger) 48:50.8; **4** D. Blagg (UK) 49:58.6.

High Jump: 1 D. Mogenburg (Ger) 2.11m (6' 11"); **2** T. Llewelyn (UK) 2.11m; **3** V. Clemmens (UK) 2.08m; **4** R. Moriabadi (Ger) 2.08m; **5** T. Foulger (UK – guest) 2.05m.

Pole Vault: 1 M. Fehling (Ger) 4.60m (15' 1"); **2** A. Jackson (UK) 4.50m; **3** T. Anstiss (UK) 4.30m; **4** B. Muller (Ger) 4.30m.

Long Jump: 1 J. Klocke (Ger) 7.45m (24' 5½"); **2** R. McKenzie (UK) 7.34m; **3** J. Rigsinger (Ger) 7.15m; **4** A. Slack (UK) 6.75m.

Triple Jump: 1 E. McCalla (UK) 15.55m (51′ 0¼″); **2** D. Stotz (Ger) 15.30m; **3** S. Metcalfe (UK) 15.28m(w); **4** P. Bouschen (Ger) 14.69m(w).

Shot: 1 K. Muller (Ger) 14.19m (46′ 6¾″); **2** A. Zaidman (UK) 14.18m; **3** A. Hannecker (Ger) 13.94m; **4** G. Savory (UK) 13.86m; **5** D. Smedley (UK – guest) 13.82m.

Discus: 1 A. Hannecker (Ger) 46.08m (151′ 2″); **2** F. Ressel (Ger) 45.28m; **3** R. Weir (UK) 44.30m; **4** C. Dinsdale (UK) 44.22m.

Hammer: 1 M. Girvan (UK) 60.04m (197′ 0″); **2** A. Meyer (Ger) 57.88m; **3** T. Schiller (Ger) 55.14m; **4** R. Earle (UK) 49.74m.

Javelin: 1 R. Schemminger (Ger) 70.86m (232′ 6″); **2** I. Marsh (UK) 70.58m; **3** W. Kalb (Ger) 67.04m; **4** T. Newenham (UK) 63.86m.

4 × 100m Relay: 1 Germany 40.67; **2** UK (P. Brown, J. Stark, P. Cooke, I. Loftman) 41.17.

4 × 400m Relay: 1 UK (N. Kitchen, M. Fowell, R. Dickens, N. Jackson) 3:11.1; **2** Germany 3:13.3.

Match Result: UK 115, Germany 108.

WOMEN

100m: 1 L. Stewart (UK) 12.0; **2** E. Vollmer (Ger) 12.03; **3** P. Baker (UK) 12.09; **4** M. Wagner (Ger) 12.23.

200m: 1 J. Parry (UK) 24.27; **2** E. Vollmer (Ger) 24.34; **3** M. Wagner (Ger) 24.38; **4** R. Richards (UK) 25.20.

400m: 1 C. Stickel (Ger) 55.91; **2** A. Dunn (UK – guest) 55.97; **3** S. Magerl (Ger) 56.12; **4** J. Mgbezeh (UK) 56.67; **5** S. Morgan (UK) 56.71.

800m: 1 D. Kiernan (UK) 2:06.7; **2** S. Ludlam (UK) 2:07.9; **3** B. Pastoors (Ger) 2:09.1; **4** R. Gerdes (Ger) 2:10.7.

1500m: 1 S. Arthurton (UK) 4:20.3; **2** G. Schulz (Ger) 4:22.9; **3** S. Bungener (Ger) 4:26.3; **4** K. Timson (UK) 4:32.1.

100m Hurdles: 1 M. Feller (Ger) 14.23w; **2** S. Morley (UK – guest) 14.25; **3** H. Ross (UK) 14.27; **4** U. Brennecke (Ger) 14.52; **5** A. Stacey (UK) 14.98.

High Jump: 1 S. Serk (Ger) 1.85m (6′ 0¾″); **2** D. Elliott (UK) 1.82m; **3** B. Simmonds (UK) 1.79m; **4** A. Dimke (Ger) 1.76m; **5** L. Miller (UK – guest) 1.70m.

Long Jump: 1 A. Seehaus (Ger) 6.12m (20′ 1″); **2** S. French (UK) 5.94m; **3** B. Dorobiala (Ger) 5.73m; **4** K. Hagger (UK) 5.52m.

Shot: 1 B. Wright (UK) 13.13m (43′ 1″); **2** U. Sturzebecher (Ger) 12.83m; **3** D. Galler (Ger) 12.77m; **4** C. Pryce (UK) 12.45m. Guest: H. Clarke (UK) 13.40m.

Discus: 1 K. Seedorf (Ger) 44.86m (147′ 2″); **2** F. Condon (UK) 44.62m; **3** D. Galler (Ger) 43.28m; **4** J. Picton (UK) 42.14m.

Javelin: 1 M. Jervis (UK) 53.32m (174′ 11″); **2** H. Adametz (Ger) 51.74m; **3** U. Sturzebecher (Ger) 49.04m; **4** S. Fry (UK) 39.50m.

4 × 100m Relay: UK (L. Stewart, J. Parry, D. Bunn, P. Baker) 45.54; Germany did not finish.

4 × 400m Relay: 1 UK (J. Mgbezeh, D. Kiernan, L. Callow, C. Pendleton) 3:46.0; **2** Germany 3:55.1.

Match Result: UK 69; Germany 64.

Ours is a Winning Team.

International athletes need team spirit. So do footballers and cricketers. And so, in a different way, do Master Butchers. Call in at any of our 1500 branches, and you can see our team spirit in action, giving you friendly service and a consistently high standard of quality and value. There isn't just one Master Butcher, there are <u>hundreds</u>...selling Great British Meat right round the country.

29 August – 3 September

EUROPEAN CHAMPIONSHIPS

With Marita Koch (GDR), Tatyana Zelentsova (Sov), Sara Simeoni (Ita) and Vilma Bardauskiene (Sov) achieving world records and Ruth Fuchs (GDR) accounting for a European mark, it was the women who stole the show at the European Championships staged in Prague. The overall standard in their events was higher even than at the last Olympics. Despite abysmal weather conditions for most of the week, the winning performances in Prague were better than the corresponding marks in Montreal in eight of the 13 events common to both.

The record-breaking spree was started by Vilma Bardauskiene on 29 August. A 25-year-old Lithuanian who had already created a sensation just 11 days earlier when she became the first woman ever to leap beyond the seven-metre barrier with a jump of 7.07 metres (23' 2½"), she dispelled any lingering doubts as to her ability by reaching 7.09 metres (23' 3¼") in the qualifying round! It was a quite extraordinary performance, for there was not a breath of wind as she jumped, whereas her earlier record was assisted by a breeze of 1.8 metres per second. It was as well that she produced that great leap when she did, even if it was caught only by the most alert spectators, for in the final on the following day the weather was decidedly unpleasant and she had to be content with a winning mark of 'only' 6.88 metres (22' 7").

Two of the world records came about on 31 August, truly an auspicious date in the history of women's athletics. It was the day that one great East German athlete, Marita Koch, stepped out from the shadow of Irena Szewinska, and another (Rosi Ackermann) was supplanted – at least for the time being – as the world's number one in her speciality by Sara Simeoni.

Italy's Sara Simeoni equals her own world high jump record of 2.01 metres (6' 7") in Prague.   Tony Duffy

Koch wasn't quite ready to take on the legendary Szewinska in 1977, the Pole defeating her in the World Cup 400 metres (49.52 to 49.76), but further improvement on her part coupled to a regression through injury of Szewinska drastically altered the situation in 1978. Koch broke Szewinska's world records for 200 and 400 metres during the earlier part of the season and the only real doubt as to the outcome in Prague was whether the 21-year-old East German medical student could cope with the mental pressure of starting favourite. 'The world records I have beaten this season have given me confidence', she said before the race, 'but I remain on guard because I know perfectly well the resources of Irena Szewinska. Even though she is 11 years older than I am, I know she is capable of beating me, as she did last year.' But, in the race itself, Koch gave her rival no chance. Off to a rocket start, she whistled through the first 200 metres in 22.9 and reached 300 metres, the proverbial 'street' ahead, in an unprecedented 34.9. At the finish she was almost a dozen metres clear in the momentous, barrier-breaking time of 48.94. While the men's 400 metres record has remained Lee Evans' property at 43.86 ever since the Mexico City Olympics of 1968, the women's record has advanced three seconds during the past decade. Szewinska, just edged out of second position by Christina Brehmer (GDR), collected her ninth European Championships medal – a figure she increased to 10 with another bronze in the 4 × 400 metres relay. That race was notable for Koch's split on the anchor leg . . . 48.21!

In contrast to the 400 metres world record, which was produced in virtually a competitive vacuum, the world record equalling height of 2.01 metres (6' 7") scaled by Sara Simeoni was the climax to one of the greatest duels the event has ever known. It's tough to jump 1.99 metres (6' 6¼") and lose – but that was the unique distinction suffered by Rosi Ackermann in Prague. On a chilly, wet evening, five girls were still left in at 1.91 metres (6' 3¾"), and it took a leap of 1.95 metres (6' 4¾") to assure Brigitte Holzapfel (Ger) of a medal. Holzapfel took her leave with the bar at 1.97 metres (6' 5½"), a height which Ackermann straddled at the first attempt and Simeoni flopped over on the second. The situation swung in Simeoni's favour at the next height, though, when the Italian succeeded first time at 1.99 metres whereas Ackermann needed two tries. As the bar was raised to 2.01 metres, equal to Simeoni's recently-established world record, the atmosphere was electric. Both girls tipped the bar off on the first attempt, but second time around Simeoni made it! Ackermann, an equally resolute competitor, wasn't conceding the title yet and with her final leap she too cleared . . . or so it seemed, until well after she had completed the jump the bar fell down. It could well have been the vibration against the foot of the uprights caused by Ackermann when landing, rather than bodily contact, which shook off the bar. So, a famous victory for Simeoni, and a marvellous fight to the finish by the Olympic champion Ackermann, in a competition marked also by the friendly and sporting manner in which it was contested.

The record breaker on the next day (1 September) was Ruth Fuchs who, at the age of 31, unleashed the longest throw of her entire career, adding 4cm to her own European record with 69.16 metres (226' 11"). The big toss came in the fourth round, Fuchs having earlier gained a huge lead with 67.56 metres (221' 8") in the second round. Tessa Sanderson, the Commonwealth champion, found her opening throw of 62.40 metres (204' 9") stood up for the silver medal and thereby achieved the distinction of becoming the first British girl ever to win a European championship medal in any of the throwing events.

The last of the major records occurred on 2 September in the women's 400 metres hurdles, making its first appearance in the European Championships programme. Just a year earlier, Karin Rossley (GDR) set a world record of 55.63 in the European Cup Final, but such is the rapid progress being made in this event that the same time sufficed only for sixth place in Prague! Another important landmark was reached as 55 seconds was broken for the first time; Tatyana Zelentsova – holder of the previous record of 55.31 – clocked 54.89, with Silvia Hollmann (Ger) also inside the old figures. Zelentsova (30), who took up the event in 1976 after a long and diverse career during which she set such personal bests as 13.6 for 100 metres hurdles and 6.32 metres (20' 9") for the long jump, is clearly not the last word in 400 metres hurdling and the future of the event rests with girls like Brigitte Kohn (née Rohde) of East Germany, a 50.26 performer on the flat who, though virtually a novice, finished fourth in 55.46.

Even though, in addition to Koch, Fuchs and the 4 × 400 metres team, East German women athletes scored victories in the 100 metres (Marlies Gohr), 100 metres hurdles (Johanna Klier), shot (Ilona Slupianek) and discus (Evelin Jaal), the GDR were less dominant than usual. The USSR countered with gold medals from Bardauskiene, Zelentsova, Lyudmila Kondratyeva (200 metres), the 4 × 100 metres squad and – in a remarkable display of middle distance power – from Tatyana Providokhina (800 metres), Giana Romanova (1500 metres) and Svetlana Ulmasova (3000 metres).

The Soviet Union's gold medal haul in the women's events was originally eight, but world record holder Nadyezhda Tkachenko was stripped of the pentathlon title after a doping test revealed she had been using anabolic steroids. She was not the only offender to be caught; also disqualified (and suspended from international competition for a minimum of 18 months from the date of the test) were Yekaterina Gordienko (Sov), fifth in the pentathlon; Elena Stoyanova (Bul), fifth in the shot; and two men – Yevgeniy Mironov (Sov), second in the shot; and Vasiliy Yershov (Sov), fifth in the javelin.

Britain's top women athletes, so successful in Edmonton, found the level of European competition a totally different proposition. Despite setting a worthy Commonwealth record of 8:48.7, Paula Fudge finished eighth in the 3000 metres, while in the 100 metres hurdles none of the girls who scored a clean sweep of the Commonwealth medals even reached the final in Prague (which, incidentally, was re-run after Polish world record holder Grazyna Rabsztyn crashed out of her lane and impeded another competitor in the original race). All credit, though, to Tessa Sanderson and to the sprint relay team of Bev Goddard, Kathy Smallwood, Sharon Colyear and Sonia Lannaman (they set a Commonwealth record of 42.72) for their silver medals in such company.

On the men's side it was a Briton, Steve Ovett, who was arguably the outstanding athlete of the championships. He followed up a silver medal in the 800 metres, on 31 August, with a resoundingly comfortable victory three days later in the 1500 metres – Britain's only gold medal in Prague. Of the two runs

Right: *Pietro Mennea of Italy won both the 100 and 200 metres – and contributed a 44.2 400 metres relay leg for good measure!* Tony Duffy

the 800 metres was probably the more outstanding in the context of Ovett's career. If Ovett can be faulted as an athlete it is through his reluctance to run faster than strictly necessary, to push himself to the limit. But in the European 800 metres final he did just that by following team-mate Sebastian Coe through one of the fastest first laps in the history of the event. Coe, who headed the 1978 world rankings with his UK record time of 1:44.3, had planned a fast first lap . . . but not the incredible time of 49.3 with which he was credited! 'I didn't want anything slower than 50.5, 50.0 would have been okay, but 49.3? No way.' Ovett, who rarely covers the first 400 metres much faster than 52 seconds, knew he couldn't afford to let Coe get too far ahead and thus went through in under 50 seconds too, as did East Germany's Olaf Beyer who must have been under orders to stick with the British pair – the clear favourites – no matter what. Coe continued to hammer out a world record pace, passing 600 metres in 76.2, but still he couldn't shake off his pursuers and shortly after entering the finishing straight he was overtaken by Ovett. Steve had run the perfect race, it seemed, and was destined for victory – but no one had reckoned on Beyer still being in contention at this late stage of the game. The East German, whose previous best was 1:45.8, was inspired to put it mildly – chugging past a bemused Ovett to win in 1:43.8, only 0.4 outside Juantorena's world record. Ovett relieved Coe of the British record with 1:44.1, Coe placing third in 1:44.8. After such a full-blooded race the 1500 metres proved just a little of an anti-climax, the other 11 finalists (including Beyer) seemingly handing Ovett the race on a plate. Ovett was able to launch his famous kick at

A dramatic finish to the 800 metres as unheralded Olaf Beyer (GDR) wins from Steve Ovett and Sebastian Coe.   Mark Shearman

precisely his favourite spot with 200 metres to go, and that was that. A 53.2 last lap carried Ovett to victory in 3:35.6, as Ireland's Eamonn Coghlan narrowly got the better of Commonwealth champion Dave Moorcroft for second place for a British Isles clean sweep.

Britain gained one other medal: a silver by Daley Thompson in the decathlon. But for a disastrous showing in one of his normally strong events, the pole vault, Thompson might have won his second gold medal of the summer, but by any standards his was an admirable performance and his final score of 8289 points constituted a Commonwealth record. His individual marks included a legal personal best long jump of 7.93 metres (26' 0¼") and best-evers of 14.69 metres (48' 2½") in the shot, 43.52 metres (142' 9") in the discus and 59.80 metres (196' 2") in the javelin. No fewer than 288 points up on Aleksandr Grebenyuk (Sov) at the end of the first day with 4459 points, Thompson eventually lost by 51. Unfortunately, European record holder Guido Kratschmer (Ger) injured himself in the first few steps of the 100 metres and took no further part in the competition. Other hopes of medals for the British men's team fell by the wayside as Geoff Capes was disqualified prior to the shot final for failing to wear a competitor's number on his chest, David Jenkins fell in a heat of the 4 × 400 metres relay, and a number of other Edmonton heroes such as Brendan Foster, Keith Connor, Roy Mitchell and Allan Wells were at less than 100 per cent effectiveness through injury or sheer fatigue. Nevertheless, in spite of only one gold medal, the championships were by no means a disaster for the British who, in terms of points awarded to athletes finishing in the first eight, ranked fourth in the men's events behind the USSR, GDR and Germany.

Steve Ovett, we suggested earlier, was arguably the outstanding athlete in the men's events, but certainly there are other strong contenders for that honour. Among them: Pietro Mennea, a convincing winner of both sprints who in his tenth race of the championships contributed a 44.2 leg in the 4 × 400 metres relay; another Italian, Venanzio Ortis, who sprinted to victory in the 5000 metres after finishing a close second to Martti Vainio (Fin) in a fast and magnificent 10,000 metres race which saw Brendan Foster and Dave Black run superb times and yet go unrewarded; Harald Schmid (Ger), head and shoulders clear of his opposition in the 400 metres hurdles and who would probably have won the flat title too had the timetable permitted doubling; and Vladimir Yashchenko (Sov), who successfully draped himself over a high jump bar set at 2.30 metres (7' 6½") and gamely tried for a world record 2.35 metres (7' 8½") despite cold and fatigue. The 1982 Championships are to be staged in Athens.

MEN'S EVENTS

100 METRES

Heats *(1st 4 to semis)* **Heat 1:** (nil wind) **1** A. Wells (UK) 10.40; **2** V. Borzov (Sov) 10.50; **3** J. Arame (Fra) 10.59; **4** L. Micha (Bel) 10.63; **5** F. Fahndrich (Swi) 10.64; **6** L. Latocha (Cze) 10.73; **7** I. Karanyotov (Bul) 10.78. **Heat 2:** (nil) **1** P. Mennea (Ita) 10.19 *(Championship record)*; **2** L. Dunecki

(Pol) 10.31; **3** V. Ignatenko (Sov) 10.38; **4** D. Zaric (Yug) 10.59; **5** R. Desruelles (Bel) 10.60; **6** S. Nilsson (Swe) 10.62; **7** O. Wild (Cze) 10.73. **Heat 3:** (nil) **1** E. Ray (GDR) 10.30; **2** M. Woronin (Pol) 10.50; **3** S. Curini (Ita) 10.58; **4** K. Ronn (Swe) 10.58; **5** P. Thessard (Fra) 10.79; **6** G. Massing (Aut) 10.86; **7** V. Panov (Bul) 10.90. **Heat 4:** (nil) **1** P. Petrov (Bul) 10.44; **2** N. Kolesnikov (Sov) 10.49; **3** L. Kefalas (Gre) 10.53; **4** G. Grazioli (Ita) 10.55; **5** A. Thieme (GDR) 10.55; **6** Z. Mazur (Cze) 10.73; **7** V. Vilhjalmsson (Ice) 10.76.

Semi-finals (*1st 4 to final*) **Heat 1:** (nil) **1** Mennea 10.26; **2** Ignatenko 10.45; **3** Petrov 10.46; **4** Borzov 10.53; **5** Woronin 10.54; **6** Ronn 10.63; **7** Curini 10.72; **8** Micha 10.74. **Heat 2:** (−0.8m) **1** Ray 10.30; **2** Dunecki 10.38; **3** Wells 10.38; **4** Kolesnikov 10.43; **5** Grazioli 10.58; **6** Kefalas 10.60; **7** Arame 10.64; **8** Zaric 10.69.

Final: (nil) **1** Pietro Mennea (Ita) 10.27; **2** Eugen Ray (GDR) 10.36; **3** Vladimir Ignatenko (Sov) 10.37; **4** Petar Petrov (Bul) 10.41; **5** Leszek Dunecki (Pol) 10.34; **6** Allan Wells (UK) 10.45; **7** Nikolay Kolesnikov (Sov) 10.46; **8** Valeriy Borzov (Sov) 10.55.

200 METRES

Heats (*1st 4 to semis*) **Heat 1:** (+0.5m) **1** P. Mennea (Ita) 20.70; **2** L. Dunecki (Pol) 21.01; **3** D. Zaric (Yug) 21.13; **4** D. Jenkins (UK) 21.16; **5** R. Bombardella (Lux) 21.17; **6** L. Micha (Bel) 21.36. **Heat 2:** (−1.5m) **1** A. Aksinin (Sov) 20.97; **2** J. Arame (Fra) 21.32; **3** A. Rajamaki (Fin) 21.34; **4** K. Thiele (GDR) 21.36; **5** L. Bohman (Cze) 21.39; **6** M. Bayle (Lux) 21.48; **7** V. Vilhjalmsson (Ice) 21.80. **Heat 3:** (−0.2m) **1** Pascal Barre (Fra) 20.78; **2** V. Ignatenko (Sov) 20.98; **3** L. Sarria (Spa) 21.18; **4** M. Pelach (Cze) 21.48; **5** P. Pavlov (Bul) 21.50; R. Roelandt (Bel) did not finish. **Heat 4:** (+0.2m) **1** Z. Licznerski (Pol) 20.82; **2** V. Ivanov (Bul) 20.96; **3** O. Prenzler (GDR) 20.97; **4** P. Muster (Swi) 21.04; **5** T. Hoyte (UK) 21.24; **6** Patrick Barre (Fra) 21.27; **7** M. Kralik (Cze) 21.47.

Semi-finals (*1st 4 to final*) **Heat 1:** (−0.2m) **1** Mennea 20.40; **2** Muster 20.63; **3** Dunecki 20.64; **4** Prenzler 20.69; **5** Ignatenko 20.74; **6** Arame 21.08; **7** Rajamaki 21.19; **8** Pelach 21.59. **Heat 2:** (nil) **1** Pascal Barre 20.96; **2** Ivanov 20.96; **3** Aksinin 21.08; **4** Licznerski 21.10; **5** Sarria 21.24; **6** Zaric 21.28; **7** Jenkins 21.59; Thiele did not finish.

Final: (−0.2m) **1** Pietro Mennea (Ita) 20.16 (*Championship record*); **2** Olaf Prenzler (GDR) 20.61; **3** Peter Muster (Swi) 20.64; **4** Lech Dunecki (Pol) 20.68; **5** Pascal Barre (Fra) 20.70; **6** Zenon Licznerski (Pol) 20.74; **7** Aleksandr Aksinin (Sov) 20.87; **8** Vladimir Ivanov (Bul) 20.92.

400 METRES

Heats (*1st 3 and 4 fastest losers to semis*) **Heat 1:** **1** K. Kolar (Cze) 46.33; **2** J. Pietrzyk (Pol) 46.75; **3** V. Burakov (Sov) 47.18; **4** Z. Knapic (Yug) 47.51; **5** C. Gombault (Fra) 47.91; **6** M. Bayle (Lux) 48.71; **7** A. Brydenbach (Bel) 53.05. **Heat 2:** **1** F-P. Hofmeister (Ger) 46.28; **2** R. Ashton (UK) 46.63; **3** M. Tulis (Cze) 46.77; **4** M. Volmar (Fra) 46.94; **5** E. De Leeuw (Bel) 47.27; **6** K. Gijsbers (Hol) 47.65. **Heat 3:** **1** L. Krieg (Ger) 46.57; **2** F. Demarthon (Fra) 46.73; **3** G. Cohen (UK) 47.05; **4** J. Hansen (Den) 47.28; **5** R. Vandenberghe (Bel) 47.55; **6** O. Karttunen (Fin) 48.02. **Heat 4:** **1** B. Herrmann (Ger) 46.50; **2** T. Whitehead (UK) 46.51; **3** R. Podlas (Pol) 46.81; **4** S. Malinverni (Ita) 47.03; **5** M. Kukkoaho (Fin) 47.33; **6** F. Schaffer (GDR) 47.59.

Semi-finals (*1st 4 to final*) **Heat 1:** **1** Pietrzyk 46.27; **2** Kolar 46.28; **3** Krieg 46.33; **4** Whitehead 46.69; **5** Cohen 46.91; **6** De Leeuw 47.17; **7** Malinverni 47.18; **8** Volmar 47.50. **Heat 2:** **1** Herrmann 46.09; **2** Hofmeister 46.18; **3** Demarthon 46.26; **4** Ashton 46.32; **5** Tulis 46.37; **6** Podlas 46.59; **7** Burakov 46.91; **8** Hansen 47.35.

Final: **1** Franz-Peter Hofmeister (Ger) 45.73; **2** Karel Kolar (Cze) 45.77; **3** Francis Demarthon (Fra) 45.97; **4** Lothar Krieg (Ger) 46.22; **5** Terry Whitehead (UK) 46.23; **6** Richard Ashton (UK) 46.34; **7** Bernd Herrmann (Ger) 46.69; J. Pietrzyk (Pol) scratched.

800 METRES

Heats (*1st 3 and 4 fastest losers to semis*) **Heat 1: 1** S. Ovett (UK) 1:47.8; **2** H-P. Ferner (Ger) 1:48.1; **3** M. Taskinen (Fin) 1:48.3; **4** D. Wagenknecht (GDR) 1:48.4; **5** V. Malozemlin (Sov) 1:48.6; **6** C. Grippo (Ita) 1:48.6. **Heat 2: 1** O. Beyer (GDR) 1:47.7; **2** A. Kormeling (Hol) 1:48.1; **3** G. Hasler (Lie) 1:48.5; **4** J. Gloden (Lux) 1:49.0; **5** P. Hoffmann (UK) 1:49.3; W. Wulbeck (Ger) non-starter. **Heat 3: 1** A. Busse (GDR) 1:49.1; **2** J. Marajo (Fra) 1:49.4; **3** A. Reshetnyak (Sov) 1:49.5; **4** M. Savic (Yug) 1:50.0; **5** M. Timko (Cze) 1:50.5; **6** P. Pallikaris (Gre) 1:51.6. **Heat 4: 1** S. Coe (UK) 1:46.8; **2** R. Milhau (Fra) 1:47.1; **3** U. Becker (Ger) 1:47.1; **4** D. Zivotic (Yug) 1:47.2; **5** V. Podolyakov (Sov) 1:47.2; **6** S. Timurlenk (Tur) 1:47.2; **7** J. Didriksson (Ice) 1:50.4.

Semi-finals (*1st 4 to final*) **Heat 1: 1** Coe 1:47.4; **2** Busse 1:47.6; **3** Marajo 1:47.7; **4** Podolyakov 1:47.8; **5** Taskinen 1:47.9; **6** Becker 1:48.2; **7** Wagenknecht 1:48.5; **8** Kormeling 1:49.2. **Heat 2: 1** Ovett 1:46.5; **2** Beyer 1:46.7; **3** Zivotic 1:46.9; **4** Reshetnyak 1:47.2; **5** Ferner 1:47.4; **6** Timurlenk 1:47.9; **7** Milhau 1:48.9; **8** Hasler 1:49.3.

Final: 1 Olaf Beyer (GDR) 1:43.8 (*Championship record*); **2** Steve Ovett (UK) 1:44.1 (*UK national record*); **3** Sebastian Coe (UK) 1:44.8; **4** Anatoliy Reshetnyak (Sov) 1:45.8; **5** Vladimir Podolyakov (Sov) 1:46.2; **6** Andreas Busse (GDR) 1:47.1; **7** Dragan Zivotic (Yug) 1:47.4; **8** Jose Marajo (Fra) 1:53.4.

1500 METRES

Heats (*1st 3 and 3 fastest losers to final*) **Heat 1: 1** E. Coghlan (Eir) 3:40.0; **2** D. Moorcroft (UK) 3:40.0; **3** O. Beyer (GDR) 3:40.1; **4** T. Wessinghage (Ger) 3:40.1; **5** J. Marajo (Fra) 3:40.6; **6** V. Abramov (Sov) 3:40.9; **7** B. Vifian (Swi) 3:42.5; **8** R. Nemeth (Aut) 3:44.1; **9** A. Paunonen (Fin) 3:45.0; **10** J. Abascal (Spa) 3:47.6; **11** M. Pierrard (Lux) 3:52.8; K. Lok (Hol) did not finish. **Heat 2: 1** S. Ovett (UK) 3:42.9; **2** J. Straub (GDR) 3:43.1; **3** R. Gysin (Swi) 3:43.2; **4** M. Nevens (Bel) 3:43.2; **5** R. Flynn (Eir) 3:44.1; **6** D. Millonig (Aut) 3:44.8; **7** V. Seronov (Sov) 3:45.1; **8** G. Hasler (Lie) 3:46.7; **9** P. Dien (Fra) 3:47.4; **10** B. Nilsson (Swe) 3:47.9; **11** J. Didriksson (Ice) 3:48.1. **Heat 3: 1** A. Loikkanen (Fin) 3:39.7; **2** J. Robson (UK) 3:40.0; **3** F. Gonzalez (Fra) 3:40.4; **4** J. Plachy (Cze) 3:40.6; **5** P. Deleze (Swi) 3:40.7; **6** G. Ruth (GDR) 3:41.4; **7** L. Ericsson (Swe) 3:42.5; **8** V. Toropov (Sov) 3:45.1; **9** S. Timurlenk (Tur) 3:45.8; **10** F. Kourtis (Gre) 3:45.9; K. Fleschen (Ger) did not finish.

Final: 1 Steve Ovett (UK) 3:35.6 (*Championship record*); **2** Eamonn Coghlan (Eir) 3:36.6; **3** Dave Moorcroft (UK) 3:36.7; **4** Thomas Wessinghage (Ger) 3:37.2; **5** Antti Loikkanen (Fin) 3:37.5; **6** Jose Marajo (Fra) 3:38.2; **7** Jurgen Straub (GDR) 3:38.9; **8** John Robson (UK) 3:39.6; **9** O. Beyer (GDR) 3:39.7; **10** F. Gonzalez (Fra) 3:40.1; **11** R. Gysin (Swi) 3:41.0; **12** J. Plachy (Cze) 3:42.2.

5000 METRES

Heats (*1st 4 and 3 fastest losers to final*) **Heat 1: 1** F. Zimmermann (Ger) 13:32.4; **2** M. Vainio (Fin) 13:33.6; **3** L. Schots (Bel) 13:34.1; **4** J. Peter (GDR) 13:34.3; **5** B. Kuznyetsov (Sov) 13:34.8; **6** B. Foster (UK) 13:38.3; **7** K. Kvalheim (Nor) 13:43.6; **8** R. Bouster (Fra) 14:09.3; **9** J. Charvetto (Gib) 14:18.4; K. Gaba (Cze) did not finish. **Heat 2: 1** K. Fleschen (Ger) 13:34.5; **2** F. Mamede (Por) 13:34.8; **3** N. Rose (UK) 13:35.7; **4** E. Sellik (Sov) 13:36.3; **5** G. Tebroke (Hol) 13:37.0; **6** F. Cerrada (Spa) 13:40.4; **7** P. Levisse (Fra) 13:44.1; **8** S. Tabor (Cze) 13:45.0; **9** D. Millonig (Aut) 13:50.4; **10** N. Ayaz (Tur) 13:55.7; J. Gloden (Lux) did not finish. **Heat 3: 1** A. Fedotkin (Sov) 13:24.1; **2** M. Ryffel (Swi) 13:24.7; **3** V. Ortis (Ita) 13:26.7; **4** J. Treacy (Eir) 13:28.9; **5** C. Herle (Ger) 13:30.6; **6** I. Floroiu (Rom) 13:32.5; **7** M. McLeod (UK) 13:42.9; **8** J. Kowol (Pol) 13:49.1; **9** A. Simoes (Por) 13:52.1; **10** W. Polleunis (Bel) 14:24.5; K. Lok (Hol) did not finish.

Final: 1 Venanzio Ortis (Ita) 13:28.5; **2 eq** Markus Ryffel (Swi) and Aleksandr Fedotkin (Sov) 13:28.6; **4** John Treacy (Eir) 13:28.8; **5** Ilie Floroiu (Rom) 13:29.3; **6** Martti Vainio (Fin) 13:29.7; **7** Nick Rose (UK) 13:32.8; **8** Enn Sellik (Sov) 13:35.8; **9** B. Kuznyetsov (Sov) 13:36.5; **10** F. Zimmermann (Ger) 13:39.1; **11** L. Schots (Bel) 13:47.4; **12** J. Peter (GDR) 13:48.6; **13** K. Fleschen (Ger) 13:50.3; **14** C. Herle (Ger) 13:55.4; **15** F. Mamede (Por) 13:58.2.

10,000 METRES

1 Martti Vainio (Fin) 27:31.0 (*Championship record*); **2** Venanzio Ortis (Ita) 27:31.5; **3** Aleksandr Antipov (Sov) 27:31.5; **4** Brendan Foster (UK) 27:32.7; **5** David Black (UK) 27:36.3; **6** Gerard Tebroke (Hol) 27:36.6; **7** Ilie Floroiu (Rom) 27:40.1; **8** Enn Sellik (Sov) 27:40.6; **9** K. Kvalheim (Nor) 27:41.3; **10** J. Kowol (Pol) 27:53.6; **11** J. Treacy (Eir) 28:17.0; **12** L. Schots (Bel) 28:19.6; **13** C. Andreica (Rom) 28:29.4; **14** M. McLeod (UK) 28:38.0; **15** O. Dahl (Nor) 28:43.2; **16** F. Grillaert (Bel) 28:43.5; **17** R. Kopijasz (Pol) 28:44.2; **18** K. Lismont (Bel) 28:49.2; **19** W. Cierpinski (GDR) 28:58.9; **20** K. Gaba (Cze) 29:56.3; P. Copu (Rom), P. Levisse (Fra), D. Uhlemann (Ger) and J. Hermens (Hol) did not finish.

MARATHON

1 Leonid Moseyev (Sov) 2:11:57.5 (*Championship record*); **2** Nikolay Penzin (Sov) 2:11:59.0; **3** Karel Lismont (Bel) 2:12:07.7; **4** Waldemar Cierpinski (GDR) 2:12:20.0; **5** Catalin Andreica (Rom) 2:12:29.4; **6** Massimo Magnani (Ita) 2:12:45.3; **7** Hans-Joachim Truppel (GDR) 2:12:54.3; **8** Jurgen Eberding (GDR) 2:13:39.7; **9** D. Cannon (UK) 2:14:31.7; **10** M. Koussis (Gre) 2:14:41.3; **11** S. Dzumanazarov (Sov) 2:14:43.3; **12** G. Bengtsson (Swe) 2:15:01.9; **13** A. Simmons (UK) 2:15:31.5; **14** F. Szekeres (Hun) 2:15:45.0; **15** R. Marczak (Pol) 2:15:47.8; **16** M. Arena (Ita) 2:16:09.2; **17** V. Zwiefelhofer (Cze) 2:16:37.6; **18** H. Schoofs (Bel) 2:16:49.5; **19** J. Jansky (Cze) 2:16:53.0; **20** R. Leibold (Ger) 2:16:56.3; **21** J-M. Ancion (Bel) 2:17:24.5; **22** K. Van den Weyden (Hol) 2:17:32.8; **23** B. Bobes (Fra) 2:17:48.0; **24** A. Ristimaki (Fin) 2:18:17.8; **25** C. Taylor (UK) 2:18:44.5; **26** A. Romero (Spa) 2:19:26.4; **27** P. Hooper (Eir) 2:20:28.5; **28** M. Paiva (Por) 2:20:49.4; **29** R. Hooper (Eir) 2:21:00.2; **30** C. Vriend (Hol) 2:21:25.2; **31** H. Olsen (Nor) 2:21:35.1; **32** S. Salman (Tur) 2:22:47.4; **33** J. Lauenborg (Den) 2:23:14.8; **34** R. Veld (Hol) 2:23:38.3; **35** A. Fancsali (Hun) 2:23:39.7; **36** V. Balli (Tur) 2:25:56.2; **37** K. Lazaridis (Gre) 2:32:16.9; J. Fjaerstad (Nor), M. Krsek (Cze), H. Spik (Fin), F. Kolbeck (Fra), J. Schirmer (Ger), P. Accaputo (Ita), J. Hein (Den), L. Enqvist (Swe), B. Brondum (Den), P. Kopijarz (Pol), A. Simoes (Por) and O. Dahl (Nor) did not finish.

3000 METRES STEEPLECHASE

Heats (*1st 3 and 3 fastest losers to final*) **Heat 1: 1** G. Gerbi (Ita) 8:29.1; **2** I. Toukonen (Fin) 8:29.5; **3** K. Wesolowski (Pol) 8:30.0; **4** F. Bartos (Cze) 8:31.9; **5** M. Schoeneberg (Ger) 8:34.2; **6** D. Glans (Swe) 8:34.5; **7** D. Betini (Rom) 8:34.9; **8** V. Filonov (Sov) 8:39.0; **9** P. Thys (Bel) 8:34.8; **10** W. Konrad (Aut) 8:43.9. **Heat 2: 1** P. Copu (Rom) 8:33.3; **2** M. Karst (Ger) 8:33.7; **3** D. Coates (UK) 8:34.7; **4** S. Olizarenko (Sov) 8:36.7; **5** R. Volpi (Ita) 8:39.1; **6** D. Moravcik (Cze) 8:43.2; **7** K. Maranda (Pol) 8:48.4; **8** B. Lafranchi (Swi) 8:51.7; **9** C. Strom (Swe) 8:53.8; **10** H. Koeleman (Hol) 8:59.6; **11** D. Ramon (Spa) 9:07.8. **Heat 3: 1** V. Bichea (Rom) 8:25.4; **2** B. Malinowski (Pol) 8:25.6; **3** P. Ilg (Ger) 8:30.4; **4** V. Lisovskiy (Sov) 8:31.4; **5** G. Wetzig (GDR) 8:36.1; **6** J-L. Lemire (Fra) 8:38.0; **7** A. Campos (Spa) 8:38.2; **8** M. Slovak (Cze) 8:41.4; **9** T. Kantanen (Fin) 8:46.0; **10** J. Davies (UK) 8:57.4; **11** J. Hagelbrandt (Swe) 9:21.1.

Final: 1 Bronislaw Malinowski (Pol) 8:15.1; **2** Patriz Ilg (Ger) 8:16.9; **3** Ismo Toukonen (Fin) 8:18.3; **4** Michael Karst (Ger) 8:19.0; **5** Paul Copu (Rom) 8:20.4; **6** Vasile Bichea (Rom) 8:24.9; **7** Frantisek Bartos (Cze) 8:38.0; **8** Manfred Schoeneberg (Ger) 8:40.1; **9** G. Gerbi (Ita) 8:42.8; **10** D. Coates (UK) 8:44.0; **11** K. Wesolowski (Pol) 8:46.4; **12** V. Lisovskiy (Sov) 9:00.5.

110 METRES HURDLES

Heats (*1st 5 and fastest loser to semis*) **Heat 1:** (+0.7m) **1** V. Myasnikov (Sov) 13.76; **2** A. Bryggare (Fin) 13.83; **3** R. Giegiel (Pol) 13.97; **4** J. Moracho (Spa) 14.15; **5** J. Ivan (Cze) 14.22; **6** P. Vukicevic (Yug) 14.25. **Heat 2:** (−0.3m) **1** T. Munkelt (GDR) 13.62; **2** G. Buttari (Ita) 13.81; **3** E. Pereverzev (Sov) 13.86; **4** D. Gebhard (Ger) 14.05; **5** M. Holtom (UK) 14.12; **6** J. Lloveras (Spa) 14.17; **7** J. Cerovsky (Cze) 14.36. **Heat 3:** (nil) **1** J. Pusty (Pol) 13.81; **2** V. Kulebyakin (Sov) 13.95; **3** B. Price (UK) 14.00; **4** B. Pisic (Yug) 14.02; **5** P. Euripidou (Gre) 14.11; **6** P. Cech (Cze) 14.13.

Semi-finals (*1st 4 to final*) **Heat 1:** (−0.45m) **1** Munkelt 13.50; **2** Buttari 13.74; **3** Pereverzev 13.78; **4** Giegiel 13.97; **5** Pisic 14.01; **6** Moracho 14.16; **7** Cech 14.20; **8** Holtom 14.27. **Heat 2:** (nil) **1** Pusty 13.75; **2** Bryggare 13.78; **3** Kulebyakin 13.94; **4** Gebhard 13.95; **5** Price 14.01; **6** Euripidou 14.16; **7** Ivan 14.29; Myasnikov did not finish.

Final: (−0.55m) **1** Thomas Munkelt (GDR) 13.54; **2** Jan Pusty (Pol) 13.55; **3** Arto Bryggare (Fin) 13.56; **4** Giuseppe Buttari (Ita) 13.78; **5** Eduard Pereverzev (Sov) 13.83; **6** Vyacheslav Kulebyakin (Sov) 13.90; **7** Romuald Giegiel (Pol) 13.91; **8** Dieter Gebhard (Ger) 13.94.

Left: *Martti Vainio maintained Finland's illustrious reputation in major 10,000 metres championships.*

Tony Duffy

Harald Schmid of Germany was head and shoulders above his opposition in the 400 metres hurdles.

Mark Shearman

400 METRES HURDLES

Heats (*1st 3 and 4 fastest losers to semis*) **Heat 1: 1** D. Stukalov (Sov) 50.35; **2** H. Schulting (Hol) 50.39; **3** P. Haas (Swi) 50.45; **4** J. Carvalho (Por) 51.02; **5** C. Gullstrand (Swe) 51.03; **6** G. Oakes (UK) 52.08; **7** F. Rummele (Aut) 52.13. **Heat 2: 1** T. Lowe (Ger) 50.34; **2** J. Bratanov (Bul) 50.45; **3** H. Toboc (Rom) 50.75; **4** O. Bulatkin (Sov) 50.90; **5** C. Anicet (Fra) 51.68; **6** K. Kodejs (Cze) 51.98; **7** W. Hartley (UK) 52.15. **Heat 3: 1** H. Schmid (Ger) 49.78; **2** R. Kopitar (Yug) 50.43; **3** G. Parris (Gre) 50.45; **4** J-C. Nallet (Fra) 50.49; **5** A. Pascoe (UK) 50.95; **6** L. Karsky (Cze) 51.38; **7** L. Nielsen (Den) 51.48. **Heat 4: 1** V. Arkhipenko (Sov) 50.15; **2** J. Alonso (Spa) 50.27; **3** S. Tziortzis (Gre) 50.49; **4** A. Salander (Ger) 50.55; **5** F. Meier (Swi) 50.66; **6** L. Welander (Swe) 50.72.

Semi-finals (*1st 4 to final*) **Heat 1: 1** Schmid 50.07; **2** Alonso 50.32; **3** Toboc 50.42; **4** Stukalov 50.51; **5** Tziortzis 50.83; **6** Haas 51.29; **7** Salander 51.63; **8** Bratanov 52.39. **Heat 2: 1** Arkhipenko 49.92; **2** Nallet 49.98; **3** Meier 50.12; **4** Schulting 50.22; **5** Parris 50.66; **6** Kopitar 50.98; **7** Welander 50.99; **8** Lowe 51.96.

Final: 1 Harald Schmid (Ger) 48.51 (*Championship record*); **2** Dmitriy Stukalov (Sov) 49.72; **3** Vasiliy Arkhipenko (Sov) 49.77; **4** Franz Meier (Swi) 49.84; **5** Harry Schulting (Hol) 50.07; **6** Jean-Claude Nallet (Fra) 50.19; **7** Jose Alonso (Spa) 50.19; **8** Horia Toboc (Rom) 50.46.

HIGH JUMP

1 Vladimir Yashchenko (Sov) 2.30m (7′ 6½″) (*Championship record*) (2.10–1, 2.15–1, 2.21–1, 2.24–3, 2.26–1, 2.28–1, 2.30–2, 2.35–fail); **2** Aleksandr Grigoryev (Sov) 2.28m (2.10–1, 2.15–1, 2.18–1, 2.21–1, 2.24–1, 2.26–1, 2.28–3, 2.30/2.32–fail); **3** Rolf Beilschmidt (GDR) 2.28m (2.10–1, 2.15–1, 2.18–2, 2.21–2, 2.24–3, 2.26–2, 2.28–3, 2.30–1 failure, retired); **4** Henry Lauterbach (GDR)

Left: *A lap of honour for Poland's Bronislaw Malinowski, who retained the steeplechase title.*   Mike Street

2.26m; **5** Carlo Thranhardt (Ger) 2.21m; **6** Jacek Wszola (Pol) 2.21m; **7** Andre Schneider (Ger) 2.21m; **8** Josef Hrabal (Cze) 2.18m; **9** G. Moreau (Bel) 2.18m; **10** R. Almen (Swe) 2.18m; **11** W. Nachtegael (Bel) 2.18m; **12** J. Vondra (Cze) 2.15m; **13** B. Bruni (Ita) 2.15m (2.18m in qualifying); **14 eq** G. Belkov (Sov) 2.15m (2.18m qual) and T. Totland (Nor) 2.15m; **16** E. Annys-Campstein (Bel) 2.10m; **17** R. Moravec (Cze) 2.10m; **18** M. Naylor (UK) 2.10m (2.15m qual). *Non-qualifiers:* P. Poaniewa (Fra), E. Ozdamar (Tur), J. Aletti (Fra), V. Papadimitriou (Gre) and R. Bergamo (Ita) 2.10m; B. Burgess (UK) 2.00m. R. Wielart (Hol) and M. DiGiorgio (Ita) failed 2.10m.

POLE VAULT

1 Vladimir Trofimenko (Sov) 5.55m (18' 2½") (*Championship record*) (5.20–1, 5.40–1, 5.50–3, 5.55–1, 5.60–fail); **2** Antti Kalliomaki (Fin) 5.50m (5.20–1, 5.40–3, 5.50–3, 5.60–fail); **3** Rauli Pudas (Fin) 5.45m (5.10–1, 5.20–1, 5.30–2, 5.40–1, 5.45–1, 5.50–fail); **4** Wladyslaw Kozakiewicz (Pol) 5.45m (5.30–1, 5.45–2, 5.55–fail); **5** Yevgeniy Tananika (Sov) 5.40m; **6** Philippe Houvion (Fra) 5.40m; **7 eq** Francois Tracanelli (Fra) and Brian Hooper (UK) 5.30m; **9** P. Abada (Fra) 5.30m; **10** T. Haapakoski (Fin) 5.30m; **11** G. Lohre (Ger) 5.20m (5.25m qual); M. Klimczyk (Pol) failed 5.20m (5.25m qual). R. Oriol (Spa) scratched (5.15m qual). *Non-qualifiers:* D. D'Alisera (Ita), R. Zrun (Cze), E. Sakellariadis (Gre), P. Jensen (Den) and R. Lechner (Aut) 4.90m; K. Stock (UK) and T. Slusarski (Pol) failed 5.15m; P. Desruelles (Bel), A. Hadinger (Cze) and J. Lesak (Cze) failed 4.90m.

LONG JUMP

1 Jacques Rousseau (Fra) 8.18m (26' 10") (*Championship record*) (8.15, 8.11, 8.18, pass, —, pass); **2** Nenad Stekic (Yug) 8.12m (7.97, 7.96, 8.09, —, 8.12, 7.93); **3** Vladimir Tsepelev (Sov) 8.01m (7.80, —, 7.63, 8.01, 7.67, 8.01); **4** Grzegorz Cybulski (Pol) 7.96m; **5** Joachim Verschl (Ger) 7.89m; **6** Valeriy Podluzhny (Sov) 7.89m; **7** Roy Mitchell (UK) 7.88m; **8** Ake Fransson (Swe) 7.65mw; **9** J. Krivka (Cze) 7.60m (7.71m qual); **10** S. Jaskulka (Pol) 7.60m (7.64m qual); **11** J. Leitner (Cze) 7.59m (7.80m qual); **12** J. Priscak (Cze) 7.48m (7.81m qual). *Non-qualifiers:* M. Chludzinski (Pol) 7.61m; P. Deroche (Fra) 7.58m; R. Desruelles (Bel) 7.54m; L. Szalma (Hun) 7.35m; O. Stepanyan (Sov) 7.52m; W. Klepsch (Ger) 7.52m; D. Delifotis (Gre) 7.44m; M. Maffi (Ita) 7.42m; A. Solanas (Spa) 7.36m.

TRIPLE JUMP

1 Milos Srejovic (Yug) 16.94m (55' 7") (16.24, 16.48, 16.39, 16.60, 16.73, 16.94); **2** Viktor Sanyeyev (Sov) 16.93m (16.84, 16.71, 16.92, 16.50, 16.93, 16.79); **3** Anatoliy Piskulin (Sov) 16.87m (14.47, —, 16.87, —, —, 16.65); **4** Bernard Lamitie (Fra) 16.87m (16.36, 16.59, 16.55, 16.87, —, 16.27); **5** Gennadiy Valyukevich (Sov) 16.64m; **6** Keith Connor (UK) 16.64m; **7** Milan Spasojevic (Yug) 16.62m; **8** Aston Moore (UK) 16.55m; **9** J. Hegedis (Yug) 16.24m; **10** E. Biskupski (Pol) 16.23m; **11** L. Gora (GDR) 16.20m; **12** G. Katona (Hun) 16.18m; **13** K. Hradil (Cze) 16.05m; **14** C. Corbu (Rom) 16.02m; **15** B. Bakosi (Hun) 15.74m.

SHOT

1 Udo Beyer (GDR) 21.08m (69' 2") (—, 21.08, —, 20.21, —, 20.18); **2** Aleksandr Baryshnikov (Sov) 20.68m (19.73, 20.68, 20.16, 20.03, 19.84, 20.48); **3** Wolfgang Schmidt (GDR) 20.30m (19.86, 19.63, 19.92, 19.62, 20.30, 19.49); **4** Reijo Stahlberg (Fin) 20.17m (20.25m qual); **5** Anatoliy Yarosh (Sov) 20.03m; **6** Jaromir Vlk (Cze) 19.53m (19.76m qual); **7** Hreinn Halldorsson (Ice) 19.34m (19.62m qual); **8** Jaroslav Brabec (Cze) 19.27m (19.48m qual); **9** V. Stoev (Bul) 19.23m (19.26m qual); **10** M. Schmidt (GDR) 19.21m (19.38m qual). G. Capes (UK) disq (20.08m qual). Y. Mironov (Sov) disqualified after placing 2nd with 20.87m. *Non-qualifiers:* R. Reichenbach (Ger) 19.09m; J–P. Egger (Swi) 18.67m; M. Janousek (Cze) 18.61m; A. Arrhenius (Swe) 18.48m; V. Milic (Yug) 18.35m; M. Montelatici (Ita) 18.14m; A. Groppelli (Ita) 18.04m.

DISCUS

1 Wolfgang Schmidt (GDR) 66.82m (219' 3") (64.04, 61.68, 64.52, 62.08, 65.94, 66.82) 67.20m (220' 6") in qualifying (*Championship record*); **2** Markku Tuokko (Fin) 64.90m (58.84, —, 62.48, 63.16, 64.90, —); **3** Imrich Bugar (Cze) 64.66m (62.88, 64.24, 64.66, —, —, 62.98); **4** Velko Velev (Bul) 64.56m; **5** Knut Hjeltnes (Nor) 63.76m; **6** Alwin Wagner (Ger) 62.70m; **7** Dmitriy Kovchun (Sov) 61.84m; **8** Wolfgang Warnemunde (GDR) 61.28m (63.80m qual); **9** F. Tegla (Hun) 60.22m; **10** I. Duginets (Sov) 59.80m (61.52m qual); **11** O. Jakobsson (Ice) 59.44m (60.86m qual); **12** S. Simeon (Ita) 59.16m (59.28m qual). *Non-qualifiers:* W. Hartmann (Ger) 59.14m; D. Juzyszyn (Pol) 58.86m; L. Danek (Cze) 58.60m; A. De Vincentiis (Ita) 58.20m; F. Piette (Fra) 57.54m; J. Silhavy (Cze) 57.28m; J. Tuomola (Fin) 56.38m; J. Farago (Hun) 56.14m.

HAMMER

1 Yuriy Sedykh (Sov) 77.28m (253' 6") (*Championship record*) (77.28, 75.92, 75.54, 76.96, —, 77.28); **2** Roland Steuk (GDR) 77.24m (75.30, 73.24, 75.10, 76.50, 77.16, 77.24); **3** Karl-Hans Riehm (Ger) 77.02m (76.50, 76.40, 76.90, 75.66, —, 77.02); **4** Detlef Gerstenberg (GDR) 76.70m; **5** Manfred Huning (Ger) 76.46m; **6** Boris Zaichuk (Sov) 75.62m; **7** Edoardo Podberscek (Ita) 73.02m; **8** Gianpaolo Urlando (Ita) 72.62m (73.04m qual); **9** J. Sachse (GDR) 71.56m; **10** G. Tamas (Hun) 70.72m; **11** H. Huhtala (Fin) 69.92m; **12** K. Ploghaus (Ger) 69.30m (70.86m qual). *Non-qualifiers:* O. Bianchini (Ita) 69.78m; E. Dyulgerov (Bul) 68.96m; A. Malyukov (Sov) 68.78m; R. Olsen (Nor) 68.56m; J. Accambray (Fra) 67.78m; P. Suriray (Fra) 66.78m; R. Skoumal (Cze) 65.44m; C. Black (UK) 63.54m.

JAVELIN

1 Michael Wessing (Ger) 89.12m (292' 5") (82.94, —, 72.08, 89.12, 85.74, 83.66); **2** Nikolay Grebnyev (Sov) 87.82m (82.80, 80.02, 83.26, 87.82, 78.34, 79.42); **3** Wolfgang Hanisch (GDR) 87.66m (83.58, —, 87.66, 82.84, 80.90, 86.92); **4** Detlef Michel (GDR) 85.46m; **5** Helmut Schreiber (Ger) 83.58m (85.16m qual); **6** Miklos Nemeth (Hun) 83.58m; **7** Piotr Bielczyk (Pol) 81.80m; **8** Terje Thorslund (Nor) 80.42m; **9** F. Paragi (Hun) 70.08m (86.04m qual); **10** S. Boros (Hun) 78.78m (83.22m qual); **11** P. Sinersaari (Fin) 77.10m (82.46m qual); **12** S. Hovinen (Fin) 73.08m (80.94m qual); **13** A. Puranen (Fin) 72.74m (84.42m qual). V. Yershov (Sov) disqualified after placing 5th with 85.06m. *Non-qualifiers:* K. Elderbrink (Swe) 78.60m; B. Grimnes (Nor) 78.58m; J. Hanak (Cze) 78.56m; R. Pihl (Swe) 78.42m; P. Smiding (Swe) 76.36m; P. Yates (UK) 75.82m; T. Babiak (Cze) 75.20m; T. Pirvu (Rom) 75.14m; V. Marchetti (Ita) 71.80m.

DECATHLON

1 Aleksandr Grebenyuk (Sov) 8340 pts (*Championship record*) (11.02, 6.94, 15.90, 2.01, 48.88, 14.43, 48.42, 4.50, 67.74, 4:24.4); **2** Daley Thompson (UK) 8289 pts (*Commonwealth & UK national record*) (10.69, 7.93, 14.69, 2.04, 47.77, 15.28, 43.52, 4.20, 59.80, 4:22.8); **3** Siegfried Stark (GDR) 8208 pts (11.17, 7.30, 15.04, 1.95, 49.58, 15.12, 44.52, 4.90, 69.00, 4:24.0); **4** Josef Zeilbauer (Aut) 7988 pts (11.12, 7.32, 14.81, 1.92, 49.55, 14.61, 45.22, 4.70, 60.36, 4:41.6); **5** Yuriy Kutsenko (Sov) 7978 pts (11.02, 7.24, 14.82, 1.98, 49.23, 15.34, 43.76, 4.40, 57.74, 4:22.9); **6** Roger Kanerva (Fin) 7945 pts (11.18, 7.22, 13.32, 2.01, 49.62, 15.28, 41.82, 4.80, 61.60, 4:25:4); **7** Johannes Lahti (Fin) 7913 pts (10.86, 7.08, 14.06, 2.07, 49.64, 15.00, 41.36, 4.00, 67.98, 4:36.7); **8** Rainer Pottel (GDR) 7900 pts (11.05, 7.40, 15.05, 1.92, 48.04, 14.89, 32.80, 4.90, 56.24, 4:29.5); **9** H. Schmidt (Ger) 7839 pts; **10** Y. LeRoy (Fra) 7780 pts; **11** T. Dubois (Fra) 7705 pts; **12** V. Buryakov (Sov) 7670 pts; **13** R. Hingsen (Ger) 7640 pts; **14** S. Schauerhammer (GDR) 7635 pts; **15** A. Andonov (Bul) 7590 pts; **16** J. Fric (Cze) 7516 pts; **17** A. Tschenett (Swi) 7362 pts; **18** C. Lythell (Swe) 7362 pts; **19** E. Sveinsson (Ice) 7317 pts; **20** L. Pernica (Cze) 7290 pts; **21** A. Kiss (Hun) 7202 pts; **22** K. Riggberger (Swe) 7063 pts. Retired: G. Werthner (Aut); G. Kratschmer (Ger).

Following page: *Yuriy Sedykh (Sov) added the European hammer title to his Olympic laurels.* Tony Duffy

Daley Thompson finishes ahead of Aleksandr Grebenyuk in the first event, the 100 metres, but it was the Soviet athlete who triumphed overall in the decathlon.   Mike Street

---

4 × 100 METRES RELAY

Heats (*1st 3 and 2 fastest losers to final*) **Heat 1: 1** Poland 39.20; **2** Italy 39.51; **3** Switzerland 39.87; **4** UK 40.08; **5** Czechoslovakia 40.43. **Heat 2: 1** GDR 39.05; **2** USSR 39.21; **3** France 39.45; **4** Belgium 40.16; Bulgaria did not finish.

Final: 1 Poland (Zenon Nowosz, Zenon Licznerski, Leszek Dunecki, Marian Woronin) 38.58; **2** GDR (Manfred Kokot, Eugen Ray, Olaf Prenzler, Alexander Thieme) 38.78; **3** USSR (Sergey Vladimirtsev, Nikolay Kolesnikov, Aleksandr Aksinin, Vladimir Ignatenko) 38.82; **4** France (Patrick Barre, Pascal Barre, L. Sainte-Rose, H. Panzo) 38.90; **5** Italy (G. Grazioli, L. Caravani, S. Curini, P. Mennea) 39.11; **6** UK (T. Hoyte, A. Wells, C. Sharp, S. Green) 39.49; **7** Switzerland (F. Fahndrich, U. Gisler, P. Muster, H. Ziegler) 39.56; **8** Belgium (R. Desruelles, H. Van Den Daele, D. Roelandt, L. Micha) 39.73.

---

4 × 400 METRES RELAY

Heats (*1st 3 and 2 fastest losers to final*) **Heat 1: 1** Poland 3:06.5; **2** Switzerland 3:06.6; **3** Czechoslovakia 3:07.1; **4** Holland 3:07.6; **5** Belgium 3:08.0; **6** UK (T. Whitehead, G. Cohen, D. Jenkins, R. Ashton) 3:39.9. **Heat 2: 1** Germany 3:06.0; **2** Italy 3:06.5; **3** France 3.06.6; **4** GDR 3:06.8; **5** Yugoslavia 3:07.1; Finland did not finish.

Final: 1 Germany (Martin Weppler, Franz-Peter Hofmeister, Bernd Herrmann, Harald Schmid) 3:02.0; **2** Poland (Jerzy Wlodarczyk, Zbigniew Jaremski, Cezary Lapinski, Ryszard Podlas) 3:03.6; **3** Czechoslovakia (Josef Lomicky, Frantisek Brecka, Miroslav Tulis, Karel Kolar) 3:04.0; **4** Switzerland (R. Strittmatter, P. Haas, K. Vogt, R. Gisler) 3:04.3; **5** GDR (F. Richter, G. Arnold, A. Busse, J. Pfenning) 3:04.4; **6** France (M. Volmar, G. Boutier, H. Llatser, F. Demarthon) 3:05.6; **7** Italy (R. Tozzi, D. Zanini, S. Malinverni, P. Mennea) 3:06.7; **8** Yugoslavia (R. Kopitar, D. Zivotic, M. Savic, Z. Knapic) 3:06.9.

20 KILOMETRES WALK

1 Ronald Wieser (GDR) 1:23:11.5 (*Championship record*); **2** Pyotr Pochenchuk (Sov) 1:23:43.0; **3** Anatoliy Solomin (Sov) 1:24:11.5; **4** Boris Yakovlyev (Sov) 1:24:27.9; **5** Jose Marin (Spa) 1:24:38.1; **6** Maurizio Damilano (Ita) 1:24:57.5; **7** Hartwig Gauder (GDR) 1:25:15.7; **8** Roberto Buccione (Ita) 1:25:40.9; **9** B. Bulakowski (Pol) 1:25:56.8; **10** B. Gustafsson (Swe) 1:26:13.5; **11** G. Lelievre (Fra) 1:26:42.3; **12** A. Pezzatini (Ita) 1:26:44.2; **13** J. Bencik (Cze) 1:27:47.4; **14** S. Blazek (Cze) 1:27:49.3; **15** L. Faber (Lux) 1:29:19.7; **16** S. Rola (Pol) 1:29:22.0; **17** I. Stankovics (Hun) 1:29:33.3; **18** S. Petrik (Cze) 1:30:08.4; **19** O. Hemmingson (Swe) 1:30:44.2; **20** A. Schwarz (Ger) 1:31:17.6; **21** R. Mills (UK) 1:31:52.5; **22** J. Kamenov (Bul) 1:31:08.9; **23** E. Andersen (Nor) 1:32:13.0; **24** A. Brandt (Swe) 1:32:41.7; **25** B. Adams (UK) 1:33:08.2; **26** A. Seddon (UK) 1:34:17.8; **27** K–A. Stromoy (Nor) 1:36:01.9; D. Guebey (Fra) did not finish; K–H. Stadtmuller (GDR) disqualified for 'lifting', after finishing first.

50 KILOMETRES WALK

1 Jorge Llopart (Spa) 3:53:29.9 (*Championship record*); **2** Venyamin Soldatenko (Sov) 3:55:12.1; **3** Jan Ornoch (Pol) 3:55:15.9; **4** Otto Bartsch (Sov) 3:57:23.7; **5** Viktor Dorovskykh (Sov) 3:57:26.7; **6** Vittorio Visini (Ita) 3:57:42.8; **7** Alesandro Bellucci (Ita) 3:58:25.9; **8** Olaf Pilarski (GDR) 4:00:03.8; **9** M. Kroel (GDR) 4:00:11.9; **10** M. Kerber (GDR) 4:01:03.7; **11** B. Simonsen (Swe) 4:03:34.6; **12** G. Weidner (Ger) 4:04:01.9; **13** H. Binder (Ger) 4:04:12.4; **14** J. Dzurnak (Cze) 4:04:40.0; **15** P. Gregucci (Ita) 4:05:46.8; **16** L. Vitez (Cze) 4:07:55.8; **17** L. Lundgren (Swe) 4:09:54.7; **18** D. Guebey (Fra) 4:09:57.0; **19** L. Sator (Hun) 4:10:22.4; **20** S-O. Elofsson (Swe) 4:12:39.1; **21** S. Immonen (Fin) 4:16:52.5; **22** C. Patusinschi (Rom) 4:23:26.9; **23** I. Richards (UK) 4:27:09.3; A. Jorba (Spa), B. Kmieczik (Pol), J. Vanous.(Cze), D. Cotton (UK), L. Moen (Nor), G. Lelievre (Fra), L. Faber (Lux) and J. Marin (Spa) did not finish. H. Schubert (Ger) and J. Kamenov (Bul) were disqualified for 'lifting'.

WOMEN'S EVENTS

100 METRES

Heats (*1st 5 and fastest loser to semis*) **Heat 1:** (nil) **1** M. Gohr (GDR) 11.34; **2** L. Kondratyeva (Sov) 11.41; **3** L. Miano (Ita) 11.52; **4** B. Goddard (UK) 11.53; **5** H. Laihorinne (Fin) 11.58; **6** A. Alize (Fra) 11.61; **7** E. Possekel (Ger) 11.82; **8** T. Verhoef (Hol) 12.04. **Heat 2:** (nil) **1** L. Maslakova (Sov) 11.23; **2** S. Lannaman (UK) 11.54; **3** I. Valkova (Bul) 11.61; **4** M. Walsh (Eir) 11.70; **5** V. Rosset (Fra) 11.77; **6** P. Sharp (Ger) 11.84; **7** B. Haest (Aut) 11.89; **8** L. Jimramovska (Cze) 11.91. **Heat 3:** (nil) **1** L. Haglund (Swe) 11.24; **2** C. Rega (Fra) 11.38; **3** L. Storoshkova (Sov) 11.38; **4** M. Hamann (GDR) 11.52; **5** S. Popova (Bul) 11.65; **6** G. Molik (Pol) 11.90; **7** E. Henzen (Hol) 12.04.

Semi-finals (*1st 4 to final*) **Heat 1:** (−1.17m) **1** Gohr 11.27; **2** Haglund 11.43; **3** Kondratyeva 11.51; **4** Lannaman 11.54; **5** Miano 11.71; **6** Rosset 11.80; **7** Popova 11.87; **8** Alize 11.87. **Heat 2:** (−1.58m) **1** Maslakova 11.42; **2** Hamann 11.47; **3** Storoshkova 11.52; **4** Rega 11.59; **5** Goddard 11.72; **6** Valkova 11.80; **7** Laihorinne 11.82; **8** Walsh 11.95.

Final: (nil wind) **1** Marlies Gohr (GDR) 11.13 (*equals Championship record*); **2** Linda Haglund (Swe) 11.29; **3** Lyudmila Maslakova (Sov) 11.31; **4** Monika Hamann (GDR) 11.33; **5** Lyudmila Storoshkova (Sov) 11.33; **6** Lyudmila Kondratyeva (Sov) 11.38; **7** Chantal Rega (Fra) 11.49; **8** Sonia Lannaman (UK) 11.67.

200 METRES

Heats (*1st 4 to semis*) **Heat 1:** (−0.30m) **1** T. Prorochenko (Sov) 23.23; **2** K. Smallwood (UK) 23.54; **3** M. Gohr (GDR) 23.73; **4** C. Steger (Ger) 23.96; **5** M. Walsh (Eir) 23.99; **6** R. Soborova (Cze) 24.55. **Heat 2:** (nil) **1** L. Kondratyeva (Sov) 23.11; **2** M. Hamann (GDR) 23.35; **3** I. Orosz (Hun)

23.46; **4** S. Lannaman (UK) 23.48; **5** D. Schenten (Ger) 23.70; **6** H. Laihorinne (Fin) 23.84; **7** T. Verhoef (Hol) 24.12. **Heat 3:** (nil) **1** C. Rega (Fra) 23.26; **2** L. Haglund (Swe) 23.38; **3** Z. Bielczyk (Pol) 23.40; **4** B. Goddard (UK) 23.54; **5** M. Masullo (Ita) 23.62; **6** S. Schinzel (Aut) 24.30. **Heat 4:** (+0.50m) **1** L. Maslakova (Sov) 22.92; **2** L. Ivanova (Bul) 22.93; **3** C. Bodendorf (GDR) 23.11; **4** R. Naigre (Fra) 23.56; **5** J. Stalmach (Pol) 23.96; **6** E. Henzen (Hol) 23.97.

Semi-finals (*1st 4 to final*) **Heat 1:** (–0.20m) **1** Gohr 22.86; **2** Maslakova 22.86; **3** Hamann 22.99; **4** Ivanova 23.12; **5** Lannaman 23.36; **6** Bielczyk 23.41; **7** Naigre 23.89; **8** Steger 24.18. **Heat 2:** (–0.30m) **1** Kondratyeva 22.83; **2** Bodendorf 22.92; **3** Rega 22.98; **4** Haglund 23.11; **5** Smallwood 23.12; **6** Prorochenko 23.30; **7** Goddard 23.37; **8** Orosz 23.56.

Final: (–0.20m) **1** Lyudmila Kondratyeva (Sov) 22.52; **2** Marlies Gohr (GDR) 22.53; **3** Carla Bodendorf (GDR) 22.64; **4** Monika Hamann (GDR) 22.76; **5** Chantal Rega (Fra) 22.77; **6** Lyudmila Maslakova (Sov) 22.89; **7** Linda Haglund (Swe) 23.07; **8** Lilyana Ivanova (Bul) 23.23.

400 METRES

Heats (*1st 3 and 4 fastest losers to semis*) **Heat 1:** **1** M. Koch (GDR) 52.95; **2** I. Szewinska (Pol) 53.14; **3** I. Pal (Hun) 53.42; **4** P. Darbonville (Fra) 53.50; **5** R. Wallez (Bel) 53.99; **6** A. Aren (Swe) 54.37. **Heat 2:** **1** C. Marquardt (GDR) 52.12; **2** J. Hoyte (UK) 52.79; **3** G. Bussmann (Ger) 52.92; **4** J. Kratochvilova (Cze) 53.33; **5** M. Sidorova (Sov) 53.72; **6** Y. Hannus (Fin) 53.98; **7** I. Petrika (Hun) 54.01. **Heat 3:** **1** C. Brehmer (GDR) 51.71; **2** V. Elder (UK) 52.64; **3** P. Haggman (Fin) 52.68; **4** E. Decker (Ger) 52.97; **5** C. Delachanal (Fra) 53.81; **6** T. Van Amstel (Hol) 54.37. **Heat 4:** **1** M. Kulchunova (Sov) 51.55; **2** D. Fuhrmann (Ger) 53.45; **3** D. Hartley (UK) 53.61; **4** S. Schinzel (Aut) 53.80; **5** R. Halmosi (Hun) 53.93; **6** E. Rakova (Cze) 54.00.

Semi-finals (*1st 4 to final*) **Heat 1:** **1** Koch 51.76; **2** Kulchunova 51.88; **3** Hartley 52.14; **4** Haggman 52.24; **5** Decker 52.92; **6** Hoyte 52.92; **7** Kratochvilova 53.93; **8** Darbonville 54.47. **Heat 2:** **1** Brehmer 52.01; **2** Marquardt 52.29; **3** Szewinska 52.37; **4** Elder 52.65; **5** Bussmann 52.66; **6** Fuhrmann 53.23; **7** Pal 53.50; **8** Sidorova 54.08.

Final: **1** Marita Koch (GDR) 48.94 (*world record*); **2** Christina Brehmer (GDR) 50.38; **3** Irena Szewinska (Pol) 50.40; **4** Maria Kulchunova (Sov) 51.25; **5** Christiane Marquardt (GDR) 51.99; **6** Donna Hartley (UK) 52.31; **7** Pirjo Haggman (Fin) 52.46; **8** Verona Elder (UK) 52.53.

800 METRES

Heats (*1st 5 and fastest loser to semis*) **Heat 1:** **1** T. Providokhina (Sov) 2.00.0; **2** F. Lovin (Rom) 2:00.0; **3** U. Bruns (GDR) 2:00.4; **4** G. Dorio (Ita) 2:00.4; **5** A. Van Nuffel (Bel) 2:01.3; **6** J. Colebrook (UK) 2:03.0; **7** M. Ritter (Lie) 2:09.0. **Heat 2:** **1** H. Ullrich (GDR) 2:01.4; **2** Z. Rigel (Sov) 2:01.6; **3** T. Petrova (Bul) 2:01.8; **4** I. Lipcsei (Hun) 2:02.3; **5** E. Tarita (Rom) 2:02.9; **6** J. Prictoe (UK) 2:03.7; **7** E. van Hulst (Hol) 2:03.9; **8** J. Kubeckova (Cze) 2:04.0. **Heat 3:** **1** N. Mushta (Sov) 2:01.7; **2** A. Weiss (GDR) 2:01.8; **3** J. Cerchlanova (Cze) 2:02.0; **4** E. Barnes (UK) 2:02.1; **5** M. Suman (Rom) 2:02.2; **6** M. Verhoeven (Bel) 2:04.5; **7** F. Schmitt (Lux) 2:04.7.

Semi-finals (*1st 4 to final*) **Heat 1:** **1** Weiss 1:58.8; **2** Mushta 1:58.8; **3** Lovin 1:58.8; **4** Rigel 1:58.9; **5** Dorio 2:00.5; **6** Tarita 2:01.7; **7** Van Nuffel 2:06.2; **8** Lipcsei 2:06.8. **Heat 2:** **1** Providokhina 2:00.1; **2** Petrova 2:00.2; **3** Bruns 2:00.3; **4** Ullrich 2:00.6; **5** Suman 2:01.6; **6** Barnes 2:01.7; **7** Colebrook 2:02.9; **8** Cerchlanova 2:07.0.

Final: **1** Tatyana Providokhina (Sov) 1:55.8 (*Championship record*); **2** Nadyezhda Mushta (Sov) 1:55.8 (*Championship record*); **3** Zoya Rigel (Sov) 1:56.6; **4** Totka Petrova (Bul) 1:56.6; **5** Hildegard Ullrich (GDR) 1:57.5; **6** Anita Weiss (GDR) 1:57.7; **7** Ulrike Bruns (GDR) 1:58.6; **8** Fita Lovin (Rom) 1:58.8.

A Soviet clean-sweep in the women's 800 metres as Tatyana Providokhina (329) wins from Nadyezhda Mushta (324) and Zoya Rigel (331). Mike Street

1500 METRES

Heats (*1st 5 and 2 fastest losers to final*) **Heat 1: 1** U. Bruns (GDR) 4:11.5; **2** G. Dorio (Ita) 4:11.5; **3** V. Yatsinska (Bul) 4:11.7; **4** G. Romanova (Sov) 4:11.8; **5** C. Burki (Swi) 4:11.8; **6** B. Kraus (Ger) 4:11.9; **7** M. Stewart (UK) 4:17.5; **8** T. Kluft (Hol) 4:17.7; **9** I. Lipcsei (Hun) 4:20.2; **10** F. Schmitt (Lux) 4:31.3. **Heat 2: 1** N. Marasescu (Rom) 4:05.8; **2** M. Puica (Rom) 4:06.1; **3** V. Ilyinykh (Sov) 4:06.3; **4** G. Waitz (Nor) 4:06.3; **5** L. Kalnitskaya (Sov) 4:06.7; **6** T. Petrova (Bul) 4:07.2; **7** C. Benning (UK) 4:11.8; **8** M. Lazar (Hun) 4:14.4; **9** D. Zvonickova (Cze) 4:19.2; **10** V. Renties (Fra) 4:40.3.

Final: 1 Giana Romanova (Sov) 3:59.0 (*Championship record*); **2** Natalia Marasescu (Rom) 3:59.8; **3** Totka Petrova (Bul) 4:00.2; **4** Valentina Ilyinykh (Sov) 4:00.2; **5** Grete Waitz (Nor) 4:00.6; **6** Gabrielle Dorio (Ita) 4:01.3; **7** Ulrike Bruns (GDR) 4:02.2; **8** Cornelia Burki (Swi) 4:04.6; **9** V. Yatsinska (Bul) 4:04.7; **10** L. Kalnitskaya (Sov) 4:06.6; **11** M. Puica (Rom) 4:09.3; **12** C. Benning (UK) 4:11.5.

3000 METRES

1 Svetlana Ulmasova (Sov) 8:33.2 (*Championship record*); **2** Natalia Marasescu (Rom) 8:33.5; **3**

Another success for the USSR came in the 3000 metres where Svetlana Ulmasova prevailed over Natalia Marasescu (Rom) and Grete Waitz (Nor). Mark Shearman

Grete Waitz (Nor) 8:34.3; **4** Maricica Puica (Rom) 8:40.9; **5** Giana Romanova (Sov) 8:45.7; **6** Cornelia Burki (Swi) 8:46.1; **7** Raisa Belousova (Sov) 8:48.7; **8** Paula Fudge (UK) 8:48.7 (*Commonwealth and UK national record*); **9** A. Ford (UK) 8:53.1; **10** I. Christensen (Nor) 9:02.9; **11** M. Lazar (Hun) 9:05.1; **12** J. Debrouwer (Fra) 9:05.2; **13** G. Penny (UK) 9:08.9; **14** H. Ledvinova (Cze) 9:10.9; **15** M. Purcell (Eir) 9:11.9; **16** L. Olafsson (Den) 9:12.0; **17** B. Sudicka (Cze) 9:12.9; **18** B. Van Roy (Bel) 9:13.9; **19** D. Nagle (Eir) 9:21.9; **20** D. Gustin (Bel) 9:24.0; **21** C. Beurskens (Hol) 9:25.5; **22** T. Kluft (Hol) 9:31.0; **23** C. Valero (Spa) 9:34.0; **24** M. Margoldova (Cze) 9:36.1; **25** C. Olsen (Den) 9:40.6; B. Friedmann (Ger) did not finish.

100 METRES HURDLES

Heats (*1st 4 to semi-finals*) **Heat 1:** (−0.30m) **1** G. Rabsztyn (Pol) 12.94; **2** N. Morgulina (Sov) 13.04; **3** G. Berend (GDR) 13.26; **4** X. Siska (Hun) 13.48; **5** S. Strong (UK) 13.56; **6** L. Elloy (Fra) 14.07. **Heat 2:** (+1.80m) **1** J. Klier (GDR) 12.85; **2** L. Langer (Pol) 13.13; **3** S. Colyear (UK) 13.23; **4** S. Kempin (Ger) 13.40; **5** L. Lebeau (Fra) 13.60; **6** H. Fredriksen (Nor) 13.63. **Heat 3:** (−1.90m) **1** E. Rabsztyn (Pol) 13.20; **2** L. Boothe (UK) 13.46; **3** L. Guseva (Bul) 13.52; **4** M. Schonauerova (Cze) 13.61; **5** L. Spoof (Fin) 13.63. **Heat 4:** (+0.40m) **1** T. Anisimova (Sov) 12.85; **2** A. Fiedler (GDR) 13.43; **3** I. Ongar (Ita) 13.74; **4** E. Pantazi (Gre) 13.84; **5** D. Rasmussen (Den) 13.95; **6** H. Chocova (Cze) 14.04.

Tatyana Zelentsova (Sov), who captured the 400 metres hurdles in a world record of 54.89.   Tony Duffy

Semi-finals (*1st 4 to final*) **Heat 1:** (−0.20m) **1** G Rabsztyn 12.60 (*Championship record*); **2** Klier 12.90; **3** Morgulina 13.00; **4** Fiedler 13.07; **5** Colyear 13.25; **6** Siska 13.36; **7** Schonauerova 13.72; **8** Ongar 13.90. **Heat 2:** (+0.20m) **1** Berend 12.90; **2** Anisimova 12.92; **3** Langer 13.00; **4** E. Rabsztyn 13.14; **5** Boothe 13.44; **6** Pantazi 13.82; S. Kempin did not finish; Guseva scratched.

Final (re-run after Grazyna Rabsztyn was disqualified) (+0.60m) **1** Johanna Klier (GDR) 12.62; **2** Tatyana Anisimova (Sov) 12.67; **3** Gudrun Berend (GDR) 12.73; **4** Nina Morgulina (Sov) 12.86; **5** Lucyna Langer (Pol) 12.98; **6** Annerose Fiedler (GDR) 13.09; **7** Elzbieta Rabsztyn (Pol) 13.17.

400 METRES HURDLES

Heats (*1st 3 and 4 fastest losers to semis*) **Heat 1: 1** B. Kohn (GDR) 56.83; **2** K. Kacperczyk (Pol) 57.18; **3** E. Weinstein (Ger) 57.56; **4** M. Appleby (Eir) 57.66; **5** E. Mohacsi (Hun) 59.61; **6** R-M. Colorado (Spa) 59.76; **7** K. Staut (Bel) 68.51. **Heat 2: 1** S. Hollmann (Ger) 57.50; **2** K. Rossley (GDR) 58.07; **3** H. Fredriksen (Nor) 58.12; **4** I. Barkane (Sov) 58.29; **5** D. Badescu (Rom) 59.72; **6** W. Hillen (Hol) 59.97; **7** K. Josefikova (Cze) 60.61. **Heat 3: 1** E. Sutherland (UK) 57.61; **2** M. Makeyeva (Sov) 57.66; **3** L. Alaerts (Bel) 57.74; **4** G. Blaszak (Pol) 58.11; **5** A. Aren (Swe) 59.32; **6** M. Pujol (Spa) 60.21; **7** D. Wildova (Cze) 60.97. **Heat 4: 1** A. Weiss (GDR) 56.19; **2** T. Zelentsova (Sov) 56.44; **3** A. Michel (Bel) 58.19; **4** S. Filipova (Bel) 58.31; **5** D. Lairloup (Fra) 58.47; **6** L. Helbling (Swi) 58.57; **7** H. Slamova (Cze) 60.77.

Semi-finals (*1st 4 to final*) **Heat 1: 1** Hollmann 56.08; **2** Weiss 56.19; **3** Kacperczyk 56.20; **4** Rossley 56.27; **5** Appleby 57.36; **6** Makeyeva 57.49; **7** Alaerts 57.68; Filipova did not finish. **Heat 2: 1** Zelentsova 55.89; **2** Barkane 56.32; **3** Kohn 56.55; **4** Blaszak 56.67; **5** Weinstein 57.22; **6** Fredriksen 58.35; **7** Michel 58.67; **8** Sutherland 62.83.

Final: 1 Tatyana Zelentsova (Sov) 54.89 (*world record*); **2** Silvia Hollmann (Ger) 55.14; **3** Karin Rossley (GDR) 55.36; **4** Brigitte Kohn (GDR) 55.46; **5** Krystyna Kacperczyk (Pol) 55.55; **6** Anita Weiss (GDR) 55.63; **7** Ingrida Barkane (Sov) 55.97; **8** Genowefa Blaszak (Pol) 57.72.

HIGH JUMP

1 Sara Simeoni (Ita) 2.01m (6' 7") (*equals world record*) (1.80–1, 1.85–1, 1.91–1, 1.95–1, 1.97–2, 1.99–1, 2.01–2, 2.03–fail); **2** Rosi Ackermann (GDR) 1.99m (1.75–1, 1.80–1, 1.85–1, 1.88–1, 1.91–1, 1.93–1, 1.95–1, 1.97–1, 1.99–2, 2.01–fail); **3** Brigitte Holzapfel (Ger) 1.95m (1.80–1, 1.85–1, 1.88–2, 1.91–1, 1.93–1, 1.95–2, 1.97–fail); **4** Jutta Kirst (GDR) 1.93m; **5** Ulrike Meyfarth (Ger) 1.91m; **6** Andrea Matay (Hun) 1.85m; **7** Snezana Hrepevnik (Yug) 1.85m; **8** Urszula Kielan (Pol) 1.85m; **9** A. Harnack (Ger) 1.80m (1.85m qual); **10** A. Tveit (Nor) 1.80m (1.83m qual); **11** K. Nitzsche (GDR) 1.80m (1.85m qual); **12** L. Klimentyonok (Sov) 1.80m (1.85m qual); **13** M. Mracnova (Cze) 1.80m (1.83m qual); **14** M. Karbanova (Cze) 1.80m (1.85m qual). *Non-qualifiers:* A. Tannander (Swe) and G. Ejstrup (Den) 1.80m; M. Van Laar (Hol), M. Rehorovska (Cze), D. Bulkowska (Pol), G. Hitchen (UK) and C. Popa (Rom) 1.75m; A-M. Pira (Bel) and S. Dini (Ita) 1.70m.

LONG JUMP

1 Vilma Bardauskiene (Sov) 6.88m (22' 7") (6.57, 6.63, 6.69, 6.88, 6.57, 6.76); 7.09m (23' 3¼") in qualifying round (*world record*); **2** Angela Voigt (GDR) 6.79m (—, 6.48, 6.66, 6.55, 6.33, 6.79); **3** Jarmila Nygrynova (Cze) 6.69m (6.60, 6.69, —, 6.51, 6.39, 6.61); **4** Brigitte Wujak (GDR) 6.60m (6.65m qual); **5** Gina Panait (Rom) 6.52m (6.61m qual); **6** Sue Reeve (UK) 6.48m; **7** Karin Hanel (Ger) 6.48m; **8** Heidi Wycisk (GDR) 6.44m; **9** J. Curtet (Fra) 6.24m (6.54m qual); **10** D. Anton (Rom) 6.22m (6.31m qual); **11** L. Guseva (Bul) 6.20m (6.40m qual); **12** M. Lambrou (Gre) 6.12m (6.31m qual). *Non-qualifiers:* L. Alfeyeva (Sov) 6.29m, M. Papp (Hun) 6.28m, T. Marciniak (Pol) 6.26m, S. Hearnshaw (UK) 6.25m, S. Vlad (Rom) 6.19m, I. Keller (Swi) 6.15m, S. Barlag (Hol) 6.12m, A. Weigt (Ger) 6.08m, D. Rasmussén (Den) 5.85m; E. Suranova (Cze) 3 fouls.

SHOT

1 Ilona Slupianek (GDR) 21.41m (70' 3") (*Championship record*) (—, 19.98, 20,87, 20.23, 20.44, 21.41); **2** Helena Fibingerova (Cze) 20.86m (19.89, 20.86, —, –, –, 19.64); **3** Margitte Droese (GDR) 20.58m (18.06, 19.59, 20.28, 20.58, 20.48, 20.31); **4** Svetlana Krachevskaya (Sov) 20.13m; **5** Eva Wilms (Ger) 19.20m; **6** Ivanka Petrova (Bul) 18.85m; **7** Svetlana Melnikova (Sov) 18.63m; **8** Mihaela Loghin (Rom) 17.35m; **9** Z. Bartonova (Cze) 17.23m; **10** B. Philipp (Ger) 17.13m; N. Isayeva (Sov) 3 fouls. E. Stoyanova (Bul) disqualified after placing 5th with 19.43m.

DISCUS

1 Evelin Jahl (GDR) 66.98m (219' 9") (62.02, —, 65.74, 66.98, 65.26, 63.26); **2** Margitte Droese (GDR) 64.04m (63.76, 63.32, —, 64.04, 63.34, 63.96); **3** Natalia Gorbachova (Sov) 63.58m (63.58, —, 60.66, 62.90, 61.04, 60.38); **4** Sabine Engel (GDR) 63.46m; **5** Faina Veleva (Sov) 62.30m; **6** Svetla Boshkova (Bul) 61.94m; **7** Lyudmila Isayeva (Sov) 61.56m; **8** Jitka Prouzova (Cze) 59.90m; **9** A. Menis (Rom) 58.36m; **10** A. Herczeg (Hun) 57.94m; **11** R. Pfister (Swi) 53.78m; **12** I. Manecke (Ger) 52.92m; **13** M. Ritchie (UK) 52.64m; **14** M. Pilarova (Cze) 50.34m.

Following page: left: *Vilma Bardauskiene (Sov) took the long jump gold medal after setting a world record of 7.09 metres (23' 3¼") in the qualifying round.*   Mike Street

Following page: right: *The indestructible Ruth Fuchs (GDR) struck gold yet again – and with her longest-ever throw!*   Tony Duffy

JAVELIN

1 Ruth Fuchs (GDR) 69.16m (226′ 11″) (*European record*) (56.10, 67.56, 51.56, —, 69.16, 62.84); **2** Tessa Sanderson (UK) 62.40m (62.40, —, —, 58.76, 60.62, 57.96); **3** Ute Hommola (GDR) 63.32m (62.32, —, 55.74, 56.16, 55.16, 58.44); **4** Ute Richter (GDR) 62.04m; **5** Eva Raduly (Rom) 61.14m; **6** Eva Helmschmidt (Ger) 60.96m; **7** Ingrid Thyssen (Ger) 60.18m; **8** Bernadetta Blechacz (Pol) 60.14m; **9** N. Nikanorova (Sov) 57.50m (63.18m qual); **10** J. Putiniene (Sov) 57.28m (59.84m qual); **11** E. Burgarova (Cze) 57.22m (57.40m qual); **12** I. Vantseva (Bul) 53.10m (59.34m qual). *Non-qualifiers:* S. Sakorafa (Gre) 56.76m, C. Mikhailova (Bul) 54.72m, G. Amici (Ita) 52.66m, L. Berkhout (Hol) 52.14m.

PENTATHLON

1 Margit Papp (Hun) 4655 (13.70, 15.41, 1.81, 6.22, 2:16.2); **2** Burglinde Pollak (GDR) 4600 (13.48, 16.64, 1.65, 6.17, 2:15.0); **3** Kristine Nitzsche (GDR) 4599 (14.02, 12.77, 1.93, 6.13, 2:12.7); **4** Beatrix Philipp (Ger) 4554 (14.65, 17.95, 1.77, 6.03, 2:19.2); **5** Yekaterina Smirnova (Sov) 4534 (13.43, 14.10, 1.79, 6.13, 2:19.7); **6** Ramona Neubert (GDR) 4380 (14.14, 13.29, 1.75, 6.33, 2:21.3); **7** Ina Losch (Ger) 4319 (15.03, 12.24, 1.79, 6.23, 2:14.0); **8** Florence Picaut (Fra) 4307 (13.98, 13.16, 1.83, 5.80, 2:25.0); **9** M. Koblasova (Cze) 4210; **10** C. Sulek (Ger) 4202; **11** E. Stolk (Hol) 4190; **12** S. Barlag (Hol) 4184; **13** Y. Wray (UK) 4171; **14** A. Weiss (Swi) 4165; **15** G. Ionescu (Rom) 4145; **16** B. Lorenci (Yug) 4144; **17** S. Mapstone (UK) 3993; A. Tannander (Swe) and D. Cally (Pol) retired. N. Tkachenko (Sov) and Y. Gordienko (Sov) disqualified after placing 1st (4744) and 5th (4572).

Nadyezhda Tkachenko (Sov) seen leading in the final event of the pentathlon, the 800 metres. She was later deprived of the gold medal after doping tests proved she had been taking anabolic steroids.　　　Mark Shearman

The British team which collected silver medals in the 4 × 100 metres relay; left to right — Sonia Lannaman, Sharon Colyear, Bev Goddard and Kathy Smallwood. Tony Duffy

4 × 100 METRES RELAY

Heats (*1st 3 and 2 fastest losers to final*) **Heat 1: 1** GDR 43.05; **2** France 43.78; **3** Bulgaria 43.97; **4** Poland 44.20; **5** Italy 44.95. **Heat 2: 1** USSR 43.35; **2** UK 43.90; **3** Sweden 44.31; **4** Germany 44.58; **5** Czechoslovakia 45.03.

Final: 1 USSR (Vera Anisimova, Lyudmila Maslakova, Lyudmila Kondratyeva, Lyudmila Storoshkova) 42.54; **2** UK (Bev Goddard, Kathy Smallwood, Sharon Colyear, Sonia Lannaman) 42.72 (*Commonwealth and UK national record*); **3** GDR (Johanna Klier, Monika Hamann, Carla Bodendorf, Marlies Gohr) 43.07; **4** Bulgaria (S. Popova, L. Ivanova, Z. Sipoklyeva, I. Valkova) 43.47; **5** Poland (G. Rabsztyn, Z. Bielczyk, J. Stalmach, I. Szewinska) 43.83; **6** Germany (E. Possekel, D. Schenten, C. Steger, P. Sharp) 44.34; **7** Sweden (L. Haglund, H. Pihl, J. Rangeby, L. Moller) 44.37; France (V. Rosset, A. Alize, C. Rega, R. Naigre) did not finish.

4 × 400 METRES RELAY

Heats (*1st 3 and 2 fastest losers to final*) **Heat 1: 1** USSR 3:24.2 (*Championship record*); **2** UK 3:29.0; **3** Hungary 3:30.7; **4** Czechoslovakia 3:31.2; **5** France 3:33.8; **6** Netherlands 3:34.7. **Heat 2: 1** GDR 3:27.7; **2** Germany 3:30.9; **3** Poland 3:31.2; **4** Romania 3:31.8; **5** Finland 3:32.2; **6** Belgium 3:33.4.

Final: 1 GDR (Christine Marquardt, Barbara Krug, Christine Brehmer, Marita Koch) 3:21.2 (*Championship record*); **2** USSR (Tatyana Prorochenko, Nadyezhda Mushta, Tatyana Providokhina, Maria Kulchunova) 3:22.5; **3** Poland (Malgorzata Gajewska, Krystyna Kacperczyk, Genowefa Blaszak, Irena Szewinska) 3:26.8; **4** UK (K. Williams, J. Hoyte, V. Elder, D. Hartley) 3:27.2; **5** Germany (E. Decker, E. Barth, G. Bussmann, S. Hollmann) 3:28.0; **6** Czechoslovakia (J. Kratochvilova, J. Kubeckova, E. Rakova, J. Cerchlanova) 3:30.4; **7** Romania (M. Samungi, D. Badescu, M. Suman, E. Tarita) 3:30.7; **8** Hungary (E. Mohacsi, R. Halmosi, I. Orosz, I. Pal) 3:32.2.

AUGUST HIGHLIGHTS

Rarely have so many women's world records tumbled in a single month as during August 1978. Sara Simeoni (Ita) high jumped 2.01 metres (6' 7") at Brescia on the 4th; Evelin Jahl (GDR) threw the discus 70.72 metres (232' 0") at Dresden on the 12th; Vilma Bardauskiene (Sov) long jumped 7.07 metres (23' 2½") at Kishinyov, Krystyna Kacperczyk (Pol) ran 400 metres hurdles in 55.44 and Ulrike Bruns (GDR) clocked 2:32.0 for 1000 metres – the latter not yet an official world record event – in West Berlin, all on the 18th; while next day Tatyana Zelentsova (Sov) improved on the 400 metres hurdles figures with 55.31 at Donetsk, and in Potsdam Marita Koch (GDR) recorded 49.02 on the flat and an East German squad of Johanna Klier, Monika Hamann, Carla Bodendorf and Marlies Gohr registered 42.27 for the 4 × 100 metres relay. One day after all that, Tatyana Providokhina (Sov) clipped the 1000 metres mark to 2:30.6 in Moscow; and the month's activities concluded spectacularly in Prague with further world record exploits by Bardauskiene, Koch and Simeoni.

The men were not entirely idle during this record blitz. Karl-Hans Riehm (Ger) whirled the hammer out to 80.32 metres (263' 6") at Heidenheim on the 6th; Wolfgang Schmidt (GDR) hurled the discus 71.16 metres (233' 5") in East Berlin on the 9th; and a Soviet foursome of Vladimir Podolyakov, Nikolay Kirov, Vladimir Malozemlin and Anatoliy Reshetnyak averaged a shade over 1:47 each to record a 4 × 800 metres time of 7:08.1 at Podolsk on the 12th.

There were a couple of other notable happenings at 800 metres prior to the Prague classic. Running in the Ivo Van Damme Memorial Meeting in Brussels on 18 August, Sebastian Coe established himself as favourite for the European title with a UK record breaking time of 1:44.3, leading throughout the second lap after a pacemaker towed him through 400 metres in 50.5. Two days earlier, in Zurich, Olympic champion and world record holder Alberto Juantorena suffered his first defeat in the two-lap event. Proving, to the relief of his rivals, that he is human after all, the Cuban faded in the finishing straight to sixth place in 1:47.1 as victory went to James Robinson (USA) in 1:45.9, one-tenth ahead of Mike Boit (Ken). 'I am not a superman', said Juantorena. 'I had to lose sometime.' Also at Zurich, Renaldo Nehemiah (USA) lowered his world junior record for 110 metres hurdles from 13.25 (in Warsaw on 13 August) to 13.23 – that's just two-hundredths of a second away from Alejandro Casanas's world record proper!

That Warsaw meeting was significant also for a European junior 1500 metres record of 3:37.7 by Scotsman Graham Williamson, the fastest-ever by any 18-year-old in the world. Six days later, in Edinburgh, Williamson again embarrassed the Scottish Commonwealth Games selectors (who neglected to pick him for Edmonton) by defeating a crack mile field in 3:58.3. He was followed home by Frank Clement (3:58.4), John Robson (3:58.6), Nick Rose (3:58.9) and New Zealand's Rod Dixon (4:00.4). At the same meeting, the Glenlivet Edinburgh Highland Games, Brian Hooper beat strong North American opposition in setting a UK pole vault record of 5.41 metres (17' 9"). Another record to note: Louise Miller (18) high jumped exactly six feet (1.83

Right: *Daley Thompson in discus action in Prague. He gained the silver medal in the decathlon with a UK record score.*
Tony Duffy

metres) for a UK junior mark at Woodford on 12 August.

Four-time Olympic discus champion Al Oerter (USA), a month short of his forty-second birthday, threw 62.62 metres (205′ 5″) at State College, Pennsylvania, on 5 August – his longest effort for 10 years!

Italy dominated Britain in a road walking international match, 42 points to 21, at Hove on 6 August.

Results: 20km: 1 M. DaMilano (Ita) 1:29:41; **2** R. Mills (UK) 1:30:18; **3** R. Buccione (Ita) 1:30:55; **4** A. Zambaldo (Ita) 1:31:29; **5** C. Mattioli (Ita) 1:31:51; **6** C. Harvey (UK) 1:34:10; **7** S. Gower (UK) 1:36:16; **8** K. Carter (UK) 1:38:05. **35km: 1** S. Bellucci (Ita) 2:43:10; **2** P. Gregucci (Ita) 2:43:37; **3** V. Visini (Ita) 2:47:00; **4** D. Cotton (UK) 2:53:25; **5** S. Lightman (UK) 2:54:53; **6** R. Dobson (UK) 2:58:55; **7** D. Carpentieri (Ita) 2:59:34; **8** I. Richards (UK) 3:02:27. **Junior 10km: 1** G. Gandossi (Ita) 44:03; **2** S. Grosselle (Ita) 44:17; **3** G. Morris (UK) 44:55; **4** D. Scognamiglio (Ita) 45:33; **5** M. Miley (UK) 45:41; **6** M. Wordsworth (UK) 47:30; **7** I. McCombie (UK) 47:35; P. Poggi (Ita) disq.

England finished second to Sweden in the 5km road event in the international women's race walking competition at Fredrikstad (Nor) on 12 August.

Result: 1 B–M. Carlsson (Swe) 23:05.0; **2** T. Gylder (Nor) 23:08.6; **3** M. Fawkes (Eng) 23:31.7; **4** C. Tyson (Eng) 23:35.2; **5** S. Gustavsson (Swe) 23:44.3; **6** E. Karlsson (Swe) 23:46.0 . . . **12** I. Bateman (Eng) 25:21.0. **Teams: 1** Sweden 64; **2** England 57; **3** Norway 50.

Wolverhampton and Bilston AC romped away with the GRE British League championship for the fourth consecutive year, scoring 23 out of a possible 24 points from the four matches contested.

Final tables: (Division 1) 1 Wolverhampton and Bilston 23 pts; **2** Cardiff 17; **3** Stretford 16; **4** Thames Valley 13; **5** Sale 10; **6** Woodford Green 5. **(Division 2) 1** Birchfield 20 (977 match points); **2** Essex Beagles 20 (959); **3** Southampton and Eastleigh 16; **4** Edinburgh Southern 13; **5** Bristol 11; **6** Enfield 4. **(Division 3) 1** Edinburgh AC 21; **2** Shaftesbury 19; **3** Liverpool 14 (850½); **4** Polytechnic 14 (813½); **5** Metropolitan Police 12; **6** Brighton and Hove 4. **(Division 4) 1** Haringey 23; **2** Sheffield 18; **3** Oxford 17½; **4** Luton 12; **5** Swansea 9½; **6** Hillingdon 4.

The top and bottom two clubs in each division are, as applicable, promoted or relegated. The two new members of Division 4 in 1979 are Bedford and County and Epsom and Ewell. The League will be expanded this year to include a fifth division, comprising: Swansea, Leicester Coritanian, Leeds City, Windsor Slough and Eton, Blackburn and Chelmsford.

Sale Harriers won the Singer UK Women's League title for the third year running.

Final placings: 1 Sale 17; **2** Stretford 15; **3** Glasgow 9 (687½); **4** Edinburgh Southern 9 (671); **5** Feltham 7; **6** Bristol 6.

The Master Butcher is highly rated in athletics... by athletes.

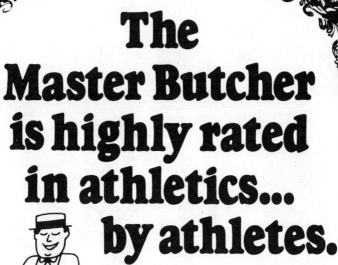

Many athletes, both famous and not so famous, get their weekly meat from Dewhurst. Why? Well, it isn't just because Dewhurst are avid supporters of British athletics Nor just because there are Dewhurst shops in most high streets. No, they shop at Dewhurst because they, like so many thousands of housewives, know that they'll get high quality meat, genuine value and friendly service from the Master Butcher.

September

9, 10 September

UK v FINLAND

On the same day that Alan Pascoe (30) made his final appearance for Britain, 11 years after his first, Graham Williamson (18) made his début for the senior national team at Crystal Palace. Partnered in the 1500 metres by the even younger Steve Cram against the formidable Finnish pairing of European indoor champion Antti Loikkanen (who had placed fifth in Prague the previous weekend in 3:37.5) and European junior champion Ari Paunonen, Williamson demonstrated that his armoury includes a prolonged kick. Leading at the bell after a slow early pace, he scorched through a 53.1 last lap for an impressive victory, with Cram also excelling by finishing very close behind his Finnish rivals.

The one newly-crowned European champion present, a race-weary Martti Vainio, had his hands full to finish ahead of Bernie Ford in the 10,000 metres – almost half a minute down on guest runner Henry Rono. Others seized the chance to put bad memories of Prague behind them. Geoff Capes despatched the shot 20.68 metres (67' 10¼"), equal to the silver medal distance at the European Championships, and Pentti Sinersaari – a bitterly disappointed twelfth in Prague – threw the javelin 88.90 metres (291' 8"), which would have placed him second. An excellent pole vault contest was won jointly by American guest Jeff Taylor, who even went on to attempt the world record height of 5.72 metres (18' 9¼"). The match, sponsored by British Meat, was originally scheduled to be a triangular affair, but the USSR withdrew without explanation.

MEN

100m: 1 H. Crawford (Tri-guest) 10.59; **2** M. McFarlane (UK) 10.68; **3** S. Green (UK) 10.79; **4** A. Bryggare (Fin) 10.82; **5** M. Juhola (Fin) 11.14.

200m: 1 T. Hoyte (UK) 21.84; **2** P. Cooke (UK) 22.09; **3** J. Sulalampi (Fin) 22.34; **4** T. Turunen (Fin) 22.86.

400m: 1 D. Laing (UK) 47.15; **2** R. Jenkins (UK) 47.84; **3** H. Hamalainen (Fin) 47.85; **4** J. Kemola (Fin) 49.39.

800m: 1 G. Cook (UK) 1:49.2; **2** J. Harkonen (Fin) 1:49.9; **3** G. Grant (UK) 1:50.2; **4** H. Lipsanen (Fin) 1:53.3.

1500m: 1 G. Williamson (UK) 3:47.2; **2** A. Paunonen (Fin) 3:47.9; **3** A. Loikkanen (Fin) 3:48.0; **4** S. Cram (UK) 3:48.3.

5000m: 1 H. Okkola (Fin) 14:04.5; **2** C. Spedding (UK) 14:10.5; **3** P. Paivarinta (Fin) 14:19.2; **4** L. Spence (UK) 14:24.5.

10,000m: 1 H. Rono (Ken-guest) 27:53.8; **2** M. Vainio (Fin) 28:22.9; **3** B. Ford (UK) 28:25.3; **4** G. Smith (UK) 28:40.0; **5** M. Kilholma (Fin) 30:56.7.

3000m Steeplechase: 1 I. Toukonen (Fin) 8:37.4; **2** I. Gilmour (UK) 8:40.1; **3** T. Kantanen (Fin) 8:44.5; **4** M. Morris (UK) 9:11.0.

110m Hurdles: 1 A. Bryggare (Fin) 14.22; **2** M. Holtom (UK) 14.31; **3** R. Byman (Fin) 14.59; **4** D. Wilson (UK) 14.77.

Left: *Steve Ovett triumphs in the European 1500 metres.*   Mike Street

400m Hurdles: 1 A. Pascoe (UK) 50.87; **2** G. Oakes (UK) 51.85; **3** R. Alanen (Fin) 52.45; **4** K. Lille (Fin) 53.32.

High Jump: 1 M. Naylor (UK) 2.17m (7' 1½"); **2** J. Porkka (Fin) 2.11m; **3** T. Llewelyn (UK) 2.11m; **4** S. Varjonen (Fin) 2.08m.

Pole Vault: 1 eq J. Taylor (USA-guest) and A. Kalliomaki (Fin) 5.50m (18' 0½"); **3** B. Hooper (UK) 5.40m; **4** R. Pudas (Fin) 5.30m; **5** J. Gutteridge (UK) 5.10m.

Long Jump: 1 E. Elsila (Fin) 7.50m (24' 7¼"); **2** P. Raitanen (Fin) 7.48m(w); **3** W. Kirkpatrick (UK) 7.46m; **4** K. Cocks (UK) 7.39m.

Triple Jump: 1 A. Moore (UK) 16.25m (53' 3¾"); **2** D. Johnson (UK) 16.11m; **3** S. Von Gerich (Fin) 15.84m; **4** H. Puhakka (Fin) 15.63m.

Shot: 1 G. Capes (UK) 20.68m (67' 10¼"); **2** R. Stahlberg (Fin) 20.49m; **3** M. Yrjola (Fin) 19.07m; **4** R. Dale (UK) 17.04m.

Discus: 1 M. Tuokko (Fin) 64.64m (212' 1"); **2** J. Tuomola (Fin) 61.18m; **3** P. Tancred (UK) 54.82m; **4** P. Gordon (UK) 54.48m.

Hammer: 1 H. Huhtala (Fin) 70.86m (232' 6"); **2** P. Dickenson (UK) 66.26m (217' 5"); **3** I. Chipchase (UK) 62.52m; **4** M. Auvinen (Fin) 20.08m.

Javelin: 1 P. Sinersaari (Fin) 88.90m (291' 8"); **2** M. Auvinen (Fin) 82.60m; **3** P. Yates (UK) 80.62m; **4** D. Ottley (UK) 74.02m.

4 × 100m Relay: 1 UK (L. Hoyte, M. McFarlane, C. Sharp, S. Green) 41.47; **2** Finland 41.79.

4 × 400m Relay: 1 UK (R. Dickens, C. Hamilton, R. Jenkins, D. Laing) 3:10.0; **2** Finland 3:11.3.

Match Result: UK 111, Finland 101.

WOMEN

100m: 1 S. Lannaman (UK) 11.59; **2** B. Goddard (UK) 11.72; **3** H. Laihorinne (Fin) 12.04; **4** B. Lindstrom (Fin) 12.47.

200m: 1 J. Hoyte (UK) 24.19; **2** V. Elder (UK) 24.37; **3** H. Laihorinne (Fin) 24.62; **4** M-L. Pursiainen (Fin) 25.14.

400m: 1 J. Hoyte (UK) 52.65; **2** K. Williams (UK) 53.84; **3** B. Lindstrom (Fin) 54.47; **4** M-L. Pursiainen (Fin) 54.60.

800m: 1 E. Barnes (UK) 2:04.3; **2** J. Prictoe (UK) 2:06.5; **3** S. Tyynela (Fin) 2:09.7; **4** I. Lusikka (Fin) 2:10.7.

1500m: 1 S. Tyynela (Fin) 4:13.4; **2** M. Stewart (UK) 4:14.4; **3** C. Boxer (UK) 4:18.5; **4** I. Lusikka (Fin) 4:35.9.

3000m: 1 P. Fudge (UK) 9:04.7; **2** A. Ford (UK) 9:04.7; **3** E. Pulkkinen (Fin) 9:24.2; **4** A. Virkberg (Fin) 10:17.3.

100m Hurdles: 1 L. Boothe (UK) 13.80; **2** S. Strong (UK) 13.92; **3** L. Spoof (Fin) 14.03; **4** E. Ristola (Fin) 14.61.

400m Hurdles: 1 V. Langley (UK) 59.55; **2** T. Heinonen (Fin) 59.78; **3** D. Heath (UK) 59.83; **4** T. Helander (Fin) 60.30.

High Jump: 1 B. Simmonds (UK) 1.78m (5' 10"); **2** S. Sundqvist (Fin) 1.78m; **3** M. Vehmasto (Fin) 1.73m; **4** D. Elliott (UK) 1.73m.

Long Jump: 1 S. Colyear (UK) 6.42m (21' 0¾")w; **2** S. Hearnshaw (UK) 6.29m; **3** H. Saarinen (Fin) 6.01m; **4** L. Pylkkanen (Fin) 5.96m.

Shot: 1 A. Littlewood (UK) 15.84m (51' 11¼"); **2** T. Kivi (Fin) 15.62m; **3** E. Tulikanto (Fin) 14.88m; **4** V. Redford (UK) 14.78m.

Discus: 1 M. Ritchie (UK) 58.16m (190' 10"); **2** S. Salminen (Fin) 54.84m; **3** U. Lundholm (Fin) 54.38m; **4** J. Thompson (UK) 54.02m.

Javelin: 1 T. Sanderson (UK) 61.58m (202′ 0″); **2** F. Whitbread (UK) 51.06m; **3** S. Kopiloff (Fin) 48.76m; **4** T. Lillak (Fin) 46.10m.

4 × 100m Relay: 1 UK (W. Clarke, B. Goddard, S. Colyear, S. Lannaman) 44.34; **2** Finland 46.47.

4 × 400m Relay: 1 UK (K. Williams, J. Hoyte, V. Elder, D. Hartley) 3:37.0; **2** Finland 3:47.1.

Match Result: UK 104, Finland 53.

15 September

IAC–COCA COLA INVITATION MEETING

All 17,000-plus tickets for the final international meeting of the season at Crystal Palace were sold even before any of the competitors were announced – such is the reputation of this fixture. The fans were not disappointed, for as usual there was a glittering array of talent set before them and one event – the 2 miles – will long live in the memories of all present. It was a smashing race, involving a momentous duel between the world's top miler Steve Ovett and the world's best at almost everything else, Henry Rono. A first mile of 4:08.8 had appeared to rule out the chance of a 'world record' (Brendan Foster passed in 4:05.4 when he set his world record – now no longer included on the official IAAF list – of 8:13.7), but the pace really hotted up in the last three laps during which Rono threw in everything to shake off Ovett. It was all in vain, for Ovett followed comfortably, biding his time until the start of the final straight. At that point he zipped past to gain an ecstatically acclaimed victory in 8:13.5 – the fastest-ever time outdoors, although 0.3 shy of the absolute quickest achieved indoors by Emiel Puttemans (Bel). Ovett covered the last quarter-mile in 55.8, clocking an exceptional 3:00.1 for the final three-quarters. His mile splits were 4:09.1 and 4:04.4.

Earlier in the evening, Ovett lost the UK 800 metres record he had accomplished when finishing second in Prague. Sebastian Coe regained the mark with 1:44.0; in fact he just dipped inside 1:44 for the electrical timing showed 1:43.97. Helped by the pacemaking on the first lap of Steve Scutt, Coe was bang on schedule with a split of 51.0 at 400 metres and 77.1 at 600 metres. The mile was notable too as Dave Moorcroft (3:55.4), ever-improving Graham Williamson (with a UK junior record of 3:55.8) and Frank Clement (3:56.1) all steamed past Filbert Bayi in the finishing straight.

MEN

100m: 1 H. Crawford (Tri) 10.41; **2** J. Gilkes (Guy) 10.47; **3** E. Obeng (Gha) 10.55; **4** C. Edwards (USA) 10.59; **5** D. Quarrie (Jam) 10.64; **6** S. Green 10.65.

200m: 1 J. Gilkes (Guy) 20.36; **2** D. Quarrie (Jam) 20.63; **3** C. Edwards (USA) 20.64; **4** S. Green 21.27.

800m: 1 S. Coe 1:44.0 (*UK all-comers and national record*); **2** J. Maina (Ken) 1:46.3; **3** D. Joseph 1:47.7; **4** R. Ashton 1:49.3.

Mile: 1 D. Moorcroft 3:55.4; **2** G. Williamson 3:55.8 (*UK junior record*); **3** F. Clement 3:56.1; **4** F. Bayi (Tan) 3:56.1; **5** L. Ericsson (Swe) 3:59.3; **6** T. Hutchings 4:01.2.

2 Miles: 1 S. Ovett 8:13.5 (*world outdoor best*); **2** H. Rono (Ken) 8:14.7; **3** B. Malinowski (Pol) 8:18.4; **4** W. Polleunis (Bel) 8:22.2; **5** N. Rose 8:22.4; **6** M. McLeod 8:25.8.

5000m: 1 S. Nyambui (Tan) 13:28.5; **2** M. Vainio (Fin) 13:28.9; **3** G. Tebroke (Hol) 13:29.0; **4** J. Goater 13:31.8; **5** B. Ford 13:34.9; **6** K. Penny 13:37.2.

110m Hurdles: 1 M. Holtom 14.04; **2** B. Price 14.18; **3** P. Sang (Ken) 14.51; **4** D. Wilson 14.57.

400m Hurdles: 1 A. Pascoe 49.63; **2** J. King (USA) 49.71; **3** C. Anicet (Fra) 49.96; **4** G. Oakes 51.38.

Pole Vault: 1 R. Pullard (USA) 5.50m (18′ 0¼″); **2** B. Hooper 5.35m; **3** L. Jessee (USA) 5.30m; **4** J. Taylor (USA) 5.20m.

Shot: 1 G. Capes 20.00m (65′ 7½″); **2** A. Feuerbach (USA) 19.59m; **3** R. Dale 16.34m.

Mile Walk: 1 R. Buccione (Ita) 6:00.0 (*UK all-comers best*); **2** R. Mills 6:01.8 (*UK national best*); **3** C. Lawton 6:30.2.

WOMEN

200m: 1 S. Lannaman 22.88; **2** I. Szewinska (Pol) 23.14; **3** B. Goddard 23.52; **4** S. Colyear 23.52.

400m: 1 D. Hartley 51.47; **2** J. Hoyte 52.15; **3** V. Elder 52.71; **4** C. Dawkins 55.26.

800m: 1 K. Kacperczyk (Pol) 1:59.8; **2** J. Colebrook 2:01.6; **3** E. Barnes 2:01.9; **4** C. Boxer 2:03.3.

High Jump: 1 A. Tveit (Nor) 1.81m (5′ 11¼″); **2** D. Elliott 1.78m; **3** A-M. Devally 1.78m; **4** L. Miller 1.78m.

Long Jump: 1 J. Davies 6.05m (19′ 10¼″); **2** S. Mapstone 6.00m; **3** J. Frank-Lynch 6.00m.

Javelin: 1 T. Sanderson 63.24m (207′ 6″); **2** I. Thyssen (Ger) 58.22m; **3** A. Farquhar 50.48m.

25 September

TOKYO INTERNATIONAL AND 'GOLDEN MILE'

This was Steve Ovett's month, with a vengeance. In Prague on 3 September he dominated Europe's best 1500 metres runners in 3:35.6; at Crystal Palace on the 15th he defeated Henry Rono in an epic two miles; in Oslo five days later he regained the UK mile record by defying dreadful conditions (it was very cold, wet and windy) to clock the extraordinary time of 3:52.8, just three-tenths away from the European record. On his own from before the halfway mark, he won by the length of the straight. His intermediate times were 55.0 at 440 yards, 1:55.2 at 880 yards and 2:54.5 at three-quarters of a mile. Finally, in Tokyo on 25 September he outclassed the opposition in what was dubbed the Dubai International 'Golden Mile', clocking 3:55.5 to have his name inscribed on a gold trophy valued at nearly $10,000. An ailing Henry Rono failed to finish.

The mile also formed part of an eight-nations match (which lacked a men's shot and five of the usual women's events), won by the USSR by a single point from Poland. The British team, which in common with most of the others was nowhere near full strength, finished fifth overall. The men came last in their match, but the girls were second in theirs – a mere point behind the USSR.

Right: *Sebastian Coe races to a UK 800 metres record of 1:44.0 in the Coca Cola Meeting.*   Mark Shearman

Sonia Lannaman and Tessa Sanderson won their events, while in the triple jump Aston Moore (second to Olympic champion Viktor Sanyeyev) bounded to a lifetime best of 16.76 metres (55' 0"), the following wind being just over the limit at 2.4 metres per second.

MEN

100m: 1 V. Ignatenko (Sov) 10.40; **2** M. Woronin (Pol) 10.45; **3** H. Panzo (Fra) 10.55; **4** S. Green (UK) 10.57; **5** L. Caravani (Ita) 10.57; **6** A. Harada (Jap) 10.75; **7** F-P. Hofmeister (Ger) 10.88; **8** D. Merrick (USA) 10.96.

200m: 1 L. Dunecki (Pol) 20.78; **2** A. Rogers (USA) 21.32; **3** T. Hoyte (UK) 21.34; **4** S. Curini (Ita) 21.35; **5** L. Sainte-Rose (Fra) 21.43; **6** A. Aksinin (Sov) 21.47; **7** F-P. Hofmeister (Ger) 21.56; **8** T. Toyoda (Jap) 21.61.

400m: 1 S. Vinson (USA) 46.05; **2** D. Laing (UK) 46.39; **3** F. Demarthon (Fra) 46.49; **4** M. Weppler (Ger) 46.59; **5** Z. Jaremski (Pol) 47.07; **6** Y. Harada (Jap) 47.44; **7** S. Malinverni (Ita) 47.84; **8** D. Stukalov (Sov) 48.20.

800m: 1 J. Marajo (Fra) 1:47.6; **2** W. Wulbeck (Ger) 1:47.9; **3** S. Clark (USA) 1:48.4; **4** G. Cook (UK) 1:48.5; **5** A. Reshetnyak (Sov) 1:48.5; **6** T. Nakamura (Jap) 1:49.2; **7** S. Zingales (Ita) 1:49.3; **8** G. Lapinski (Pol) 1:51.5.

Mile: 1 S. Ovett (UK) 3:55.5; **2** F. Gonzalez (Fra) 3:57.3; **3** G. Williamson (UK) 3:59.2; **4** S. Scott (USA) 4:01.1; **5** T. Ishii (Jap) 4:01.5; **6** T. Wessinghage (Ger) 4:02.8; **7** G. Jones (USA) 4:03.1; **8** R. Dixon (NZ) 4:04.0.

5000m: 1 A. Fedotkin (Sov) 13:31.5; **2** J. Kowol (Pol) 13:35.5; **3** T. Kamata (Jap) 13:35.8; **4** F. Zimmermann (Ger) 13:35.9; **5** M. Centrowitz (USA) 13:37.7; **6** C. Spedding (UK) 13:52.8; **7** P. Levisse (Fra) 14:18.8; **8** G. Gerbi (Ita) 14:39.5.

10,000m: 1 V. Ortis (Ita) 29:14.9; **2** T. Seko (Jap) 29:20.8; **3** D. Uhlemann (Ger) 29:28.5; **4** J-P. Gomez (Fra) 29:37.4; **5** A. Antipov (Sov) 29:38.8; **6** K. Penny (UK) 29:39.8; **7** R. Kopijarz (Pol) 29:53.7; **8** K. Misner (USA) 29:58.4.

3000m Steeplechase: 1 B. Malinowski (Pol) 8:19.3; **2** H. Iwabuchi (Jap) 8:30.8; **3** J-L. Lemire (Fra) 8:33.8; **4** M. Karst (Ger) 8:39.4; **5** I. Gilmour (UK) 8:40.0; **6** R. Volpi (Ita) 8:47.1; **7** J. Johnson (USA) 9:10.2.

110m Hurdles: 1 K. Bethel (USA) 13.89; **2** G. Buttari (Ita) 13.94; **3** B. Price (UK) 14.01; **4** J. Pusty (Pol) 14.04; **5** D. Gebhard (Ger) 14.11; **6** E. Raybois (Fra) 14.51; **7** Y. Fujimori (Jap) 14.67.

400m Hurdles: 1 V. Arkhipenko (Sov) 49.45; **2** T. Nagao (Jap) 49.59; **3** T. Andrews (USA) 50.65; **4** H. Schmid (Ger) 51.14; **5** J-C. Nallet (Fra) 51.46; **6** R. Minetti (Ita) 51.59; **7** J. Wlodarczyk (Pol) 53.53; **8** G. Oakes (UK) 53.93.

High Jump: 1 V. Yashchenko (Sov) 2.28m (7' 5¾"); **2** B. Fields (USA) 2.26m; **3** B. Bruni (Ita) 2.23m; **4** K. Kagei (Jap) 2.15m; **5** L. Kalek (Pol) 2.15m; **6** C. Thranhardt (Ger) 2.15m; **7** T. Llewelyn (UK) 2.15m (*equals UK junior record*); **8** P. Poaniewa (Fra) 2.10m.

Pole Vault: 1 V. Trofimenko (Sov) 5.50m (18' 0½"); **2** W. Buciarski (Pol) 5.40m; **3** G. Lohre (Ger) 5.30m; **4** R. Haynie (USA) 5.10m; **5** P. Houvion (Fra) 5.00m; **6** I. Takanasawa (Jap) 5.00m; **7** D. D'Alisera (Ita) 4.80m; B. Hooper (UK) failed opening height of 5.20m.

Long Jump: 1 G. Cybulski (Pol) 7.99m (26' 2¾"); **2** J. Rousseau (Fra) 7.87m; **3** A. Robinson (USA) 7.84m; **4** R. Mitchell (UK) 7.83m; **5** V. Tsepelev (Sov) 7.77m; **6** J. Usui (Jap) 7.74m; **7** J. Verschl (Ger) 7.57m; **8** C. Arrighi (Ita) 7.48m.

Triple Jump: 1 V. Sanyeyev (Sov) 17.02m (55' 10¼"); **2** A. Moore (UK) 16.76m(w); **3** R. Livers (USA) 16.54m; **4** E. Biskupski (Pol) 16.42m; **5** B. Lamitie (Fra) 16.26m; **6** M. Nakanishi (Jap) 16.12m; **7** K. Kubler (Ger) 16.03m; **8** P. Piapan (Ita) 15.90m.

Discus: 1 A. De Vincentiis (Ita) 60.82m (199' 6"); **2** A. Wagner (Ger) 60.48m; **3** S. Wolodko (Pol)

59.90m; **4** F. Piette (Fra) 56.56m; **5** A. Baryshnikov (Sov) 56.44m; **6** K. Kawasaki (Jap) 53.76m; **7** P. Dickenson (UK) 42.46m; D. Voorhees (USA) 53.74m, disq for refusing to take doping test.

Hammer: 1 Y. Sedykh (Sov) 74.44m (244' 3"); **2** G. Urlando (Ita) 72.06m; **3** K-H. Riehm (Ger) 71.84m; **4** S. Murofushi (Jap) 69.36m; **5** I. Golda (Pol) 68.88m; **6** P. Suriray (Fra) 68.10m; **7** E. Berry (USA) 63.72m; **8** P. Dickenson (UK) 62.16m.

Javelin: 1 N. Grebnyev (Sov) 87.46m (286' 11"); **2** M. Wessing (Ger) 85.34m; **3** P. Bielczyk (Pol) 84.80m; **4** T. Takeda (Jap) 76.20m; **5** V. Marchetti (Ita) 75.06m; **6** W. Schmidt (USA) 73.14m; **7** P. Yates (UK) 72.68m; **8** Leroy (Fra) 65.70m.

4 × 100m Relay: 1 Poland 39.10; **2** USSR 39.48; **3** France 39.67; **4** Italy 39.69; **5** Germany 39.80; **6** USA 39.89; **7** Japan 39.96; UK scr.

4 × 400m Relay: 1 USA 3:04.9; **2** Germany 3:05.4; **3** Japan 3:06.5; **4** France 3:06.9; **5** UK 3:07.2; **6** Italy 3:07.4.

Match Result: 1 Poland 95; **2** USSR 91; **3 equal** USA and Germany 89; **5** France 88; **6** Japan 79; **7** Italy 74; **8** UK 70.

WOMEN

100m: 1 S. Lannaman (UK) 11.26; **2** L. Maslakova (Sov) 11.27; **3** G. Rabsztyn (Pol) 11.57; **4** V. Rosset (Fra) 11.71; **5** E. Possekel (Ger) 11.82; **6** M. Masullo (Ita) 11.94; **7** K. Hawkins (USA) 11.98; **8** S. Kaibara (Jap) 12.24.

200m: 1 L. Kondratyeva (Sov) 22.81; **2** B. Goddard (UK) 23.24; **3** V. Rosset (Fra) 23.56; **4** Z. Bielczyk (Pol) 23.63; **5** M. Masullo (Ita) 23.82; **6** D. Schenten (Ger) 24.12; **7** S. Kaibara (Jap) 24.96; **8** S. Brown (USA) 25.20.

400m: 1 I. Szewinska (Pol) 50.97; **2** M. Kulchunova (Sov) 51.27; **3** V. Elder (UK) 52.66; **4** E. Rossi (Ita) 53.42; **5** P. Darbonville (Fra) 53.68; **6** G. Bussmann (Ger) 54.10; **7** S. Dabney (USA) 54.27; **8** K. Nagasawa (Jap) 55.90.

1500m: 1 S. Ulmasova (Sov) 4:10.8; **2** B. Kraus (Ger) 4:11.3; **3** G. Dorio (Ita) 4:11.8; **4** M. Stewart (UK) 4:12.4; **5** D. Heald (USA) 4:14.4; **6** V. Renties (Fra) 4:16.3; **7** E. Szydlowska (Pol) 4:18.6; **8** S. Ohkawa (Jap) 4:45.0.

100m Hurdles: 1 T. Anisimova (Sov) 13.03; **2** D. Perka (Pol) 13.11; **3** L. Boothe (UK) 13.46; **4** L. Elloy (Fra) 13.68; **5** I. Ongar (Ita) 13.80; **6** E. Akimota (Jap) 14.06; **7** E. Possekel (Ger) 14.23; **8** M. Smith (USA) 14.25.

High Jump: 1 S. Simeoni (Ita) 1.93m (6' 4"); **2** B. Holzapfel (Ger) 1.91m; **3** L. Ritter (USA) 1.88m; **4** U. Kielan (Pol) 1.88m; **5** T. Yagi (Jap) 1.85m; **6** F. Picaut (Fra) 1.80m; **7** N. Tkachenko (Sov) 1.80m; **8** G. Hitchen (UK) 1.75m.

Long Jump: 1 V. Bardauskiene (Sov) 6.53m (21' 5¼"); **2** J. Curtet (Fra) 6.50m; **3** S. Reeve (UK) 6.36m; **4** K. Hanel (Ger) 6.23m; **5** T. Marciniak (Pol) 6.20m; **6** S. Awara (Jap) 6.07m; **7** J. Anderson (USA) 5.93m; **8** C. Graziella (Ita) 5.90m.

Shot: 1 M. Seidler (USA) 17.83m (58' 6"); **2** B. Philipp (Ger) 17.63m; **3** B. Habrzyk (Pol) 17.20m; **4** L. Bertimon (Fra) 16.08m; **5** C. Petrucci (Ita) 15.99m; **6** A. Littlewood (UK) 15.84m; **7** N. Tkachenko (Sov) 15.31m; **8** K. Hayashi (Jap) 15.25m.

Javelin: 1 T. Sanderson (UK) 62.66m (205' 7"); **2** I. Thyssen (Ger) 59.52m; **3** S. Calvert (USA) 57.52m; **4** N. Shibusawa (Jap) 56.20m; **5** B. Blechacz (Pol) 55.16m; **6** G. Amici (Ita) 49.24m; **7** N. Besson (Fra) 41.58m.

4 × 100m Relay: 1 USSR 43.04; **2** UK 43.65; **3** Poland 43.95; **4** France 44.10; **5** Italy 45.05; **6** Germany 45.10; **7** Japan 46.21; **8** USA 46.51.

Match Result: 1 USSR 58; **2** UK 57; **3** Poland 53; **4** Germany 48; **5** France 45; **6** Italy 42; **7** USA 33; **8** Japan 23.

Combined Result: 1 USSR 149; **2** Poland 148; **3** Germany 137; **4** France 133; **5** UK 127; **6** USA 122; **7** Italy 116; **8** Japan 102.

SEPTEMBER HIGHLIGHTS

A 20-year-old Norwegian, Thorill Gylder, claimed her second world's best within six weeks when she walked 10,000 metres in 48:40.0 at Softeland on 16 September. She had, in Oslo on 4 August, covered 5000 metres in 23:17.5. Roberto Buccione of Italy, eighth in the European 20 kilometres walk, set a world best of 12:32.7 for two miles at Ravenna on 21 September. Britain scored a splendid victory, 38–28, over Germany in a walks match at Sheffield on 17 September.

20km: 1 O. Flynn (UK) 1:32:26; **2** C. Harvey (UK) 1:33:40; **3** H. Michalski (Ger) 1:34:30; **4** A. Seddon (UK) 1:35:08; **5** A. Schwarz (Ger) 1:36:45; **6** W. Werner (Ger) 1:37:13; **7** S. Gower (UK) 1:37:38; **8** W. Wiedermann (Ger) 1:39:29. **50km: 1** G. Weidner (Ger) 4:06:11; **2** H. Binder (Ger) 4:13:09; **3** B. Adams (UK) 4:15:22; **4** K. Degener (Ger) 4:17:39; **5** C. Maddocks (UK) 4:21:06; **6** S. Lightman (UK) 4:24:09; **7** A. James (UK) 4:24:32; H. Schubert (Ger) disq. **Junior 10km: 1** M. Miley (UK) 47:14; **2** M. Wordsworth (UK) 47:15; **3** I. McCombie (UK) 48:11; **4** F. Helms (Ger) 48:29; **5** U. Jacob (Ger) 48:56; **6** R. Sheppard (UK) 49:19.

Liesel Albert (Ger) amassed the highest total yet for the women's heptathlon – the all rounders' contest which will replace the traditional pentathlon as from 1981 – when she scored 5761 points for the seven-event competition at Dillingen on 9 and 10 September. She reeled off marks of 14.0 for 100 metres hurdles, 14.14 metres (46' 4¾") for the shot, 1.60 metres (5' 3") for the high jump, 24.5 for 200 metres, 6.13 metres (20' 1½") for the long jump, 33.44 metres (109' 8") for the javelin and 2:24.8 for 800 metres. Winner of Britain's first heptathlon, staged in Birmingham on 23 and 24 September was Ruth Howell with 5126 points.

Results of a decathlon/pentathlon match at Antony (Paris) on 16 and 17 September were as follows:

Senior Decathlon: 1 B. Schindelholz (Swi) 7488 pts; **2** S. Miklaus (Swi) 7239 pts; **3** T. Staubli (Swi) 7230 pts . . . **5** B. McStravick (UK) 7165 pts; P. Zeniou (UK) 7034 pts; **12** J. Howell 6826 pts; **15** P. Bredin 6465 pts. **Junior Decathlon: 1** M. Rutenacht (Swi) 6861 pts; **2** C. Gugler (Swi) 6556 pts; **3** K. Lobb (UK) 6490 pts . . . **6** P. Edwards (UK) 6273 pts; **8** F. Obikwu (UK) 6139 pts; **9** L. Shakes (UK) 6082 pts. **Overall Men's Scores: 1** Switzerland 41,454 pts; **2** France 40,172 pts; **3** UK 39,927 pts. **Senior Pentathlon: 1** A. Weiss (Swi) 4200 pts; **2** G. Howell (UK) 4006 pts; **3** S. Baumann (Swi) 3956 pts . . . **6** V. Langley (UK) 3794 pts; **11** A. Manley (UK) 3239 pts; V. Mullin (UK) retired. **Junior Pentathlon: 1** K. Hagger (UK) 3844 pts; **2** E. Jeker (Swi) 3800 pts; **3** C. Schneider (Swi) 3763 pts; **4** V. Kelly (UK) 3707 . . . **6** J. Livermore (UK) 3654 pts; **8** M. Somerville (UK) 3455 pts. **Overall Women's Scores: 1** Switzerland 23,146 pts; **2** UK 22,244 pts; **3** France 21,084 pts.

Rosemary Cox clipped one second off Christine Readdy's UK women's marathon best with a time of 2:50:54 at Rugby on 3 September.

The last official UK record of the season fell at Gateshead on 17 September when Brian Hooper vaulted 5.42 metres (17' 9½") in conditions so windy that he very nearly decided not to compete at all.

Shaftesbury Harriers won the GRE Gold Cup for men and Stretford AC the Jubilee Cup for women (for the third year running) in the finals at Cwmbran on 23 September.

Right: *Commonwealth walking champion Olly Flynn, a winner also in the match against Germany.*

Mike Street

Men: 1 Shaftesbury 107; **2** Cardiff 101; **3** Edinburgh Southern 97; **4** Wolverhampton and Bilston 95; **5** Birchfield 94; **6** Sale 85; **7** Thames Valley 82; **8** Edinburgh AC 77. **Women: 1** Stretford 99; **2** Edinburgh Southern 95; **3** Sale 83; **4** Southampton 60; **5** Liverpool 57; **6** London Olympiades 55; **7** Essex Ladies 54; **8** Bristol 51.

Birchfield (461) won the National Young Athletes League Final at Crystal Palace on 17 September, ahead of Haringey (406) and Cardiff (399).

OCTOBER HIGHLIGHTS

Liesel Albert (Ger) improved upon her own best on record score for the new women's heptathlon event with a total of 5831 points at Dillingen on 7 and 8 October. Her individual marks: 100 metres hurdles – 13.6, shot – 14.19 metres (46′ 6¾″), high jump – 1.58 metres (5′ 2¼″), 200 metres – 24.1, long jump – 6.09 metres (19′ 11¾″), javelin – 30.46 metres (99′ 11″), 800 metres – 2:19.6.

A 19-year-old Japanese girl, Tamami Yagi, high jumped an Asian record of 1.90 metres (6′ 2¾″) at Matsumoto on 19 October – leaping higher over her own head (26 centimetres or 10¼″) than any other woman in history.

Norway's Grete Waitz, the IAAF cross-country champion and European 3000 metres bronze medallist, made a spectacular marathon début in New York on 22 October . . . slicing over two minutes from the women's world best with a time of 2:32:30! Overall, she finished 104th in a record field of 11,000 (including 1,000 women), the race being won for the third year running by Bill Rodgers (USA) in 2:12:12, followed by the British pair of Ian Thompson (2:14:12) and Trevor Wright (2:14:35). Margaret Lockley, sixth woman to finish, clocked 2:50:58 – just four seconds away from the UK record. An estimated two million spectators lined the course.

Despite having to leave the track at one stage because of stomach trouble, Scotsman Don Ritchie took over quarter of an hour from Cavin Woodward's previous world best for the 100 kilometres track run with a time of 6:10:20 on 28 October at Crystal Palace . . . that's 250 laps of the track! He also set a world best of 4:53:28 for 50 miles *en route*. Ritchie had, on 1 October, won the London to Brighton race in 5:13:02.

Bob Dobson broke his own UK best for the 50 kilometres road walk by a minute with a mark of 4:08:39 at Aigen in Austria on 28 October. At the same meeting, Carol Tyson recorded 49:26.7 for 10 kilometres, also a UK road best performance.

Cambridge and Coleridge AC won the AAA national six-stage road relay title at Crystal Palace on 14 October.

Result: 1 Cambridge and Coleridge AC 76:56; 2 Shaftesbury H 77:27; 3 Aldershot Farnham and District AC 77:31; 4 Sheffield AC 77:37; 5 Airedale and Spen Valley AC 77:57; 6 Bingley H 78:00. **Fastest laps:** S. Kenyon 12:20; K. Penny, J. Goater and B. Ford 12:21.

The dramatic upsurge in jogging in Britain was reflected by the turn-out for the first *Sunday Times* National Fun Run in Hyde Park on 1 October: a total of 11,822 participants, ages ranging from 4 to 80, attempted the four kilometre course.

NOVEMBER HIGHLIGHTS

Only three weeks after finishing second in the New York Marathon, Britain's Ian Thompson notched up his first significant international marathon win for four years, in Auckland on 12 November, clocking 2:13:49 despite a strong

Left: *Irishmen Gerry Deegan (62) and John Treacy (68) and Welshman Steve Jones in December's IAC cross-country race.*
Peter Tempest

wind which he estimated added two and a half to three minutes to his time. Gillian File (NZ) was the first woman home, in a Commonwealth best of 2:44:11.

Christa Vahlensieck (Ger) gained a little consolation for the loss of her world marathon best to Grete Waitz by setting a world's best 25 kilometres road time of 1:28:33 at Griesheim on 22 November.

Feltham AC (since renamed as Borough of Hounslow AC) dominated the women's national road relay championship at Coventry on 12 November.

Result: 1 Feltham AC 27:50; **2** Feltham 'B' 29:01; **3** Bracknell AC 29:41; **4** Cambridge H 29:43; **5** Birchfield H 30:02; **6** Bolton United H 30:11.
Fastest laps: A. Roberts 9:13, P. Fudge 9:17, A. Ford 9:20.

The first big event of the 1978–79 cross-country season, the Schweppes International at Gateshead on 25 November, was won by Mike McLeod, despite an attack of stomach cramp. He clocked 23:38, ahead of Steve Jones (23:40) and Bernie Ford (23:42). Grete Waitz (Nor) took the women's race in 13:07, followed by Cherry Hanson (13:53) and Ann Ford (13:57).

Squire Yarrow (73), silver medallist in the 1938 European marathon championship, was elected president of the AAA in succession to the late Harold Abrahams.

DECEMBER HIGHLIGHTS

Japanese runners scored a clean sweep in their own classic Fukuoka Marathon on 3 December, Toshihiko Seko winning in 2:10:21 from Hideki Kita (2:11:05) and Shigeru Sou (2:11:41). Britain's Trevor Wright was fourth in a personal best of 2:12:32, followed by European champion Leonid Moseyev (Sov), 2:12:44, and Bill Rodgers (USA), 2:12:51. Olympic champion Waldemar Cierpinski (GDR) could finish no higher than thirty-second in 2:22:49.

Japan were less successful in the eighth Asian Games, staged in Bangkok from 14 to 19 December, where China – newly welcomed into membership of the IAAF in place of Taiwan – gained 12 gold medals to the previously all-conquering Japan's 10. The Games went ahead despite the insistence of the IAAF that all competitors would be suspended from further international competition because of the organisers' refusal to invite Israel to compete.

Winners: Men: 100m: S. Chairsuvaparb (Tha) 10.44; **200m:** R. Gnanasekharan (Ind) 21.42; **400m:** Abbas el Saybi (Irq) 46.71; **800m:** Sri Ram Singh (Ind) 1:48.8; **1500m:** T. Ishii (Jap) 3:47.5; **5000m/10,000m:** H. Chand (Ind) 14:22.0/30:07.7; **Marathon:** M. Sakamoto (Jap) 2:15:30; **3000m Steeplechase:** M. Shintaku (Jap) 8:40.7; **110m Hurdles:** Wang Hsu-hua (Chi) 14.28; **400m Hurdles:** K. Bassan (Irq) 50.81; **High Jump:** T. Sakamoto (Jap) 2.20m (7' 2½"); **Pole Vault:** Y. Kigawa (Jap) 5.15m (16' 10¾"); **Long Jump:** S. Babu (Ind) 7.85m (25' 9¼"); **Triple Jump:** M. Nakanishi (Jap) 16.56m (54' 4"); **Shot:** Bahadur Singh (Ind) 17.61m (57' 9½"); **Discus:** Lee Wei-nan (Chi) 56.26m (184' 7"); **Hammer:** S. Murofushi (Jap) 68.26m (223' 11"); **Javelin:** Chen Mao-mao (Chi) 79.24m (260' 0"); **Decathlon:** H. Iwai (Jap) 7003; **20km Walk:** Hakam Singh (Ind) 1:31:55; **4 x 100m:** Thailand 40.32; **4 x 400m:** Japan 3:08.3.
Women: 100m: Ya Pin-yin (Chi) 12.20; **200m:** U. Laopinkarn (Tha) 24.81; **400m:** Shaik (Mal) 55.08; **800m:** G. Zutchi (Ind) 2:07.7; **1500m/3000m:** Kim Ok Sem (NK) 4:18.9/9:24.1; **100m**

Hurdles: Tsai Chien-hua (Chi) 13.98; **400m Hurdles:** Hsin Chen (Chi) 61.32; **High Jump:** Cheng Ta-chen (Chi) 1.88m (6′ 2″); **Long Jump:** Chou Wa (Chi) 6.28m (20′ 7¼″); **Shot:** Hsen Lee-chuan (Chi) 17.70m (58′ 1″); **Discus:** Lee Chiao-hui (Chi) 55.92m (183′ 5″); **Javelin:** Yao Sui-ying (Chi) 57.22m (187′ 9″); **Pentathlon:** Yeh Pei-su (Chi) 4133; **4 × 100m:** N. Korea 46.20; **4 × 400m:** Japan 3:46.3.

Carol Tyson retained the national women's 5000 metres road walk title at Melksham on 3 December.

Result: **1** C. Tyson 24:08; **2** K. Eden 24:20; **3** I. Bateman 24:26; **4** J. Farr 24:29; **5** B. Francis 25:54; **6** S. Till 26:26. **Team:** Brighton.

Irish runners scored a one-two in the Philips-sponsored IAC cross-country at Crystal Palace on 9 December. Gerry Deegan won in 26:16, ahead of the reigning IAAF champion John Treacy (26:17), with Welshmen Steve Jones (26:18) and Tony Simmons (26:20) next to finish. Norway's Grete Waitz gained another unpressed victory in the women's race, clocking 14:37 far in front of Kathy Binns (15:14) and Ruth Smeeth (15:39).

OBITUARY

Among well-known athletics personalities who died during 1978 were:
Harold Abrahams (78), Olympic 100 metres champion in 1924 who continued to make a massive contribution to the sport in Britain and world-wide as a writer, broadcaster and administrator. (January)
Kitty Dyer (63), five times WAAA shot champion between 1934 and 1946. (February)
Sir Lancelot Royle (80), a member – along with Harold Abrahams – of the British team which placed second in the 1924 Olympic 4 × 100 metres relay. (June)
Ralph Metcalfe (68), world record-setting American sprinter who was second in the 100 metres at both the 1932 and 1936 Olympic Games, and who later became a Congressman. (October)
Jiri Skobla (48), a Czech who held the European shot record for many years and was Olympic bronze medallist in 1956. (November)

Daley Thompson on the Way to Fulfilling his Destiny

Ever since, at the age of 16, he scored the remarkable total of 6685 points in his decathlon début, Francis Morgan (Daley) Thompson has appeared destined to become the world's greatest all-round athlete. Barely a year after that precocious start he was British senior and world junior record holder with 7905 points, having earlier made a promising showing in the Montreal Olympics where he impressed gold medallist and world record smasher Bruce Jenner (USA) as a likely successor to himself.

Daley has continued to close in on Jenner's monumental score of 8618 points. He topped 8000 for the first time in 1977, and in 1978 – at the Commonwealth Games in Edmonton, a week after his twentieth birthday – he piled up the third highest score (using electrical timing) in decathlon history . . . 8467. That couldn't be ratified as a Commonwealth and UK record because of excessive wind assistance in the long jump, where he achieved the sensational distance of 8.11 metres (26′ 7¼″), but three weeks later he put together a fully official total of 8289 points in placing second to Aleksandr Grebenyuk (Sov) in the European Championships.

Thompson is his own sternest critic. While everyone else was drooling over his performance in Edmonton, Daley himself was far from satisfied. He was happy with his 100 metres, long jump (and how!), 400 metres and pole vault, reasonably content with his 1500 metres . . . and thoroughly displeased with everything else despite equalling his lifetime best in the high jump and going close to his personal bests in the shot, discus and hurdles. He knows that he must improve considerably in his weaker events – the throws and hurdles – before his dream of succeeding Jenner can be realised.

Born in London of a Nigerian father and Scottish mother, Daley Thompson has one of the most engaging personalities in athletics. He delights in his own immense talent, and that joy is communicated to the spectators. By 1980, he could be ready to fulfil his destiny . . . and where better than in the Olympic Stadium in Moscow.

Daley Thompson's Decathlons in Chronological Order

(Individual marks are for, in order, 100m, long jump, shot, high jump, 400m, 110m hurdles, discus, pole vault, javelin and 1500m)

28–29.6.1975, Cwmbran: *6685* – 1st Welsh Open Championship (3764 first day); (11.0, 6.99, 10.74, 1.97, 50.2, 16.8, 31.42, 2.90, 51.88, 4:31.0).

Daley Thompson – destined to become the world's greatest all-round athlete?   George Herringshaw

30–31.8.1975, Cwmbran: *7008* – 1st AAA Junior Championship (3880); (10.7w, 7.21, 10.80, 1.93, 49.6, 15.8, 32.20, 3.30, 53.28, 4:36.5).

4–5.10.1975, Cwmbran: *7100* – 2nd UK v France (3886); (10.8w, 7.11w, 11.77, 1.90, 49.3, 16.0, 31.84, 3.40, 57.04, 4:30.9).

22–23.5.1976, Cwmbran: *7684* – 1st AAA Championship (4092); (10.8, 7.40, 12.79, 1.98, 49.1, 15.5, 38.78, 3.80, 56.92, 4:20.3).

26–27.6.1976, Copenhagen: *6639* – 10th International Match (4040); (10.6, 7.26, 11.94, 1.93, 48.6, 15.3, 36.47, no height, 51.34, 4:41.2).

29–30.7.1976, Montreal: *7434* – 18th Olympic Games (4055); (10.79, 7.19, 13.10, 1.91, 48.15, 15.98, 36.36, 4.20, 45.18, 4:29.6).

4–5.9.1976, Talence: *7905* – 4th International Meeting (4275); (10.5, 7.57, 13.59, 1.95, 48.1, 15.4, 37.70, 4.40, 51.92, 4:25.9).

21–22.5.1977, Gotzis: *7921* – 3rd International Meeting (4282); (10.71w, 7.72, 13.59, 2.00, 48.35, 15.24, 37.28, 4.20, 55.78, 4:23.4).

25–26.6.1977, Madrid: *8190* – 1st International Match (4437); (10.5, 7.60, 13.85, 2.07, 47.4, 15.1, 39.60, 4.80, 50.32, 4:29.0).

30–31.7.1977, Sittard: *8124* – 1st European Cup Semi-Final (4324); (10.70, 7.54, 13.84, 2.01, 47.31, 15.26, 41.70, 4.70, 54.48, 4:30.4).

19–20.8.1977, Donetsk: *7647* – 1st European Junior Championship (4207); (11.02, 7.25, 13.72, 2.06, 47.60, 14.95, 38.22, 3.80, 49.72, 4:35.5).

27–28.5.1978, Gotzis: *8238* – 2nd International Meeting (4385); (10.77, 7.95w, 13.89, 2.03, 47.76, 14.85, 41.40, 4.60, 56.90, 4.29.1).

7–8.8.1978, Edmonton: *8467w* – 1st Commonwealth Games (4550); (10.50w, 8.11w, 14.43, 2.07, 47.85, 14.92, 41.68, 4.80, 56.60, 4:25.8).

30–31.8.1978, Prague: *8289* – 2nd European Championships (4459); (10.69, 7.93, 14.69, 2.04, 47.77, 15.28, 43.52, 4.20, 59.80, 4:22.8).

Personal bests: 100m – 10.65/10.50w and 10.5 (hand); **200m** – 21.8; **400m** – 47.31; **1500m** – 4:20.3; **110m hurdles** – 14.85; **400m hurdles** – 52.6; **High jump** – 2.07m (6′ 9½″); **Pole vault** – 4.90m (16′ 0¾″); **Long jump** – 7.93m (26′ 0¼″) and 8.11m (26′ 7¼″)w; **Shot** – 14.69m (48′ 2½″); **Discus** – 44.46m (145′ 10″); **Javelin** – 59.80m (196′ 2″); **Decathlon** – 8289 and 8467w.

Who's Who in the British Team

Compiled by **Jon Wigley**

Brief biographical and career details of 198 men and women who represented the UK senior team during 1978. The information provided includes athletes' personal best performances in a variety of events, and positions in major international championships (when placed in the first eight in Olympic, European, or Commonwealth Games; first three in relays).

Abbreviations:
i = indoor performance;
w = wind-assisted performance.

BRIAN ADAMS
Leicester WC. *Born* Leicester, 13.3.1949; *Height:* 1.83m (6' 0"), *Weight:* 70kg (154lb); Teacher. *Best performances:* 3000m walk – 12:02.2, 20km walk – 1:27:46, 50km walk – 4:15:22. *Championships:* 1978 Commonwealth – 4th 30km walk.

RICHARD ASHTON
Polytechnic H. *Born* Wolverhampton, 9.12.1955; *Height:* 1.84m (6' 0¼"), *Weight:* 76kg (168lb); Teacher. *Best performances:* 400m – 46.27, 800m – 1:49.3. *Championships:* 1978 Commonwealth – 6th 400m; 1978 European – 6th 400m.

FRANK ATTOH
Shaftesbury H. *Born* Accra (Ghana), 21.8.1956; *Height:* 1.76m (5' 9½"), *Weight:* 70kg (154lb); Maintenance engineer. *Best performance:* Triple jump – 15.87m (52' 0¾")w and 15.85m (52' 0")i.

DAVID BAPTISTE
Essex Beagles. *Born* London, 16.1.1959; *Height:* 1.74m (5' 8½"), *Weight:* 73kg (161lb); Student. *Best performances:* 100m – 10.66, 200m – 21.36.

LIZ BARNES
Cambridge H. *Born* Woolwich, 3.8.1951; *Height:* 1.62m (5' 4"), *Weight:* 54kg (120lb); Student radiographer. *Best performances:* 100m – 11.6w, 200m – 24.0, 400m – 52.2, 800m – 2:01.4. *Championships:* 1978 Commonwealth – 4th 800m.

BRENDA BEDFORD (née Sawyer)
Mitcham AC. *Born* London 4.9.1937; *Height:* 1.75m (5' 9"), *Weight:* 82kg (182lb); Secretary. *Best performances:* Shot – 16.29m (53' 5¼"), Discus – 50.58m (165' 11"). *Championships:* 1966 Commonwealth – 6th shot and discus; 1970 Commonwealth – 5th shot, 6th discus; 1974 Commonwealth – 6th shot.

ALAN BELL
Wakefield H. *Born* Wakefield, 10.6.1957; *Height:* 1.90m (6' 3"), *Weight:* 79kg (175lb); Medical student. *Best performances:* 200m – 21.36, 400m – 46.96.

CHRIS BENNING (née Tranter)
Stretford AC. *Born* Urmston, 30.3.1955; *Height:* 1.60m (5' 3"), *Weight:* 55kg (122lb); Teacher. *Best performances:* 800m – 2.03.5, 1500m – 4:07.5, 3000m – 8:52.3. *Championships:* 1978 Commonwealth – 2nd 1500m.

CHRIS BLACK
Edinburgh Southern H. *Born* Edinburgh, 1.1.1950; *Height:* 1.88m (6' 2"), *Weight:* 108kg (238lb); Draughtsman. *Best performances:* Discus – 50.94m (167' 1"), Hammer – 74.98m (246' 0") (UK record). *Championships:* 1974 Commonwealth – 6th hammer; 1976 Olympics – 7th; 1978 Commonwealth – 3rd.

DAVE BLACK
Small Heath H. *Born* Tamworth (Staffs), 2.10.1952; *Height:* 1.83m (6' 0"), *Weight:* 66kg (146lb); Security officer. *Best performances:* Mile – 4:00.2, 3000m – 7:46.6, 5000m – 13:23.6, 10,000m – 27:36.3. *Championships:* 1974 Commonwealth – 3rd 5000m, 2nd 10,000m; 1978 Commonwealth – 4th 10,000m; 1978 European – 5th 10,000m.

TIM BONSOR
Coventry Godiva H. *Born* Coventry,
20.12.1954; *Height:* 1.78m (5' 10"), *Weight:*
73kg (161lb); Design draughtsman. *Best
performances:* 100m – 10.67, 200m – 21.47
(20.89w).

LORNA BOOTHE
Borough of Hounslow AC. *Born* Kingston
(Jamaica), 5.12.1954; *Height:* 1.62m (5' 4"),
Weight: 51kg (112lb); Bank clerk. *Best
performances:* 200m – 24.03, 100m hurdles –
13.08 (UK record) and 12.98w, 400m hurdles –
61.5, Long jump – 6.00m (19' 8¼").
Championships: 1978 Commonwealth – 1st
100m hurdles.

CHRIS BOXER
Aldershot, Farnham and District AC. *Born*
Northolt (Middx), 25.3.1957; *Height:* 1.62m
(5' 4"), *Weight:* 53kg (118lb); Trainee pensions
consultant. *Best performances:* 800m – 2:03.1,
1500m – 4:10.0.

PAT BREDIN
Luton United AC. *Born* Bedford, 18.9.1954;
Height: 1.83m (6' 0"), *Weight:* 81kg (180lb);
Teacher. *Best performance:* Decathlon – 6856.

PETE BROWNE
Thames Valley H. *Born* London, 3.2.1949;
Height: 1.76m (5' 9½"), *Weight:* 63kg (140lb);
Accountant. *Best performances:* 400m – 48.0,
800m – 1:46.2, 1500m – 3:46.6, 400m hurdles –
55.1. *Championships:* 1971 European – 5th
800m.

BRIAN BURGESS
Edinburgh AC. *Born* Edinburgh, 30.9.1957;
Height: 1.87m (6' 1¾"), *Weight:* 70kg (154lb);
Laboratory assistant. *Best performance:* High
jump – 2.20m (7' 2½") (UK record).
Championships: 1978 Commonwealth – 3rd
equal.

MIKE BUTTERFIELD
Cardiff AAC. *Born* Staincliff (Yorks), 4.5.1953;
Height: 1.94m (6' 4½"), *Weight:* 76kg (167lb);
RAF electronic technician. *Best performances:*
110m hurdles – 14.7, High jump – 2.16m (7'
1")i.

BLONDELLE CAINES (née Thompson)
Birchfield H. *Born* St Kitts (West Indies),
5.9.1953; *Height:* 1.68m (5' 6"), *Weight:* 59kg
(130lb); Video display operator. *Best
performance:* 100m hurdles – 13.49 (and 13.0 –
hand timing).

DAVE CANNON
Gateshead H. *Born* 7.8.1950; *Height:* 1.83m (6'

0"), *Weight:* 67kg (147lb); Electricity linesman.
Best performances: 10,000m – 29:23.2, Marathon
– 2:13:29.

GEOFF CAPES
Borough of Enfield H. *Born* Holbeach (Lincs),
23.8.1949; *Height:* 1.98m (6' 6"), *Weight:* 137kg
(302lb); Policeman. *Best performances:* Shot –
21.55m (70' 8½") (UK record), Discus – 58.34m
(191' 5"), Javelin – 60.56m (198' 8").
Championships: 1970 Commonwealth – 4th
shot; 1974 Commonwealth – 1st; 1974
European Indoor – 1st; 1974 European – 3rd;
1975 European Indoor – 2nd; 1975 European
Cup – 1st; 1976 European Indoor – 1st; 1976
Olympics – 6th; 1977 European Indoor – 2nd;
1978 European Indoor – 3rd; 1978
Commonwealth – 1st.

KEN CARTER
Southend AC. *Born* 7.3.1947. *Best performances:*
10,000m walk – 46:21.0, 20km walk – 1:33:57.

IAN CHIPCHASE
North Shields Poly. *Born* Hebburn, 26.2.1952;
Height: 1.76m (5' 9½"), *Weight:* 101kg (224lb);
Teacher. *Best performance:* Hammer – 71.00m
(232' 11"). *Championships:* 1970 European
Junior – 8th; 1974 Commonwealth – 1st; 1978
Commonwealth – 6th.

THERESA CHIPP
Lincoln City and Colleges AC. *Born* Boscombe
(Hants), 17.11.1959; *Height:* 1.62m (5' 4"),
Weight: 52kg (116lb); Student. *Best performance:*
100m hurdles – 14.23 (and 14.01w).

JILL CLARKE
Sheffield AC. *Born* 20.6.1958; *Height:* 1.67m (5'
6"). *Best performance:* 3000m – 9:20.3.

WENDY CLARKE
Highgate H. *Born* London, 17.12.1957; *Height:*
1.60m (5' 3"), *Weight:* 52kg (115lb); Clerk. *Best
performances:* 100m – 11.54 (and 11.38w), 200m
– 23.48. *Championships:* 1975 European Junior –
3rd 100m, 2nd 200m; 1978 Commonwealth –
8th 100m.

DENNIS COATES
Gateshead H. *Born* Sunderland, 11.2.1953;
Height: 1.75m (5' 9"), *Weight:* 66kg (147lb); Air
conditioning engineer. *Best performances:* 1500m
– 3:45.5, Mile – 4:00.7, 3000m – 7:45.3, 5000m
– 13:53.5, 3000m steeplechase – 8:19.0 (UK
record). *Championships:* 1978 Commonwealth –
6th 3000m steeplechase.

KEN COCKS
West Cornwall AC. *Born* Truro, 23.5.1951;

Height: 1.67m (5' 6"), *Weight:* 66kg (145lb); Floor coverings manager. *Best performance:* Long jump – 7.75m (25' 5¼").

SEBASTIAN COE
Loughborough Univ and Hallamshire H. *Born* London, 29.9.1956; *Height:* 1.76m (5' 9½"), *Weight:* 56kg (123lb); Student. *Best performances:* 400m – 47.7, 800m – 1:44.0 (UK record), 1500m – 3:42.7, Mile – 3:57.7, 3000m – 8:14.8. *Championships:* 1975 European Junior – 3rd 1500m; 1977 European Indoor – 1st 800m; 1978 European – 3rd 800m.

GLEN COHEN
Wolverhampton and Bilston AC. *Born* St Catherine (Jamaica), 22.4.1954; *Height:* 1.85m (6' 1"), *Weight:* 76kg (168lb); Student. *Best performances:* 200m – 20.90, 400m – 45.49. *Championships:* 1973 European Junior – 4th 400m, 3rd 4 × 400m; 1974 European – 1st 4 × 400m; 1975 European Cup – 1st 4 × 400m; 1978 Commonwealth – 5th 400m.

JANE COLEBROOK
Cannock AC. *Born* Caistor (Lincs), 8.11.1957; *Height:* 1.65m (5' 5"), *Weight:* 52kg (115lb); Laboratory assistant. *Best performances:* 100m – 12.0, 200m – 24.6, 400m – 53.6, 800m – 2:00.6, 1500m – 4:17.6, 400m hurdles – 59.2. *Championships:* 1977 European Indoor – 1st 800m (equalled world indoor record of 2:01.1); 1978 Commonwealth – 3rd 800m.

SHARON COLYEAR
Stretford AC. *Born* Manchester, 22.4.1955; *Height:* 1.70m (5' 7"), *Weight:* 59kg (130lb); Bank clerk. *Best performances:* 100m – 11.35, 200m – 23.40, 400m – 55.4, 100m hurdles – 13.11, 400m hurdles – 62.4, Long jump – 6.44m (21' 1½"). *Championships:* 1978 Commonwealth – 3rd 100m hurdles, 1st 4 × 100m; 1978 European – 2nd 4 × 100m.

KEITH CONNOR
Wolverhampton and Bilston AC. *Born* Anguilla (West Indies), 16.9.1957; *Height:* 1.85m (6' 1"), *Weight:* 74kg (163lb); Electrician. *Best performance:* Triple jump – 16.76m (55' 0") (UK record) and 17.21m (56' 5¾")w. *Championships:* 1978 European Indoor – 2nd; 1978 Commonwealth – 1st; 1978 European – 6th.

GARRY COOK
Wolverhampton and Bilston AC. *Born* Wednesbury, 10.1.1958; *Height:* 1.83m (6' 0"), *Weight:* 70kg (154lb); Student. *Best performances:* 400m – 47.6, 800m – 1:45.8. *Championships:* 1977 European Junior – 4th

800m; 1978 Commonwealth – 5th 800m.

PHILIP COOKE
City of Hull AC. *Born* Ferriby (near Hull), 26.11.1960; *Height:* 1.82m (5' 11½"), *Weight:* 66kg (147lb). *Best performance:* 200m – 21.30.

MARGARET COOMBER (née MacSherry)
Cambridge H. *Born* Dartford, 13.5.1950; *Height:* 1.71m (5' 7½"), *Weight:* 57kg (127lb); Copy typist. *Best performances:* 400m – 55.3, 800m – 2:02.0, 1500m – 4:18.2. *Championships:* 1970 Commonwealth – 7th 1500m.

MIKE CORDEN
Sheffield AC. *Born* Sheffield, 15.4.1948; *Height:* 1.88m (6' 2"), *Weight:* 86kg (189lb); Teacher. *Best performance:* Decathlon – 7750.

DAVID COTTON
Holloway Polytechnic. *Born* Birmingham, 16.9.1956; *Height:* 1.79m (5' 10½"), *Weight:* 74kg (164lb); Estimator. *Best performances:* 3000m walk – 12:38.0, 20km walk – 1:33:32, 50km walk – 4:14:25.

STEVE CRAM
Jarrow and Hebburn AC. *Born* Gateshead, 14.10.1960; *Height:* 1.83m (6' 0"), *Weight:* 65kg (143lb); Schoolboy. *Best performances:* 800m – 1:53.5, 1500m – 3:42.7, Mile – 3:57.4, 3000m – 8:05.8.

ANGELA CREAMER
Rotherham H. *Born* Rotherham, 30.1.1956; *Height:* 1.62m (5' 4"), *Weight:* 53kg (118lb); Local government officer. *Best performances:* 400m – 55.2, 800m – 2:03.5.

ALAN DAINTON
Harlow AC. *Born* Harlow, 6.1.1956; *Height:* 1.87m (6' 1½"), *Weight:* 78kg (172lb); Student. *Best performance:* High jump – 2.14m (7' 0¼").

GILLIAN DAINTY
Birchfield H. *Born* Birmingham, 24.11.1958; *Height:* 1.60m (5' 3"), *Weight:* 48kg (106lb); Bank clerk. *Best performance:* 1500m – 4:16.3.

BOB DALE
City of Stoke AC. *Born* Macclesfield, 24.6.1948; *Height:* 1.98m (6' 6"), *Weight:* 120kg (266lb); Housing assistant. *Best performance:* Shot – 18.94m (62' 1¾"). *Championships:* 1978 Commonwealth – 6th.

JOHN DAVIES
Thames Valley H. *Born* Rhondda Valley (South Wales), 20.11.1952; *Height:* 1.68m (5' 6"), *Weight:* 55kg (122lb); Teacher. *Best*

performances: 1500m – 3:45.3, Mile – 4:02.6,
3000m – 7:54.0, 5000m – 13:39.8, 3000m
steeplechase – 8:22.6. *Championships:* 1974
Commonwealth – 2nd 3000m steeplechase.

ROY DICKENS

Herne Hill H. *Born* 30.3.1958; *Height:* 1.80m
(5′ 11″), *Weight:* 66kg (147lb). *Best performance:*
400m – 47.88.

PAUL DICKENSON

Borough of Enfield H. *Born* North Shields,
4.12.1949; *Height:* 1.83m (6′ 0″), *Weight:* 104kg
(229lb); Teacher. *Best performances:* Discus –
50.66m (166′ 2″), Hammer – 73.20m (240′ 2″).
Championships: 1978 Commonwealth – 4th
hammer.

BOB DOBSON

Ilford AC. *Born* London, 4.11.1942; *Height:*
1.80m (5′ 11″), *Weight:* 68kg (150lb);
Government service. *Best performances:* 3000m
walk – 12:40.4, 20km walk – 1:30:02, 50km
walk – 4:08:39 (UK best). *Championships:* 1970
Commonwealth – 4th 20M walk.

LIZ EDDY

Birchfield H. *Born* Birmingham, 24.6.1957;
Height: 1.67m (5′ 6″), *Weight:* 62kg (137lb);
Student. *Best performances:* 200m – 23.8, 400m –
53.88.

VERONA ELDER (née Bernard)

Wolverhampton and Bilston AC. *Born*
Wolverhampton, 5.4.1953; *Height:* 1.67m (5′
6″), *Weight:* 60kg (133lb); Laboratory
technician. *Best performances:* 100m – 11.7,
200m – 23.29, 400m – 51.4, 800m – 2:04.3i.
Championships: 1973 European Indoor – 1st
400m; 1974 Commonwealth – 2nd 400m, 1st 4
× 400m; 1974 European – 7th 400m; 1975
European Indoor – 1st 400m; 1977 European
Indoor – 2nd 400m; 1978 Commonwealth –
2nd 400m, 1st 4 × 400m; 1978 European – 8th
400m.

DIANA ELLIOTT

Leicester Coritanian AC. *Born* Catworth
(Hunts), 7.5.1961; *Height:* 1.72m (5′ 7¾″),
Weight: 57kg (126lb); Office junior. *Best
performance:* High jump – 1.82m (5′ 11½″).

STEVE EMSON

Tipton H. *Born* West Bromwich, 5.11.1956;
Height: 1.75m (5′ 9″), *Weight:* 57kg (127lb);
Student. *Best performances:* 1500m – 3:43.7,
3000m – 8:01.6i.

ROS FEW

Mitcham AC. *Born* Andover, 20.1.1955;

Height: 1.72m (5′ 8″), *Weight:* 57kg (126lb);
Bank clerk. *Best performance:* High jump –
1.83m (6′ 0″).

OLLY FLYNN

Basildon AC. *Born* Ipswich, 30.6.1950; *Height:*
1.90m (6′ 3″), *Weight:* 77kg (170lb); Insurance
broker. *Best performance:* 20km walk – 1:27:35.
Championships: 1978 Commonwealth – 1st
30km walk.

ANN FORD (née Yeoman)

Borough of Hounslow AC. *Born* Isleworth
(Middx), 30.3.1952; *Height:* 1.66m (5′ 5½″),
Weight: 49kg (108lb); Technical clerk. *Best
performances:* 800m – 2:10.6, 1500m – 4:15.3,
3000m – 8:52.8. *Championships:* 1974 European
– 7th 3000m; 1978 Commonwealth – 3rd
3000m.

BERNIE FORD

Aldershot Farnham and District AC. *Born*
Woking, 3.8.1952; *Height:* 1.78m (5′ 10″),
Weight: 61kg (134lb); Civil servant. *Best
performances:* 1500m – 3:46.6, 5000m – 13:26.0,
10,000m – 27:43.7. *Championships:* 1976
Olympics – 8th 10,000m.

BRENDAN FOSTER

Gateshead H. *Born* Hebburn, 12.1.1948;
Height: 1.80m (5′ 11″), *Weight:* 66kg (145lb);
Local government officer. *Best performances:*
800m – 1:51.1, 1500m – 3:37.6, Mile – 3:55.9,
3000m – 7:35.2 (UK record), 2 Miles – 8:13.7,
5000m – 13:14.6 (UK record), 10,000m –
27:30.3 (European record). *Championships:*
1970 Commonwealth – 3rd 1500m; 1971
European – 3rd 1500m; 1972 Olympics – 5th
1500m; 1973 European Cup – 1st 5000m; 1974
Commonwealth – 7th 1500m, 2nd 5000m;
1974 European – 1st 5000m; 1975 European
Cup – 1st 5000m; 1976 Olympics – 5th 5000m,
3rd 10,000m; 1978 Commonwealth – 3rd
5000m, 1st 10,000m; 1978 European – 4th
10,000m.

MARTIN FRANCIS

Stretford AC. *Born* Salford, 11.1.1958; *Height:*
1.85m (6′ 1″), *Weight:* 73kg (161lb); Student.
Best performance: 400m – 48.16. *Championships:*
1977 European Junior – 3rd 4 × 400m.

MIKE FROMANT

Mitcham AC. *Born* Tooting (London),
26.4.1952; *Height:* 1.78m (5′ 10″), *Weight:* 71kg
(156lb); Bank clerk. *Best performances:* 800m –
1:49.7, 1500m – 3:43.7.

PAULA FUDGE (née Yeoman)

Borough of Hounslow AC. *Born* Isleworth

Right: Twins Ann Ford (2) and Paula Fudge (4).

Tony Duffy

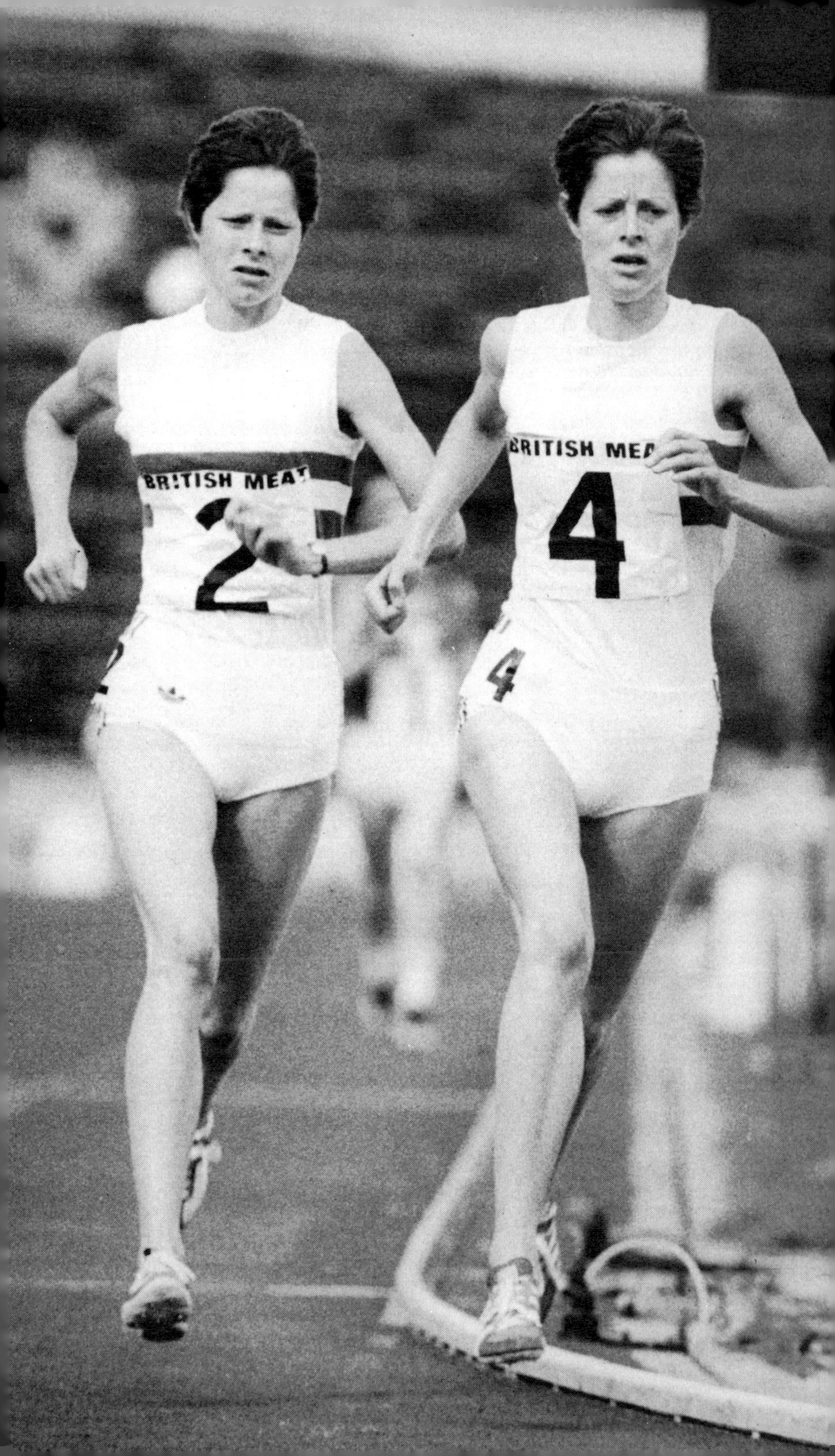
BRITISH MEAT
2
BRITISH MEA
4

(Middx), 30.3.1952; *Height:* 1.68m (5' 6"), *Weight:* 54kg (120lb); Clerk typist. *Best performances:* 800m – 2:08.7, 1500m – 4:17.5, 3000m – 8:48.7 (UK record). *Championships:* 1978 Commonwealth – 1st 3000m; 1978 European – 8th 3000m.

BRENDA GIBBS
Leicester Coritanian AC. *Born* Normanton-le-Heath, 19.7.1957; *Height:* 1.73m (5' 8¼"), *Weight:* 54kg (119lb); Medical secretary. *Best performance:* High jump – 1.85m (6' 0¾").

IAN GILMOUR
Wolverhampton and Bilston AC. *Born* Salisbury, 27.1.1952; *Height:* 1.78m (5' 10"), *Weight:* 59kg (130lb); Chemist. *Best performance:* 3000m steeplechase – 8:31.1. *Championships:* 1978 Commonwealth – 8th.

JULIAN GOATER
Shaftesbury H. *Born* Southampton, 12.1.1953; *Height:* 1.83m (6' 0"), *Weight:* 68kg (150lb); RAF officer. *Best performances:* 1500m – 3:43.5, 5000m – 13:27.1, 10,000m – 27:55.2.

BEVERLEY GODDARD
Reading AC. *Born* Barbados, 28.8.1956; *Height:* 1.70m (5' 7"), *Weight:* 55kg (121lb); Secretary. *Best performances:* 100m – 11.49 (and 11.30w), 200m – 23.11 (and 22.95w), 400m – 53.08, Long jump – 5.82m (19' 1¼")w. *Championships:* 1978 Commonwealth – 5th 100m, 4th 200m, 1st 4 × 100m; 1978 European – 2nd 4 × 100m.

HELEN GOLDEN
Edinburgh Southern H. *Born* Edinburgh, 16.5.1953; *Height:* 1.65m (5' 5"), *Weight:* 52kg (115lb); Clerk. *Best performances:* 100m – 11.40, 200m – 23.14 (and 22.97w), 400m – 54.3. *Championships:* 1970 Commonwealth – 5th 100m, 4th 200m; 1970 European Junior – 3rd 100m, 1st 200m; 1974 European – 5th 200m; 1978 Commonwealth – 6th 200m.

JOHN GOODACRE
Notts AC. *Born* Nottingham, 31.3.1955; *Height:* 1.80m (5' 11"), *Weight:* 74kg (163lb); Student. *Best performance:* 800m – 1:48.4.

PETER GORDON
Metropolitan Police AC. *Born* 2.7.1951. *Best performances:* Discus – 57.02m (187' 1"), Hammer – 62.84m (206' 2").

STEVE GOWER
Ilford AC. *Born* 7.10.1950. *Best performance:* 20km walk – 1:30:27.

GLEN GRANT
Cambridge H. *Born* Farnborough (Kent), 16.7.1953; *Height:* 1.79m (5' 10½"), *Weight:* 60kg (133lb); Army officer. *Best performances:* 800m – 1:48.0, 1500m – 3:38.1, Mile – 3:59.2, 5000m – 13:55.9. *Championships:* 1978 Commonwealth – 8th 800m, 6th 1500m.

STEVE GREEN
Thames Valley H. *Born* London, 13.10.1955; *Height:* 1.78m (5' 10"), *Weight:* 70kg (154lb). *Best performances:* 100m – 10.49 (and 10.40w), 200m – 21.05.

JEFF GRIFFITHS
Swansea H. *Born* Port Talbot, 20.3.1957; *Height:* 1.78m (5' 10"), *Weight:* 75kg (165lb); Clerk. *Best performances:* 200m – 21.4, 400m – 46.74.

PETER GRIFFITHS
Tipton H. *Born* London, 1.9.1948; *Height:* 1.86m (6' 1½"), *Weight:* 76kg (169lb); Social worker. *Best performances:* 5000m – 13:52.8, 3000m steeplechase – 8:30.6.

JEFF GUTTERIDGE
Windsor, Slough and Eton AC. *Born* Slough, 28.10.1956; *Height:* 1.83m (6' 0"), *Weight:* 76kg (168lb); Sales representative. *Best performance:* Pole vault – 5.20m (17' 0¾"). *Championships:* 1978 Commonwealth – 4th.

TONY HADLEY
Birchfield H. *Born* Birmingham, 23.5.1953; *Height:* 1.75m (5' 9"), *Weight:* 71kg (158lb); Teacher. *Best performances:* 100m – 10.6, 200m – 21.5.

CARL HAMILTON
Sale H. *Born* 20.11.1956; *Height:* 1.80m (5' 11"), *Weight:* 72kg (159lb); Travel agent. *Best performance:* 400m – 47.05.

CHERRY HANSON
Derby Ladies AC. *Born* Derby, 13.11.1956; *Height:* 1.70m (5' 7"), *Weight:* 57kg (126lb); Student. *Best performances:* 800m – 2:05.5, 1500m – 4:11.6.

ANN HARLEY (née Robertson)
Central Region AC. *Born* Falkirk, 2.12.1957; *Height:* 1.72m (5' 8"), *Weight:* 58kg (128lb); Bank officer. *Best performance:* 400m – 54.0.

BILL HARTLEY
Liverpool H and AC. *Born* Liverpool, 27.6.1950; *Height:* 1.88m (6' 2"), *Weight:* 81kg (180lb); Horticulturist. *Best performances:* 200m – 21.6, 400m – 47.1, 400m hurdles – 49.65.

Championships: 1974 Commonwealth – 6th 400m hurdles, 2nd 4 × 400m; 1974 European – 1st 4 × 400m; 1975 European Cup – 1st 4 × 400m.

DONNA HARTLEY (née Murray)
Stretford AC. *Born* Southampton, 1.5.1955; *Height:* 1.70m (5' 7"), *Weight:* 55kg (122lb); Bank clerk. *Best performances:* 100m – 11.46, 200m – 22.75 (UK record), 400m – 51.28 (UK record), 800m – 2:07.8. *Championships:* 1977 European Cup – 3rd 400m; 1977 World Cup – 2nd 4 × 400m; 1978 Commonwealth – 1st 400m, 1st 4 × 400m; 1978 European – 6th 400m.

CHRIS HARVEY
Lancashire WC. *Born* 14.10.1956. *Best performance:* 20km walk – 1:32:45.

LINDA HAYSMAN
London Olympiades. *Born* Hammersmith (London), 11.3.1958; *Height:* 1.71m (5' 7½"), *Weight:* 59kg (131lb); Art student. *Best performance:* High jump – 1.79m (5' 10½").

SUSAN HEARNSHAW
Hull Spartan AC. *Born* Liversedge (Yorks), 26.5.1961; *Height:* 1.78m (5' 10"), *Weight:* 63kg (140lb); Schoolgirl. *Best performance:* Long jump – 6.40m (21' 0") and 6.59m (21' 7½")w. *Championships:* 1978 Commonwealth – 4th.

DIANE HEATH
Stretford AC. *Born* Cheshire, 29.4.1956; *Height:* 1.62m (5' 4"), *Weight:* 52kg (116lb); Clerical officer. *Best performance:* 400m hurdles – 59.64.

TONY HENRY
Shaftesbury H. *Born* London, 14.6.1957; *Height:* 1.83m (6' 0"), *Weight:* 76kg (168lb); Mechanical engineer. *Best performances:* 200m – 21.52, Long jump – 7.66m (25' 1¾").

GILLIAN HITCHEN
Wigan AC. *Born* Wigan, 9.4.1959; *Height:* 1.78m (5' 10"), *Weight:* 64kg (142lb); Student. *Best performance:* High jump – 1.85m (6' 0¾"). *Championships:* 1978 Commonwealth – 4th.

PETER HOFFMANN
Edinburgh AC. *Born* Edinburgh, 1.7.1956; *Height:* 1.78m (5' 10"), *Weight:* 67kg (148lb); Student. *Best performances:* 100m – 10.8, 200m – 21.81, 400m – 46.76, 800m – 1:46.6, 400m hurdles – 54.2. *Championships:* 1975 European Junior – 2nd 400m.

HILARY HOLLICK (née Tanner)
Sale H. *Born* Sidcup (Kent), 10.8.1951; *Height:* 1.60m (5' 3"), *Weight:* 48kg (106lb); Teacher. *Best performances:* 800m – 2:04.7, 1500m – 4:12.7. *Championships:* 1978 Commonwealth – 5th 1500m.

MARK HOLTOM
City of Stoke AC. *Born* Burton, 6.2.1958; *Height:* 1.88m (6' 2"), *Weight:* 82kg (182lb); Student. *Best performances:* 200m – 21.8, 110m hurdles – 14.01. *Championships:* 1977 European Junior – 2nd 110m hurdles.

BRIAN HOOPER
Woking AC. *Born* Woking, 18.5.1953; *Height:* 1.74m (5' 8½"), *Weight:* 72kg (160lb); Teacher. *Best performance:* Pole vault – 5.42m (17' 9¼") (UK record). *Championships:* 1974 Commonwealth – 3rd; 1978 Commonwealth – 3rd; 1978 European – 7th equal.

GILLIAN HOWELL
Leeds University AC and City of Hull AC. *Born* 16.12.1956; *Height:* 1.76m (5' 9¼"), *Weight:* 59kg (131lb); Student. *Best performances:* High jump – 1.79m (5' 10½"), Long jump – 6.04m (19' 9¾"), Pentathlon – 4070.

JOHN HOWELL
City of Stoke AC. *Born* Stoke, 17.6.1955; *Height:* 1.85m (6' 1"), *Weight:* 82kg (182lb); Store employee. *Best performances:* Discus – 50.98m (167' 3"), Decathlon – 7239.

RUTH HOWELL (née Martin-Jones)
Birchfield H. *Born* Criccieth (Wales), 28.1.1947; *Height:* 1.75m (5' 9"), *Weight:* 63kg (140lb); Office manager. *Best performances:* Long jump – 6.51m (21' 4¼") and 6.54m (21' 5½")w, Pentathlon – 4022. *Championships:* 1970 Commonwealth – 6th pentathlon; 1974 Commonwealth – 3rd long jump; 1978 Commonwealth – 7th long jump, 6th pentathlon.

JOSLYN HOYTE
Dorothy Hyman TC. *Born* Barbados, 16.12.1954; *Height:* 1.62m (5' 4"), *Weight:* 52kg (114lb); Cashier. *Best performances:* 200m – 23.61 (and 23.45w), 400m – 52.15. *Championships:* 1978 Commonwealth – 4th 400m, 1st 4 × 400m.

LES HOYTE
Thames Valley H. *Born* Trinidad, 4.2.1956; *Height:* 1.80m (5' 11"), *Weight:* 65kg (144lb); Bank clerk. *Best performances:* 100m – 10.60 (and 10.54w), 200m – 21.17, 400m – 48.7, Long jump – 7.23m (23' 8¾")w and 7.18m (23' 6¾").

Sue Hearnshaw.

George Herringshaw

TREVOR HOYTE
Thames Valley H. *Born* Trinidad, 5.1.1957;
Height: 1.83m (6' 0"), *Weight:* 82kg (182lb);
Trainee plasterer. *Best performances:* 100m –
10.70 (and 10.58w), 200m – 21.15 (20.90w).
Championships: 1978 Commonwealth – 7th
200m.

HEATHER HUNTE
Haringey AC. *Born* Hackney (London),
14.8.1959; *Height:* 1.65m (5' 5"), *Weight:* 58kg
(129lb); Clerk. *Best performances:* 100m – 11.58
(and 11.3), 200m – 24.04. *Championships:* 1977
European Junior – 4th 100m, 3rd 4 × 100m.

TIM HUTCHINGS
Crawley AC. *Born* Highgate (London),
4.12.1958; *Height:* 1.83m (6' 0"), *Weight:* 72kg
(159lb); Technical librarian. *Best performances:*
1500m – 3:40.6, mile – 3:57.8, 3000m – 7:57.7.

ALLISTER HUTTON
Edinburgh Southern H. *Born* Edinburgh,
18.7.1954; *Height:* 1.67m (5' 6"), *Weight:* 53kg
(117lb); Laboratory technician. *Best
performances:* 5000m – 13:41.6, 10,000m –
28:13.1. *Championships:* 1978 Commonwealth –
8th 10,000m.

NEIL JACKSON
Wolverhampton and Bilston AC. *Born* Leicester, 13.8.1960; *Height:* 1.78m (5' 10"), *Weight:* 66kg (146lb); Student. *Best performance:* 400m – 47.6.

DAVID JENKINS
Gateshead H. *Born* Point a Pierre (Trinidad), 25.5.1952; *Height:* 1.90m (6' 3"), *Weight:* 82kg (182lb); Marketing consultant. *Best performances:* 100m – 10.1, 200m – 20.3 and 20.66, 400m – 44.93 (UK record), 800m – 1:53.5, 400m hurdles – 53.0. *Championships:* 1971 European – 1st 400m; 1972 Olympics – 2nd 4 × 400m; 1974 Commonwealth – 4th 400m; 1974 European – 2nd 400m, 1st 4 × 400m; 1975 European Cup – 1st 400m, 1st 4 × 400m; 1976 Olympics – 7th 400m; 1977 World Cup – 2nd 4 × 400m; 1978 Commonwealth – 1st 4 × 100m.

ROGER JENKINS
Racing Club de France. *Born* Liverpool, 30.9.1955; *Height:* 1.89m (6' 2¼"), *Weight:* 76kg (168lb); Teacher. *Best performances:* 100m – 10.5, 200m – 21.3, 400m – 46.49, 400m hurdles – 51.88. *Championships:* 1973 European Junior – 5th 400m, 3rd 4 × 400m.

DAVE JOHNSON
Hallamshire H. *Born* Skirlaugh (Yorks), 18.5.1953; *Height:* 1.88m (6' 2"), *Weight:* 79kg (175lb); Newsagent. *Best performances:* Long jump – 7.34m (24' 1"), Triple jump – 16.33m (53' 7")w and 16.29m (53' 5¼")i. *Championships:* 1978 Commonwealth – 8th triple jump.

RUTH KENNEDY
Notts AC. *Born* Nottingham, 13.1.1957; *Height:* 1.67m (5' 6"), *Weight:* 59kg (131lb); Student. *Best performances:* 200m – 23.7, 400m – 52.9, 800m – 2:09.3. *Championships:* 1973 European Junior – 2nd 4 × 400m; 1974 Commonwealth – 1st 4 × 400m; 1975 European Junior – 3rd 4 × 400m; 1978 Commonwealth – 1st 4 × 400m.

LESLEY KIERNAN
Havering AC. *Born* London, 9.8.1957; *Height:* 1.65m (5' 5"), *Weight:* 52kg (114lb); Receptionist. *Best performances:* 400m – 53.9, 800m – 2:01.5, 1500m – 4:24.8. *Championships:* 1973 European Junior – 2nd 800m.

BILLIE KIRKPATRICK
Ballymena AC. *Born* Ballymena (N. Ireland), 29.1.1949; *Height:* 1.85m (6' 1"), *Weight:* 76kg (168lb); Teacher. *Best performance:* Long jump – 7.71m (25' 3½").

DANNY LAING
South London H. *Born* Jamaica, 1.4.1949; *Height:* 1.74m (5' 8½"), *Weight:* 70kg (154lb); Electrician. *Best performances:* 100m – 10.79, 200m – 21.27, 400m – 46.39.

VERONICA LANGLEY
Sheffield AC. *Born* 23.12.1958; *Height:* 1.67m (5' 6"). *Best performances:* 400m hurdles – 59.53 High jump – 1.76m (5' 9¼"), Pentathlon – 3936.

SONIA LANNAMAN
Wolverhampton and Bilston AC. *Born* Birmingham, 24.3.1956; *Height:* 1.62m (5' 4"), *Weight:* 57kg (126lb); Receptionist. *Best performances:* 100m – 11.22 (and 10.93w), 200m – 22.81 (and 22.69w). *Championships:* 1973 European Junior – 1st 100m, 3rd 4 × 100m; 1974 Commonwealth – 2nd 4 × 100m; 1976 European Indoor – 2nd 60m; 1977 European Cup – 2nd 100m, 2nd 200m; 1977 World Cup – 2nd 100m, 1st 4 × 100m; 1978 Commonwealth – 1st 100m, 2nd 200m, 1st 4 × 100m; 1978 European – 8th 100m, 2nd 4 × 100m.

JANET LAWRENCE
Pilkington H and AC. *Born* St Helens, 9.12.1958; *Height:* 1.65m (5' 5"), *Weight:* 54kg (119lb); Bank clerk. *Best performances:* 800m – 2:04.6, 1500m – 4:14.4.

PHIL LEWIS
Haringey AC. *Born* London, 31.1.1951; *Height:* 1.89m (6' 2¼"), *Weight:* 93kg (205lb); Physical training instructor (Royal Marines). *Best performance:* Decathlon – 7104.

SHAUN LIGHTMAN
Metropolitan WC. *Born* Hounslow (Middx), 15.4.1943; *Height:* 1.71m (5' 7¼"), *Weight:* 70kg (154lb); Teacher. *Best performances:* 10,000m walk – 44:17.0, 20km walk – 1:31:10, 50km walk – 4:15:13. *Championships:* 1970 Commonwealth – 7th 20 miles walk.

PETER LITTLE
Edinburgh AC. *Born* Edinburgh, 2.12.1960; *Height:* 1.80m (5' 11"), *Weight:* 70kg (154lb); British Airways apprentice. *Best performances:* 100m – 10.72, 200m – 21.24, 400m – 49.9, Long jump – 7.12m (23' 4½"). *Championships:* 1977 European Junior – 4th 200m.

ANGELA LITTLEWOOD
Cambridge H. *Born* Nottingham, 24.9.1949; *Height:* 1.72m (5' 8"), *Weight:* 76kg (169lb); Teacher. *Best performances:* Shot – 16.34m (53' 7½"), Discus – 48.24m (158' 3"). *Championships:* 1978 Commonwealth – 4th shot.

JUDY LIVERMORE
Rugby AC. *Born* 14.11.1960; *Height:* 1.79m (5'
10½"), *Weight:* 70kg (154lb). *Best performances:*
100m hurdles – 13.99, High jump – 1.80m (5'
10¾"), Pentathlon – 4028.

TREVOR LLEWELYN
Blackheath H. *Born* 27.4.1961; *Height:* 1.85m
(6' 1"), *Weight:* 73kg (161lb). *Best performance:*
High jump – 2.15m (7' 0½").

PAULA LLOYD
Wolverhampton and Bilston AC. *Born*
Haverfordwest (Wales), 12.9.1954; *Height:*
1.70m (5' 7"), *Weight:* 53kg (118lb); Student.
Best performances: 400m – 53.98, 800m – 2:08.8.

ANDREA LYNCH
Mitcham AC. *Born* Barbados, 24.11.1952;
Height: 1.57m (5' 2"), *Weight:* 52kg (114lb);
Student. *Best performances:* 100m – 10.9 and
11.16 (UK record), 200m – 23.15 (and
22.90w). *Championships:* 1970 European Junior
– 2nd 100m; 1974 Commonwealth – 2nd 100m,
2nd 4 × 100m; 1974 European Indoor – 2nd
60m; 1974 European – 3rd 100m; 1975
European Indoor – 1st 60m; 1976 Olympics –
7th 100m; 1977 World Cup – 1st 4 × 100m.

GLADYS McCORMACK (née Taylor)
Essex Ladies AC. *Born* Jamaica, 5.3.1953;
Height: 1.75m (5' 9"), *Weight:* 63kg (140lb);
Secretary. *Best performances:* 100m – 11.6, 200m
– 23.69, 400m – 52.5, High jump – 1.69m (5'
6½"), Long jump – 5.95m (19' 6¼").

MIKE McFARLANE
Haringey AC. *Born* 2.5.1960; *Height:* 1.78m (5'
10"), *Weight:* 70kg (154lb). *Best performances:*
100m – 10.32 (and 10.29w), 200m – 20.97.
Championships: 1978 Commonwealth – 5th
100m.

JANINE MacGREGOR
Burn Road H. *Born* Hartlepool, 6.1.1960;
Height: 1.67m (5' 6"), *Weight:* 60kg (133lb);
Student. *Best performances:* 100m – 11.91 (and
11.74w), 200m – 23.76 (and 23.54w).
Championships: 1977 European Junior – 7th
200m, 3rd 4 × 100m.

MIKE McLEOD
Elswick H. *Born* Dilston (Northumberland),
15.1.1952; *Height:* 1.80m (5' 11"), *Weight:* 62kg
(138lb); Sports goods salesman. *Best
performances:* 800m – 1:50.8, mile – 3:59.4,
3000m – 7:48.2, 5000m – 13:25.2, 10,000m –
28:04.2. *Championships:* 1978 Commonwealth –
3rd 10,000m, 4th 5000m.

Left: *Mike McFarlane.*

CHRISTINE McMEEKIN
Glasgow AC. *Born* Glasgow, 1.2.1956; *Height:*
1.62m (5' 4"), *Weight:* 48kg (107lb); Student.
Best performances: 800m – 2:01.2, 1500 – 4:12.4.
Championships: 1978 Commonwealth – 4th
800m.

BRAD McSTRAVICK
Sheffield AC. *Born* Plymouth, 25.5.1956;
Height: 1.83m (6' 0"), *Weight:* 79kg (175lb);
Student. *Best performance:* Decathlon – 7165.

CHRIS MADDOCKS
Dawlish WC. *Born* 28.3.1957. *Best performances:*
20km walk – 1:36:03, 50km walk – 4:21:06.

LESLEY MALLIN
Torbay AC. *Born* Totnes, 12.4.1956; *Height:*
1.72m (5' 8"), *Weight:* 75kg (165lb); Teacher.
Best performance: Discus – 51.04m (167' 5").
Championships: 1978 Commonwealth – 6th.

ALLISON MANLEY
Croydon H. *Born* Croydon, 16.6.1957; *Height:*
1.67m (5' 6"), *Weight:* 62kg (140lb); Student
teacher. *Best performances:* High jump – 1.78m
(5' 10")i, Long jump – 6.11m (20' 0½"),
Pentathlon – 3826.

SUE MAPSTONE
Harlow AC. *Born* London, 16.12.1956; *Height:*
1.69m (5' 6¾"), *Weight:* 60kg (133lb); Student.
Best performances: 100m hurdles – 14.01, High
jump – 1.75m (5' 8¾"), Long jump – 6.12m (20'
1") and 6.15m (20' 2¼")w, Pentathlon – 4222.
Championships: 1973 European Junior – 2nd
pentathlon; 1974 Commonwealth – 7th; 1978
Commonwealth – 2nd.

ROGER MILLS
Ilford AC. *Born* Romford, 11.2.1948; *Height:*
1.82m (5' 11½"), *Weight:* 74kg (164lb). *Best
performances:* Mile walk – 6:01.8 (UK best),
3000m walk – 11:59.1, 20km walk – 1:28:50,
50km walk – 4:35:12. *Championships:* 1974
European – 3rd 20km walk.

ROY MITCHELL
Enfield H. *Born* Jamaica, 1.1.1955; *Height:*
1.90m (6' 3"), *Weight:* 85kg (187lb);
Electrician. *Best performances:* 100m – 10.6w,
High jump – 2.02m (6' 7½"), Long jump –
8.04m (26' 4½") and 8.16m (26' 9¼")w,
Decathlon – 7088. *Championships:* 1977
European Cup – 3rd long jump; 1978
Commonwealth – 1st; 1978 European – 7th.

DAVE MOORCROFT
Coventry Godiva H. *Born* Coventry, 10.4.1953;
Height: 1.80m (5' 11"), *Weight:* 68kg (150lb);

Mark Shearman

Teacher. *Best performances:* 800m – 1:49.0, 1500m – 3:35.5, Mile – 3:55.3, 3000m – 7:43.5, 5000m – 13:58.4. *Championships:* 1976 Olympics – 7th 1500m; 1978 Commonwealth – 1st; 1978 European – 3rd.

ASTON MOORE

Birchfield H. *Born* Jamaica, 8.2.1956; *Height:* 1.80m (5′ 11″), *Weight:* 81kg (178lb); Sheet metal worker. *Best performances:* Long jump – 7.76m (25′ 5½″)w, Triple jump – 16.69m (54′ 9¼″) and 16.76m (55′ 0″)w. *Championships:* 1975 European Junior – 1st triple jump; 1978 Commonwealth – 3rd; 1978 European – 8th.

MICKY MORRIS

Cwmbran Olympiades. *Born* Pontypool, 11.12.1956; *Height:* 1.78m (5′ 10″), *Weight:* 63kg (140lb); Student. *Best performance:* 3000m steeplechase – 8:35.5. *Championships:* 1975 European Junior – 1st 2000m steeplechase.

CECIL MOVEN

Wolverhampton and Bilston AC. *Born* Nevis (West Indies), 8.11.1956; *Height:* 1.67m (5′ 6″), *Weight:* 68kg (150lb); Apprentice tool maker. *Best performances:* 100m – 10.72 (and 10.68w), 200m – 21.63.

VAL MULLIN

Liverpool H and AC. *Born* Liverpool, 29.9.1957; *Height:* 1.74m (5′ 8½″), *Weight:* 60kg (133lb); Bank clerk. *Best performance:* Pentathlon – 4013.

MARK NAYLOR

Hillingdon AC. *Born* York, 10.9.1957; *Height:* 1.85m (6′ 1″), *Weight:* 74kg (163lb); Customer services assistant. *Best performance:* High jump – 2.19m (7′ 2¼″)i. *Championships:* 1978 Commonwealth – 6th.

PAULA NEWNHAM

Oxford City AC. *Born* Wolverhampton, 2.2.1959; *Height:* 1.71m (5′ 7¼″), *Weight:* 59kg (130lb); Student. *Best performances:* 800m – 2:03.2, 1500m – 4:16.4.

KEN NEWTON

Sheffield AC. *Born* Sheffield, 5.6.1954; *Height:* 1.80m (5′ 11″), *Weight:* 66kg (147lb). *Best performances:* 1500m – 3:45.4i, Mile – 3:59.8, 3000m – 8:01.4i, 5000m – 13:58.4.

GARY OAKES

Haringey AC. *Born* London, 21.9.1958; *Height:* 1.77m (5′ 9¾″), *Weight:* 69kg (153lb); Student. *Best performances:* 400m – 48.4, 400m hurdles – 50.96. *Championships:* 1977 European Junior – 3rd 400m hurdles; 1978 Commonwealth – 7th.

JUDITH OAKES

Croydon H. *Born* Lewisham (London), 14.2.1958; *Height:* 1.65m (5′ 5″), *Weight:* 74kg (164lb); Bank clerk. *Best performance:* Shot – 16.74m (54′ 11¼″)i (UK best). *Championships:* 1978 Commonwealth – 3rd.

COLIN O'NEILL

Bristol AC. *Born* Bristol, 14.8.1948; *Height:* 1.82m (5′ 11¾″), *Weight:* 74kg (164lb); University technician. *Best performances:* 400m – 47.28, 400m hurdles – 50.6, Long jump – 7.20m (23′ 7½″), Triple jump – 14.15m (46′ 5″). *Championships:* 1974 Commonwealth – 8th 400m hurdles.

DAVID OTTLEY

Thurrock H. *Born* Thurrock, 5.8.1955; *Height:* 1.88m (6′ 2″), *Weight:* 89kg (196lb); Teacher. *Best performance:* Javelin – 81.50m (267′ 5″). *Championships:* 1978 Commonwealth – 5th.

STEVE OVETT

Brighton and Hove AC. *Born* Brighton, 9.10.1955; *Height:* 1.83m (6′ 0″), *Weight:* 70kg (154lb). *Best performances:* 400m – 47.5, 800m – 1:44.1, 1500m – 3:34.5 (UK record), Mile – 3:52.8 (UK record), 2000m – 4:57.8 (UK record), 3000m – 7:41.3, 2 miles – 8:13.5 (world outdoor best), 5000m – 13:25.0. *Championships:* 1973 European Junior – 1st 800m; 1974 European – 2nd 800m; 1975 European Cup – 1st 800m; 1976 Olympics – 5th 800m; 1977 European Cup – 1st 1500m; 1977 World Cup – 1st 1500m; 1978 European – 2nd 800m, 1st 1500m.

ALAN PASCOE

Polytechnic H. *Born* Portsmouth, 11.10.1947; *Height:* 1.85m (6′ 1″), *Weight:* 76kg (168lb); Company director. *Best performances:* 100m – 10.6w, 200m – 20.9, 400m – 46.8, 110m hurdles – 13.7, 400m hurdles – 48.59. *Championships:* 1969 European Indoor – 1st 50m hurdles; 1969 European – 3rd 110m hurdles; 1971 European – 2nd 110m hurdles; 1972 Olympics – 2nd 4 × 400m; 1973 European Cup final – 1st 400m hurdles; 1974 Commonwealth – 1st 400m hurdles, 2nd 4 × 400m; 1974 European – 1st 400m hurdles, 1st 4 × 400m; 1975 European Cup – 1st 400m hurdles; 1976 Olympics – 8th 400m hurdles; 1977 European Cup – 3rd 400m hurdles; 1977 World Cup – 4th 400m hurdles; 1978 Commonwealth – 3rd 400m hurdles.

GLYNIS PENNY (née Goodburn)

Cambridge H. *Born* Eltham, 28.1.1951; *Height:* 1.65m (5′ 5″), *Weight:* 51kg (112lb); Dental nurse. *Best performances:* 800m – 2:08.2, 1500m – 4:12.5, 3000m – 9:06.4, marathon – 2:53:40.

KEITH PENNY
Cambridge H. *Born* 29.1.1950. *Best performances:* 3000m – 7:53.9, 5000m – 13:37.2, 10,000m – 28:37.4, marathon – 2:16:57.

BERWYN PRICE
Cardiff AAC. *Born* Tredegar (Wales), 15.8.1951; *Height:* 1.90m (6' 3"), *Weight:* 81kg (178lb); Sports centre manager. *Best performances:* 100m – 10.8, 110m hurdles – 13.69 (UK record) and 13.65w, 400m hurdles – 52.8. *Championships:* (all 110m hurdles) 1970 European Junior – 1st; 1973 World Student Games – 1st; 1974 Commonwealth – 2nd; 1974 European – 7th; 1976 European Indoor – 2nd (60m hurdles); 1978 Commonwealth – 1st.

JANET PRICTOE
Lincoln City and Colleges AC. *Born* Marlborough, 15.1.1959; *Height:* 1.75m (5' 9"), *Weight:* 54kg (119lb); Student. *Best performance:* 800m – 2:03.1.

IAN RATCLIFFE
Wolverhampton and Bilston AC. *Born* Stoke-on-Trent, 19.9.1957; *Height:* 1.80m (5' 11"), *Weight:* 73kg (161lb); Student. *Best performance:* 110m hurdles – 14.60.

VANESSA REDFORD
Cambridge H. *Born* Woolwich (London), 9.3.1954; *Height:* 1.65m (5' 5"), *Weight:* 80kg (177lb); Teacher. *Best performances:* Shot – 15.03m (49' 3¾"), Discus – 49.00m (160' 9").

SUE REED
Wigmore LAC. *Born* Bromley (Kent), 5.6.1956; *Height:* 1.64m (5' 4¼"), *Weight:* 59kg (130lb); Architectural technician. *Best performance:* 400m hurdles – 60.5.

SUE REEVE (née Scott)
Birchfield H. *Born* Birmingham, 17.9.1951; *Height:* 1.78m (5' 10"), *Weight:* 70kg (154lb); Civil servant. *Best performances:* 200m – 24.3, 100m hurdles – 13.7, Long jump – 6.84m (22' 5¼")w and 6.61m (21' 8¼"), Shot – 13.17m (43' 2½"). *Championships:* (long jump) 1969 European Indoor – 2nd; 1977 European Cup – 3rd; 1978 European Indoor – 3rd; 1978 Commonwealth – 1st; 1978 European – 6th.

GILLIAN REGAN
Cardiff AAC. *Born* Cardiff, 28.11.1956; *Height:* 1.60m (5' 3"), *Weight:* 54kg (120lb); Dietician. *Best performance:* Long jump – 6.14m (20' 1¾").

IAN RICHARDS
Coventry Godiva H. *Born* 2.4.1948. *Best performances:* 20km walk – 1:33:00, 50km walk – 4:18:32.

MARGARET RITCHIE
Edinburgh Southern H. *Born* Kirkcaldy (Scotland), 6.7.1952; *Height:* 1.78m (5' 10"), *Weight:* 91kg (202lb); Teacher. *Best performances:* Shot – 16.40m (53' 9¾") (UK record), Discus – 60.80m (199' 6") (UK record). *Championships:* 1974 Commonwealth – 6th discus; 1978 Commonwealth – 8th shot, 4th discus.

DAVID ROBERTS
Cardiff AAC. *Born* Bangor (Wales), 5.6.1949; *Height:* 1.75m (5' 9"), *Weight:* 66kg (147lb); Solicitor. *Best performances:* 100m – 10.64 (and 10.51w), 200m – 21.3.

JOHN ROBSON
Edinburgh Southern H. *Born* Kelso, 31.1.1957; *Height:* 1.75m (5' 9"), *Weight:* 63kg (140lb); Electrician. *Best performances:* 800m – 1:47.8, 1500m – 3:35.6, Mile – 3:54.3. *Championships:* 1978 Commonwealth – 3rd 1500m; 1978 European – 8th.

JANNETTE ROSCOE (née Champion)
Stretford AC. *Born* Tunbridge Wells, 10.6.1946; *Height:* 1.69m (5' 6¼"), *Weight:* 56kg (124lb); Lecturer. *Best performances:* 100m – 11.6, 200m – 23.7, 400m – 52.9, 400m hurdles – 58.31. *Championships:* 1970 Commonwealth – 4th 400m; 1974 Commonwealth – 4th 400m, 1st 4 × 400m.

NICK ROSE
Bristol AC. *Born* Bristol, 30.12.1951; *Height:* 1.75m (5' 9"), *Weight:* 60kg (132lb); Post-graduate student. *Best performances:* 800m – 1:51.0, 1500m – 3:40.8, Mile – 3:58.4, 2000m – 4:59.6, 3000m 7:40.4, 2 miles – 8:18 4i, 5000m – 13:20.4, 10,000m – 28:49.0. *Championships:* 1977 European Cup – 1st 5000m; 1977 World Cup – 4th; 1978 European – 7th.

VAL RUTTER (née Harrison)
Liverpool H and AC. *Born* Liverpool, 30.10.1954; *Height:* 1.64m (5' 4½"), *Weight:* 56kg (123lb); Teacher. *Best performance:* High jump – 1.83m (6' 0"). *Championships:* 1974 Commonwealth – 5th; 1978 Commonwealth – 7th.

TESSA SANDERSON
Wolverhampton and Bilston AC. *Born* Jamaica, 14.3.1956; *Height:* 1.68m (5' 6"), *Weight:* 60kg (133lb); Typist/information assistant. *Best performances:* 400m – 57.3, 100m hurdles – 13.9, 400m hurdles – 60.46, High jump – 1.69m (5' 6¼"), Javelin – 67.20m (220' 6") (UK record). *Championships:* 1974

Commonwealth – 5th javelin; 1977 European
Cup – 2nd; 1977 World Cup – 3rd; 1978
Commonwealth – 1st; 1978 European – 2nd.

AMOS SEDDON
Borough of Enfield H. *Born* Leek (Staffs),
22.1.1941; *Height:* 1.76m (5′ 9½″), *Weight:* 77kg
(171lb); Policeman. *Best performance:* 20km
walk – 1:28:50. *Championships:* 1974 European
– 6th 20km walk; 1978 Commonwealth – 5th
30km walk.

CAMERON SHARP
Shettleston H. *Born* 3.6.1958; *Height:* 1.81m (5′
11½″), *Weight:* 71kg (156lb); Student. *Best
performances:* 100m – 10.65, 200m – 21.52 and
21.2. *Championships:* 1978 Commonwealth – 1st
4 x 100m.

PETER SHAW
Manchester H and AC. *Born* Manchester,
2.9.1961; *Height:* 1.75m (5′ 9″), *Weight:* 65kg
(144lb); Teacher. *Best performance:* 3000m –
7:55.2i.

ANN SIMMONDS (née Wilson)
Southend AC. *Born* Rochford (Essex),
29.9.1949; *Height:* 1.70m (5′ 7″), *Weight:* 58kg
(128lb); Bank clerk. *Best performances:* 100m
hurdles – 13.3, High jump – 1.77m (5′ 9¾″),
Long jump – 6.55m (21′ 6″). *Championships:*
1966 Commonwealth – 6th 80m hurdles, 7th
high jump; 1970 Commonwealth – 2nd High
jump, 2nd Long jump, 2nd Pentathlon; 1974
Commonwealth – 7th High jump, 3rd
Pentathlon.

BARBARA SIMMONDS
Oxford AC. *Born* 6.10.1961; *Height:* 1.76m (5′
9½″), *Weight:* 68kg (151lb); Student. *Best
performance:* High jump – 1.81m (5′ 11¼″).
Championships: 1978 Commonwealth – 5th.

TONY SIMMONS
Luton United H. *Born* Maesteg (Wales),
6.10.1948; *Height:* 1.67m (5′ 6″), *Weight:* 55kg
(121lb); Paint technician. *Best performances:*
800m – 1:52.0, 1500m – 3:41.1, Mile – 4:00.5,
3000m – 7:51.6, 5000m – 13:21.2, 10,000m –
27:43.6, Marathon – 2:12:33, 3000m
steeplechase – 8:55.0. *Championships:* 1974
Commonwealth – 7th 10,000m; 1974
European – 2nd 10,000m; 1976 Olympics – 4th
10,000m; 1978 Commonwealth – 7th 5000m,
6th 10,000m.

KATHY SMALLWOOD
Reading AC. *Born* Winchester, 3.5.1960;
Height: 1.78m (5′ 10″), *Weight:* 62kg (136lb);
Student. *Best performances:* 100m – 11.64 (and

11.61w), 200m – 22.99 (and 22.73w), 400m –
56.0, High jump – 1.63m (5′ 4¼″).
Championships: 1977 European Junior – 3rd
100m, 3rd 200m, 3rd 4 x 100m; 1978
Commonwealth – 5th 200m, 1st 4 x 100m;
1978 European – 2nd 4 x 100m.

RUTH SMEETH
Aldershot, Farnham and District AC. *Born*
19.6.1960; *Height:* 1.62m (5′ 4″), *Weight:* 51kg
(112lb). *Best performances:* 1500m – 4:14.6,
3000m – 9:15.8.

GEOFF SMITH
Liverpool H and AC. *Born* 24.10.1953; *Height:*
1.74m (5′ 8½″); Fireman. *Best performances:*
5000m – 13:55.8, 10,000m – 28:36.5.

JOYCE SMITH (née Byatt)
Barnet Ladies AC. *Born* Stoke Newington
(London), 26.10.1937; *Height:* 1.69m (5′ 6½″),
Weight: 54kg (119lb); Housewife/part-time
clerk. *Best performances:* 800m – 2:08.0, 1500m –
4:09.4, 3000m – 8:55.6. *Championships:* 1972
International Cross Country – 1st; 1974
European – 2nd 3000m.

SUE SMITH (née Howell)
City of Hull AC. *Born* Cottingham, 9.9.1953;
Height: 1.63m (5′ 4½″), *Weight:* 55kg (122lb);
Bank clerk. *Best performances:* 400m – 53.97,
800m – 2:04.5, 1500m – 4:39.8, 400m hurdles –
59.02.

ADRIENNE SMYTH (née Lynch)
Ballymena AC. *Born* 27.7.1950; *Height:* 1.75m
(5′ 9″), *Weight:* 57kg (126lb); Teacher. *Best
performances:* 400m – 53.96, 800m – 2:06.0.

CHARLIE SPEDDING
Gateshead H. *Born* Bishop Auckland,
19.3.1952; *Height:* 1.74m (5′ 8½″), *Weight:* 63kg
(140lb); Pharmacist. *Best performances:* 3000m –
7:52.1, 5000m – 13:28.7.

LAWRIE SPENCE
Shettleston H. *Born* Greenock, 16.7.1953;
Height: 1.75m (5′ 8¾″), *Weight:* 59kg (130lb);
Graduate engineer. *Best performances:* 1500m –
3:44.0, Mile – 3:58.8, 3000m – 7:52.8, 5000m –
13:37.7.

MARY STEWART
Birchfield H. *Born* Birmingham, 25.2.1956;
Height: 1.67m (5′ 6″), *Weight:* 52kg (116lb);
Clerical officer. *Best performances:* 800m –
2:03.1, 1500m – 4:06.0, Mile – 4:36.1 (UK
record), 3000m – 9:09.4i. *Championships:* 1973
European Junior – 5th 1500m; 1974
Commonwealth – 4th 1500m; 1977 European

Indoor – 1st 1500m; 1978 Commonwealth – 1st 1500m.

KEITH STOCK
Croydon H. *Born* Woolwich (London), 18.3.1957; *Height:* 1.72m (5′ 8″), *Weight:* 61kg (134lb); Student. *Best performance:* Pole vault – 5.25m (17′ 2¾″).

SHIRLEY STRONG
Stretford AC. *Born* Northwich (Cheshire), 18.11.1958; *Height:* 1.67m (5′ 6″), *Weight:* 62kg (136lb); Laboratory technician. *Best performances:* 100m – 11.83, 100m hurdles – 13.41 (and 13.08w). *Championships:* 1978 Commonwealth – 2nd.

LIZ SUTHERLAND (née Toulalan)
Edinburgh SH. *Born* St Andrews, 5.2.1947; *Height:* 1.74m (5′ 8½″), *Weight:* 57kg (126lb); Housewife/mother. *Best performances:* 100m – 11.4, 200m – 23.6w and 24.0, 400m – 54.28, 100m hurdles – 13.2w and 13.5, 400m hurdles – 57.43 (UK record).

PETER TANCRED
Wolverhampton and Bilston AC. *Born* Quetta (India), 20.10.1949; *Height:* 1.90m (6′ 3″), *Weight:* 108kg (238lb); Teacher. *Best performances:* Shot – 18.35m (60′ 2½″), Discus – 61.62m (202′ 2″), Hammer – 53.50m (175′ 6″). *Championships:* 1978 Commonwealth – 6th discus.

COLIN TAYLOR
Airedale and Spen Valley AC. *Born* Dewsbury, 15.10.1949; *Height:* 1.79m (5′ 10½″), *Weight:* 63kg (140lb); Civil engineer. *Best performance:* Marathon – 2:15:47.

ELEANOR THOMAS
Selsonia LAC. *Born* Kingston (Jamaica), 24.11.1958; *Height:* 1.57m (5′ 2″), *Weight:* 49kg (109lb); Clerk/typist. *Best performances:* 100m – 11.73 (and 11.50w), 200m – 23.51.

DALEY THOMPSON
Essex Beagles. *Born* London, 30.7.1958; *Height:* 1.86m (6′ 1¼″), *Weight:* 82kg (181lb); Student. *Best performances:* 100m – 10.65 (and 10.50w), 200m – 21.8, 400m – 47.31, 1500m – 4:20.3, 110m hurdles – 14.85, 400m hurdles – 52.6, High jump – 2.07m (6′ 9½″), Pole vault – 4.90m (16′ 0¾″), Long jump – 7.93m (26′ 0¼″) and 8.11m (26′ 7¼″)w, Shot – 14.69m (48′ 2½″), Discus – 44.46m (145′ 10″), Javelin – 59.80m (196′ 2″), Decathlon – 8289 (UK record) and 8467w. *Championships:* 1977 European Junior – 1st decathlon, 5th long jump; 1978

Commonwealth – 1st decathlon; 1978 European – 2nd decathlon.

JANET THOMPSON
Bracknell AC. *Born* Woking (Surrey), 21.2.1954; *Height:* 1.85m (6′ 1″), *Weight:* 86kg (190lb); Teacher. *Best performances:* Shot – 14.54m (47′ 8½″), Discus – 55.06m (180′ 8″). *Championships:* 1978 Commonwealth – 5th discus.

DAVE TRAVIS
Surrey AC. *Born* Twickenham (Middx), 9.9.1945; *Height:* 1.83m (6′ 0″), *Weight:* 86kg (190lb); Teacher. *Best performances:* Triple jump – 14.15m (46′ 5″), Javelin – 83.44m (273′ 9″), Decathlon – 7067. *Championships:* (all javelin) 1966 Commonwealth – 6th; 1970 Commonwealth – 1st; 1974 Commonwealth – 2nd.

EARL TULLOCH
Sale H. *Born* Jamaica, 13.9.1957; *Height:* 1.72m (5′ 8″), *Weight:* 71kg (156lb); Student. *Best performances:* 100m – 10.71w, 200m – 21.51w, 400m – 48.4.

MOIRA WALLS
Edinburgh Southern H. *Born* Glasgow, 4.5.1952; *Height:* 1.78m (5′ 10″), *Weight:* 63kg (139lb); Teacher. *Best performances:* High jump 1.83m (6′ 0″), Long jump – 6.48m (21′ 3¼″)w and 6.43m (21′ 1¼″), Pentathlon – 4227 (with 200m). *Championships:* 1970 Commonwealth – 3rd high jump.

DAVE WARREN
Epsom and Ewell H. *Born* 11.2.1956. *Best performances:* 800m – 1:47.4, 1500m – 3:49.2, 2000m steeplechase – 5:41.4.

GRAEME WATSON
Polytechnic H. *Born* 19.11.1957; *Height:* 1.85m (6′ 1″), *Weight:* 80kg (176lb). *Best performances:* 100m – 10.75 (and 10.72w), Long jump – 7.37m (24′ 2¼″)w, Decathlon – 7381. *Championships:* 1978 Commonwealth – 4th decathlon.

ALLAN WELLS
Edinburgh Southern H. *Born* Edinburgh, 3.5.1952; *Height:* 1.83m (6′ 0″), *Weight:* 74kg (163lb); Marine engineer. *Best performances:* 100m – 10.15 (UK record) and 10.07w, 200m – 20.61 (UK record) and 20.12w, Long jump – 7.32m (24′ 0¼″). *Championships:* 1978 Commonwealth – 2nd 100m, 1st 200m, 1st 4 × 100m; 1978 European – 6th 100m.

FATIMA WHITBREAD
Thurrock H. *Born* Hackney (London),
3.3.1961; *Height:* 1.67m (5' 6"), *Weight:* 58kg
(129lb); Student. *Best performance:* Javelin –
53.88m (176' 9"). *Championships:* 1978
Commonwealth – 6th.

JIM WHITEHEAD
Birchfield H. *Born* Walkern (Herts), 22.8.1949;
Height: 1.90m (6' 3"), *Weight:* 108kg (238lb);
Teacher. *Best performance:* Hammer – 69.00m
(226' 4"). *Championships:* 1978 Commonwealth
– 5th.

TERRY WHITEHEAD
Chelmsford AC. *Born* Braintree, 10.1.1957;
Height: 1.85m (6' 1"), *Weight:* 72kg (160lb);
Bank clerk. *Best performances:* 200m – 21.28,
400m – 46.23. *Championships:* 1978 European –
5th 400m.

JANEEN WILLIAMS
Cannock Chase AC. *Born* Birmingham,
18.7.1956; *Height:* 1.75m (5' 9"), *Weight:* 76kg
(168lb); Student. *Best performance:* Javelin –
50.20m (164' 8").

KAREN WILLIAMS
Pitreavie AC. *Born* Kirkcaldy, 10.1.1960;
Height: 1.72m (5' 7¾"), *Weight:* 60kg (132lb);
Clerical assistant. *Best performance:* 400m –
52.98. *Championships:* 1978 Commonwealth –
6th 400m.

GRAHAM WILLIAMSON
Springburn H. *Born* Glasgow, 15.6.1960;
Height: 1.80m (5' 11"), *Weight:* 63kg (140lb);
Student. *Best performances:* 800m – 1:50.5,
1500m – 3:37.7 (European Junior record),
Mile – 3:55.8, 3000m – 8:00.7.

DAVE WILSON
Edinburgh AC. *Born* Edinburgh, 7.9.1951;
Height: 1.90m (6' 3"), *Weight:* 79kg (174lb);
Chemical engineer. *Best performances:* 110m
hurdles – 14.10w and 14.3, High jump – 2.05m
(6' 8¾").

MIKE WINCH
Blackheath H. *Born* Que-Que (Rhodesia),
20.7.1948; *Height:* 1.82m (5' 11½"), *Weight:*
105kg (231lb); Teacher. *Best performances:* Shot
– 20.43m (67' 0½"), Discus – 58.08m (190' 7").
Championships: 1974 Commonwealth – 2nd
shot; 1978 Commonwealth – 5th shot.

YVETTE WRAY
Shrewsbury and District AC. *Born* Scraptoft
(Leicester), 18.10.1958; *Height:* 1.69m (5' 6½"),
Weight: 62kg (136lb); Student. *Best
performances:* 100m hurdles – 13.77, Long jump
– 6.04m (19' 9¾")w and 5.96m (19' 6¾"), Shot –
12.71m (41' 8½"), Pentathlon – 4292.
Championships: 1978 Commonwealth – 3rd
pentathlon.

PETER YATES
Exeter H. *Born* London, 15.6.1957; *Height:*
1.80m (5' 11"), *Weight:* 79kg (175lb); Student.
Best performance: Javelin – 80.62m (264' 6").
Championships: 1978 Commonwealth – 3rd.

PENNY YULE
Portsmouth Atalanta AC. *Born* Chichester
(Sussex), 7.6.1949; *Height:* 1.69m (5' 6½"),
Weight: 52kg (116lb); Civil servant. *Best
performances:* 800m – 2:04.1, 1500m – 4:10.3,
3000m – 9:08.6.

PANAYIOTIS ZENIOU
North London AC. *Born* Cyprus, 7.2.1953;
Height: 1.82m (5' 11½"), *Weight:* 80kg (176lb);
Play leader. *Best performance:* Decathlon – 7443.

The Commonwealth Champions

DON QUARRIE (Jamaica)
(100 metres – 10.03w)

The reigning Olympic 200 metres champion became the first sprinter to win the Commonwealth 100 metres title three times in succession, and increased his tally of Commonwealth gold medals to six – unique among male athletes. Injury ruined his Olympic chances in 1972 but he won the silver medal in the Montreal Olympic 100 metres as well as the gold he achieved in the 200 metres. He is Commonwealth record holder at 200 metres with 19.86 – second-fastest on the world all-time list.

Born Kingston, 25.2.1951; *Height* 1.72m (5' 8"), *Weight* 70kg (155lb). *Best marks* 100 metres – 10.07 (10.03w); 200 metres – 19.86.

ALLAN WELLS (Scotland)
(200 metres – 20.12w)

Allan Wells climaxed a meteoric rise into the world's sprinting élite by becoming the first British male athlete to win a Commonwealth sprint title for 40 years. Earlier in the season he eclipsed Peter Radford's long-standing UK 100 metres record when he clocked a sensational 10.15 in the UK Championship before his home crowd in Edinburgh, and in Edmonton he gained two other medals: a gold in the sprint relay and silver in the 100 metres. Until 1976, at the age of 24, he had never broken 22 seconds for 200 metres!

Born Edinburgh, 3.5.1952; *Height* 1.83m (6' 0"), *Weight* 74kg (163lb). *Best marks* 100 metres – 10.15 (10.07w); 200 metres – 20.61 (20.12w); Long jump – 7.32m (24' 0¼").

RICK MITCHELL (Australia)
(400 metres – 46.34)

Rick Mitchell proved himself to be a 'Big Games' competitor, producing his best form to win the Commonwealth title after a quiet season in 1977. He had in 1976 finished sixth in the Montreal Olympic final in 45.40 – his personal best. His fastest in 1978 was 45.6 hand-timed, and he may move up-distance to 800 metres in a couple of years time.

Born 24.3.1955; *Height* 1.83m (6' 0"), *Weight* 72kg (158lb). *Best mark* 400 metres – 45.40.

MIKE BOIT (Kenya)
(800 metres – 1:46.4)

After a lengthy international career, the Commonwealth record holder (1:43.6) finally captured a major title. He had been so close to

gold so many times that most fans were willing him to success, particularly in view of the African boycott of the Montreal Olympics. He was bronze medallist in the 1972 Olympics and silver medallist in the 1974 Commonwealth Games.

Born 1.1.1949; *Height* 1.80m (5' 11"), *Weight* 68kg (150lb). *Best marks* 800 metres – 1:43.6; 1500 metres – 3:36.8.

DAVE MOORCROFT (England)
(1500 metres – 3:35.5)

Following his fine seventh place in the Montreal Olympic 1500 metres final, Dave Moorcroft had his 1977 season wiped out by a recurring back injury. A teaching post in New Zealand enabled him to re-establish himself and eradicate his back problem. His range – 800 metres in 1:49.0 to second place in the English National Cross-Country Championships of 1976 – suggests a serious move up to 5000 metres may be his next step.

Born Coventry, 10.4.1953; *Height* 1.80m (5' 11"), *Weight* 68kg (150lb). *Best marks* 800 metres – 1:49.0; 1500 metres – 3:35.5; 3000 metres – 7:43.5; 5000 metres – 13:58.4.

HENRY RONO (Kenya)
(5000 metres – 13:23.0; steeplechase – 8:26.5)

Possibly never in the history of athletics has a distance runner so dominated a season – clocking world records in four different events in the space of four months. He raced incessantly all over the world and many observers doubted his ability to sustain the pressure up to and including the Commonwealth Games, yet he was still running fast times on the European circuit in late September! In Edmonton he emulated the 5000 metres and steeplechase double achieved in 1974 by his illustrious countryman, Ben Jipcho. Rono predicts that he can run under 8 minutes for the steeplechase and 27 minutes for 10,000 metres.

Born Rift Valley, 12.2.1952; *Height* 1.70m (5' 7"), *Weight* 63kg (139lb). *Best marks* 3000 metres – 7:32.1 (World record); 5000 metres – 13:08.4 (World record); 10,000 metres – 27:22.5 (World record); Half marathon (road) – 1:04.46; 3000 metres steeplechase – 8:05.4 (World record).

BRENDAN FOSTER (England)
(10,000 metres – 28:13.7)

'Big Bren' made athletics history by becoming

the first man ever to win Commonwealth Games medals in the 1500, 5000 and 10,000 metres – 1500 bronze in 1970, 5000 silver in 1974. The European 5000 metres champion in 1974 and an Olympic bronze medallist in the Montreal 10,000 metres, he is a former world record holder at 3000 metres and 2 miles. His uncompromising tactic of surging in mid-race and leaving his opponents trailing has made him a huge favourite with crowds all over the world and a folk hero in his home town of Gateshead, where he has created a huge following for athletics.

Born Hebburn, 12.1.1948; *Height* 1.80m (5′ 11″), *Weight* 66kg (145lb). *Best marks* 1500 metres – 3:37.6; 3000 metres – 7:35.2 (European record); 2 miles – 8:13.7; 5000 metres – 13:14.6; 10,000 metres – 27:30.3 (European record).

BERWYN PRICE (Wales)
(110 metres hurdles – 13.70w)
Berwyn Price has waited a long time to add another major title to those won in the European Junior Championships in 1970 and World Student Games in 1973. It was third time lucky for Price in these Championships, having reached the semi-finals in 1970 and won the silver medal in 1974. He became the first Welshman to win a Commonwealth Games gold medal on the track for 40 years.

Born Tredegar, 15.8.1951; *Height* 1.90m (6′ 3″), *Weight* 81kg (178lb). *Best mark* 110 metres hurdles – 13.69.

DANIEL KIMAIYO (Kenya)
(400 metres hurdles – 49.48)
Daniel Kimaiyo served notice of his fine form by clocking a personal best of 49.20 in the semi-finals. A few weeks earlier he had won the African Games event in 49.48 – identical to his winning time in the Edmonton final – ahead of 1972 Olympic champion John Akii-Bua of Uganda. He picked up another gold medal in the 4 × 400 metres relay.

Born 11.1.1948; *Height* 1.78m (5′ 10″), *Weight* 68kg (150lb). *Best mark* 400 metres hurdles – 49.20.

GIDEMAS SHAHANGA (Tanzania)
(Marathon – 2:15:39.8)
Just as Abebe Bikila's 1960 Olympic victory in Rome took everyone by surprise, so the Commonwealth triumph of this slim Tanzanian hailing from high altitude Arusha threw the experts into confusion. A complete unknown, his previous best time was 2:22:41 and he had, a mere 15 days before the Edmonton race, finished seventh in the African Games marathon in 2:32:50!

Born Arusha, 1957–59(?); *Height* 1.77m (5′ 9¾″), *Weight* 57kg (125lb). *Best mark* Marathon – 2:15:39.8.

OLLY FLYNN (England)
(30 kilometres walk – 2:22:03.7)
Olly Flynn, England's third winner of the Commonwealth walk title since the event was introduced in 1966, following Ron Wallwork (1966) and John Warhurst (1974), announced afterwards that 1978 might have been his last international season. 'I feel I'm as good as the best in the world, but I can't compete against full-time professional athletes like I'd meet at the Olympics in Moscow.'

Born Ipswich, 30.6.1950; *Height* 1.90m (6′ 3″), *Weight* 77kg (170lb). *Best mark* 20 kilometres walk – 1:27:35.

CLAUDE FERRAGNE (Canada)
(High jump – 2.20m/7′ 2½″)
In the last competition of his career – he announced his retirement immediately afterwards ('after 12 years of this I want to live a normal life') – Claude Ferragne got the better of his more famed compatriot, Olympic silver medallist, Greg Joy. The French-Canadian straddle jumper finally broke a chain of Australian winners that goes back to 1962.

Born Montreal, 14.10.1952; *Height* 1.86m (6′ 1½″), *Weight* 75kg (165lb). *Best mark* High jump – 2.25m (7′ 4½″).

BRUCE SIMPSON (Canada)
(Pole vault – 5.10m/ 16′ 8¾″)
Bruce Simpson became the first Canadian to win the pole vault since S. Apps cleared 3.81m (12′ 6″) to take the gold medal in 1934. Simpson had waited a long time to win his first major title in a career which has fluctuated from a promising fifth in the 1972 Olympics to failing to clear his opening height four years later in the Montreal final.

Born Toronto, 6.3.1950; *Height* 1.76m (5′ 9¼″), *Weight* 68kg (150lb). *Best mark* Pole vault – 5.38m (17′ 7¾″).

ROY MITCHELL (England)
(Long jump – 8.06m/26′ 5¼″w)
Roy Mitchell has developed into a very consistent performer on the big occasion. As in the 1977 European Cup Final, where he finished a distinguished third, he was able to respond to a strong challenge with cool determination. 'When Chris (Commons) did 8.04m in the second round I knew I had to pull all the stops out' – and that he did with a leap of 8.06m in the next round.

Born Jamaica, 1.1.1955; *Height* 1.90m (6′ 3″), *Weight* 85kg (187lb). *Best mark* Long jump – 8.16m (26′ 9¼″)w and 8.04m (26′ 4½″).

KEITH CONNOR (England)

(Triple jump – 17.21m/56' 5¾"w)

After his superb silver medal in the European Indoor Championships in Milan earlier in 1978, Keith Connor had said that the target of 17 metres 'is possible for me by 1980 if not before'. In Edmonton the highly competitive Connor improved from 16.54m (54' 3¼") to a staggering 17.21m (56' 5¾") – aided by a wind of just over the limit at 2.32 metres per second – the longest jump by a European in 1978. His wind-free second round jump of 16.76m (55' 0") was a new UK record.

Born Anguilla (West Indies), 16.9.1957; *Height* 1.85m (6' 1"), *Weight* 74kg (163lb). *Best mark* Triple jump – 17.21m (56' 5¾")w and 16.76m (55' 0").

GEOFF CAPES (England)

(Shot – 19.77m/64' 10½")

Competing in his third Commonwealth Games, Geoff Capes became one of only two athletes from the 1974 Games to defend successfully their Commonwealth title – Don Quarrie in the 100 metres being the other. It was the fourth international gold medal of his career, he having twice won the European indoor championship. He has dominated British shot putting for almost a decade and in recent years has turned his experience into positive benefit for young athletes by becoming a BAAB Staff Coach in shot putting and forming the Dewhurst Shot Squad.

Born Holbeach, 23.8.1949; *Height* 1.98m (6' 6"), *Weight* 137kg (302lb). *Best mark* Shot – 21.55m (70' 8½").

BORYS CHAMBUL (Canada)

(Discus – 59.70m/195' 10")

The Commonwealth record holder at 65.40m (214' 7"), Borys Chambul, won a depressed competition that saw the bronze medal go for little more than it did back in 1966. In world terms, the discus remains one of the Commonwealth's weakest events. Chambul failed to get beyond the qualifying round in the 1976 Olympics.

Born Toronto, 17.2.1953; *Height* 1.91m (6' 3¼"), *Weight* 130kg (287lb). *Best mark* Discus – 65.40m (214' 7").

PETER FARMER (Australia)

(Hammer – 71.10m/233' 3")

Top-tanked Commonwealth hammer thrower, Peter Farmer, improved from his third place in 1974 to defeat the opposition with a Games record of 71.10m (233' 3") in a contest which lasted over two and a half hours due to constant interruptions. 'It was the worst-run competition I've ever competed in.' His most notable international performance occurred in 1977 when he finished third in the World Cup in Dusseldorf, ahead of Olympic champion Yuriy Sedykh.

Born 25.6.1952; *Height* 1.84m (6' 0½"), *Weight* 108kg (238lb). *Best mark* Hammer – 74.08m (243' 0").

PHIL OLSEN (Canada)

(Javelin – 84.00m/275' 7")

Phil Olsen regained some of the form that made him such an exciting young talent in 1976. Lack of experience (he was only 19) and the pressure of an expectant crowd was his undoing in the Montreal Olympics; he threw a Commonwealth and world junior record of 87.76m (287' 11") to qualify, but on the day when it mattered he could throw no further than 77.70m (254' 11") for eleventh place.

Born Nanaimo, BC, 31.1.1957; *Height* 1.85m (6' 0¾"), *Weight* 86kg (190lb). *Best mark* Javelin – 87.76m (287' 11").

DALEY THOMPSON (England)

(Decathlon – 8467w)

The 1977 European Junior champion – just one week past his twentieth birthday – continued to make gigantic progress towards becoming the world's top decathlete. A massive score of 4550 at the end of the first day set the possibility of surpassing Bruce Jenner's world record total, but a patchy second day saw valuable points lost and by the ninth event, although he had already broken the Games record(!), he had fallen behind schedule. Nevertheless he amassed a brilliant total of 8467 to move to Number 3 on the world all-time list.

Born London, 30.7.1958; *Height* 1.86m (6' 1¼"), *Weight* 82kg (181lb). *Best marks* 100 metres – 10.65 (10.50w); 400 metres – 47.31; High jump – 2.07m (6' 9½"); Pole vault – 4.90m (16' 0¾"); Long jump – 7.93m (26' 0¼") and 8.11m (26' 7¼")w; Decathlon – 8289 (8467w).

SONIA LANNAMAN (England)

(100 metres – 11.27w)

Sonia Lannaman overcame her previously indifferent form in 1978 to secure her first major Games title as a senior. Ever injury-prone, it was a hamstring injury in the final days before her event in Montreal that robbed Sonia of the chance of Olympic honours. The following year she established herself firmly as Number 2 in the world.

Born Birmingham, 24.3.1956; *Height* 1.62m (5' 4"), *Weight* 57kg (126lb). *Best marks* 100 metres – 11.22 (10.93w); 200 metres – 22.81 (22.69w).

DENISE BOYD (Australia)
(200 metres – 22.82w)
Having finished a disappointed third in the 100
metres, as she had done four years before in
Christchurch, Denise Boyd (née Robertson)
was hungry for gold and she took her
opportunity in the 200 metres to improve on
her silver medal from 1974. In winning, she
maintained an unbroken run of Australian
successes in the event stretching back to 1966.
   Born 15.12.1952; *Height* 1.75m (5′ 8¾″),
Weight 60kg (131lb). *Best marks* 100 metres –
11.0; 200 metres – 22.5.

DONNA HARTLEY (England)
(400 metres – 51.69)
Donna Hartley (née Murray), for many years
dubbed Britain's 'golden girl', finally secured
her first major Games gold medal. Despite
UK records at 200 and 400 metres and a
lengthy international career, she had never
previously reached a major Games final. She
attributed her new-found confidence to her
husband Bill – the international 400 metres
hurdler; 'because of him I'm much more
mature now'.
   Born Southampton, 1.5.1955; *Height* 1.70m
(5′ 7″), *Weight* 55kg (122lb). *Best marks* 100
metres – 11.46; 200 metres – 22.75; 400 metres
– 51.28; 800 metres – 2:07.8.

JUDY PECKHAM (Australia)
(800 metres – 2:02.8)
Judy Peckham (née Canty), criticised in the
past for below-par performances in major
Games, finally produced her best form when it
counted to secure an important title. The
former Australian 400 metres record holder at
51.7 commented: 'This is just a little kid's
game compared with the Olympics, but still
it's fantastic'. Husband Lawrie was
Commonwealth high jump champion in 1966
and 1970.
   Born 9.12.1950; *Height* 1.78m (5′ 10″), *Weight*
63kg (140lb). *Best marks* 400 metres – 51.7; 800
metres – 2:02.8.

MARY STEWART (England)
(1500 metres – 4:06.3)
Not to be outdone by her illustrious brothers,
Ian and Peter, Mary improved from her fourth
place in 1974 to extend the famous Stewart
family's collection of medals to one Olympic
bronze, one European gold, two
Commonwealth gold, one IAAF Cross-
Country gold and four European Indoor gold!
Setting a new Games record and running close
to her personal best she joined Ian (winner of
the 1970 5000 metres for Scotland) as a
Commonwealth champion.

Born Birmingham, 25.2.1956; *Height* 1.67m
(5′ 6″), *Weight* 52kg (116lb). *Best marks* 800
metres – 2:03.1; 1500 metres – 4:06.0; 3000
metres – 9:09.4i.

PAULA FUDGE (England)
(3000 metres – 9:13.0)
Previously better known as a road and cross-
country runner, Paula Fudge (née Yeoman)
moved out of the shadow of her more successful
twin sister – Ann Ford – when she won the UK
3000 metres title in 8:53.6, cutting 14 seconds
from her previous best. Very windy conditions
slowed her winning time in Edmonton to a
seemingly modest 9:13.0. Paula clocked 8:48.7
for a Commonwealth record in finishing eighth
in the European Championships a month later.
   Born Isleworth, 30.3.1952; *Height* 1.68m (5′
6″), *Weight:* 54kg (120lb). *Best marks* 1500
metres – 4:17.5; 3000 metres – 8:48.7.

LORNA BOOTHE (England)
(100 metres hurdles – 12.98w)
The UK record holder and favourite, Lorna
Boothe, became the first Briton to dip under
the 13-second barrier (admittedly, with wind
assistance) and she led the English trio to a
clean sweep of the medals for the first time in
any women's event since 1934. She started in
athletics as a cross-country runner, progressed
to long jump and then took up hurdling in
1967.
   Born Kingston (Jamaica), 5.12.1954; *Height*
1.62m (5′ 4″), *Weight* 51kg (112lb). *Best mark*
100 metres hurdles – 13.08, (12.98w).

KATRINA GIBBS (Australia)
(High jump – 1.93m/6′ 4″)
For Katrina Gibbs it was a case of being in the
wrong event. Until 1976 she was just a
moderately successful hurdler; then she turned
to the 'flop'. Starting with a best of 1.52m (4′
11¾″) she made a meteoric rise to 1.89m (6′
2¼″) early in 1978, improved to 1.90m (6′ 2¾″)
in Europe a few weeks prior to these Games,
and her winning jump in Edmonton – a
Commonwealth record of 1.93m (6′ 4″) – put
her amongst the world élite.
   Born 7.4.1959; *Height* 1.75m (5′ 9″), *Weight*
56kg (123lb). *Best mark* High jump – 1.93m (6′
4″).

SUE REEVE (England)
(Long jump – 6.59m/21′ 7½″)
Her 17-year career has been plagued by injury
to the ankles, and the jinx struck Sue Reeve
(née Scott) again in the final days before this
competition. It must have seemed like a *déja vu*
experience, for as an 18-year-old in 1970 she

damaged ligaments in her ankle just one week before the Edinburgh Commonwealth Games and managed to compete only with the help of pain-killing injections. 'I'll get down the runway on one leg if I have to', she resolved in Edmonton, and her bravery was justly rewarded with the gold medal.

Born Birmingham, 17.9.1951; *Height* 1.78m (5' 10"), *Weight* 70kg (154lb). *Best mark* Long jump – 6.84m (22' 5¼")w and 6.61m (21' 8¼").

GAEL MULHALL (Australia)
(*Shot – 17.31m/56' 9¼"*)
Despite undergoing an operation two months previously which caused her to drop 11 pounds in bodyweight, Commonwealth record holder Gael Mulhall was far superior to her rivals. All six of her puts were in excess of anything achieved by the other competitors, and her winning throw was quite an improvement on her 1974 performance when she finished eleventh with 13.57m (44' 6¼").

Born 27.8.1956; *Height* 1.70m (5' 7"), *Weight* 89kg (196lb). *Best marks* Shot – 18.16m (59' 7"); Discus – 58.48m (191' 10").

CARMEN IONESCO (Canada)
(*Discus – 62.16m/203' 11"*)
It took Carmen Ionesco just one throw to give her victory as she smashed the Games record in the opening round, coming close to the new Commonwealth record of 62.34m (204' 6") which she set just two weeks before. The former Romanian defected after placing seventh in the 1972 Munich Olympics, settling in Canada later that year. She only took up throwing again in the winter of 1977–78 after the birth of her second child and became eligible to represent Canada internationally.

Born Bucharest, 28.7.1951; *Height* 1.77m (5' 9¾"), *Weight* 84kg (185lb). *Best mark* Discus – 64.92m (213' 0").

TESSA SANDERSON (England)
(*Javelin – 61.34m/201' 3"*)
The strongest of favourites in the women's events, Commonwealth record holder Tessa Sanderson wrapped up the competition as expected with her opening throw – which was over six metres better than anyone else achieved throughout the entire contest. A few weeks later she claimed the European silver medal in Prague. 'I'm shooting for 70 metres and I hope by the Moscow Olympics that I'll have my technique all down to hit that peak.'

Born Jamaica, 14.3.1956; *Height* 1.68m (5' 6"), *Weight* 60kg (133lb). *Best mark* Javelin – 67.20m (220' 6").

DIANE KONIHOWSKI (Canada)
(*Pentathlon – 4768*)
Diane Konihowski (née Jones) completely dominated the competition in her home town, and won by the largest margin ever achieved in a major championship. She even surprised herself with a new Commonwealth record of 4768 which moved her to Number 3 on the world all-time list. Particularly notable was her high jump clearance of 1.88 metres (6' 2"), a Games record at the time.

Born Vancouver, 1.3.1951; *Height* 1.78m (5' 10"), *Weight* 72kg (159lb). *Best marks* 800 metres – 2:12.1; 100 metres hurdles – 13.76; High jump – 1.88m (6' 2"); Long jump – 6.55m (21' 6"); Shot – 16.24m (53' 3½"); Pentathlon – 4768.

The European Champions

PIETRO MENNEA (Italy)
(100 metres – 10.27 and 200 metres – 20.16)
Pietro Mennea retained his 200 metres title and added the 100 metres – his self-confessed weaker distance – to gain the sprint double which he had been planning since securing the European indoor 400 metres title the previous winter. The endurance cultivated by 400 metres training and specific work on his starting – another weak point – gave the Italian a clear edge over arch-rival Eugen Ray (GDR) throughout an exhausting week where he contested the 100, 200 and both relays!
Born Barletta, 28.6.1952; *Height* 1.79m (5′ 10½″), *Weight* 68kg (150lb). *Best marks* 100 metres – 10.19; 200 metres – 20.11; 400 metres – 45.87.

FRANZ-PETER HOFMEISTER (Germany)
(400 metres – 45.73)
Running himself to a state of collapse, Franz-Peter Hofmeister finally secured an individual gold medal after a lengthy international career that had begun with a European Junior 100/200 metres double back in 1970. Hofmeister topped the rankings prior to Prague but his task was made comparatively easier when the favoured Fons Brydenbach (Bel) was eliminated in the heats with a recurrence of injury.
Born Kerpen, 5.8.1951; *Height* 1.86m (6′ 1¼″), *Weight* 74kg (163lb). *Best marks* 100 metres – 10.1; 200 metres – 20.57; 400 metres – 45.45.

OLAF BEYER (GDR)
(800 metres – 1:43.8)
Olaf Beyer shook everyone with his victory. The East German's second placings in the 1977 European Cup Final and 1978 European Indoor Championships had marked him as a runner of promise, but in the process of outlasting a classy European field through a blistering pace he slashed two seconds from his previous best and came within 0.4 of Alberto Juantorena's world record.
Born Grimma, 18.6.1957; *Height* 1.86m (6′ 1¼″), *Weight* 70kg (154lb). *Best marks* 400 metres – 47.53; 800 metres – 1:43.8; 1500 metres – 3:37.1.

STEVE OVETT (UK)
(1500 metres – 3:35.6)
Since his fine victories in the European and World Cup Finals in 1977, Steve Ovett had

been a clear favourite for the European title, but he could scarcely have envisaged a more co-operative set of finalists who provided a tailor-made race for which Ovett's lethal kick in the last 200 metres was most highly suited. In winning the title Ovett maintained a fine British tradition, following Sydney Wooderson (1938), Roger Bannister (1954), Brian Hewson (1958) and John Whetton (1969).
Born Brighton, 9.10.1955; *Height* 1.83m (6′ 0″), *Weight* 70kg (154lb). *Best marks* 400 metres – 47.5; 800 metres – 1:44.1; 1500 metres – 3:34.5; Mile – 3:52.8; 3000 metres – 7:41.3; 2 miles – 8:13.5 (World best); 5000 metres – 13:25.0.

VENANZIO ORTIS (Italy)
(5000 metres – 13:28.5)
Having already finished a spectacular runner-up in the 10,000 metres with a new national record (27:31.5), Venanzio Ortis came of age at these Championships. He was one of seven runners at the bell in the 5000 metres final but had the strength and confidence in the last 150 metres to win the title. His great progress in 1978 followed several years in the doldrums after finishing second in the 1973 IAAF Junior Cross-Country Championship.
Born Paluzza, 29.1.1955; *Height* 1.78m (5′ 10″), *Weight* 64kg (141lb). *Best marks* 1500 metres – 3:43.2; 5000 metres – 13:20.8; 10,000 metres – 27:31.5.

MARTTI VAINIO (Finland)
(10,000 metres – 27:31.0)
Martti Vainio maintained the heritage of the Flying Finns by claiming for his native land yet another major 10,000 metres title. Vainio considered to be a front-runner by nature, but in the final he adopted similar tactics to those of his legendary compatriot Lasse Viren and hung back, allowing the field to be reduced to a few contenders before he moved into the fray with 800 metres of the race remaining.
Born Vehkalahti, 30.12.1950; *Height* 1.91m (6′ 3¼″), *Weight* 71kg (157lb). *Best marks* 1500 metres – 3:45.5; 5000 metres – 13:28.0; 10,000m – 27:31.0.

THOMAS MUNKELT (GDR)
(110 metres hurdles – 13.54)
The 1977 European and World Cup winner, Thomas Munkelt, secured his first major title but it was a close-run thing as two-hundredths of a second covered the first three. The elimination of top-ranked European, Viktor

194

Myasnikov (Sov), in the semi-finals gave Munkelt all the opportunity he needed to claim the Championship.

Born Zedlitz, 3.8.1952; *Height* 1.85m (6' 0¾"), *Weight* 80kg (176lb). *Best marks* 100 metres – 10.49; 110 metres hurdles – 13.37.

HARALD SCHMID (Germany)
(400 metres hurdles – 48.51)
The prodigiously talented Harald Schmid must have been one of the hottest favourites of the Championships. Blessed with superb flat speed plus the strength to run 800 metres in 1:46.9, he could have chosen to contest the 400 metres flat with equal confidence. He is one of the few athletes to have defeated Olympic champion Ed Moses and his best of 48.43 is the second-fastest ever by a European.

Born Hanau, 29.9.1957; *Height* 1.87m (6' 1½"), *Weight* 82kg (181lb). *Best marks* 100 metres – 10.3; 200 metres – 21.01; 400 metres – 45.06; 800 metres – 1:46.9; 400 metres hurdles – 48.43.

BRONISLAW MALINOWSKI (Poland)
(3000 metres steeplechase – 8:15.1)
Bronislaw Malinowski, the first steeplechaser to retain a European title, has been one of the world's leading exponents for eight seasons. He won the European Junior title in 1970, finished fourth in the 1972 Olympic final and second in 1976. Born of a Polish father and Scottish mother, Malinowski is also a massively talented runner on the flat.

Born Newe, 4.6.1951; *Height* 1.81m (5' 11¼"), *Weight* 70kg (154lb). *Best marks* 1500 metres – 3:37.4; Mile – 3:55.4; 3000 metres – 7:42.4; 5000 metres – 13:17.7; 10,000 metres – 28:25.2; 3000 metres steeplechase – 8:09.1.

LEONID MOSEYEV (USSR)
(Marathon – 2:11:57.5)
It has taken the USSR 20 years to find a successor to Sergey Popov, winner of the European title in 1958 with a then-astounding 2:15:17; but in Leonid Moseyev they have found at last another marathoner of the highest calibre. He improved his personal best by almost five minutes to 2:12:20 in finishing seventh in Montreal, cut that still further to 2:11:57 in placing second to Bill Rodgers (USA) in the 1977 Fukuoka marathon and matched that time when winning in Prague on a much more difficult course.

Born 21.10.1952; *Height* 1.73m (5' 8"), *Weight* 55kg (121lb). *Best marks* 5000 metres – 13:38.6; 10,000 metres – 28:03.6; Marathon – 2:11:57.

ROLAND WIESER (GDR)
(20 kilometres walk – 1:23:11.5)
Roland Wieser has made steady progress since winning the European Junior 10,000 metres walk title in 1975. In 1976 he reduced his 20 kilometres time by nearly three minutes to 1:27:28, and a year later he finished a solid seventh in the Lugano Trophy Final at Milton Keynes. Wieser's time in Prague was the fastest ever recorded, although doubts have been expressed over the accuracy of the distance.

Born Berlin, 6.5.1956; *Height* 1.87m (6' 1½"), *Weight* 71kg (157lb). *Best mark* 20 kilometres walk – 1:23:11.5.

JORGE LLOPART (Spain)
(50 kilometres walk – 3:53:29.9)
Mexico's walkers have dominated the world scene in recent years and their influence was felt in Prague when the diminutive Jorge Llopart won Spain's first European title, looking like a replica of Bautista and Co! He had spent some weeks earlier in the year training with the Mexicans and evidently absorbed much of what he learnt.

Born 5.5.1952; *Height* 1.67m (5' 5¾"), *Weight* 63kg (139lb). *Best mark* 50 kilometres walk – 3:53:29.9.

VLADIMIR YASHCHENKO (USSR)
(High jump – 2.30m/7' 6½")
The Soviet youngster, one of athletics' genuine superstars, twice in 1978 electrified European audiences with his cool approach in the final stages of tense competition. He claimed the European indoor title in Milan with an absolute world best of 2.35 metres (7' 8½"), and added the outdoor title after a marathon four and three-quarter hour competition in very chilly conditions. He has twice broken the world outdoor record: 2.33 metres (7' 7¾") in 1977, aged 18, and 2.34 metres (7' 8") in 1978.

Born Zaperozhye (Ukraine), 12.1.1959; *Height* 1.93m (6' 4"), *Weight* 84kg (185lb). *Best mark* High jump – 2.35m (7' 8½") (World record).

VLADIMIR TROFIMENKO (USSR)
(Pole vault – 5.55m/18' 2¼")
Vladimir Trofimenko, the Soviet record holder at 5.61 metres (18' 4¾") was close to his best in Prague despite the length of the competition (five hours), the cold and the damp. In a nerve-racking contest he cleared 5.55 metres (18' 2¼") for victory. It was his second big international success of the year, for in March he had won in the Europe v USA indoor match.

Born 22.5.1953; *Height* 1.86m (6' 1¼"), *Weight* 78kg (172lb). *Best mark* Pole vault – 5.61m (18' 4¾").

JACQUES ROUSSEAU (France)
(Long jump – 8.18m/26' 10")
He had problems even qualifying for the final,

but everything turned out just fine for Rousseau. Twice a European indoor champion (1975 and 1976) he finally made it big outdoors, jumping well over 8 metres on all three of his valid jumps in the final. An excellent sprinter, Rousseau placed fourth at the Montreal Olympics.

Born Guadeloupe, 10.3.1951; *Height* 1.86m (6' 1¼"), *Weight* 79kg (174lb). *Best marks* 100 metres – 10.3; 200 metres – 20.9; 400 metres – 47.5; Long jump – 8.26m (27' 1¼") and 8.37m (27' 5½")w.

MILOS SREJOVIC (Yugoslavia)
(Triple jump – 16.94m/55' 7")
One of the major surprises of the Championships was Milos Srejovic's last-round winning effort over three-time Olympic champion Viktor Sanyeyev (Sov). Ranked a mere sixty-fourth in Europe in 1977 with 16.11 metres (52' 10¼"), he made a meteoric rise during the 1978 season to 16.75 metres (54' 11½") and finally to 16.94 metres (55' 7") in Prague.

Born Kragujevac, 12.4.1956; *Height* 1.91m (6' 3¼"), *Weight* 79kg (174lb). *Best mark* Triple jump – 16.94m (55' 7").

UDO BEYER (GDR)
(Shot – 21.08m/69' 2")
Always the man for the big occasion, Udo Beyer duly added the European title to his 1976 Olympic crown and wins in the 1977 European Cup Final and World Cup competitions. Prior to these Championships, Beyer had broken Aleksandr Baryshnikov's world record with a mighty put of 22.15 metres (72' 8").

Born Eisenhuttenstadt, 9.8.1955; *Height* 1.94m (6' 4¼"), *Weight* 112kg (247lb). *Best mark* Shot – 22.15m (72' 8") (World record).

WOLFGANG SCHMIDT (GDR)
(Discus – 66.82m/219' 3")
World Cup winner, Wolfgang Schmidt, started outright favourite for the title having recently set a new world record of 71.16 metres (233' 5"). He emphasised his position by leading the qualifiers with a throw of 67.20 metres (220' 6") but unexpectedly he was only third at the start of the fifth round of the final. His last two throws, however, won him the title comfortably. Schmidt also gained a bronze medal in the shot.

Born Berlin, 16.1.1954; *Height* 1.97m (6' 5½"), *Weight* 110kg (243lb). *Best marks* Shot – 20.76m (68' 1½"); Discus – 71.16m (233' 5") (World record).

YURIY SEDYKH (USSR)
(Hammer – 77.28m/253' 6")
Olympic champion Yuriy Sedykh retained the USSR's hold on the hammer title. Below form in 1977 when he finished third in the European Cup final and fourth in the World Cup, Sedykh roared back to top form shortly before the European Championships with a personal best of 79.76 metres (261' 8"), defeating world record holder Karl-Hans Riehm (Ger) in the process. He is coached by the former Olympic champion, Anatoliy Bondarchuk.

Born Novocherkask, 11.6.1955; *Height* 1.87m (6' 1½"), *Weight* 115kg (253lb). *Best mark* Hammer – 79.76m (261' 8").

MICHAEL WESSING (Germany)
(Javelin – 89.12m/292' 5")
Michael Wessing has worked long and hard at his career and his reward was a major title. An inspired winner of the 1977 World Cup competition in Dusseldorf, Wessing's most dramatic improvement came the following season when he threw 94.22 metres (309' 1") to place second on the world all-time list.

Born Recklinghausen, 29.8.1952; *Height* 1.83m (6' 0"), *Weight* 91kg (201lb). *Best mark* Javelin – 94.22m (309' 1").

ALEKSANDR GREBENYUK (USSR)
(Decathlon – 8340)
The 1977 European Combined Events Cup final winner, Aleksandr Grebenyuk – the world's highest-scoring decathlete in 1977 – proved the value of experience and consistency by progressing steadily through the two days of competition in demanding conditions. Nearly 300 points behind Daley Thompson at the halfway mark, he took the lead in the ninth event. Grebenyuk scored 4171 points on the first day, 4169 on the second!

Born Zelenokumsk, 2.5.1951; *Height* 1.89m (6' 2¼"), *Weight* 92kg (203lb). *Best marks* 100 metres – 10.89; 400 metres – 48.63; 1500 metres – 4:24.4; 110 metres hurdles – 14.32; High jump – 2.04m (6' 8¼"); Pole vault – 4.70m (15' 5"); Long jump – 7.34m (24' 1"); Shot – 17.10m (56' 1¼"); Discus – 52.24m (171' 5"); Javelin – 73.60m (241' 6"); Decathlon – 8478.

MARLIES GOHR (GDR)
(100 metres – 11.13)
World record holder (10.88) Marlies Gohr (née Oelsner) claimed her first major outdoor title to add to the two European indoor gold medals she won earlier. In previous championships she was second in the 1975 **European Junior and eighth in the 1976** Olympics, but in 1977 she clocked her phenomenal world record and was the winner of both the European and World Cup events.

Born Gera, 21.3.1958; *Height* 1.64m (5' 4½"), *Weight* 52kg (115lb). *Best marks* 100 metres – 10.88 (World record); 200 metres – 22.38.

LYUDMILA KONDRATYEVA (USSR)
(200 metres – 22.52)
Lyudmila Kondratyeva improved beyond recognition to become a surprise winner over 100 metres champion Marlies Gohr. Coming to Prague with a personal best of 22.90 she won her semi-final in an impressive 22.83 and then progressed still further in the final to record a new Soviet record of 22.52. She had finished sixth in the 100 metres final.

Born 17.4.1958; *Height* 1.69m (5' 6¼"), *Weight* 58kg (128lb). *Best marks* 100 metres – 11.35; 200 metres – 22.52.

MARITA KOCH (GDR)
(400 metres – 48.94)
Marita Koch's devastating form – highlighted by world records of 22.06 for 200 metres and 49.02 for 400 metres – confirmed her ability to win both events in Prague. The timetable did not permit a 'double', though, so the East German girl concentrated on the longer event and avenged her defeat at the hands of Irena Szewinska (Pol) in the previous year's World Cup, setting another world record (48.94) in the process.

Born Wismar, 18.2.1957; *Height* 1.71m (5' 7¼"), *Weight* 60kg (132lb). *Best marks* 100 metres – 11.16; 200 metres – 22.06 (World record); 400 metres – 48.94 (World record).

TATYANA PROVIDOKHINA (USSR)
(800 metres – 1:55.8)
Following a relatively disappointing 1977 season, Tatyana Providokhina served warning of her outstanding form when she clocked a 'world record' 2:30.6 for 1000 metres shortly before the Championships – where her winning time of 1:55.8 was a personal best. In 1976 she ran 1:57.0 but such was the depth of talent in Soviet middle-distance running that she did not make the Olympic team!

Born Leningrad, 26.3.1953; *Height* 1.67m (5' 5¾"), *Weight* 51kg (112lb). *Best marks* 800 metres – 1:55.8; 1000 metres – 2:30.6 (World best).

GIANA ROMANOVA (USSR)
(1500 metres – 3:59.0)
Upset after placing only fifth in the 3000 metres, which she regarded as her stronger event, Giana Romanova more than made amends in the 1500 metres, in which she ran a full four seconds faster than ever before to clock 3:59.0. She has also been a major force in the Soviet cross-country team, finishing third in the 1977 IAAF Championship.

Born 10.3.1955; *Height* 1.60m (5' 3"), *Weight* 48kg (106lb). *Best marks* 1500 metres – 3:59.0; 3000 metres – 8:43.0.

SVETLANA ULMASOVA (USSR)
(3000 metres – 8:33.2)
Part of a new wave of Soviet distance running talent, Svetlana Ulmasova – who hails from high altitude Uzbekhistan – was seemingly out of contact in fourth place at the bell but a spectacular last lap of about 61 seconds carried her to a thrilling victory in very fast time. Her previous best stood at 8:42.6 in winning against the USA in July.

Born 4.2.1953; *Height* 1.62m (5' 3¾"), *Weight* 62kg (126lb). *Best marks* 1500 metres – 4:05.1; 3000 metres – 8:33.2.

JOHANNA KLIER (GDR)
(100 metres hurdles – 12.62)
Johanna Klier (née Schaller), the reigning Olympic champion, claimed the European title to add to the indoor honours she won in Milan earlier in the year. She won the 1977 European Cup final in the absence of arch-rival Grazyna Rabsztyn, but the Polish girl got the better of Klier in the World Cup. Rabsztyn, the world record holder, was disqualified from competing in the re-run final in Prague.

Born Erfurt, 3.9.1952; *Height* 1.76m (5' 9¼"), *Weight* 70kg (154lb). *Best mark* 100 metres hurdles – 12.62.

TATYANA ZELENTSOVA (USSR)
(400 metres hurdles – 54.89)
Despite a long and varied career, Tatyana Zelentsova was internationally practically unknown before 1978. Starting the season with a best of 57.6 she leapt to prominence with a new world record of 55.31, improving to 54.89 in Prague to become the first woman to break 55 seconds for the event. Zelentsova's 14-year career began with the 80 metres hurdles. She took up 400 metres hurdling in 1976 (58.73).

Born Moscow, 5.8.1948; *Height* 1.68m (5' 6"), *Weight* 59kg (130lb). *Best mark* 400 metres hurdles – 54.89 (World record).

SARA SIMEONI (Italy)
(High jump – 2.01m/6' 7")
Sara Simeoni made a timely emergence from the shadow of Olympic champion Rosi Ackermann (GDR) – for so long the supreme competitor in women's high jumping – to clinch a major title other than the European indoor successes she gained in 1977 and 1978. She leapt to a new world record of 2.01 metres (6' 7") prior to these Championships, and duplicated that dizzy height in Prague.

Born Verona, 19.4.1953; *Height* 1.78m (5' 10"), *Weight* 61kg (134lb). *Best mark* High jump – 2.01m (6' 7") (World record).

197

VILMA BARDAUSKIENE (USSR)
(Long jump – 6.88m/22' 7")

Having topped the 1977 world rankings, Vilma Bardauskiene proved a disappointment in the 1978 European Indoor Championship, finishing merely ninth of 12 competitors. But that reverse was forgotten when she jumped to a world record of 7.07 metres (23' 2½"), improving that to 7.09 metres (23' 3¼") in the qualifying round in Prague. She possesses 11.5 sprinting speed.

Born Vilnius (Lithuania), 15.6.1953; *Height* 1.75m (5' 8¾"), *Weight* 65kg (143lb). *Best mark* Long jump – 7.09m (23' 3¼") (World record).

ILONA SLUPIANEK (GDR)
(Shot – 21.41m/70' 3")

The 1973 European Junior champion as Ilona Schoknecht came back after a one year IAAF ban for taking anabolic steroids to secure the European title. She was disqualified after a dope test at the 1977 European Cup Final in Helsinki. Prior to Prague she moved to second on the world all-time list with a put of 22.06 metres (72' 4½").

Born Demmin, 24.9.1956; *Height* 1.80m (5' 10¾"), *Weight* 85kg (187lb). *Best marks* Shot – 22.06m (72' 4½"); Discus – 64.40m (211' 3").

EVELIN JAHL (GDR)
(Discus – 66.98m/219' 9")

Olympic champion Evelin Jahl (née Schlaak) proved herself to be a perfect 'big-time' competitor by returning to add the European title after a quiet season in 1977 when she married shot-putter Norbert Jahl. She signalled her return to top form in the accustomed GDR style – by posting a new world record of 70.72 metres (232' 0") in August 1978.

Born Annaberg, 28.3.1956; *Height* 1.79m (5' 10½"), *Weight* 84kg (185lb). *Best mark* Discus – 70.72m (232' 0") (World record).

RUTH FUCHS (GDR)
(Javelin – 69.16m/226' 11")

Rarely has one athlete so dominated an event as has Ruth Fuchs the women's javelin. Her ultra-consistency at major championships is unparalleled. Of the 10 most important competitions in her eight-year career at the top – including two Olympics, three European Championships, four European Cup Finals and the World Cup – she has only lost one, when she finished third in the 1971 European. In Prague, at the age of 31, she produced the longest throw of her career, a European record of 69.16 metres (226' 11").

Born Egeln, 14.12.1946; *Height* 1.69m (5' 6½"), *Weight* 67kg (148lb). *Best mark* Javelin – 69.16m (226' 11") (European record).

MARGIT PAPP (Hungary)
(Pentathlon – 4655)

It was not until two months after the competition that Margit Papp became European pentathlon champion. In Prague she finished second but it transpired that the winner, Nadyezhda Tkachenko (Sov), had been taking anabolic steroids and she was disqualified. The Hungarian set personal bests during the contest in the hurdles and 800 metres. Her strongest individual event – the long jump.

Born 30.4.1948; *Height* 1.77m (5' 9¾"), *Weight* 72kg (159lb). *Best marks* 800 metres – 2:16.2; 100 metres hurdles – 13.70; High jump – 1.84m (6' 0½"); Long jump – 6.54m (21' 5½"); Shot – 15.75m (51' 8¼"); Pentathlon – 4675.

Records and Ranking Lists

Compiled by Peter Matthews *National Union of Track Statisticians*

Records
(W) World; (E) European; (C) Commonwealth; (UK) United Kingdom;
(WJ) World Junior; (EJ) European Junior; (UKJ) UK Junior.

MEN

---

100 METRES
(W)	9.95	Jim Hines (USA); 1968
(E)	10.07	Valeriy Borzov (Sov); 1972
(C)	10.04	Lennox Miller (Jam); 1968
(UK)	10.15	Allan Wells; 1978
(WJ)	10.11	Harvey Glance (USA); 1976
(EJ)	10.16i	Eugen Ray (GDR); 1976
(UKJ)	10.29	Peter Radford; 1958

200 METRES
(W)	19.83	Tommie Smith (USA); 1968
(E)	20.00	Valeriy Borzov (Sov); 1972
(C)	19.86	Don Quarrie (Jam); 1971
(UK)	20.61	Allan Wells; 1978
(WJ)	20.22	Dwayne Evans (USA); 1976
(EJ)	20.59	Bernhard Hoff (GDR); 1977
(UKJ)	20.67	David Jenkins; 1971

400 METRES
(W)	43.86	Lee Evans (USA); 1968
(E)	44.70	Karl Honz (Ger); 1972
(C)	44.92	Julius Sang (Ken); 1972
(UK)	44.93	David Jenkins; 1975
(WJ)	45.04	Wayne Collett (USA); 1968
(EJ, UKJ)	45.45	David Jenkins; 1971

800 METRES
(W)	1:43.4	Alberto Juantorena (Cub); 1977
(E)	1:43.7	Marcello Fiasconaro (Ita); 1973
(C)	1:43.6	Mike Boit (Ken); 1976
(UK)	1:44.0	Sebastian Coe; 1978
(WJ)	1:44.2	Jim Ryun (USA); 1966
(EJ)	1:45.5	Andreas Busse (GDR); 1978
(UKJ)	1:45.8	Steve Ovett; 1974

1000 METRES
(W)	2:13.9	Rick Wohlhuter (USA); 1974
(E)	2:15.5	Ivo van Damme (Bel); 1976
(C)	2:15.3	Mike Boit (Ken); 1977
(UK)	2:18.2	John Boulter; 1969
(WJ, EJ)	2:18.3	Andreas Busse (GDR); 1977
(UKJ)	2:20.0	Steve Ovett; 1973

1500 METRES
(W, C)	3:32.2	Filbert Bayi (Tan); 1974
(E)	3:34.0	Jean Wadoux (Fra); 1970
(UK)	3:34.5	Steve Ovett; 1977
(WJ)	3:36.1	Jim Ryun (USA); 1966
(EJ, UKJ)	3:37.7	Graham Williamson; 1978

1 MILE
(W, C)	3:49.4	John Walker (NZ); 1975
(E)	3:52.5	Thomas Wessinghage (Ger); 1978
(UK)	3:52.8	Steve Ovett; 1978
(WJ)	3:51.3	Jim Ryun (USA); 1966
(EJ)	3:55.7	Ari Paunonen (Fin); 1977
(UKJ)	3:55.8	Graham Williamson; 1978

2000 METRES
(W, C)	4:51.4	John Walker (NZ); 1976
(E)	4:56.2	Michel Jazy (Fra); 1966
(UK)	4:57.8	Steve Ovett; 1978
(WJ, EJ)	5:04.4	Harald Hudak (Ger); 1976
(UKJ)	5:10.1	Julian Goater; 1972

3000 METRES
(W, C)	7:32.1	Henry Rono (Ken); 1978
(E, UK)	7:35.2	Brendan Foster; 1974
(WJ, EJ)	7:43.2	Ari Paunonen (Fin); 1977
(UKJ)	8:00.1	Michael Morton; 1978

5000 METRES
(W, C)	13:08.4	Henry Rono (Ken); 1978
(E)	13:13.0	Emiel Puttemans (Bel); 1972
(UK)	13:14.6	Brendan Foster; 1974
(WJ, EJ, UKJ)	13:37.4	David Black; 1971

10,000 METRES
(W, C)	27:22.5	Henry Rono (Ken); 1978
(E, UK)	27:30.3	Brendan Foster; 1978
(WJ)	28:32.8	Rudy Chapa (USA); 1976
(EJ)	29:08.0	Konstantin Lebedyev (Sov); 1976
(UKJ)	29:38.6	Ray Crabb; 1973

1 HOUR
(W, E)	20,944m	Jos Hermens (Hol); 1976
(C, UK)	20,472m	Ron Hill; 1968

20,000 METRES
(W, E)	57:24.2	Jos Hermens (Hol); 1976
(C, UK)	58:39.0	Ron Hill; 1968

25,000 METRES
(W, E)	1:14:16.8	Pekka Paivarinta (Fin); 1975
(C, UK)	1:15:22.6	Ron Hill; 1965

30,000 METRES
(W, E, C, UK)	1:31:30.4	Jim Alder; 1970

3000 METRES STEEPLECHASE
(W, C)	8:05.4	Henry Rono (Ken); 1978
(E)	8:08.0	Anders Garderud (Swe); 1976
(UK)	8:19.0	Dennis Coates; 1976
(WJ, EJ)	8:29.5	Ralf Ponitzsch (GDR); 1976
(UKJ)	8:48.4	Graeme Fell; 1978

110 METRES HURDLES
(W)	13.21	Alejandro Casanas (Cub); 1977
(E)	13.28	Guy Drut (Fra); 1975
(C)	13.69	Berwyn Price; 1973 (and UK)
	13.69	Fatwell Kimaiyo (Ken); 1974
	13.69	Godwin Obasogie (Nig); 1976
(WJ)	13.23	Renaldo Nehemiah (USA); 1978
(EJ)	13.66	Arto Bryggare (Fin); 1977
(UKJ)	14.06	Mark Holtom; 1977

400 METRES HURDLES
(W)	47.45	Edwin Moses (USA); 1977
(E, UK)	48.12	David Hemery (UK); 1968
(C)	47.82	John Akii-Bua (Uga); 1972
(WJ, EJ)	49.61	Harald Schmid (Ger); 1976
(UKJ)	51.15	Andy Todd; 1967

HIGH JUMP
(W, E)	2.34m (7' 8½")	Vladimir Yashchenko (Sov); 1978
(C)	2.26m (7' 5")	Greg Joy (Can); 1976
(UK)	2.20m (7' 2¾")	Brian Burgess; 1978
(WJ, EJ)	2.33m (7' 7¾")	Vladimir Yashchenko (Sov); 1977
(UKJ)	2.15m (7' 0½")	Brian Burgess; 1976 and Trevor Llewelyn; 1978

POLE VAULT
(W)	5.71m (18' 8¾")	Mike Tully (USA); 1978
(E)	5.66m (18' 6¾")	Wladyslaw Kozakiewicz (Pol); 1977
(C)	5.53m (18' 2")	Don Baird (Aus); 1977
(UK)	5.42m (17' 9¼")	Brian Hooper; 1978
(WJ)	5.43m (17' 10")	Mike Tully (USA); 1975
(EJ)	5.40m (17' 8½")	Francois Tracanelli (Fra); 1970
	5.40m (17' 8½")	Viktor Spasov (Sov); 1978
(UKJ)	5.10m (16' 8¾")	Brian Hooper; 1972

LONG JUMP
(W)	8.90m (29' 2½")	Bob Beamon (USA); 1968
(E)	8.45m (27' 8¾")	Nenad Stekic (Yug); 1975
(C, UK)	8.23m (27' 0")	Lynn Davies; 1968
(WJ)	8.34m (27' 4½")	Randy Williams (USA); 1972
(EJ)	8.05m (26' 5")	Antonio Corgos (Spa); 1978
(UKJ)	7.72m (25' 4")	Daley Thompson; 1977

TRIPLE JUMP
(W)	17.89m (58' 8¼")	Joao Carlos de Oliveira (Bra); 1975
(E)	17.44m (57' 2¾")	Viktor Sanyeyev (Sov); 1972
(C)	17.02m (55' 10")	Phil May (Aus); 1968
(UK)	16.76m (55' 0")	Keith Connor; 1978

(WJ)   17.40m   Pedro Perez (Cub); 1971
(57′ 1″)
(EJ)   17.00m (55′Aleksandr Lisichonok
9¼″)   (Sov); 1978
(UKJ)   16.24m   Aston Moore; 1975
(53′ 3½″)

SHOT
(W, E)   22.15m   Udo Beyer (GDR); 1978
(72′ 8″)
(C, UK)   21.55m Geoff Capes; 1976
(70′ 8¼″)
(WJ)   20.38m   Terry Albritton (USA);
(66′ 10¼″)   1974
(EJ)   20.20m (66′ Udo Beyer (GDR); 1974
3¼″)
(UKJ)   16.80m   Geoff Capes; 1968
(55′ 1½″)

DISCUS
(W, E)   71.16m   Wolfgang Schmidt (GDR);
(233′ 5″)   1976
(C)   65.40m   Borys Chambul (Can);
(214′ 7″)   1976
(UK)   64.94m   Bill Tancred; 1974
(213′ 1″)
(WJ, EJ) 63.64m Werner Hartmann (Ger);
(208′ 9″)   1978
(UKJ)   53.32m   Paul Buxton; 1975
(174′ 11″)

HAMMER
(W, E)   80.32m   Karl-Hans Riehm (Ger);
(263′ 6″)   1978
(C, UK)   74.98m Chris Black; 1976
(246′ 0″)
(WJ, EJ) 78.14m Roland Steuk (GDR); 1978
(256′ 4″)
(UKJ)   64.14m   Ian Chipchase; 1971
(210′ 5″)

JAVELIN
(W, E)   94.58m   Miklos Nemeth (Hun);
(310′ 4″)   1976
(C, WJ)   87.76m Phil Olsen (Can); 1976
(287′ 11″)
(UK, UKJ)   Charles Clover; 1974
84.92m
(278′ 7″)
(EJ)   85.70m   Arto Harkonen (Fin); 1978
(281′ 2″)

DECATHLON *(with fully automatic timing)*
(W)   8618   Bruce Jenner (USA); 1976
(E)   8498   Guido Kratschmer (Ger);
                  1978
(C, UK)   8289   Daley Thompson; 1978
(WJ, EJ, UKJ)   Daley Thompson; 1977
8124

4 × 100 METRES RELAY
(W)   38.03   United States; 1977
(E)   38.42   France; 1968
(C)   38.39   Jamaica; 1968
(UK)   39.24   Scotland; 1978
(WJ)   39.51   United States; 1978
(EJ)   39.67   Soviet Union; 1978
(UKJ)   40.74   National Team; 1976

4 × 200 METRES RELAY
(W)   1:20.3   Univ. of Southern
                  California, USA; 1978
(E)   1:21.5   Italy; 1972
(C)   1:22.5   Trinidad and Tobago; 1972
(UK)   1:24.1   National Team; 1971

4 × 400 METRES RELAY
(W)   2:56.2   United States; 1968
(E, UK)   3:00.5 United Kingdom; 1972
(C)   2:59.6   Kenya; 1968
(WJ, EJ)   3:06.8 GDR; 1973
(UKJ)   3:07.3   National Team; 1973

4 × 800 METRES RELAY
(W, E)   7:08.1   Soviet Union; 1978
(C)   7:11.6   Kenya; 1970
(UK)   7:14.6   National Team; 1966

4 × 1500 METRES RELAY
(W, E)   14:38.8 Germany; 1977
(C)   14:40.4   New Zealand; 1973
(UK)   15:04.6   National Team; 1976

TRACK WALKING
20,000 METRES
(W)   1:23:31.9   Daniel Bautista (Mex); 1977
(E)   1:24:22.8   Hartwig Gauder (GDR);
                  1978
(C, UK)   Ken Matthews; 1964
1:28:45.8

2 HOURS
(W)   27,247m   Raul Gonzales (Mex); 1978
(E)   27,154m   Bernd Kannenberg (Ger);
                  1974
(C)   26,118m   Ted Allsopp (Aus); 1956
(UK)   26,037m   Ron Wallwork; 1971

30,000 METRES WALK
(W)   2:11:53.4   Raul Gonzales (Mex); 1978
(E)   2:12:58.0   Bernd Kannenberg (Ger);
                  1974
(C, UK)   Roy Thorpe; 1974
2:24:18.2

50,000 METRES WALK
(W)	3:52:23.5	Raul Gonzales (Mex); 1978
(E)	3:56:51.4	Bernd Kannenberg (Ger); 1975
(C, UK) 4:11:22.0		Bob Dobson; 1974

BESTS AT OTHER EVENTS 2 MILES
(W, E, C, UK) 8:13.5		Steve Ovett; 1978
(WJ)	8:25.2	Jim Ryun; 1966
(EJ, UKJ) 8:35.3		Ian Stewart; 1968

MARATHON
(W, C)	2:08:34	Derek Clayton (Aus); 1969
(E, UK)	2:09:12	Ian Thompson; 1974
(WJ)	2:17:44	Kirk Pfeffer (USA); 1975

20,000 METRES ROAD WALK
(W, E)	1:23:12	Roland Wieser (GDR); 1978
(C, UK)	1:24:50	Paul Nihill; 1972

50,000 METRES ROAD WALK
(W)	3:41:20	Raul Gonzales (Mex); 1978
(E)	3:51:39	Reima Salonen (Fin); 1978
(C)	4:05:34	Willie Sawall (Aus); 1977
(UK)	4:08:39	Bob Dobson; 1978

2000 METRES STEEPLECHASE
(W)	5:21.2	Eshetu Tura (Eth); 1976
(E, WJ, EJ) 5:28.1		Frank Baumgartl (GDR); 1977
(UK, C)	5:30.6	Dennis Coates; 1978
(UKJ)	5:32.6	Colin Reitz; 1978

WOMEN

100 METRES
(W, E)	10.88	Marlies Gohr (GDR); 1977
(C)	11.14	Lilieth Hodges (Jam); 1978
(UK)	11.16	Andrea Lynch; 1975
(WJ)	11.13	Chandra Cheeseborough (USA); 1976
(EJ)	11.17	Marlies Gohr (GDR); 1976
(UKJ)	11.45	Sonia Lannaman; 1972

200 METRES
(W, E)	22.06	Marita Koch (GDR); 1978
(C)	22.45	Raelene Boyle (Aus); 1972
(UK)	22.75	Donna Hartley; 1978
(WJ)	22.74	Raelene Boyle (Aus); 1968
(EJ)	22.81	Margit Sinzel (GDR); 1976
(UKJ)	22.99	Kathy Smallwood; 1978

400 METRES
(W, E)	48.94	Marita Koch (GDR); 1978
(C)	51.02	Marilyn Neufville (Jam); 1970
(UK)	51.28	Donna Hartley; 1975
(WJ, EJ)	49.77	Christine Brehmer (GDR); 1976
(UKJ)	52.6	Marilyn Neufville; 1970

800 METRES
(W, E)	1:54.9	Tatyana Kazankina (Sov); 1976
(C)	1:59.0	Charlene Rendina (Aus); 1976
(UK)	2:00.2	Rosemary Wright; 1972
(WJ, EJ)	1:57.5	Hildegarde Ullrich (GDR); 1978
(UKJ)	2:02.0	Jo White; 1977

1500 METRES
(W, E)	3:56.0	Tatyana Kazankina (Sov); 1976
(C, UK)	4:04.8	Sheila Carey; 1972
(WJ, EJ)	4:06.0	Birgit Friedmann (Ger); 1978
(UKJ)	4:14.6	Ruth Smeeth; 1978

3000 METRES
(W, E)	8:27.1	Lyudmila Bragina (Sov); 1976
(C, UK)	8:48.7	Paula Fudge; 1978
(WJ, EJ)	8:58.4	Inger Knutsson (Swe); 1973
(UKJ)	9:15.8	Ruth Smeeth; 1978

100 METRES HURDLES
(W, E)	12.48	Grazyna Rabsztyn (Pol); 1978
(C)	12.93	Pam Ryan (Aus); 1972
(UK)	13.08	Lorna Boothe; 1978
(WJ, EJ)	13.25	Regina Beyer (GDR); 1977
(UKJ)	13.65	Wendy McDonnell; 1978

400 METRES HURDLES
(W, E)	54.89	Tatyana Zelentsova (Sov); 1978
(C)	57.28	Marion Fisher (Aus); 1977
(UK)	57.43	Liz Sutherland; 1978
(WJ, EJ)	56.47	Hildegard Ullrich (GDR); 1978
(UKJ)	59.00	Diane Heath; 1975

HIGH JUMP
(W, E)	2.01m (6' 7")	Sara Simeoni (Ita); 1978

(C) 1.93m (6' Katrina Gibbs (Aus); 1978
4")

(UK) 1.87m (6' Barbara Lawton; 1973
1½")

(WJ, EJ) 1.92m Ulrike Meyfarth (Ger);
(6' 3½") 1972

(UKJ) 1.83m (6' Louise Miller; 1978
0")

LONG JUMP

(W, E) 7.09m Vilma Bardauskiene (Sov);
(23' 3¼") 1978

(C, UK) 6.76m Mary Rand; 1964
(22' 2¼")

(WJ, EJ) 6.77m Marianne Voelzke (GDR);
(22' 2½") 1974

(UKJ) 6.40m Susan Hearnshaw; 1978
(21' 0")

SHOT

(W, E) 22.32m Helena Fibingerova (Cze);
(73' 2¾") 1977

(C) 18.16m (59' Gael Mulhall (Aus); 1978
7")

(UK) 16.40m Margaret Ritchie; 1978
(53' 9¾")

(WJ, EJ) Ilona Slupianek (GDR);
19.23m (63' 1¼") 1974

(UKJ) 15.94m Judith Oakes; 1976
(52' 3¾")

DISCUS

(W, E) 70.72m Evelin Jahl (GDR); 1978
(232' 0")

(C) 61.70m Jane Haist (Can); 1975
(202' 5")

(UK) 60.80m Margaret Ritchie; 1978
(199' 6")

(WJ, EJ) 63.26m Evelin Jahl (GDR); 1974
(207' 6")

(UKJ) 48.82m Lesley Mallin; 1974
(160' 2")

JAVELIN

(W) 69.32m Kate Schmidt (USA); 1977
(227' 5")

(E) 69.16m Ruth Fuchs (GDR); 1978
(226' 11")

(C, UK) 67.20m Tessa Sanderson; 1977
(220' 6")

(WJ, EJ) 63.86m Lyudmila Pasternakevich
(209' 6") (Sov); 1976

(UKJ) 55.04m Tessa Sanderson; 1974
(180' 7")

PENTATHLON

(W, E) 4839 Nadyezhda Tkachenko
(Sov); 1977

(C) 4768 Diane Konihowski (Can);
1978

(UK) 4385 Susan Longden; 1977

(WJ, EJ) 4409 Kristine Nitzsche (GDR);
1977

(UKJ) 4028 Judy Livermore; 1978

4 × 100 METRES RELAY

(W, E) 42.27 GDR; 1978
(C, UK) 42.72 United Kingdom; 1978
(WJ, EJ) 44.05 GDR; 1977
(UKJ) 44.71 National Team; 1977

4 × 200 METRES RELAY

(W, E, C, UK) United Kingdom; 1977
1:31.6

4 × 400 METRES RELAY

(W, E) 3:19.2 GDR; 1976
(C) 3:25.6 Australia; 1976
(UK) 3:26.6 National Team; 1975
(WJ, EJ) 3:32.8 Germany; 1977
(UKJ) 3:37.0 National Team; 1973

4 × 800 METRES RELAY

(W, E) 7:52.3 Soviet Union; 1976
(C, UK) 8:23.8 UK National Team; 1971

BEST AT OTHER EVENTS

1000 METRES

(W, E) 2:30.6 Tatyana Providokhina
(Sov); 1978

(C) 2:36.9 Francine Gendron (Can);
1978

(UK) 2:38.4 Evelyn McMeekin; 1978
(WJ, EJ) 2:36.8 Hildegard Ullrich (GDR);
1977

(UKJ) 2:38.6 Jo White; 1977

1 MILE

(W, E) 4:23.8 Natalia Marasescu (Rom);
1977

(C) 4:35.1 Glenda Reiser (Can); 1973
(UK) 4:36.1 Mary Stewart; 1977

5000 METRES

(W, E) 15:08.8 Loa Olafsson (Den); 1978

10,000 METRES

(W, E) 31:45.4 Loa Olafsson (Den); 1978

MARATHON

(W, E) 2:32:30 Grete Waitz (Nor); 1978
(C) 2:44:11 Gillian File (NZ); 1978
(UK) 2:50:54 Rosemary Cox; 1978

3000 METRES TRACK WALK

(W, E) 13:39.6 Siv Gustavsson (Swe); 1977
(C, UK) 13:40.0 Carol Tyson; 1977 and
1978

5000 METRES TRACK WALK
(W, E)   23:17.5   Thorill Gylder (Nor); 1978
(C, UK)   23:42.4 Carol Tyson; 1977

10,000 METRES TRACK WALK
(W, E)   48:48.5   Siv Gustavsson (Swe); 1978
(C, UK)   49:59.0 Carol Tyson; 1978

World All-Time List

MEN   (wind-assisted marks not included in this section; i = indoor mark)

100 METRES *(Fully automatic timing)*

9.95	Jim Hines (USA); 1968
9.98	Silvio Leonard (Cub); 1977
10.02	Charles Greene (USA); 1968
10.04	Lennox Miller (Jam); 1968
10.05	Bob Hayes (USA), 1964
10.05	Steve Riddick (USA); 1975
10.06	Hasely Crawford (Tri); 1976
10.07	Valeriy Borzov (Sov); 1972
10.07	Don Quarrie (Jam); 1976
10.07	Clancy Edwards (USA); 1978
10.07	Eddie Hart (USA); 1978
10.07	Steve Williams (USA); 1978
10.09	Mel Lattany (USA); 1978
10.10	Hermes Ramirez (Cub); 1968
10.11	Roger Bambuck (Fra); 1968
10.11	Harvey Glance (USA); 1976
10.11	Curtis Dickey (USA); 1978
10.11	Osvaldo Lara (Cub); 1978
10.11	Mike Roberson (USA); 1978
10.11	Don Coleman (USA); 1978

Hand timing

9.8	Steve Williams (USA); 1975
9.8	Harvey Glance (USA); 1977
9.9	Jim Hines (USA); 1968
9.9	Charles Greene (USA); 1968
9.9	Eddie Hart (USA); 1968
9.9	Rey Robinson (USA); 1972
9.9	Silvio Leonard (Cub); 1975
9.9	Don Quarrie (Jam); 1975
9.9	Johnny Jones (USA); 1977
9.9	Mike Roberson (USA); 1978

200 METRES *(Fully automatic timing)*
(*220 yards time less 0.1 sec)

19.83	Tommie Smith (USA); 1968
19.86	Don Quarrie (Jam); 1971
19.92	John Carlos (USA); 1968
20.00	Valeriy Borzov (Sov); 1972
20.03	Clancy Edwards (USA): 1978
20.06	Peter Norman (Aus); 1968
20.06	Silvio Leonard (Cub); 1978
20.10	Millard Hampton (USA); 1976
20.11	Pietro Mennea (Ita); 1977
20.14	James Gilkes (Guy); 1978
20.16	Steve Williams (USA); 1975
20.19	Larry Black (USA); 1972
20.22	Dwayne Evans (USA); 1976

20.24	James Sanford (USA); 1978
20.27	Wardell Gilbreath (USA); 1976
20.27	William Snoddy (USA); 1978
20.28	Larry Questad (USA); 1968
20.29	Jerry Bright (USA); 1968
20.29	Tom Randolph (USA); 1968
20.31	Steve Riddick (USA); 1975

Hand timing

19.7	John Carlos (USA); 1968
19.8	Don Quarrie (Jam); 1975
19.8*	Steve Williams (USA); 1975
19.9	Silvio Leonard (Cub); 1977
20.0	Johnny Jones (USA); 1977
20.0	Larry Black (USA); 1972

400 METRES
(*440 yards time less 0.3 sec)

43.86	Lee Evans (USA); 1968
43.97	Larry James (USA); 1968
44.1	Wayne Collett (USA); 1972
44.2*	John Smith (USA); 1971
44.2	Fred Newhouse (USA); 1972
44.26	Alberto Juantorena (Cub); 1976
44.41	Ron Freeman (USA); 1968
44.45	Ronald Ray (USA); 1975
44.4	Vince Matthews (USA); 1972
44.4*	Curtis Mills (USA); 1969
44.5	Tommie Smith (USA); 1967
44.6*	Adolph Plummer (USA); 1963
44.70	Karl Honz (Ger); 1972
44.73	Willie Smith (USA); 1978
44.7*	Benny Brown (USA); 1973
44.7*	Maurice Peoples (USA); 1973
44.82	Maxie Parks (USA); 1976
44.8*	Ken Randle (USA); 1975
44.8*	Warren Edmondson (USA-pro); 1976
44.92	Julius Sang (Ken); 1972
44.93	David Jenkins (UK); 1975
44.9	4 athletes

800 METRES
(*880 yards time less 0.7 sec)

1:43.4	Alberto Juantorena (Cub); 1977
1:43.4*	Rick Wohlhuter (USA); 1974
1:43.6	Mike Boit (Ken); 1976
1:43.7	Marcello Fiasconaro (Ita); 1973
1:43.8	Olaf Beyer (GDR); 1978
1:43.9	John Kipkurgat (Ken); 1974

1:43.9	Ivo Van Damme (Bel); 1976
1:44.0	Sebastian Coe (UK); 1978
1:44.1	Luciano Susanj (Yug); 1974
1:44.1	Steve Ovett (UK); 1978
1:44.2*	Jim Ryun (USA); 1966
1:44.3	Peter Snell (NZ); 1962
1:44.3	Dave Wottle (USA); 1972
1:44.4	Ralph Doubell (Aus); 1968
1:44.4*	Danie Malan (Saf); 1973
1:44.5	Pekka Vasala (Fin); 1972
1:44.6	Wilson Kiprugut (Ken); 1968
1:44.7	Dicky Broberg (Saf); 1971
1:44.8	Ken Swenson (USA); 1970
1:44.8	Mark Enyeart (USA); 1977

1500 METRES

3:32.2	Filbert Bayi (Tan); 1974
3:32.4	John Walker (NZ); 1975
3:33.1	Jim Ryun (USA); 1967
3:33.2	Ben Jipcho (Ken); 1974
3:33.9	Rod Dixon (NZ); 1974
3:34.0	Jean Wadoux (Fra); 1970
3:34.2	Graeme Crouch (Aus); 1974
3:34.5	Steve Ovett (UK); 1977
3:34.8	Thomas Wessinghage (Ger); 1976
3:34.9	Kipchoge Keino (Ken); 1968
3:35.5	David Moorcroft (UK); 1978
3:35.6	Herb Elliott (Aus); 1960
3:35.6	John Robson (UK); 1978
3:35.7	Frank Clement (UK); 1978
3:36.0	Marty Liquori (USA); 1971
3:36.0	Danie Malan (Saf); 1976
3:36.0	Steve Scott (USA); 1978
3:36.1	Harald Hudak (Ger); 1977
3:36.1	Jurgen Straub (GDR); 1978
3:36.2	Dave Wottle (USA); 1973
3:36.2	Paul-Heinz Wellmann (Ger); 1976
3:36.2	Karl Fleschen (Ger); 1977
3:36.2	Abdrahamne Morsli (Alg); 1977

1 MILE

3:49.4	John Walker (NZ); 1975
3:51.0	Filbert Bayi (Tan); 1975
3:51.1	Jim Ryun (USA); 1967
3:52.0	Ben Jipcho (Ken); 1973
3:52.2	Marty Liquori (USA); 1975
3:52.5	Thomas Wessinghage (Ger); 1978
3:52.6	Jozef Plachy (Cze); 1978
3:52.8	Steve Ovett (UK); 1978
3:52.9	Steve Scott (USA); 1978
3:53.1	Kipchoge Keino (Ken); 1967
3:53.2	Tony Waldrop (USA); 1974
3:53.2	Wilson Waigwa (Ken); 1978
3:53.3	Dave Wottle (USA); 1973
3:53.3	Eamonn Coghlan (Eir); 1975
3:53.3	Rick Wohlhuter (USA); 1975
3:53.6	Michel Jazy (Fra); 1965
3:53.6	Rod Dixon (NZ); 1975
3:53.8	Jurgen May (GDR – later Ger); 1965

3:53.8	Bodo Tummler (Ger); 1968
3:54.1	Peter Snell (NZ); 1964
3:54.2	Frank Clement (UK); 1978

3000 METRES

7:32.1	Henry Rono (Ken); 1978
7:35.2	Brendan Foster (UK); 1974
7:37.6	Emiel Puttemans (Bel); 1972
7:39.6	Kipchoge Keino (Ken); 1965
7:40.3	Suleiman Nyambui (Tan); 1978
7:40.4	Nick Rose (UK); 1978
7:40.6	John Walker (NZ); 1974
7:41.0	Rod Dixon (NZ); 1974
7:41.2	Karl Fleschen (Ger); 1977
7:41.3	Steve Ovett (UK); 1977
7:41.9	Wilson Waigwa (Ken); 1978
7:42.1	Boris Kuznyetsov (Sov); 1978
7:42.2	Markus Ryffel (Swi); 1978
7:42.4	Bronislaw Malinowski (Pol); 1974
7:42.4	Knut Kvalheim (Nor); 1974
7:42.4	Peter Weigt (Ger); 1977
7:42.6	Steve Prefontaine (USA); 1974
7:43.2	Lasse Viren (Fin); 1972
7:43.2	Ari Paunonen (Fin); 1977
7:43.2	Eshetu Tura (Eth); 1977
7:43.2	Marty Liquori (USA); 1977
7:43.5	David Moorcroft (UK); 1978
7:43.8	Jacques Boxberger (Fra); 1976

5000 METRES

13:08.4	Henry Rono (Ken); 1978
13:12.9	Dick Quax (NZ); 1977
13:13.0	Emiel Puttemans (Bel); 1972
13:13.7	Klaus-Peter Hildenbrand (Ger); 1976
13:13.8	Miruts Yifter (Eth); 1977
13:13.9	Karl Fleschen (Ger); 1977
13:14.4	Ben Jipcho (Ken); 1974
13:14.5	Peter Weigt (Ger); 1977
13:14.6	Brendan Foster (UK); 1974
13:15.0	Ilie Floroiu (Rom); 1978
13:15.1	Marty Liquori (USA); 1977
13:16.4	Lasse Viren (Fin); 1972
13:16.6	Ron Clarke (Aus); 1966
13:17.2	David Bedford (UK); 1972
13:17.2	Enn Sellik (Sov); 1976
13:17.3	Rod Dixon (NZ); 1976
13:17.4	David Fitzsimons (Aus); 1977
13:17.6	Anders Garderud (Swe); 1976
13:17.7	Bronislaw Malinowski (Pol); 1976
13:17.8	Fernando Mamede (Por); 1978

10,000 METRES

27:22.5	Henry Rono (Ken); 1978
27:30.3	Brendan Foster (UK); 1978
27:30.5	Samson Kimobwa (Ken); 1977
27:30.8	David Bedford (UK); 1973
27:31.0	Martti Vainio (Fin); 1978
27:31.5	Venanzio Ortis (Ita); 1978
27:31.5	Aleksandr Antipov (Sov); 1978
27:36.3	David Black (UK); 1978

27:36.6	Gerard Tebroke (Hol); 1978	13.21	Alejandro Casanas (Cub); 1977
27:38.4	Lasse Viren (Fin); 1972*	13.22	Greg Foster (USA); 1978
27:39.6	Emiel Puttemans (Bel); 1972	13.23	Renaldo Nehemiah (USA); 1978
27:39.9	Ron Clarke (Aus); 1965	13.24	Rod Milburn (USA); 1972
27:40.1	Ilie Floroiu (Rom); 1978	13.28	Guy Drut (Fra); 1975
27:40.6	Enn Sellik (Sov); 1978	13.33	Willie Davenport (USA); 1968
27:41.0	Miruts Yifter (Eth); 1972	13.33	Frank Siebeck (GDR); 1976
27:41.3	Jos Hermens (Hol); 1977	13.37	Thomas Munkelt (GDR); 1977
27:41.3	Knut Kvalheim (Nor); 1978	13.38	Ervin Hall (USA); 1968
27:41.9	Mike Musyoki (Ken); 1977	13.38	Jerry Wilson (USA); 1975
27:42.0	Dick Quax (NZ); 1977	13.41	Charles Foster (USA); 1976
27:42.1	Detlef Uhlemann (Ger); 1977	13.42*	Thomas Hill (USA); 1970

MARATHON

2:08:34	Derek Clayton (Aus); 1969	13.43	Earl McCullouch (USA); 1967
2:09.06	Shigeru Sou (Jap); 1978	13.43*	Marcus Walker (USA); 1970
2:09:12	Ian Thompson (UK); 1974	13.43	Dedy Cooper (USA); 1978
2:09:28	Ron Hill (UK); 1970	13.45	Kerry Bethel (USA); 1978
2:09:55	Bill Rodgers (USA); 1975	13.45*	Leon Coleman (USA); 1969
2:09:55	Waldemar Cierpinski (GDR); 1976	13.46	Eddy Ottoz (Ita); 1968
2:10:08	Jerome Drayton (Can); 1975	13.46	James Owens (USA); 1978
2:10:15	Jeff Wells (USA); 1978	13.47	Viktor Myasnikov (Sov), 1978
2:10:20	David Chettle (Aus); 1974	*(Leading hand times)*	
2:10:21	Toshihiko Seko (Jap); 1978	13.0	Guy Drut (Fra); 1975
2:10:30	Frank Shorter (USA); 1972	13.0y	Rod Milburn (USA); 1971
2:10:38	Akio Usami (Jap); 1970	13.1y	Lance Babb (USA-pro); 1975
2:10:48	Bill Adcocks (UK); 1968	13.2	Martin Lauer (Ger); 1959
2:11:05	Hideki Kita (Jap); 1978	13.2	Lee Calhoun (USA); 1960
2:11:12	Eamon O'Reilly (USA); 1970	13.2	Earl McCullouch (USA); 1967
2:11:13	John Farrington (Aus); 1973	13.2	Willie Davenport (USA); 1969
2:11:13	Karel Lismont (Bel); 1974	13.2	Ervin Hall (USA); 1969
2:11:15	Esa Tikkanen (Fin); 1978	13.2	Thomas Hill (USA); 1970
2:11:16	Don Kardong (USA); 1976	13.2	Jerry Wilson (USA); 1975
2:11:17	Seiichiro Sasaki (Jap); 1967	13.2	Charles Foster (USA); 1975
2:11:17	Jack Fultz (USA); 1978		

3000 METRES STEEPLECHASE

400 METRES HURDLES
*(*440 yards time plus 0.3 sec)*

8:05.4	Henry Rono (Ken); 1978	47.45	Edwin Moses (USA); 1977
8:08.0	Anders Garderud (Swe); 1976	47.82	John Akii-Bua (Uga); 1972
8:09.1	Bronislaw Malinowski (Pol); 1976	48.12	David Hemery (UK); 1968
8:10.4	Frank Baumgartl (GDR); 1976	48.1	Jim Bolding (USA), 1974
8:12.6	Tapio Kantanen (Fin); 1976	48.43	Harald Schmid (Ger); 1978
8:13.9	Ben Jipcho (Ken); 1973	48.4	Ralph Mann (USA); 1972
8:14.1	Michael Karst (Ger); 1977	48.55	Quentin Wheeler (USA); 1976
8:15.3	Dan Glans (Swe); 1976	48.55	Tom Andrews (USA); 1976
8:16.1	Gheorghe Cefan (Rom); 1976	48.59	Alan Pascoe (UK); 1975
8:16.9	Patriz Ilg (Ger); 1978	48.64	Jim Seymour (USA); 1972
8:18.3	Ismo Tuokonen (Fin); 1978	48.6	Jean-Claude Nallet (Fra); 1970
8:18.9	Franco Fava (Ita); 1974	48.6	Dick Bruggeman (USA); 1972
8:19.0	Dennis Coates (UK); 1976	48.69	Mike Shine (USA); 1976
8:19.3	Doug Brown (USA); 1978	48.83	Volker Beck (GDR); 1977
8:19.4	Gerd Frahmcke (Ger); 1976	48.8	Geoff Vanderstock (USA); 1968
8:19.5	Krzysztof Weselowski (Pol); 1978	48.91	James Walker (USA); 1978
8:19.6	Yohannes Mohamed (Eth); 1975	48.9*	Wayne Collett (USA); 1970
8:19.8	Jurgen Straub (GDR); 1975	49.00	Wes Williams (USA); 1976
8:20.2	Boualem Rahoui (Alg); 1975	49.02	Gerhard Hennige (Ger); 1968
8:20.4	Paul Copu (Rom); 1978	49.02	Yevgeniy Gavrilenko (Sov); 1976

110 METRES HURDLES
(Fully automatic timing)
*(*120 yards time plus 0.03 sec)*

HIGH JUMP
2.35m (7' 8¼")i Vladimir Yashchenko (Sov); 1978
2.32m (7' 7¼") Dwight Stones (USA); 1976

2.32m (7′ 7$\frac{1}{4}$″)i Franklin Jacobs (USA); 1978
2.31m (7′ 7″) Rolf Beilschmidt (GDR); 1977
2.31m (7′ 7″) Greg Joy (Can); 1978
2.30m (7′ 6$\frac{1}{2}$″) Aleksandr Grigoryev (Sov); 1977
2.30m (7′ 6$\frac{1}{2}$″) Jacek Wszola (Pol); 1977
2.30m (7′ 6$\frac{1}{2}$″) Henry Lauterbach (GDR); 1978
2.30m (7′ 6$\frac{1}{2}$″) Benn Fields (USA); 1978
2.29m (7′ 6$\frac{1}{4}$″) Ni Chih-Chin (Chi); 1970
2.29m (7′ 6$\frac{1}{4}$″) Pat Matzdorf (USA); 1971
2.29m (7′ 6$\frac{1}{4}$″) Rory Kotinek (USA); 1977
2.28m (7′ 6″)i John Radetich (USA-pro); 1976
2.28m (7′ 6″) Kyle Arney (USA); 1977
2.28m (7′ 5$\frac{3}{4}$″) Valeriy Brumel (Sov); 1963
2.28m (7′ 5$\frac{3}{4}$″) Bill Jankunis (USA); 1976
2.28m (7′ 5$\frac{3}{4}$″) Sergey Senyukov (Sov); 1977
2.28m (7′ 5$\frac{3}{4}$″)i Wolfgang Killing (Ger); 1978
2.27m (7′ 5$\frac{1}{2}$″) Mike Winsor (USA); 1977
2.27m (7′ 5$\frac{1}{2}$″) Tom Woods (USA); 1975
2.27m (7′ 5$\frac{1}{4}$″)i Stanislav Molotilov (Sov); 1977
2.27m (7′ 5$\frac{1}{4}$″) Gennadiy Byelkov (Sov); 1978
2.27m (7′ 5$\frac{1}{4}$″) Ruud Wielart (Hol); 1978

POLE VAULT

5.71m (18′ 8$\frac{3}{4}$″) Mike Tully (USA); 1978
5.70m (18′ 8$\frac{1}{4}$″) Dave Roberts (USA); 1976
5.67m (18′ 7$\frac{1}{4}$″) Earl Bell (USA); 1976
5.66m (18′ 6$\frac{3}{4}$″) Wladyslaw Kozakiewicz (Pol); 1977
5.63m (18′ 5$\frac{1}{2}$″) Bob Seagren (USA); 1972
5.62m (18′ 5$\frac{1}{4}$″) Tadeusz Slusarski (Pol); 1976
5.61m (18′ 5″)i Steve Smith (USA-pro); 1975
5.61m (18′ 5″) Larry Jessee (USA); 1978
5.61m (18′ 5″) Vladimir Trofimyenko (Sov); 1978
5.60m (18′ 4$\frac{1}{2}$″) Antti Kalliomaki (Fin); 1978
5.59m (18′ 4″) Kjell Isaksson (Swe); 1972
5.59m (18′ 4″) Dan Ripley (USA); 1976
5.56m (18′ 3″) Rauli Pudas (Fin); 1978
5.55m (18′ 2$\frac{1}{2}$″) Vladimir Kishkun (Sov); 1977
5.55m (18′ 2$\frac{3}{4}$″) Jeff Taylor (USA); 1978
5.53m (18′ 2″) Don Baird (Aus); 1977
5.53m (18′ 1$\frac{3}{4}$″) Yuriy Prokhoryenko (Sov); 1976
5.53m (18′ 1$\frac{3}{4}$″) Mariusz Klimczyk (Pol); 1977
5.52m (18′ 1$\frac{1}{4}$″) Russ Rogers (USA); 1976
5.51m (18′ 1″) Vic Dias (USA); 1975
5.51m (18′ 1″) Terry Porter (USA); 1976
5.51m (18′ 1″) Gunther Lohre (Ger); 1978

LONG JUMP

8.90m (29′ 2$\frac{1}{2}$″) Bob Beamon (USA); 1968
8.45m (27′ 8$\frac{3}{4}$″) Nenad Stekic (Yug); 1975
8.35m (27′ 5″) Ralph Boston (USA); 1965
8.35m (27′ 4$\frac{3}{4}$″) Igor Ter-Ovanesyan (Sov); 1967
8.35m (27′ 4$\frac{3}{4}$″) Josef Schwarz (Ger); 1970
8.35m (27′ 4$\frac{3}{4}$″) Arnie Robinson (USA); 1976
8.34m (27′ 4$\frac{1}{2}$″) Randy Williams (USA); 1972
8.27m (27′ 1$\frac{3}{4}$″) Grzegorz Cybulski (Pol); 1975
8.26m (27′ 1$\frac{1}{4}$″)i Charlton Ehizuelen (Nig); 1975
8.26m (27′ 1$\frac{1}{4}$″) Jacques Rousseau (Fra); 1976
8.25m (27′ 1″)i Henry Hines (USA-pro); 1973
8.25m (27′ 1″) Ronald Coleman (USA); 1971
8.24m (27′ 0$\frac{1}{2}$″) James McAlister (USA); 1973
8.23m (27′ 0″) Lynn Davies (UK); 1968
8.23m (27′ 0″) James Lofton (USA); 1978
8.23m (27′ 0″) Norm Tate (USA); 1971
8.22m (26′ 11$\frac{3}{4}$″) Preston Carrington (USA); 1972
8.22m (26′ 11$\frac{3}{4}$″) Larry Doubley (USA); 1977
8.21m (26′ 11$\frac{1}{4}$″) Waldemar Stepien (Pol); 1969
8.21m (26′ 11$\frac{1}{4}$″) Aleksey Perevertsev (Sov); 1976

TRIPLE JUMP

17.89m (58′ 8$\frac{1}{2}$″) Joao Carlos de Oliveira (Bra); 1975
17.44m (57′ 2$\frac{3}{4}$″) Viktor Sanyeyev (Sov); 1972
17.40m (57′ 1″) Pedro Perez (Cub), 1971
17.31m (56′ 9$\frac{1}{2}$″) Jorg Drehmel (GDR); 1972
17.27m (56′ 8″) Nelson Prudencio (Bra); 1968
17.22m (56′ 6″) Giuseppe Gentile (Ita); 1968
17.20m (56′ 5$\frac{1}{4}$″) Mikhail Bariban (Sov); 1973
17.20m (56′ 5$\frac{1}{4}$″) Tommy Haynes (USA); 1975
17.19m (56′ 4$\frac{3}{4}$″) Ron Livers (USA); 1977
17.24m (56′ 6$\frac{3}{4}$″) James Butts (USA); 1978
17.12m (56′ 2″) Carol Corbu (Rom); 1971
17.07m (56′ 0″) Dave Smith (USA); 1972
17.07m (56′ 0″) Anatoliy Piskulin (Sov); 1978
17.06m (55′ 11$\frac{3}{4}$″) Michal Joachimowski (Pol); 1973
17.05m (55′ 11$\frac{1}{4}$″) Willie Banks (USA); 1978
17.03m (55′ 10$\frac{1}{2}$″) Josef Szmidt (Pol); 1960
17.02m (55′ 10″) Phil May (Aus); 1968
17.02m (55′ 10″) Gennadiy Valyukevich (Sov); 1978
17.01m (55′ 9$\frac{3}{4}$″) Nikolay Dudkin (Sov); 1970
17.00m (55′ 9$\frac{1}{4}$″) 3 athletes

SHOT

22.86m (75′ 0″)	Brian Oldfield (USA-pro); 1975
22.15m (72′ 8″)	Udo Beyer (GDR); 1978
22.02m (72′ 2¾″)	George Woods (USA); 1973
22.00m (72′ 2¼″)	Aleksandr Baryshnikov (Sov); 1976
21.85m (71′ 8½″)	Terry Albritton (USA); 1976
21.82m (71′ 7¼″)	Al Feuerbach (USA); 1973
21.78m (71′ 5½″)	Randy Matson (USA); 1967
21.67m (71′ 1¼″)	Hartmut Briesenick (GDR); 1973
21.55m (70′ 8½″)	Geoff Capes (UK); 1976
21.53m (70′ 7¾″)	Yevgeniy Mironov (Sov); 1976
21.42m (70′ 3½″)i	Fred De Bernardi (USA-pro); 1974
21.35m (70′ 0½″)	Ron Semkiw (USA); 1974
21.33m (70′ 0″)	Hans Hoglund (Swe); 1975
21.32m (69′ 11½″)	Heinz-Joachim Rothenburg (GDR); 1972
21.31m (69′ 11″)	Hans-Peter Gies (GDR); 1972
21.26m (69′ 9″)	Reijo Stahlberg (Fin); 1974
21.19m (69′ 6¼″)	Wladyslaw Komar (Pol); 1974
21.11m (69′ 3¼″)	Peter Shmock (USA); 1976
21.09m (69′ 2½″)	Hreinn Halldorsson (Ice); 1977
21.06m (69′ 1¼″)i	Mac Wilkins (USA); 1977

DISCUS

71.16m (233′ 5″)	Wolfgang Schmidt (GDR); 1978
70.86m (232′ 6″)	Mac Wilkins (USA); 1976
70.38m (230′ 11″)	Jay Silvester (USA); 1971
69.08m (226′ 8″)	John Powell (USA); 1975
68.48m (224′ 8″)	John Van Reenan (Saf); 1975
68.40m (224′ 5″)	Ricky Bruch (Swe); 1972
68.40m (224′ 5″)	Ken Stadel (USA); 1978
68.08m (223′ 4″)	Hein-Direck Neu (Ger); 1977
67.82m (222′ 6″)	Velko Velev (Bul); 1978
67.54m (221′ 7″)	Siegfried Pachale (GDR); 1976
67.38m (221′ 1″)	Tim Vollmer (USA); 1971
67.18m (220′ 5″)	Ludvik Danek (Cze); 1974
67.06m (220′ 0″)	Markku Tuokko (Fin); 1977
66.92m (219′ 7″)	Geza Fejer (Hun); 1971
66.90m (219′ 6″)	Norbert Thiede (GDR); 1976
66.82m (219′ 3″)	Pentti Kahma (Fin); 1975
66.52m (218′ 3″)	Alwin Wagner (Ger); 1977
66.48m (218′ 1″)	Art Swarts (USA); 1977
66.38m (217′ 9″)	Janos Muranyi (Hun); 1971
66.28m (217′ 5″)	Knut Hjeltnes (Nor); 1977

HAMMER

80.32m (263′ 6″)	Karl-Hans Riehm (Ger); 1978
80.14m (262′ 11″)	Boris Zaichuk (Sov); 1978
79.76m (261′ 8″)	Yuriy Sedykh (Sov); 1978
79.30m (260′ 2″)	Walter Schmidt (Ger); 1975
78.62m (257′ 11″)	Aleksey Spiridonov (Sov); 1976
78.32m (256′ 11″)	Aleksey Malyukov (Sov); 1978
78.14m (256′ 4″)	Roland Steuk (GDR); 1978
77.64m (254′ 9″)	Dzhumber Pkhakadze (Sov); 1975
77.60m (254′ 7″)	Vladimir Lyesovoy (Sov); 1977
77.58m (254′ 6″)	Valentin Dmitrenko (Sov); 1975
77.42m (254′ 0″)	Anatoliy Bondarchuk (Sov); 1976
76.94m (252′ 5″)	Detlef Gerstenberg (GDR); 1978
76.60m (251′ 4″)	Reinhard Theimer (GDR); 1974
76.52m (251′ 0″)	Manfred Huning (Ger); 1978
76.44m (250′ 9″)	Jochen Sachse (GDR); 1977
76.30m (250′ 4″)	Pavel Ryepin (Sov); 1976
76.24m (250′ 1″)	Viktor Korolyov (Sov); 1976
76.22m (250′ 1″)	Sergey Litvinov (Sov); 1978
75.90m (249′ 0″)	Aleksandr Kozlov (Sov); 1976
75.78m (248′ 7″)	Iosif Gamskiy (Sov); 1971
75.78m (248′ 7″)	Aleksandr Bunyeyev (Sov); 1977

JAVELIN

94.58m (310′ 4″)	Miklos Nemeth (Hun); 1976
94.22m (309′ 1″)	Michael Wessing (Ger); 1978
94.08m (308′ 8″)	Klaus Wolfermann (Ger); 1973
93.90m (308′ 1″)	Hannu Siitonen (Fin); 1973
93.80m (307′ 9″)	Janis Lusis (Sov); 1972
93.54m (306′ 11″)	Seppo Hovinen (Fin); 1976
92.70m (304′ 1″)	Jorma Kinnunen (Fin); 1969

92.64m (303'11")	Pauli Nevala (Fin); 1970	
91.92m (301'7")	Ferenc Paragi (Hun); 1977	
91.72m (300'11")	Terje Pedersen (Nor); 1964	
91.44m (300'0")	Mark Murro (USA); 1970	
91.14m (299'0")	Wolfgang Hanisch (GDR); 1978	
90.92m (298'3")	Cary Feldman (USA); 1973	
90.86m (298'1")	Jorma Jaakola (Fin); 1976	
90.78m (297'10")	Pjotr Bielczyk (Pol); 1976	
90.68m (297'6")	Manfred Stolle (GDR); 1971	
89.82m (294'8")	Nikolay Grebnyev (Sov); 1978	
89.42m (293'4")	Aimo Aho (Fin); 1977	
89.32m (293'0")	Janis Donins (Sov); 1971	
89.30m (293'0")	Bob Roggy (USA); 1978	

DECATHLON
(e = fully automatic timing)

8618e	Bruce Jenner (USA); 1976
8498e	Guido Kratschmer (Ger); 1978
8478	Aleksandr Grebenyuk (Sov); 1977
8467e	Daley Thompson (UK); 1978
8454e	Nikolay Avilov (Sov); 1972
8417	Bill Toomey (USA); 1969
8390e	Fred Dixon (USA); 1977
8319	Kurt Bendlin (Ger); 1967
8310	Sepp Zeilbauer (Aut); 1976
8280	Siegfried Stark (GDR); 1976
8279	Joachim Kirst (GDR); 1969
8249	Leonid Litvinyenko (Sov); 1976
8237	Boris Ivanov (Sov); 1971
8230	Russ Hodge (USA); 1966
8229	Yves Le Roy (Fra); 1974
8218e	Raimo Pihl (Swe); 1976
8207	Ryszard Skowronek (Pol); 1974
8188	Lennart Hedmark (Swe); 1973
8155	Phil Mulkey (USA); 1961
8134	Rudolph Sigert (Sov); 1973
8133e	Valeriy Kachanov (Sov); 1977

20,000 METRES WALK (ROAD)

1:23:12	Roland Wieser (GDR); 1978
1:23:26	Pyotr Myslivsyev (Sov); 1978
1:23:30	Anatoliy Solomin (Sov); 1978
1:23:30	Boris Yakovlyev (Sov); 1978
1:23:32	Daniel Bautista (Mex); 1977
1:23:33	Pyotr Potschenchuk (Sov); 1978
1:23:46	Domingo Colin (Mex); 1977
1:23:51	Reima Salonen (Fin); 1978
1:23:52	Viktor Semyonov (Sov); 1976
1:23:55	Vladimir Golubnichiy (Sov); 1976
1:24:00	Aleksey Troitskiy (Sov); 1976
1:24:05	Nikolay Polosov (Sov); 1978
1:24:07	Raul Gonzales (Mex); 1977
1:24:13	Otto Bartsch (Sov); 1976
1:24:18	Yevgeniy Yevsyukov (Sov); 1978
1:24:23	Hartwig Gauder (GDR); 1978
1:24:28	Pyotr Pochenchuk (Sov); 1976
1:24:32	Yevgeniy Lyungin (Sov); 1976
1:24:39	Jose Marin (Spa); 1978
1:24:43	Karl-Heinz Stadtmuller (GDR); 1978

50,000 METRES WALK (ROAD)

3:41:20	Raul Gonzales (Mex); 1978
3:51:39	Reima Salonen (Fin); 1978
3:52:44	Bernd Kannenberg (Ger); 1972
3:52:53	Christoph Hohne (GDR); 1974
3:53:16	Aleksandr Beryotsin (Sov); 1976
3:53:30	Jorge Llopart (Spa); 1978
3:54:40	Venyamin Soldatenko (Sov); 1976
3:55:16	Jan Ornoch (Pol); 1978
3:55:36	Gennadiy Agapov (Sov); 1965
3:55:52	Pedro Aroche (Mex); 1978
3:55:59	Yuriy Andryusenko (Sov); 1976
3:56:36	Otto Bartsch (Sov); 1978
3:56:36	Valeriy Fursov (Sov); 1978
3:56:38	Enrique Vera (Mex); 1977
3:56:47	Viktor Dorovskiy (Sov); 1978
3:57:28	Aleksandr Scherbina (Sov); 1965
3:57:39	Yevgeniy Lyungin (Sov); 1975
3:57:43	Vittorio Visini (Ita); 1978
3:57:59	Sergey Bondarenko (Sov); 1976
3:58:26	Sandro Bellucci (Ita); 1978

WOMEN

100 METRES *(Fully automatic timing)*

10.88	Marlies Göhr (GDR); 1976		11.13	Chandra Cheeseborough (USA); 1976
11.01	Annegret Richter (Ger); 1976		11.14	Leleith Hodges (Jam); 1978
11.03	Monika Hamann (GDR); 1977		11.15	Chantal Rega (Fra); 1976
11.04	Inge Helten (Ger); 1976		11.16	Andrea Lynch (UK); 1975
11.07	Wyomia Tyus (USA); 1968		11.16	Evelyn Ashford (USA); 1978
11.07	Renate Stecher (GDR); 1972		11.16	Marita Koch (GDR); 1978
11.08	Brenda Morehead (USA); 1976		11.18	Linda Haglund (Swe); 1978
11.11	Barbara Ferrell (USA); 1968		11.19	Raelene Boyle (Aus); 1968
11.12	Silvia Chivas (Cub); 1977		11.19	Mona-Lisa Pursiainen (Fin); 1973
11.13	Irena Szewinska (Pol); 1974		11.19	Martina Blos (GDR); 1976

Hand timing

10.8	Renate Stecher (GDR); 1973
10.8	Annegret Richter (Ger); 1976
10.9	Irena Szewinska (Pol); 1974
10.9	Inge Helten (Ger); 1976
10.9	Andrea Lynch (UK); 1977
11.0	Wyomia Tyus (USA); 1968
11.0	Chi Cheng (Tai); 1970
11.0	Ellen Streidt (GDR); 1972
11.0	Eva Gleskova (Cze); 1972
11.0	Doris Selmigkeit (GDR); 1973
11.0	Petra Kandarr (GDR); 1973
11.0	Mona-Lisa Pursiainen (Fin); 1973
11.0	Lyudmila Maslakova (Sov); 1976

200 METRES *(Fully automatic timing)*

22.06	Marita Koch (GDR); 1978
22.21	Irena Szewinska (Pol); 1974
22.37	Barbel Eckert (GDR); 1976
22.38	Renate Stecher (GDR); 1973
22.38	Marlies Göhr (GDR); 1978
22.39	Mona-Lisa Pursiainen (Fin); 1973
22.39	Annegret Richter (Ger); 1976
22.45	Raelene Boyle (Aus); 1972
22.52	Lyudmila Kondratyeva (Sov); 1978
22.60	Brenda Morehead (USA); 1978
22.62	Lyudmila Maslakova (Sov); 1978
22.62	Evelyn Ashford (USA); 1977
22.64	Carla Bodendorf (GDR); 1976
22.68	Inge Helten (Ger); 1976
22.72	Marina Sidorova (Sov); 1973
22.73	Ellen Streidt (GDR); 1973
22.73	Denise Robertson (Aus); 1974
22.74	Chantal Rega (Fra); 1976
22.75	Donna Hartley (UK); 1978
22.76	Monika Hamann (GDR); 1978

Hand timing

22.0	Irena Szewinska (Pol); 1974
22.1	Renate Stecher (GDR); 1973
22.3	Doris Maletzki (GDR); 1973
22.4	Chi Cheng (Tai); 1970
22.4	Petra Kandarr (GDR); 1973
22.5	Denise Robertson (Aus); 1976
22.6	Patti Loverock (Can); 1976

400 METRES

48.94	Marita Koch (GDR); 1978
49.29	Irena Szewinska (Pol); 1976
49.77	Christine Brehmer (GDR); 1976
50.14	Riita Salin (Fin); 1974
50.15	Ellen Streidt (GDR); 1976
50.26	Brigitte Köhn (GDR); 1976
50.34	Doris Maletzki (GDR); 1976
50.56	Pirjo Haggman (Fin); 1976
50.56	Aurelia Penton (Cub); 1978
50.62	Rosalyn Bryant (USA); 1976
50.62	Karoline Kafer (Aut); 1977
50.6	Tatyana Prorochenko (Sov); 1977
50.78	Gisela Anton (GDR); 1976
50.83	Maria Kulchunova (Sov); 1978
50.88	Rita Wilden (Ger); 1974
50.90	Sheila Ingram (USA); 1976
50.92	Margit Sinzel (GDR); 1976
50.97	Marilyn Neufville (Jam); 1970
50.98	Jelica Pavlicic (Yug); 1974
50.98	Marina Sidorova (Sov); 1977

800 METRES

1:54.9	Tatyana Kazankina (Sov); 1976
1:55.4	Nikolina Shtereva (Bul); 1976
1:55.6	Elfi Zinn (GDR); 1976
1:55.7	Anita Weiss (GDR); 1976
1:55.8	Tatyana Providokhina (Sov); 1978
1:55.8	Nadyezhda Mushta (Sov); 1978
1:56.0	Valentina Gerasimova (Sov); 1976
1:56.4	Svyetlana Styrkina (Sov); 1976
1:56.6	Zoya Rigel (Sov); 1978
1:56.8	Totka Petrova (Bul); 1978
1:57.1	Ulrike Bruns (GDR); 1976
1:57.2	Svetla Koleva (Bul); 1976
1:57.4	Ileana Silai (Rom); 1977
1:57.5	Hildegard Ullrich (GDR); 1978
1:57.5	Lyudmila Veselkova (Sov); 1978
1:57.9	Madeline Jackson (USA); 1976
1:58.0	Sin Kim Dan (NK); 1964
1:58.1	Lilyana Tomova (Bul); 1974
1:58.1	Doris Gluth (GDR); 1976
1:58.5	Hildegard Falck (Ger); 1971

1500 METRES

3:56.0	Tatyana Kazankina (Sov); 1976
3:59.0	Giana Romanova (Sov); 1978
3:59.8	Natalia Marasescu (Rom); 1978
3:59.8	Raissa Katyukova (Sov); 1976
3:59.9	Ulrike Bruns (GDR); 1976
4:00.2	Totka Petrova (Bul); 1978
4:00.2	Valentina Ilyinich (Sov); 1978
4:00.6	Grete Waitz (Nor); 1978
4:01.3	Gabrielle Dorio (Ita); 1978
4:01.4	Lyudmila Bragina (Sov); 1972
4:01.4	Gunhild Hoffmeister (GDR); 1976
4:01.5	Brigitte Kraus (Ger); 1978
4:02.1	Lyudmila Kalnitskaya (Sov); 1978
4:02.3	Nikolina Shtereva (Bul); 1976
4:02.6	Jan Merrill (USA); 1976
4:02.8	Olga Dvirna (Sov); 1978
4:02.9	Paola Cacchi (Ita); 1972
4:03.1	Gabrielle Lehmann (GDR); 1978
4:03.5	Ileana Silai (Rom); 1978
4:03.5	Svyetlana Guskova (Sov); 1978
4:03.5	Natalia Kuznyetsova (Sov); 1978

3000 METRES

8:27.1	Lyudmila Bragina (Sov); 1976
8:32.1	Grete Waitz (Nor); 1978
8:33.2	Svyetlana Ulmasova (Sov); 1978
8:33.5	Natalia Marasescu (Rom); 1978
8:40.9	Maricica Puica (Rom); 1978
8:41.8	Raissa Katyukova (Sov); 1976
8:42.3	Loa Olafsson (Den); 1978

8:42.6	Jan Merrill (USA); 1978
8:43.0	Giana Romanova (Sov); 1978
8:45.6	Raissa Byelusova (Sov); 1978
8:45.6	Valentina Ilyinich (Sov); 1978
8:46.1	Cornelia Burki (Swi); 1978
8:47.6	Svyetlana Guskova (Sov); 1978
8:48.3	Raissa Smetkina (Sov); 1978
8:48.7	Paula Fudge (UK); 1978
8:49.2	Ulrike Bruns (GDR); 1977
8:51.0	Inger Knutsson (Swe); 1975
8:52.3	Christine Benning (UK); 1978
8:52.5	Raissa Sadretdinova (Sov); 1978
8:52.6	Gabrielle Lehmann (GDR); 1978

100 METRES HURDLES
(Fully automatic timing)

12.48	Grazyna Rabsztyn (Pol); 1978
12.59	Annelie Ehrhardt (GDR); 1972
12.62	Johanna Klier (GDR); 1978
12.67	Tatyana Anisimova (Sov); 1978
12.73	Gudrun Berend (GDR); 1978
12.74	Danuta Perka (Pol); 1978
12.80	Natalya Lebedyeva (Sov); 1976
12.83	Nina Morgulina (Sov); 1978
12.84	Valeria Stefanescu (Rom); 1972
12.87	Lyubov Nikitenko (Sov); 1977
12.89	Annerose Fiedler (GDR); 1974
12.89	Lubyna Langer (Pol); 1978
12.90	Karin Balzer (GDR); 1972
12.91	Danuta Straszynska (Pol); 1972
12.91	Teresa Nowak (Pol); 1974
12.91	Bozena Szwierczynska (Pol); 1975
12.93	Pamela Ryan (Aus); 1972
12.93	Esther Rot (Isr); 1976
12.98	Elzbieta Rabsztyn (Pol); 1978
13.08	Lorna Boothe (UK); 1978

Hand timing

12.3	Annelie Ehrhardt (GDR); 1973
12.5	Pamela Ryan (Aus); 1972
12.5	Teresa Nowak (Pol); 1974
12.6	Karin Balzer (GDR); 1971
12.6	Valeria Stefanescu (Rom); 1972
12.7	Teresa Sukniewicz (Pol); 1970
12.7	Danuta Straszynska (Pol); 1972
12.7	Lyubov Nikitenko (Sov); 1977
12.8	Chi Cheng (Tai); 1970
12.8	Barbel Podeswa (GDR); 1972

400 METRES HURDLES

54.89	Tatyana Zelentsova (Sov); 1978
55.14	Silvia Hollmann (Ger); 1978
55.36	Karin Rossley (GDR); 1978
55.44	Krystyna Kacperczyk (Pol); 1978
55.46	Brigitte Köhn (GDR); 1978
55.63	Anita Weiss (GDR); 1978
55.97	Ingrida Barkane (Sov); 1978
56.19	Marina Makeyeva (Sov); 1978
56.47	Hildegarde Ullrich (GDR); 1978
56.60	Erika Weinstein (Ger); 1978
56.61	Mary Ayers (USA); 1977
56.62	Irena Szewinska (Pol); 1977
56.67	Genowefa Blaszak (Pol); 1978
56.68	Yordanka Filipova (Bul); 1978
56.71	Lea Alaerts (Bel); 1978
56.7	Danuta Piecyk (Pol); 1973
56.7	Karola Claus (Ger); 1974
56.86	Debbie Esser (USA); 1977
56.91	Elzbieta Katolik (Pol); 1977
56.97	Tatyana Zubova (Sov); 1978

HIGH JUMP

2.01m (6' 7")	Sara Simeoni (Ita); 1978
2.00m (6' 6¾")	Rosemarie Ackermann (GDR); 1977
1.95m (6' 4¾")	Brigitte Holzapfel (Ger); 1978
1.95m (6' 4¾")	Ulrike Meyfarth (Ger); 1978
1.94m (6' 4¼")	Yordanka Blagoeva (Bul); 1972
1.94m (6' 4¼")	Jutta Kirst (GDR); 1977
1.93m (6' 4")	Ilona Gusenbauer (Aut); 1972
1.93m (6' 4")	Cornelia Popa (Rom); 1976
1.93m (6' 4")	Katrina Gibbs (Aus); 1978
1.93m (6' 4")	Joni Huntley (USA); 1978
1.92m (6' 3½")i	Rita Kirst (GDR); 1974
1.92m (6' 3½")	Virginia Ioan (Rom); 1974
1.92m (6' 3½")	Maria Mracnova (Cze); 1976
1.92m (6' 3½")	Milada Karbanova (Cze); 1977
1.92m (6' 3½")	Anne-Maria Pira (Bel); 1977
1.92m (6' 3½")i	Debbie Brill (Can); 1978
1.91m (6' 3¼")	Iolanda Balas (Rom); 1961
1.90m (6' 3")	Louise Ritter (USA)
1.90m (6' 2¾")	9 athletes

LONG JUMP

7.09m (23' 3¼")	Vilma Bardauskiene (Sov); 1978
6.99m (22' 11¼")	Sigrun Siegl (GDR); 1976
6.92m (22' 8½")	Angela Voigt (GDR); 1976
6.89m (22' 7½")	Jodi Anderson (USA); 1978
6.84m (22' 5¼")	Heide Rosendahl (Ger); 1970
6.82m (22' 4½")	Viorica Viscopoleanu (Rom); 1968
6.81m (22' 4¼")	Margrit Herbst (GDR); 1971
6.79m (22' 3½")	Lidiya Alfeyeva (Sov); 1976
6.78m (22' 3")	Kathy McMillan (USA); 1976
6.77m (22' 2½")	Diana Yorgova (Bul); 1972
6.77m (22' 2½")	Marianne Voelzke (GDR); 1974
6.76m (22' 2¼")	Mary Rand (UK); 1964
6.76m (22' 2¼")	Ingrid Mickler (Ger); 1971
6.76m (22' 2¼")	Brigitte Kunzel (GDR); 1977
6.76m (22' 2¼")	Ildika Erdelyi (Hun); 1977
6.76m (22' 2¼")	Heidi Wycisk (GDR); 1977
6.74m (22' 1½")	Jarmila Nygrynova (Cze); 1978

6.73m (22' 1")   Tatyana Shchelkanova (Sov); 1966
6.73m (22' 1")   Sheila Sherwood (UK); 1970
6.73m (22' 1")   Meta Antenen (Swi); 1971

SHOT
22.50m (73' 10")   Helena Fibingerova (Cze); 1977
22.06m (72' 4½")   Ilona Slupianek (GDR); 1978
21.89m (71' 10")   Ivanka Khristova (Bul); 1976
21.67m (71' 1¼")   Marianne Adam (GDR); 1976
21.58m (70' 9¾")   Margitta Droese (GDR); 1978
21.45m (70' 4½")   Nadyezhda Chizhova (Sov); 1973
21.43m (70' 3¾")   Eva Wilms (Ger); 1977
21.26m (69' 9")   Esfir Krachevskaya (Sov); 1977
20.99m (68' 10¼")   Helma Knorrscheidt (GDR); 1978
20.33m (66' 8½")   Ivanka Petrova (Bul); 1978
20.33m (66' 8½")   Elena Stoyanova (Bul); 1978
20.22m (66' 4")   Margitta Gummel (GDR); 1972
20.12m (66' 0¼")   Vyera Zapkalenko (Sov); 1977
20.06m (65' 9¾")   Raissa Taranda (Sov); 1976
20.03m (65' 8¾")   Faina Melnik (Sov); 1976
19.92m (65' 4¼")   Tamara Bufetova (Sov); 1978
19.90m (65' 3½")   Natalya Nosyenko (Sov); 1976
19.88m (65' 2¾")   Nina Issayeva (Sov); 1977
19.80m (64' 11½")   Svyetlana Myelnikova (Sov); 1978

DISCUS
70.72m (232' 0")   Evelin Jahl (GDR); 1978
70.50m (231' 3")   Faina Veleva (Sov); 1976
69.08m (226' 8")   Carmen Romero (Cub); 1976
68.92m (226' 1")   Sabine Engel (GDR); 1977
68.62m (225' 1")   Maria Vergova (Bul); 1976
68.48m (224' 8")   Margitta Droese (GDR); 1978
67.96m (222' 11")   Argentina Menis (Rom); 1976
67.54m (221' 7")   Svyetlana Petrova (Sov); 1978
67.02m (219' 10")   Gabrielle Hinzmann (GDR); 1973
66.94m (219' 7")   Svetla Boshkova (Bul); 1978

66.60m (218' 6")   Natalya Gorbachova (Sov); 1976
66.28m (217' 5")   Lyudmila Issayeva (Sov); 1978
65.74m (215' 8")   Brigitte Sander (GDR); 1976
65.62m (215' 3")   Maria Betancourt (Cub); 1976
65.38m (214' 6")   Valentina Stepushina (Sov); 1976
65.20m (213' 11")   Vera Safonova (Sov); 1977
64.96m (213' 1")   Liesel Westermann (Ger); 1972
64.68m (212' 2")   Olga Andrianova (Sov); 1976
64.58m (211' 10")   Radostina Backchevanova (Bul); 1974
64.52m (211' 8")   Carmen Ionescu (Can); 1975

JAVELIN
69.32m (227' 5")   Kate Schmidt (USA); 1977
69.16m (226' 11")   Ruth Fuchs (GDR); 1978
67.20m (220' 6")   Tessa Sanderson (UK); 1977
65.46m (214' 9")   Sabine Sebrowski (GDR); 1976
65.14m (213' 8")   Marion Becker (Ger); 1976
64.34m (211' 1")   Jacqueline Hein (GDR); 1974
64.24m (210' 9")   Ute Richter (GDR); 1978
64.04m (210' 1")   Eva Helmschmidt (Ger); 1978
63.96m (209' 10")   Elvira Ozolina (Lusis) (Sov); 1973
63.86m (209' 6")   Lyudmila Pasternakevich (Sov); 1976
63.74m (209' 1")   Svyetlana Babich (Sov); 1976
63.66m (208' 10")   Eva Zorgo (Raduly); (Rom); 1978
63.60m (208' 8")   Ute Hommola (GDR); 1978
63.50m (208' 4")   Maria Colon (Cub); 1978
63.38m (207' 11")   Sherry Calvert (USA); 1978
63.32m (207' 9")   Karin Smith (USA); 1978
63.28m (207' 7")   Nadyezhda Yakubovich (Sov); 1976
63.22m (207' 5")   Tatyana Zhigalova (Sov); 1975
63.18m (207' 3")   Nina Nikanorova (Sov); 1978
63.08m (206' 11")   Felicia Kinder (Pol); 1974

PENTATHLON
(*With 800m e – electrical timing*)
4839e   Nadyezhda Tkachenko (Sov); 1977
4823e   Eva Wilms (Ger); 1977

4768e	Diane Konihowski (Can); 1978		4565	Ramona Neubert (GDR); 1978
4704e	Jane Frederick (USA); 1978		4550	Petra Rampf (GDR); 1977
4675	Margit Papp (Hun); 1978		4541	Nadyezhda Karyakina (Sov); 1977
4638	Burglinde Pollak (GDR); 1978		4533e	Zoya Spasovkhodskaya (Sov); 1977
4630e	Valentina Dimitrova (Bul); 1977		4531i	Natalya Prokopchenko (Sov); 1977
4621	Yekaterina Smirnova (Sov); 1977		4522	Lyudmila Popovskaya (Sov); 1977
4599e	Kristine Nitzsche (GDR); 1978		4514	Ina Losch (Ger); 1978
4592e	Beatrix Philipp (Ger); 1978		4508	Christa Kohler (Ger); 1978
4590	Yekaterina Gordienko (Sov); 1978		4440	Olga Rukavishnikova (Sov); 1977

Leading World Performers 1978

MEN (w = wind assisted; i = indoor mark)

100 METRES
(Fully automatic timing)

10.07	Clancy Edwards (USA)
10.07	Eddie Hart (USA)
10.07	Steve Williams (USA)
10.08	Silvio Leonard (Cub)
10.09	Mel Lattany (USA)
10.11	Curtis Dickey (USA)
10.11	Osvaldo Lara (Cub)
10.11	Mike Robertson (USA)
10.11	Don Coleman (USA)
10.15	Harvey Glance (USA) (10.07w)
10.15	Allan Wells (UK) (10.07w)
10.16	Guy Abrahams (Pan)
10.19	Pietro Mennea (Ita) (9.99w)
10.19	Petar Petrov (Bul)
10.19	James Gilkes (Guy) (10.15w)
10.22	Don Quarrie (Jam) (10.03w)
10.22	Steve Riddick (USA) (10.19w)
10.22	Andrew Banks (USA)
10.23	Houston McTear (USA) (10.18w)
10.24	Hasely Crawford (Tri) (10.09w)

Wind assisted

9.87w	William Snoddy (USA)
9.98w	Cole Doty (Can)
10.04w	Ray Brooks (USA)
10.06w	Jerome Deal (USA)
10.11w	Mike Kelley (USA)
10.14w	Johnny Jones (USA)

Note also hand times

9.9	Harvey Glance (USA)
9.9	Mike Roberson (USA)

200 METRES
(Fully automatic timing)

20.03	Clancy Edwards (USA)
20.06	Silvio Leonard (Cub)
20.14	James Gilkes (Guy)
20.16	Pietro Mennea (Ita)
20.24	James Sanford (USA)
20.26	Steve Williams (USA)
20.27	William Snoddy (USA)
20.35	Don Quarrie (Jam)
20.40	Greg Foster (USA)
20.44	Larry Myricks (USA)
20.48	Tony Darden (USA)
20.48	Harvey Glance (USA) (20.47w)
20.50	Ray Brooks (USA)
20.50	Fred Taylor (USA)
20.52	Millard Hampton (USA)
20.53	James Mallard (USA)
20.58	Wardell Gilbreath (USA)
20.60	Klaus Thiele (GDR)
20.61	Allan Wells (UK) (20.12w)
20.61	La Monte King (USA)
20.61	Olaf Prenzler (GDR)
20.61	Brady Crain (USA)

Wind assisted

20.43w	Colin Bradford (Jam)
20.54w	Calvin Alston (USA)

400 METRES

44.27	Alberto Juantorena (Cub)
44.73	Willie Smith (USA)
45.03	Billy Mullins (USA)
45.06	Harald Schmid (Ger)
45.12	Darrol Gatson (USA)
45.15	Maxie Parks (USA)
45.21	Adrian Rodgers (USA)
45.22	Maurice Peoples (USA)
45.23	Kasheef Hassan (Sud)
45.37	Stan Vinson (USA)
45.41	Joe Coombs (Tri)
45.43	Robert Taylor (USA)
45.45	Franz-Peter Hofmeister (Ger)
45.49	Glen Cohen (UK)
45.56	Walter McCoy (USA)
45.59	Fons Brydenbach (Bel)
45.60	Bernd Herrmann (Ger)
45.63	Herman Frazier (USA)
45.65	Cyril Etoori (Uga)
45.65	Don Thompson (USA)

45.65	Dele Udo (Nig)

Hand time

45.5	Evis Jennings (USA)

800 METRES

1:43.8	Olaf Beyer (GDR)
1:44.0	Sebastian Coe (UK)
1:44.1	Steve Ovett (UK)
1:44.4	Alberto Juantorena (Cub)
1:44.9	Mike Boit (Ken)
1:45.1	Willi Wulbeck (Ger)
1:45.4	Nikolay Kirov (Sov)
1:45.5	Andreas Busse (GDR)
1:45.5	James Robinson (USA)
1:45.7	Peter Lemashon (Ken)
1:45.7	Abderrahmane Morceli (Alg)
1:45.8	Anatoliy Reshetnyak (Sov)
1:45.8	Milovan Savic (Yug)
1:45.8	Detlef Wagenknecht (GDR)
1:45.8	Garry Cook (UK)
1:45.8	Jose Marajo (Fra)
1:45.9	Jozef Plachy (Cze)
1:45.9	Tom McLean (USA)
1:45.9	Randy Wilson (USA)
1:46.0	John Higham (Aus)

1500 METRES

3:35.5	David Moorcroft (UK)
3:35.6	Filbert Bayi (Tan)
3:35.6	John Robson (UK)
3:35.6	Steve Ovett (UK)
3:35.7	Frank Clement (UK)
3:36.0	Steve Scott (USA)
3:36.1	Jurgen Straub (GDR)
3:36.5	Wilson Waigwa (Ken)
3:36.6	Eamonn Coghlan (Eir)
3:37.0	Francis Gonzales (Fra)
3:37.1	Olaf Beyer (GDR)
3:37.2	Thomas Wessinghage (Ger)
3:37.3	Amar Brahmia (Alg)
3:37.4	Valeriy Abramov (Sov)
3:37.4	Bronislaw Malinowski (Pol)
3:37.4	Abderrahmane Morceli (Alg)
3:37.5	Vladimir Sheronov (Sov)
3:37.7	Graham Williamson (UK)
3:37.7	Antti Loikkanen (Fin)

1 MILE

3:52.5	Thomas Wessinghage (Ger)
3:52.6	Jozef Plachy (Cze)
3:52.8	Steve Ovett (UK)
3:52.9	Steve Scott (USA)
3:53.2	Wilson Waigwa (Ken)
3:53.5	Filbert Bayi (Tan)
3:54.2	Frank Clement (UK)
3:54.3	John Robson (UK)
3:54.9i	Dick Buerkle (USA)
3:55.3	David Moorcroft (UK)
3:55.8	Graham Williamson (UK)
3:56.0i	Eamonn Coghlan (Eir)

3:56.2	Antti Loikkanen (Fin)
3:56.2	Ray Flynn (Eir)
3:56.4	John Walker (NZ)
3:56.7	Ari Paunonen (Fin)
3:57.0	Brendan Foster (UK)

3000 METRES

7:32.1	Henry Rono (Ken)
7:40.3	Suleiman Nyambui (Tan)
7:40.4	Nick Rose (UK)
7:41.1	Rod Dixon (NZ)
7:41.9	Wilson Waigwa (Ken)
7:42.1	Boris Kuznyetsov (Sov)
7:42.2	Markus Ryffel (Swi)
7:42.5	Bronislaw Malinowski (Pol)
7:43.5	David Moorcroft (UK)
7:44.3	Knut Kvalheim (Nor)

5000 METRES

13:08.4	Henry Rono (Ken)
13:15.0	Ilie Floroiu (Rom)
13:16.2	Marty Liquori (USA)
13:17.4	Rod Dixon (NZ)
13:17.8	Fernando Mamede (Por)
13:18.2	Frank Zimmermann (Ger)
13:20.0	Markus Ryffel (Swi)
13:20.8	Venanzio Ortis (Ita)
13:21.7	Gerard Tebroke (Hol)
13:21.9	Jos Hermens (Hol)
13:24.0	Willi Polleunis (Bel)
13:24.1	Radhouane Bouster (Fra)
13:24.1	Aleksandr Fyedotkin (Sov)
13:24.3	Karl Fleschen (Ger)
13:24.4	Wilson Waigwa (Ken)
13:24.7	David Fitzsimons (Aus)
13:24.9	Mike Musyoki (Ken)
13:25.2	Mike McLeod (UK)
13:25.4	Brendan Foster (UK)
13:25.4	Emiel Puttemans (Bel)
13:25.4	Nick Rose (UK)
13:25.4	Craig Virgin (USA)

10,000 METRES

27:22.5	Henry Rono (Ken)
27:30.3	Brendan Foster (UK)
27:31.0	Martti Vainio (Fin)
27:31.5	Venanzio Ortis (Ita)
27:31.5	Aleksandr Antipov (Sov)
27:36.3	David Black (UK)
27:36.6	Gerard Tebroke (Hol)
27:40.1	Ilie Floroiu (Rom)
27:40.6	Enn Sellik (Sov)
27:41.3	Knut Kvalheim (Nor)
27:50.5	Jos Hermens (Hol)
27:51.4	**Gerard Barrett (Aus)**
27:51.6	Toshihiko Seko (Jap)
27:52.1	Detlef Uhlemann (Ger)
27:53.0	Domingo Tibaduiza (Col)
27:53.6	Jerzy Kowol (Pol)
27:54.2	Doug Brown (USA)

27:55.2	John Treacy (Eir)
27:56.1	Ryszard Kopijasz (Pol)
27:57.2	Craig Virgin (USA)

MARATHON

2:09:06	Shigeru Sou (Jap)
2:10:13	Bill Rodgers (USA)
2:10:15	Jeff Wells (USA)
2:10:21	Toshihiko Seko (Jap)
2:11:05	Hideki Kita (Jap)
2:11:15	Esa Tikkanen (Fin)
2:11:17	Jack Fultz (USA)
2:11:25	Randy Thomas (USA)
2:11:43	Kevin Ryan (NZ)
2:11:58	Leonid Moseyev (Sov)
2:11:59	Nikolay Penzin (Sov)
2:12:00	Shivnath Singh (Ind)
2:12:08	Karel Lismont (Bel)
2:12:20	Gerard Barrett (Aus)
2:12:20	Waldemar Cierpinski (GDR)
2:12:30	Catalin Andreica (Rom)
2:12:32	Trevor Wright (UK)
2:12:33	Tony Simmons (UK)
2:12:46	Massimo Magnani (Ita)
2:12:49	Takeshi Sou (Jap)

3000 METRES STEEPLECHASE

8:05.4	Henry Rono (Ken)
8:11.6	Bronislaw Malinowski (Pol)
8:16.9	Patriz Ilg (Ger)
8:18.3	Ismo Toukonen (Fin)
8:19.0	Michael Karst (Ger)
8:19.3	Doug Brown (USA)
8:19.5	Krzysztof Wesolowski (Pol)
8:20.4	Paul Copu (Rom)
8:21.7	George Malley (USA)
8:22.5	Henry Marsh (USA)
8:22.6	Julian Marsay (Saf)
8:22.8	Paul Thys (Bel)
8:23.5	James Munyala (Ken)
8:24.0	Sergey Olizaryenko (Sov)
8:24.5	Dan Glans (Swe)
8:24.9	Vasile Bichea (Rom)
8:25.8	Kazimierz Maranda (Pol)
8:26.0	Dennis Coates (UK)
8:26.4	Kip Rono (Ken)
8:26.4	Vladimir Lisovskiy (Sov)

110 METRES HURDLES

(Fully automatic timing)

13.22	Greg Foster (USA)
13.23	Renaldo Nehemiah (USA)
13.43	Dedy Cooper (USA)
13.45	Kerry Bethel (USA)
13.46	James Owens (USA)
13.47	Viktor Myasnikov (Sov)
13.50	Thomas Munkelt (GDR)
13.55	Alejandro Casanas (Cub)
13.55	Jan Pusty (Pol)
13.56	Arto Bryggare (Fin)

13.58	Charles Foster (USA)
13.61	Greg Robertson (USA)
13.64	Edwin Moses (USA)
13.66	**Donnie Taylor (USA)** (13.4h)
13.67	Vyacheslav Kulebyakin (Sov) (13.4h)
13.68	Andy Roberts (USA)
13.69	Dieter Gebhard (Ger)
13.71	Eduard Pereverzyev (Sov)
13.71	Romuald Giegel (Pol)

Wind assisted

13.39w	Colin Williams (USA)
13.61w	Jim Kelley (USA)
13.68w	Ricky Davenport (USA)
13.68w	Barnett Edwards (USA)
13.69w	**Dan Lavitt (USA)**

400 METRES HURDLES

47.94	Edwin Moses (USA)
48.43	Harald Schmid (Ger)
48.91	James Walker (USA)
48.91	Quentin Wheeler (USA)
49.04	Sam Turner (USA)
49.20	Daniel Kimaiyo (Ken)
49.24	Vasiliy Arkhipyenko (Sov)
49.31	Rich Graybehl (USA)
49.32	Bart Williams (USA)
49.55	John Akii-Bua (Uga)
49.59	Takashi Nagao (Jap)
49.63	Tom Andrews (USA)
49.63	Alan Pascoe (UK)
49.70	James King (USA)
49.70	Dmitriy Stukalov (Sov)
49.78	Peter Rwamuhanda (Uga)
49.82	Olyeg Bulatkin (Sov)
49.85	Gregg Byram (USA)
49.85	Harry Schulting (Hol)
49.96	Mike Shine (USA)

4 x 100 METRES RELAY

38.58	Poland
38.78	GDR
38.82	Soviet Union
38.85	United States
38.90	France
39.10	Germany
39.11	Italy
39.13	Trinidad and Tobago
39.19	Switzerland
39.24	Ghana
39.24	UK (Scotland)
39.25	Bulgaria
39.26	Nigeria
39.33	Jamaica
39.44	Cuba

4 x 400 METRES RELAY

*(*4 x 440 yards time less 1.1)*

3:02.0	Germany
3:03.2	Nigeria
3:03.4	United States

3:03.5	Kenya	
3:03.6	Poland	
3:03.8	Jamaica	
3:04.0	Czechoslovakia	
3:04.2	Soviet Union	
3:04.2	Australia	
3:04.2	Uganda	
3:04.3	Switzerland	
3:04.4	GDR	
3:05.0	Trinidad and Tobago	
3:05.6	UK (3:03.5 disq)	
3:05.6	Cuba	
3:05.6	France	

HIGH JUMP

2.35m (7' 8½")i	Vladimir Yashchenko (Sov) (2.34m)
2.32m (7' 7¼")i	Franklin Jacobs (USA) (2.28m)
2.31m (7' 7")i	Greg Joy (Can)
2.31m (7' 7")	Rolf Beilschmidt (GDR)
2.30m (7' 6½")	Dwight Stones (USA)
2.30m (7' 6½")	Henry Lauterbach (GDR)
2.30m (7' 6½")	Benn Fields (USA)
2.28m (7' 5¾")	Aleksandr Grigoryev (Sov)
2.28m (7' 5¾")i	Wolfgang Killing (Ger)
2.27m (7' 5½")	Gennadiy Byelkov (Sov)
2.27m (7' 5½")	Ruud Wielart (Hol)
2.26m (7' 5")i	Kyle Arney (USA)
2.26m (7' 5")	Melvin Baker (USA)
2.26m (7' 5")	Jozsef Jambor (Hun)
2.26m (7' 5")i	Edgar Kirst (GDR)
2.26m (7' 5")i	Gail Olsen (USA)
2.26m (7' 5")	Andre Schneider (Ger)
2.26m (7' 5")	Carlo Thranhardt (Ger)
2.26m (7' 5")	Tom Woods (USA)
2.25m (7' 4½")	Stanislav Molotilov (Sov)

POLE VAULT

5.71m (18' 8¾")	Mike Tully (USA)
5.62m (18' 5¼")	Wladyslaw Kozakiewicz (Pol)
5.61m (18' 5")	Larry Jessee (USA)
5.61m (18' 5")	Vladimir Trofimyenko (Sov)
5.60m (18' 4½")	Tadeusz Slusarski (Pol)
5.60m (18' 4½")	Antti Kalliomaki (Fin)
5.56m (18' 3")	Rauli Pudas (Fin)
5.56m (18' 3")	Dan Ripley (USA)
5.55m (18' 2¾")	Jeff Taylor (USA)
5.51m (18' 1")	Gunther Lohre (Ger)
5.50m (18' 0½")	Earl Bell (USA)
5.50m (18' 0½")	Ralph Haynie (USA)
5.50m (18' 0½")	Philippe Houvion (Fra)
5.50m (18' 0½")	Bob Pullard (USA)
5.50m (18' 0½")	Yevgeniy Tananika (Sov)
5.50m (18' 0½")	Wojciech Buciarski (Pol)
5.48m (18' 0")	Don Baird (Aus)
5.45m (17' 10¾")	Jean-Michel Bellot (Fra)
5.45m (17' 10¾")	Vladimir Kishkun (Sov)
5.45m (17' 10¾")	Billy Olson (USA)
5.45m (17' 10¾")	Yuriy Prokhoryenko (Sov)
5.45m (17' 10¾")	Nikolay Syelivanov (Sov)
5.45m (17' 10¾")	Mariusz Klimczyk (Pol)
5.45m (17' 10¾")	Vladimir Sergeyenko (Sov)

LONG JUMP

8.32m (27' 3½")	Nenad Stekic (Yug)
8.23m (27' 0")	James Lofton (USA)
8.23m (27' 0")	Joao Carlos de Oliveira (Bra)
8.22m (26' 11½")	Arnie Robinson (USA) (8.33m) (w)
8.18m (26' 10¼")	La Monte King (USA)
8.18m (26' 10¼")	Jacques Rousseau (Fra)
8.11m (26' 7½")	Charlton Ehizuelen (Nig)
8.11m (26' 7¼")	Grzegorz Cybulski (Pol)
8.08m (26' 6¼")	Chris Commons (Aus)
8.08m (26' 6")i	Tommy Haynes (USA)
8.05m (26' 5")	Antonio Corgos (Spa)
8.05m (26' 5")	Larry Myricks (USA)
8.04m (26' 4½")	Valeriy Podluzhniy (Sov)
8.03m (26' 4¼")	Philippe Deroche (Fra)
8.03m (26' 4¼")	Jan Leitner (Cze)
8.03m (26' 4¼")	Vladimir Tsepelyev (Sov)
8.02m (26' 3¾")	Stanislaw Jaskulka (Pol)
8.02m (26' 3¾")	Jochen Verschl (Ger)
8.02m (26' 3¾")	Carl Williams (USA) (8.26m) (w)

Wind assisted

8.14m (26' 8½")w	Dannie Jackson (USA)
8.13m (26' 8")w	Rick Rock (Can)
8.11m (26' 7½")w	Daley Thompson (UK)
8.10m (26' 7")w	Ken Duncan (USA)
8.05m (26' 5")w	Bob Calhoun (USA)
8.05m (26' 5")w	Eugene McCain (USA)

TRIPLE JUMP

17.44m (57' 2¾")	Joao Carlos de Oliveira (Bra)
17.24m (56' 6¾")	James Butts (USA)
17.15m (56' 3¼")	Ron Livers (USA)
17.07m (56' 0")	Anatoliy Piskulin (Sov)
17.05m (55' 11¼")	Willie Banks (USA)
17.03m (55' 10½")	Viktor Sanyeyev (Sov)
17.02m (55' 10")	Gennadiy Valyukevich (Sov)
17.00m (55' 9¼")	Aleksandr Lisichonok (Sov)
16.97m (55' 8¼")i	Ian Campbell (Aus)
16.94m (55' 7")	Gennadiy Kovtunov (Sov)
16.94m (55' 7")	Milos Srejovic (Yug)
16.92m (55' 6¼")	Bernard Lamitie (Fra)
16.90m (55' 5½")	Cheng Chen-hsien (Chi)
16.89m (55' 5")	Aleksandr Yakovlyev (Sov)
16.80m (55' 1½")	Jaak Uudmae (Sov)
16.76m (54' 11¾")	Keith Connor (UK) (17.21m) (w)
16.75m (54' 11½")	Robert Cannon (USA) (16.87m) (w)
16.69m (54' 9¼")i	Milan Tiff (USA)

The Master Butcher has helped win many a shot put event.

Most top-class shot putters are a little on the heavy side…20 stone or more. But it's all solid muscle, not flab. That's why a balanced diet is so important to athletes whose events demand great strength. And meat can be a vital part of that diet, for protein and vitamins as well as long-term energy. Shot putters at all levels have won their events with the help of meat from the Master Butcher, where good value is an ingredient too.

DEWHURST
The Master Butcher

16.69m (54' 9") Gustavo Platt (Cub)
16.69m (54' 9") Aston Moore (UK)
(16.76m) (w)

Wind assisted
16.88m (55' 4½") Tommy Haynes (USA)

SHOT
22.15m (72' 8") Udo Beyer (GDR)
21.17m (69' 5¼") Reijo Stahlberg (Fin)
21.07m (69' 1¾") Al Feuerbach (USA)
20.95m (68' 8¾") Aleksandr Baryshnikov (Sov)
20.95m (68' 8¾") Hreinn Halldorsson (Ice)
20.93m (68' 8") Yevgeniy Mironov (Sov)
20.89m (68' 6½") Anatoliy Yarosh (Sov)
20.76m (68' 1¼") Wolfgang Schmidt (GDR)
20.68m (67' 10¼") Geoff Capes (UK)
20.60m (67' 7") Valcho Stoev (Bul)
20.55m (67' 5") Bishop Dolegiewicz (Can)
20.52m (67' 4") Gerald Bergmann (GDR)
20.49m (67' 2¾") Valeriy Voikin (Sov)
20.48m (67' 2¼") Mathias Schmidt (GDR)
20.45m (67' 1")i Mac Wilkins (USA)
20.39m (66' 10¾")i Colin Anderson (USA)
20.35m (66' 9¼") Jaromir Vlk (Cze)
20.23m (66' 4½") Heino Sild (Sov)
20.18m (66' 2½") Wladyslaw Komar (Pol)
20.15m (66' 1¼") Dave Lait (USA)

DISCUS
71.16m (233' 5") Wolfgang Schmidt (GDR)
70.48m (231' 3") Mac Wilkins (USA)
68.40m (224' 5") Ken Stadel (USA)
67.82m (222' 6") Velko Velev (Bul)
65.96m (216' 5") Imrich Bugar (Cze)
65.78m (215' 10") Aleksandr Klimyenko (Sov)
65.44m (214' 8") Knut Hjeltnes (Nor)
64.96m (213' 1") Jim McGoldrick (USA)
64.92m (213' 0") Markku Tuokko (Fin)
64.90m (212' 11") Janos Farago (Hun)
64.80m (212' 7") Stanislaw Wolodko (Pol)
64.60m (211' 11") Alwin Wagner (Ger)
64.48m (211' 6") Wolfgang Warnemunde (GDR)
64.16m (210' 6") Igor Duginyets (Sov)
64.08m (210' 3") Gunnar Muller (GDR)
64.02m (210' 0") Kenth Gardenkrans (Swe)
64.00m (210' 0") Ludvik Danek (Cze)
63.98m (209' 11") Pyotr Mikhailov (Sov)
63.94m (209' 9") Silvano Simeon (Ita)
63.94m (209' 9") Nikolay Vikhov (Sov)

HAMMER
80.32m (263' 6") Karl-Hans Riehm (Ger)
80.14m (262' 11") Boris Zaichuk (Sov)
79.76m (261' 8") Yuriy Sedykh (Sov)
78.32m (256' 11") Aleksey Malyukov (Sov)
78.14m (256' 4") Roland Steuk (GDR)
76.94m (252' 5") Detlef Gerstenberg (GDR)

76.64m (251' 5") Valentin Dmitrenko (Sov)
76.52m (251' 0") Manfred Huning (Ger)
76.30m (250' 4") Aleksandr Bunyeyev (Sov)
76.22m (250' 1") Sergey Litvinov (Sov)
75.76m (248' 7") Gian Paolo Urlando (Ita)
75.32m (247' 1") Jochen Sachse (GDR)
75.02m (246' 1") Aleksey Spiridonov (Sov)
74.98m (246' 0") Karl-Heinz Reissmuller (GDR)
74.60m (244' 9") Emanuil Dyulgerov (Bul)
74.58m (244' 8") Peter Farmer (Aus)
74.58m (244' 8") Juri Tamm (Sov)
73.98m (242' 8") Fyodor Palyekhin (Sov)
73.84m (242' 3") Hannu Polvi (Fin)
73.66m (241' 8") Harri Huhtala (Fin)

JAVELIN
94.22m (309' 1") Michael Wessing (Ger)
91.14m (299' 0") Wolfgang Hanisch (GDR)
89.82m (294' 8") Nikolay Grebnyev (Sov)
89.30m (293' 0") Bob Roggy (USA)
88.90m (291' 8") Pentti Sinersaari (Fin)
88.64m (290' 10") Herman Potgieter (Saf)
88.64m (290' 10") Antero Puranen (Fin)
88.60m (290' 8") Sandor Boros (Hun)
88.32m (289' 9") Bjorn Grimnes (Nor)
87.86m (288' 3") Vasiliy Yershov (Sov)
87.40m (286' 9") Miklos Nemeth (Hun)
86.88m (285' 0") Raimo Pihl (Swe)
86.78m (284' 9") Seppo Hovinen (Fin)
86.72m (284' 6") Antero Toivonen (Fin)
86.44m (283' 7") Rod Ewaliko (USA)
86.12m (282' 6") Detlef Michel (GDR)
86.04m (282' 3") Ferenc Paragi (Hun)
86.00m (282' 2") Klaus Tafelmeier (Ger)
85.84m (281' 7") Aimo Aho (Fin)
85.70m (281' 2") Arto Härkonen (Fin)

DECATHLON
(h = hand timed, others auto-timed)
8498 Guido Kratschmer (Ger)
8467w Daley Thompson (UK)
8340 Aleksandr Grebenyuk (Sov)
8208 Siegfried Stark (GDR)
8165h Nikolay Avilov (Sov)
8137h Bob Coffman (USA)
8134 Sepp Zeilbauer (Aut)
8121 Valeriy Kachanov (Sov)
8109 Johannes Lahti (Fin)
8086h Tonu Kaukis (Sov)
8083 Rainer Pottel (GDR)
8080h Yuriy Kutyenko (Sov) (8041)
8075h Holger Schmidt (Ger)
8062 Dietmar Schauerhammer (GDR)
8061 Anatoliy Kartashov (Sov)
8034 Fred Dixon (USA)
8034h Richard George (USA)
8026h Tito Steiner (Arg)
8017h Vladimir Buryakov (Sov) (8009)
8011h John Warkentin (USA)

218

20,000 METRES WALK
(Road, t = track)

1:23:12	Roland Wieser (GDR)
1:23:26	Pyotr Myslivsyev (Sov)
1:23:30	Anatoliy Solomin (Sov)
1:23:30	Boris Yakovlyev (Sov)
1:23:33	Pyotr Potschenchuk (Sov)
1:23:38	Daniel Bautista (Mex)
1:23:51	Reima Salonen (Fin)
1:24:05	Nikolay Polosov (Sov)
1:24:18	Yevgeniy Yevsyukov (Sov)
1:24:23t	Hartwig Gauder (GDR)
1:24:36t	Raul Gonzales (Mex)
1:24:39	Jose Marin (Spa)
1:24:43	Karl-Heinz Stadtmuller (GDR)
1:24:53	Mikhail Alekseyev (Sov)
1:24:57	Gerard Lelievre (Fra)
1:24:58	Maurizio DaMilano (Ita)
1:25:29	Felix Gomez (Mex)
1:25:34	Boguslaw Duda (Pol)
1:25:36	Alvars Rumbenieks (Sov)
1:25:41	Roberto Buccione (Ita)

50,000 METRES WALK

3:41:20	Raul Gonzales (Mex)
3:51:39	Reima Salonen (Fin)
3:53:30	Jorge Llopart (Spa)
3:55:13	Venyamin Soldatenko (Sov)
3:55:16	Jan Ornoch (Pol)
3:55:52	Pedro Aroche (Mex)
3:56:36	Otto Bartsch (Sov)
3:56:36	Valeriy Fursov (Sov)
3:56:47	Viktor Dorovskiy (Sov)
3:57:43	Vittorio Visini (Ita)
3:58:26	Sandro Bellucci (Ita)
3:58:36	Ralf Knutter (GDR)
3:58:37	Anatoliy Beryosin (Sov)
3:58:48	Martin Bermudes (Mex)
3:58:55	Hans Binder (Ger)
3:59:27	Domingo Colin (Mex)
4:00:04	Olaf Pilarski (Sov)
4:00:08	Steffan Muller (GDR)
4:00:12	Matthias Kroel (GDR)
4:00:19	Ivan Tikhonov (Sov)

WOMEN

100 METRES

10.94	Marlies Gohr (GDR)
11.14	Leleith Hodges (Jam)
11.14	Brenda Morehead (USA)
11.16	Evelyn Ashford (USA)
11.16	Marita Koch (GDR)
11.16	Annegret Richter (Ger)
11.17	Silvia Chivas (Cub)
11.18	Linda Haglund (Swe)
11.20	Monika Hamann (GDR)
11.23	Lyudmila Maslakova (Sov)
11.26	Sonia Lannaman (UK) (11.24w)
11.27	Lyudmila Storoshkova (Sov)
11.30	Romy Schneider (GDR)
11.32	Andrea Lynch (UK)
11.34	Patti Loverock (Can)
11.35	Lyudmila Kondratyeva (Sov)
11.35	Marjorie Bailey (Can)
11.35	Emma Sulter (Fra)
11.36	Chantal Rega (Fra) (11.27w)
11.36	Carla Bodendorf (GDR)
11.36	Ingrid Auerswald (GDR)

Wind assisted

11.30w	Beverley Goddard (UK)

200 METRES

22.06	Marita Koch (GDR)
22.38	Marlies Gohr (GDR)
22.52	Lyudmila Kondratyeva (Sov)
22.60	Brenda Morehead (USA)
22.62	Lyudmila Maslakova (Sov)
22.64	Carla Bodendorf (GDR)
22.66	Evelyn Ashford (USA)
22.75	Donna Hartley (UK)
22.76	Monika Hamann (GDR)
22.77	Christine Brehmer (GDR)
22.77	Chantal Rega (Fra)
22.84	Annegret Richter (Ger)
22.86	Irena Szewinska (Pol)
22.88	Sonia Lannaman (UK)
22.89	Barbel Lockhoff (GDR)
22.90	Linda Haglund (Swe)
22.93	Lilyana Ivanova (Bul) (22.89w)
22.99	Kathy Smallwood (UK) (22.73w)
23.01	Hannah Afriyie (Gha)
23.01	Silvia Chivas (Cub)

Wind assisted

22.82w	Denise Boyd (Aus)
22.93w	Coleen Beasley (Aus)

400 METRES

48.94	Marita Koch (GDR)
50.15	Christine Brehmer (GDR)
50.40	Irena Szewinska (Pol)
50.56	Aurelia Penton (Cub)
50.83	Maria Kulchunova (Sov)
50.85	Ellen Streidt (GDR)
50.93	Rosalyn Bryant (USA)
51.04	Lorna Forde (USA/Bar)
51.09	Jarmila Kratochvilova (Cze)
51.11	Patricia Jackson (USA)
51.13	Tatyana Prorochenko (Sov)
51.27	Beatriz Castillo (Cub)
51.29	Pirjo Haggmann (Fin)
51.31	Sharon Dabney (USA)
51.36	Barbara Krug (GDR)

51.40	June Griffith (Guy)
51.41	Nadyezhda Mushta (Sov)
51.43	Donna Hartley (UK) (51.2h)
51.45	Christine Marquardt (GDR)
51.59	Brigitte Köhn (GDR)

800 METRES

1:55.8	Tatyana Providokhina (Sov)
1:55.8	Nadyezhda Mushta (Sov)
1:56.2	Anita Weiss (GDR)
1:56.6	Zoya Rigel (Sov)
1:56.6	Totka Petrova (Bul)
1:57.5	Hildegard Ullrich (GDR)
1:57.5	Lyudmila Veselkova (Sov)
1:57.9	Svyetlana Styrkina (Sov)
1:58.1	Ulrike Bruns (GDR)
1:58.7	Raissa Byelusova (Sov)
1:58.8	Rafira Lovin (Rom)
1:59.2	Bettina Buse (GDR)
1:59.2	Lyubov Ivanova (Sov)
1:59.3	Martina Kämpfert (GDR)
1:59.4	Rommy Schmidt (GDR)
1:59.4	Eleonora Tarita (Rom)
1:59.5	Svyetlana Guskova (Sov)
1:59.5	Valentina Ilyinich (Sov)
1:59.8	Ileana Silai (Rom)
1:59.8	Vesela Yatsinska (Bul)
1:59.8	Heike Roock (GDR)
1:59.8	Krystyna Kacperczyk (Pol)

1500 METRES

3:59.0	Giana Romanova (Sov)
3:59.8	Natalia Marasescu (Rom)
4:00.2	Totka Petrova (Bul)
4:00.2	Valentina Ilyinich (Sov)
4:00.6	Grete Waitz (Nor)
4:01.3	Gabrielle Dorio (Ita)
4:01.5	Brigitte Kraus (Ger)
4:02.0	Ulrike Bruns (GDR)
4:02.1	Lyudmila Kalnitskaya (Sov)
4:02.8	Olga Dvirna (Sov)
4:03.1	Gabriele Lehmann (GDR)
4:03.5	Ileana Silai (Rom)
4:03.5	Svyetlana Guskova (Sov)
4:03.5	Natalia Kuznyetsova (Sov)
4:03.9	Zoya Rigel (Sov)
4:04.1	Nadyezhda Mushta (Sov)
4:04.5	Samira Zaitseva (Sov)
4:04.6	Cornelia Burki (Swi)
4:04.7	Lyudmila Veselkova (Sov)
4:04.7	Vesela Yatsinska (Bul)

3000 METRES

8:32.1	Grete Waitz (Nor)
8:33.2	Svyetlana Ulmasova (Sov)
8:33.5	Natalia Marasescu (Rom)
8:40.9	Maricica Puica (Rom)
8:42.3	Loa Olafsson (Den)
8:42.6	Jan Merrill (USA)
8:43.0	Giana Romanova (Sov)

8:45.6	Raissa Byelusova (Sov)
8:45.6	Valentina Ilyinich (Sov)
8:46.1	Cornelia Burki (Swi)
8:47.6	Svyetlana Guskova (Sov)
8:48.3	Raissa Smetkina (Sov)
8:48.7	Paula Fudge (UK)
8:52.3	Christine Benning (UK)
8:52.6	Gabrielle Lehmann (GDR)
8:53.1	Ann Ford (UK)
8:53.2	Raissa Sadretdinova (Sov)
8:58.4	Mary Purcell (Eir)
9:00.4	Nikolina Shtereva (Bul)
9:00.9	Carmen Valero (Spa)

MARATHON

2:32:30	Grete Waitz (Nor)
2:36:24	Julie Brown (USA)
2:38:33	Christa Vahlensieck (Ger)
2:41:32	Patty Lyons (USA)
2:41:46	Celia Peterson (USA)
2:41:49	Martha Cooksey (USA)

100 METRES HURDLES

12.48	Grazyna Rabsztyn (Pol)
12.62	Johanna Klier (GDR)
12.67	Tatyana Anisimova (Sov)
12.73	Gudrun Berend/Wakan (GDR)
12.74	Danuta Perka (Pol)
12.83	Nina Morgulina (Sov)
12.89	Lubyna Langer (Pol)
12.98	Natalya Lebedyeva (Sov)
12.98	Elzbieta Rabsztyn (Pol)
13.02	Annerose Fiedler (GDR)
13.04	Bozena Szwierczynska (Pol)
13.08	Lorna Boothe (UK) (12.98w)
13.13	Deby LaPlante (USA)
13.14	Zofia Bielczyk (Pol) (13.00w)
13.14	Patty van Wolvelaere (USA)
13.16	Silvia Kempin (Ger)
13.19	Regina Beyer (GDR)
13.19	Mariana Dumitrescu (Rom)
13.23	Ester Rot (Isr)
13.23	Sharon Colyear (UK) (13.12w)

400 METRES HURDLES

54.89	Tatyana Zelentsova (Sov)
55.14	Silvia Hollmann (Ger)
55.36	Karin Rossley (GDR)
55.44	Krystyna Kacperczyk (Pol)
55.46	Brigitte Köhn (GDR)
55.63	Anita Weiss (GDR)
55.97	Ingrida Barkane (Sov)
56.19	Marina Makeyeva (Sov)
56.47	Hildegarde Ullrich (GDR)
56.60	Erika Weinstein (Ger)
56.67	Genowefa Blaszak (Pol)
56.68	Yordanka Filipova (Bul)
56.71	Lea Alaerts (Bel)
56.97	Tatyana Zubova (Sov)
57.09	Anna Kostetskaya (Sov)

57.12	Lilyana Ivanova (Bul)
57.21	Yelena Kolesnik (Sov)
57.23	Doina Badescu (Rom)
57.36	Mary Appleby (Eir)
Hand time	
57.0	Christine Warden (UK)

4 × 100 METRES RELAY

42.27	GDR
42.54	Soviet Union
42.72	UK
43.47	Bulgaria
43.78	France
43.83	Poland
43.97	USA
44.15	Canada
44.18	Germany
44.31	Sweden
44.37	Cuba
44.41	Jamaica
44.63	Nigeria
44.78	Australia
44.89	Italy

4 × 400 METRES RELAY

3:21.2	GDR
3:22.5	Soviet Union
3:26.8	Poland
3:27.2	UK
3:28.0	Germany
3:28.2	United States
3:28.7	Australia
3:30.4	Czechoslovakia
3:30.7	Hungary
3:30.7	Romania
3:31.3	Cuba
3:32.2	Finland
3:32.7	Bulgaria
3:33.4	Belgium
3:33.8	France

HIGH JUMP

2.01m (6′7″)	Sara Simeoni (Ita)
1.99m (6′6¼″)	Rosi Ackermann (GDR)
1.95m (6′4¾″)	Brigitte Holzapfel (Ger)
1.95m (6′4¾″)	Ulrike Meyfarth (Ger)
1.93m (6′4″)	Katrina Gibbs (Aus)
1.93m (6′4″)	Joni Huntley (USA)
1.93m (6′4″)	Jutta Kirst (GDR)
1.93m (6′4″)	Kristine Nitzsche (GDR)
1.92m (6′3¾″)i	Debbie Brill (Can) (1.90m)
1.91m (6′3¼″)	Cornelia Popa (Rom)
1.90m (6′3″)	Louise Ritter (USA)
1.90m (6′2¾″)	Nadyezhda Marinenko (Sov)
1.90m (6′2¾″)i	Urszula Kielan (Pol) (1.89m)
1.90m (6′2¾″)	Tamami Yagi (Jap)
1.89m (6′2½″)	Sandra Dini (Ita)
1.89m (6′2½″)	Larisa Klementyenok (Sov)
1.89m (6′2½″)i	Marina Serkova (Sov)
1.89m (6′2½″)	Andrea Matay (Hun)
1.88m (6′2″)	13 girls

LONG JUMP

7.09m (23′3¼″)	Vilma Bardauskiene (Sov)
6.89m (22′7½″)	Jodi Anderson (USA)
6.79m (22′3¼″)	Angela Voigt (GDR) (6.87m)(w)
6.74m (22′1½″)	Jarmila Nygrynova (Cze)
6.72m (22′0¾″)	Kathy McMillan (USA)
6.71m (22′0¼″)	Gina Panait (Rom)
6.70m (21′11¾″)	Lyn Jacenko (Aus)
6.69m (21′11½″)	Anita Stukane (Sov)
6.65m (21′10″)	Brigitte Wujak (GDR) (6.71m)(w)
6.65m (21′10″)	Heide Wycisk (GDR)
6.65m (21′10″)	Lidia Alfeyeva (Sov)
6.62m (21′8¾″)	Jacqueline Curtet (Fra)
6.61m (21′8¼″)	Maryna van Niekerk (Saf)
6.59m (21′7½″)	Susan Reeve (UK)(6.64m)(w)
6.59m (21′7½″)	Ramona Neubert (GDR)
6.58m (21′7¼″)	Erica Hooker (Aus)
6.58m (21′7¼″)	Anke Weigt (Ger)
6.58m (21′7¼″)	Anna Wlodarczyk (Pol)
6.57m (21′6¾″)	Maria Papp (Hun)
6.56m (21′6¼″)	Jane Frederick (USA) (6.58m)(w)
6.56m (21′6¼″)	Karin Hänel (Ger)
6.56m (21′6¼″)	Modupe Oshikoya (Nig)
6.56m (21′6¼″)	Doina Anton (Rom)
Wind assisted	
6.79m (22′3¼″)	Sigrun Siegl (GDR)

SHOT

22.06m (72′4½″)	Ilona Slupianek (GDR)
21.87m (71′9″)	Helena Fibingerova (Cze)
21.59m (70′10″)	Marianne Adam (GDR)
21.58m (70′9¾″)	Margitta Droese (GDR)
20.99m (68′10½″)	Helma Knorrscheidt (GDR)
20.70m (66′5¼″)	Svyetlana Krachevskaya (Sov)
20.33m (66′8½″)	Yelena Stoyanova (Bul)
20.33m (66′8½″)	Ivanka Petrova (Bul)
20.10m (65′11½″)	Eva Wilms (Ger)
19.92m (65′4¼″)	Tamara Bufetova (Sov)
19.80m (64′11½″)	Svyetlana Myelnikova (Sov)
19.74m (64′9¼″)	Nina Issayeva (Sov)
19.42m (63′8¾″)	Zdena Bartonova (Cze)
19.24m (63′1½″)	Karin Fitzner (GDR)
19.22m (63′0¾″)	Simone Michel (GDR)
19.16m (62′10½″)	Verzhinia Veselinova (Bul)
19.09m (62′7¾″)	Natalya Akrimyenko (Sov)
19.05m (62′6″)	Cordula Schulze (GDR)
19.01m (62′4½″)	Vyera Kot (Sov)
18.99m (62′3¾″)	Mihaela Loghin (Rom)

DISCUS

70.72m (232′0″)	Evelin Jahl (GDR)
70.34m (230′9″)	Faina Veleva (Sov)

68.48m (224' 8")	Margitta Droese (GDR)	61.80m (202' 9")	Eva Janko (Aut)
67.54m (221' 7")	Svyetlana Petrova (Sov)	61.66m (202' 3")	Heidi Repser (Ger)
66.94m (219' 7")	Svetla Boshkova (Bul)	61.20m (200' 9")	Bernadetta Blechacz (Pol)
66.28m (217' 5")	Lyudmila Issayeva (Sov)	61.20m (200' 9")	Jadwiga Putinene (Sov)
66.24m (217' 4")	Natalya Gorbachova (Sov)	60.52m (198' 7")	Valentina Litvinova (Sov)
66.10m (216' 10")	Sabine Engel (GDR)	60.42m (198' 3")	Ingrid Thyssen (Ger)
64.40m (211' 3")	Tatyana Bereshnaya (Sov)	60.38m (198' 1")	Ivanka Vansheva (Bul)
64.04m (210' 1")	Jitka Prouzova (Cze)		
63.00m (206' 8")	Brigitte Sander (GDR)		
63.00m (206' 8")	Ilona Slupianek (GDR)		

PENTATHLON
(h – hand timing)

62.92m (206' 5")	Helgi Parts (Sov)
62.88m (206' 3")	Donka Khristova (Bul)
62.46m (204' 11")	Ute Rekeschat (GDR)
62.40m (204' 9")	Argentina Menis (Rom)
62.34m (204' 6")	Carmen Ionescu (Can)
62.16m (203' 11")	Nadyezhda Jerocha (Sov)
62.00m (203' 5")	Kharchenko (Sov)

4768	Diane Konihowski (Can)
4746	Nadyezhda Tkachenko (Sov)
4704	Jane Frederick (USA)
4675h	Margit Papp (Hun) (4655)
4638h	Burglinde Pollak (GDR) (4600)
4599	Kristine Nitzsche (GDR)
4596	Yekaterina Smirnova (Sov)
4592	Beatrix Philipp (Ger)
4590	Yekaterina Gordienko (Sov)
4565h	Ramona Neubert (GDR) (4520)
4514	Ina Losch (Ger)
4501	Nadyezhda Karyakina (Sov)
4385h	Tatyana Shlapakova (Sov)
4379	Modupe Oshikoya (Nig)

JAVELIN

69.16m (226' 11")	Ruth Fuchs (GDR)
64.24m (210' 9")	Ute Richter (GDR)
64.04m (210' 1")	Eva Helmschmidt (Ger)
64.02m (210' 0")	Kate Schmidt (USA)
64.00m (210' 0")	Tessa Sanderson (UK)
63.66m (208' 10")	Eva Zorgo/Raduly (Rom)
63.60m (208' 8")	Ute Hommola (GDR)
63.50m (208' 4")	Maria Colon (Cub)
63.38m (207' 11")	Sherry Calvert (USA)
63.32m (207' 9")	Karin Smith (USA)
63.18m (207' 3")	Nina Nikanorova (Sov)
61.92m (203' 2")	Angelika Fuchs (GDR)
61.90m (203' 1")	Petra Felke (GDR)

4371h	Gabriela Ionescu (Rom)
4368	Galina Schuschenko (Sov)
4366	Sabine Everts (GDR)
4363	Liesel Albert (Ger)
4359h	Olga Rukavishnakova (Sov)
4352h	Themis Zambryzcki (Bra)
4351	Breda Lorenci (Yug)
4343	Sivija Orja (Sov)

UK All-Time Top 10

MEN (w = wind assisted; i = indoor mark)

100 METRES
(Fully automatic timing)

10.15	Allan Wells; 1978		10.3	Roy Sandstrom; 1956
10.29	Peter Radford; 1958		10.3	David Jones; 1961
10.32	Mike McFarlane; 1978 (10.29w)		10.3	Berwyn Jones; 1963
10.33	Brian Green; 1972 (10.32w)		10.3	Ron Jones; 1968
10.35	Barrie Kelly; 1968		10.3	Martin Reynolds; 1968
10.36	David Jenkins; 1972		10.3	Barrie Kelly; 1968
10.42	Ron Jones; 1968		10.3	Don Halliday; 1968
10.46	Les Piggot; 1972 (10.36w)		10.3	Les Piggot; 1972
10.47	Ainsley Bennett; 1977			
10.49	David Jones; 1960			
10.49	Steve Green; 1978 (10.40w)			

Wind assisted

10.38w	Ian Green; 1970
10.38w	Don Halliday; 1970

Note also hand timing

10.1	David Jenkins; 1972
10.1	Brian Green; 1972
10.2	McDonald Bailey; 1951
10.2	Menzies Campbell; 1967

200 METRES
(Fully automatic timing)
*(* 220 yards time less 0.1 sec)*

20.61	Allan Wells; 1978 (20.12w)
20.66	Dick Steane; 1968
20.66	David Jenkins; 1973
20.70	Chris Monk; 1973
20.73	Ralph Banthorpe; 1968
20.83	Martin Reynolds; 1970 (20.61w)
20.84	Brian Green; 1971

20.86	Ainsley Bennett; 1975 (20.85w)	
20.90	Glen Cohen; 1976	
20.92	Alan Pascoe; 1972	

Wind assisted

20.89w	Tim Bonsor; 1978
20.90w	Trevor Hoyte; 1978

Note also hand timing

20.3	David Jenkins; 1972
20.4*	Peter Radford; 1960
20.5	Allan Wells; 1978
20.7*	Menzies Campbell; 1967
20.7	Martin Reynolds; 1970
20.7	Brian Green; 1972
20.8	Howard Davies; 1968
20.8	Don Halliday; 1972
20.9	McDonald Bailey; 1950
20.9	David Jones; 1961
20.9	Robbie Brightwell; 1962
20.9	Drew McMaster; 1976

400 METRES

*(* 440 yards time less 0.3 sec)*

44.93	David Jenkins; 1975
45.49	Glen Cohen; 1978
45.6*	Robbie Brightwell; 1962
45.7	Adrian Metcalfe; 1961
45.91	Martin Winbolt-Lewis; 1968
45.9	Colin Campbell; 1968
46.0	Tim Graham; 1964
46.10	Peter Gabbett; 1972
46.11	Martin Reynolds; 1972
46.15	Ainsley Bennett; 1975

800 METRES

1:44.0	Sebastian Coe; 1978
1:44.1	Steve Ovett; 1978
1:45.1	Andy Carter; 1973
1:45.8	Frank Clement; 1976
1:45.8	Garry Cook; 1978
1:46.1	Colin Campbell; 1972
1:46.2	Peter Browne; 1973
1:46.3	Chris Carter; 1966
1:46.3	Phil Lewis; 1974
1:46.5	John Boulter; 1966

1500 METRES

3:34.5	Steve Ovett; 1977
3:35.5	David Moorcroft; 1978
3:35.6	John Robson; 1978
3:35.7	Frank Clement; 1978
3:36.8	Mike Kearns; 1977
3:37.6	Brendan Foster; 1974
3:37.7	Graham Williamson; 1978
3:38.1	Glen Grant; 1978
3:38.1	Jim McGuinness; 1977
3:38.2	Peter Stewart; 1972

1 MILE

3:52.8	Steve Ovett; 1978
3:54.2	Frank Clement; 1978
3:54.3	John Robson; 1978
3:55.0	Jim McGuinness; 1977
3:55.3	Peter Stewart; 1972
3:55.3	David Moorcroft; 1978
3:55.7	Alan Simpson; 1965
3:55.8	Graham Williamson; 1978
3:55.9	Brendan Foster; 1972
3:56.0	Jim Douglas; 1972

3000 METRES

7:35.2	Brendan Foster; 1974
7:40.4	Nick Rose; 1978
7:41.3	Steve Ovett; 1977
7:43.5	David Moorcroft; 1978
7:45.3	Dennis Coates; 1977
7:46.4	David Bedford; 1972
7:46.6	David Black; 1973
7:46.8	Ian Stewart; 1976
7:47.0i	Ricky Wilde; 1969
7:47.6	Dick Taylor; 1969

5000 METRES

13:14.6	Brendan Foster; 1974
13:17.2	David Bedford; 1972
13:19.7	Ian McCafferty; 1972
13:20.4	Nick Rose; 1977
13:21.2	Tony Simmons; 1976
13:22.8	Ian Stewart; 1970
13:23.6	David Black; 1974
13:25.0	Steve Ovett; 1977
13:25.2	Mike McLeod; 1977
13:26.0	Bernie Ford; 1977

10,000 METRES

27:30.3	Brendan Foster; 1978
27:30.8	David Bedford; 1973
27:36.3	David Black; 1978
27:43.0	Ian Stewart; 1977
27:43.6	Tony Simmons; 1977
27:43.7	Bernie Ford; 1977
27:55.2	Julian Goater; 1977
28:00.6	Jim Brown; 1975
28:04.2	Mike McLeod; 1978
28:06.6	Dick Taylor; 1969

MARATHON

2:09:12	Ian Thompson; 1974
2:09:28	Ron Hill; 1970
2:10:48	Bill Adcocks; 1968
2:12:04	Jim Alder; 1970
2:12:19	Don Faircloth; 1970
2:12:32	Trevor Wright; 1978
2:12:33	Tony Simmons; 1978
2:12:50	Jeff Norman; 1978
2:13:12	Chris Stewart; 1974
2:13:29	David Cannon; 1978

3000 METRES STEEPLECHASE

8:19.0	Dennis Coates; 1976
8:22.5	John Davies; 1974

8:22.8	John Bicourt; 1976
8:26.4	Andrew Holden; 1972
8:27.8	Steve Hollings; 1973
8:28.5	Tony Staynings; 1976
8:28.6	David Bedford; 1971
8:30.6	Peter Griffiths; 1977
8:30.8	Gerry Stevens; 1969
8:31.1	Ian Gilmour; 1978

110 METRES HURDLES
(Fully automatic timing)

13.69	Berwyn Price; 1973 (13.65w)
13.72	David Hemery; 1970 (13.66w)
13.79	Alan Pascoe; 1972
14.01	Mark Holtom; 1978
14.10	Graham Gower; 1972
14.10	Bob Danville; 1976 (13.99w)
14.14	Mike Hogan; 1963
14.16	Mike Parker; 1968
14.19	C. J. Kirkpatrick; 1973 (14.17w)
14.10w	David Wilson; 1977

Hand timing

13.5	Berwyn Price; 1973 (13.4w)
13.6	David Hemery; 1969
13.7	Alan Pascoe; 1969
13.7	C. J. Kirkpatrick; 1974
13.9	Mike Parker; 1963
13.9	David Wilson; 1974
14.1	Laurie Taitt; 1963 (14.0w)
14.1	Stuart Storey; 1967

400 METRES HURDLES

48.12	David Hemery; 1968
48.59	Alan Pascoe; 1975
49.03	John Sherwood; 1968
49.65	Bill Hartley; 1975
49.9	Andrew Todd; 1969
50.1	John Cooper; 1964
50.58	Colin O'Neill; 1974
50.68	Peter Warden; 1966
50.7	Stewart McCallum; 1976
50.7	Steve Black; 1974

HIGH JUMP

2.20m (7' 2½")	Brian Burgess; 1978
2.19m (7' 2¼")i	Mark Naylor; 1978
2.16m (7' 1")	Mike Butterfield; 1976
2.15m (7' 0½")	Trevor Llewelyn; 1978
2.14m (7' 0¼")	Angus McKenzie; 1975
2.14m (7' 0¼")	Alan Dainton; 1977
2.14m (7' 0¼")	Colin Harris; 1978
2.11m (6' 11")	Colin Boreham; 1974
2.11m (6' 11")	Milton Palmer; 1976
2.11m (6' 11")	George Roberton; 1978

POLE VAULT

5.42m (17' 9¼")	Brian Hooper; 1978
5.25m (17' 2¾")	Mike Bull; 1973
5.25m (17' 2¾")	Allan Williams; 1977
5.25m (17' 2¾")	Keith Stock; 1978

5.20m (17' 0¾")	Jeff Gutteridge; 1976
5.18m (17' 0")	Steve Chappell; 1978
4.98m (16' 4")	Dick Williamson; 1978
4.90m (16' 0¾")	Stuart Tufton; 1972
4.90m (16' 0¾")	Daley Thompson; 1977
4.87m (15' 11¾")	Mike Bryant; 1971

LONG JUMP

8.23m (27' 0")	Lynn Davies; 1968
8.04m (26' 4½")	Roy Mitchell; 1977 (8.16m) (w)
7.98m (26' 2¼")	Alan Lerwill; 1974 (8.15m) (w)
7.93m (26' 0¼")	Daley Thompson; 1978 (8.11m) (w)
7.89m (25' 10¾")	John Morbey; 1966
7.79m (25' 6¾")	Geoff Hignett; 1971
7.79m (25' 6¾")	Don Porter; 1975
7.75m (25' 5¼")	Ken Cocks; 1978
7.74m (25' 4¾")	Fred Alsop; 1964
7.74m (25' 4¾")	Phil Scott; 1972

Wind assisted

7.82m (25' 8")	Peter Reed; 1968
7.76m (25' 5½")	Aston Moore; 1977

TRIPLE JUMP

16.76m (55' 0")	Keith Connor; 1978 (17.21m) (w)
16.69m (54' 9¼")	Aston Moore; 1978 (16.76m) (w)
16.46m (54' 0")	Fred Alsop; 1964 (16.65m) (w)
16.29m (53' 5½")	David Johnson; 1978 (16.33m) (w)
16.22m (53' 2¾")	Derek Boosey; 1968
16.18m (53' 1")	Tony Wadhams; 1969 (16.49m) (w)
16.10m (52' 10")	Alan Lerwill; 1971 (16.21m) (w)
15.97m (52' 4¾")	Mike Ralph; 1964
15.92m (52' 2¾")	John Slaney; 1977
15.88m (52' 1¼")	John Phillips; 1978

Wind assisted

16.17m (53' 0¾")	Chris Colman; 1978

SHOT

21.55m (70' 8½")	Geoff Capes; 1976
20.43m (67' 0½")	Mike Winch; 1974
19.56m (64' 2")	Arthur Rowe; 1961
19.43m (63' 9")	Bill Tancred; 1974
19.18m (62' 11")	Jeff Teale; 1968
18.94m (62' 1¼")	Bob Dale; 1976
18.93m (62' 1¼")	Paul Buxton; 1977
18.62m (61' 1¼")	Martyn Lucking; 1962
18.59m (61' 0")i	Alan Carter; 1965
18.50m (60' 8½")	Mike Lindsay; 1963

DISCUS

64.94m (213' 1")	Bill Tancred; 1974
61.62m (202' 2")	Peter Tancred; 1976

61.00m (200′1″) Allan Seatory; 1974
60.42m (198′3″) Mike Cushion; 1975
59.84m (196′4″) Colin Sutherland; 1978
59.76m (196′1″) John Hillier; 1974
59.70m (195′10″) John Watts; 1972
58.34m (191′5″) Geoff Capes; 1973
58.08m (190′7″) Mike Winch; 1975
57.58m (188′11″) Arthur McKenzie; 1969

HAMMER
74.98m (246′0″) Chris Black; 1976
73.86m (242′4″) Barry Williams; 1976
73.20m (240′2″) Paul Dickenson; 1976
71.00m (232′11″) Ian Chipchase; 1974
70.88m (232′6″) Howard Payne; 1974
69.34m (227′6″) Paul Buxton; 1977
69.00m (226′4″) Jim Whitehead; 1978
65.86m (216′1″) Matthew Mileham; 1978
64.96m (213′1″) Mike Ellis; 1959
64.80m (212′7″) Bruce Fraser; 1973

JAVELIN
84.92m (278′7″) Charles Clover; 1974
83.44m (273′9″) David Travis; 1970
81.92m (268′9″) John Fitzsimons; 1969
81.50m (267′5″) David Ottley; 1977
80.90m (265′5″) **Peter De Kremer**; 1978
80.62m (264′6″) Peter Yates; 1978
80.20m (263′1″) Kevin Sheppard; 1974
79.48m (260′9″) Brian Roberts; 1974
79.26m (260′0″) John McSorley; 1962
79.26m (260′0″) John Greasley; 1963

DECATHLON
8467pts Daley Thompson; 1978
8040pts Peter Gabbett; 1972
7750pts Mike Corden; 1976
7676pts Barry King; 1972
7532pts Nicholas Phipps; 1976
7484pts Alan Drayton; 1978
7451pts Clive Longe; 1969
7443pts Panayiotis Zeniou; 1978
7417pts Mike Bull; 1974
7381pts Graeme Watson; 1978

20 KILOMETRES WALK (ROAD)
1:24:50 Paul Nihill; 1972
1:27:35 Olly Flynn; 1976
1:27:46 Brian Adams; 1975
1:27:59 Phil Embleton; 1971
1:28:15 Ken Matthews; 1960
1:28:50 Amos Seddon; 1974
1:28:50 Roger Mills; 1977
1:29:37 John Warhurst; 1973
1:29:49 Peter Marlow; 1974
1:29:59 John Webb; 1968

50 KILOMETRES WALK (ROAD)
4:08:39 Bob Dobson; 1978
4:11:31 Paul Nihill; 1964
4:12:19 Don Thompson; 1959
4:12:37 John Warhurst; 1972
4:14:03 Tom Misson; 1959
4:14:25 David Cotton; 1978
4:15:13 Shaun Lightman; 1973
4:15:22 Brian Adams; 1978
4:15:51 Ray Middleton; 1972
4:17:52 Stuart Elms; 1976

WOMEN

100 METRES
(Fully automatic timing)
11.16 Andrea Lynch; 1975
11.22 Sonia Lannaman; 1977 (10.93w)
11.35 Sharon Colyear; 1977
11.36 Della Pascoe; 1968
11.39 Val Peat; 1968
11.40 Helen Golden; 1974
11.46 Donna Hartley; 1975
11.49 **Beverley Goddard**; 1978 (11.30w)
11.5e Dorothy Hyman; 1964 (11.43w)
11.5e Daphne Arden; 1964
11.54 Wendy Clarke; 1975 (11.38w)
Hand timing
10.9 Andrea Lynch; 1977
11.2 Helen Golden; 1974
11.2 Sharon Colyear; 1977 (11.1w)
11.3 Dorothy Hyman; 1963

11.3 Anita Neil; 1971
11.3 Beverley Goddard; 1978
11.3 Heather Hunte; 1978
11.4 Wendy Clarke; 1978
11.4 Margot Wells; 1978
11.4 Liz Sutherland; 1973
Wind assisted
10.8w Sonia Lannaman; 1976
11.2w Wendy Clarke; 1976

200 METRES
(Fully automatic timing)
22.75 Donna Hartley; 1978
22.81 Sonia Lannaman; 1976 (22.69w)
22.99 Kathryn Smallwood; 1978 (22.73w)
23.11 Beverley Goddard; 1978 (22.95w)
23.14 Helen Golden; 1973 (22.97w)
23.15 Andrea Lynch; 1975 (22.90w)

23.29	Verona Elder; 1978
23.34	Val Peat; 1969
23.40	Dorothy Hyman; 1962
23.40	Sharon Colyear; 1977

Wind assisted

23.15w	Margaret Williams; 1970

Hand timing

23.0	Helen Golden; 1974
23.1	Andrea Lynch; 1977
23.2	Dorothy Hyman; 1963
23.2	Margaret Williams; 1970 (23.1w)
23.3	Sharon Colyear; 1974 (23.1w)
23.4	Helen Barnett; 1976

400 METRES

51.2	Donna Hartley; 1978
51.4	Verona Elder; 1976
52.12	Lillian Board; 1968
52.15	Joslyn Hoyte; 1978
52.2	Ann Packer; 1964
52.2	Liz Barnes; 1976
52.5	Gladys McCormack; 1976
52.57	Janet Simpson; 1968
52.6	Marilyn Neufville; 1970
52.85	Jannette Roscoe; 1974

800 METRES

2:00.2	Rosemary Wright; 1972
2:00.6	Jane Colebrook; 1977
2:01.1	Ann Packer; 1964
2:01.2	Joan Allison; 1973
2:01.2	Christine McMeekin; 1978
2:01.4	Lillian Board; 1969
2:01.4	Liz Barnes; 1976
2:01.5	Lesley Kiernan; 1977
2:01.7	Pat Cropper; 1971
2:02.0	Margaret Coomber; 1973
2:02.0	Jo White; 1977

1500 METRES

4:04.8	Sheila Carey; 1972
4:06.0	Mary Stewart; 1978
4:07.5	Christine Benning; 1978
4:09.4	Joyce Smith; 1972
4:10.0	Christina Boxer; 1978
4:10.3	Penny Yule; 1978
4:10.7	Joan Allison; 1974
4:11.6	Cherry Hanson; 1978
4:12.4	Christine McMeekin; 1978
4:12.7	Rita Ridley; 1971

1 MILE

4:36.1	Mary Stewart; 1977
4:36.2	Joan Allison; 1973
4:36.5	Penny Yule; 1977
4:37.0	Anne Smith; 1967
4:37.2	Sheila Carey; 1973
4:37.4	Rita Ridley; 1971
4:38.1	Hilary Hollick; 1977
4:38.8	Cherry Hanson; 1977

4:39.3	Paula Fudge; 1975
4:39.4	Christina Boxer; 1977

3000 METRES

8:48.7	Paula Fudge; 1978
8:52.3	Christine Benning; 1978
8:52.8	Ann Ford; 1977
8:55.5	Joyce Smith; 1974
9:06.4	Glynis Penny; 1978
9:07.6i	Mary Stewart; 1976
9:08.6	Penny Yule; 1978
9:13.3	Joan Allison; 1975
9:13.6	Rita Ridley; 1973
9:15.8	Ruth Smeeth; 1978

100 METRES HURDLES

13.08	Lorna Boothe; 1978 (12.98w)
13.11	Sharon Colyear; 1976
13.29	Mary Peters; 1972
13.34	Judy Vernon; 1973
13.41	Shirley Strong; 1978 (13.08w)
13.45	Lorna Drysdale; 1974
13.49	Blondelle Caines; 1977
13.53	Ann Simmonds; 1972
13.65	Wendy McDonnell; 1978
13.75	Susan Reeve; 1970

Hand timing

13.0	Judy Vernon; 1974 (12.9w)
13.0	Blondelle Caines; 1974
13.3	Ann Simmonds; 1972 (13.2w)
13.4	Christine Bell; 1970
13.5	Pat Pryce; 1972
13.5	Liz Sutherland; 1976 (13.2w)
13.5	Susan Longden; 1976

Wind assisted

13.1w	Mary Peters; 1972
13.1w	Lorna Boothe; 1976
13.5w	Myra Nimmo; 1974
13.6w	Lynne Ilott; 1974

400 METRES HURDLES

57.0	Christine Warden; 1978
57.43	Liz Sutherland; 1978
58.31	Jannette Roscoe; 1975
58.55	Jackie Stokoe; 1975
59.00	Diane Heath; 1975
59.02	Susan Smith; 1978
59.42	Frances McCall; 1977
59.53	Veronica Langley; 1978
59.87	Judy Vernon; 1973
59.90	Denise Kiernan; 1978

HIGH JUMP

1.87m (6' 1½")	Barbara Lawton; 1973
1.85m (6' 0¾")	Brenda Gibbs; 1977
1.85m (6' 0¾")	Gillian Hitchen; 1978
1.83m (6' 0")	Linda Hedmark; 1971
1.83m (6' 0")	Valerie Rutter; 1974
1.83m (6' 0")i	Ros Few; 1975
1.83m (6' 0")	Moira Walls; 1977

1.83m (6′0″)	Louise Miller; 1978
1.82m (5′11½″)	Mary Peters; 1972
1.82m (5′11½″)	Denise Brown; 1976
1.82m (5′11½″)	Diane Elliott; 1978

LONG JUMP

6.76m (22′2¼″)	Mary Rand; 1964
6.73m (22′1″)	Sheila Sherwood; 1970
6.61m (21′8¼″)	Susan Reeve; 1977 (6.84m)(w)
6.55m (21′6″)	Ann Simmonds; 1970 (6.57m)(w)
6.51m (21′4¼″)i	Ruth Howell; 1974 (6.54m)(w)
6.44m (21′1½″)	Sharon Colyear; 1977
6.43m (21′1¼″)	Myra Nimmo; 1973 (6.54m)(w)
6.40m (21′0″)	Susan Hearnshaw; 1978 (6.59m)(w)
6.39m (20′11¾″)	Moira Walls; 1970 (6.48m)(w)
6.39m (20′11¾″)	Maureen Chitty; 1972
6.39m (20′11¾″)	Susan Longden; 1976

SHOT

16.74m (54′11¼″)i	Judith Oakes; 1978
16.40m (53′9¾″)i	Mary Peters; 1970
16.40m (53′9¾″)	Margaret Ritchie; 1978
16.34m (53′7½″)	Angela Littlewood; 1978
16.29m (53′5½″)	Brenda Bedford; 1976
16.05m (52′8″)	Janis Kerr; 1976
15.72m (51′7″)	Venissa Head; 1977
15.18m (49′9¾″)	Suzanne Allday; 1964
15.09m (49′6¼″)	Lana Newton; 1978
15.03m (49′3¾″)	Vanessa Redford; 1978

DISCUS

60.80m (199′6″)	Margaret Ritchie; 1978
58.02m (190′4″)	Rosemary Payne; 1972
55.06m (180′8″)	Janet Thompson; 1978
51.60m (169′3″)	Dorothy Swinyard; 1973
51.04m (167′5″)	Lesley Mallin; 1978
50.58m (165′11″)	Brenda Bedford; 1968
49.84m (163′6″)	Janis Kerr; 1977
49.66m (162′11″)	Gay Porter; 1970
49.58m (162′8″)	Jackie Elsmore; 1975
49.12m (161′2″)	Jean Fielding; 1974

JAVELIN

67.20m (220′6″)	Tessa Sanderson; 1977
55.60m (182′5″)	Susan Platt; 1968
54.18m (177′9″)	Rosemary Morgan; 1964
53.88m (176′9″)	Sharon Avann; 1973
53.88m (176′9″)	Fatima Whitbread; 1978
53.32m (174′11″)	Maxine Jervis; 1978
52.16m (171′1″)	Sandra O'Toole; 1978
52.10m (170′11″)	Anne Norton; 1973
52.04m (170′9″)	Jackie Zaslona; 1978
51.74m (169′9″)	Diane Williams; 1978

PENTATHLON

4385pts	Susan Longden; 1977
4292pts	Yvette Wray; 1978
4227pts	Moira Walls; 1977
4222pts	Susan Mapstone; 1978
4070pts	Gillian Howell; 1978
4067pts	Susan Wright; 1977

Best performances with 200 metres, not the 800 metres now included

4801pts	Mary Peters; 1972
4433pts	Ann Simmonds (Wilson); 1972
4422pts	Susan Longden; 1976
4294pts	Ruth Howell; 1972
4229pts	Hazel Oakes; 1976
4161pts	Janet Honour; 1972
4141pts	Susan Scott (Reeve); 1969

3000 METRES WALK (TRACK)

13:40.0	Carol Tyson; 1977
14:19.4	Marion Fawkes; 1976
14:34.0	Irene Bateman; 1978
14:41.3	Beverley Francis; 1978
14:46.0	Judy Farr; 1978
14:46.6	Pamela Branson; 1976
14:56.0	Virginia Lovell/Birch 1978
14:58.0	Christine Coleman; 1973
14:59.4	Betty Jenkins; 1973
15:00.6	Sallyann Wish; 1972

5000 METRES WALK (TRACK)

23:42.4	Carol Tyson; 1977
23:59.6	Marion Fawkes; 1977
24:37.7	Judy Farr; 1977
24:45.0	Karen Eden; 1978
24:46.2	Irene Bateman; 1978
24:49.4	Beverley Francis; 1978
25:02.8	Virginia Lovell; 1975
25:34.0	Sallyann Wish; 1973
25:38.4	Pamela Branson; 1974
25:46.8	Sylvia Saunders; 1974

Following page: *Richard Ashton.*

Mike Street

United Kingdom Top 20 1978

Note that wind-assisted marks are included in brackets after an athlete's best under 'legal' conditions, or as a subsidiary list.

MEN

100 METRES
(Fully automatic timing)

10.15	Allan Wells (10.07w)
10.29	Ernest Obeng (Ghana)
10.32	Mike McFarlane (10.29w)
10.49	Steve Green (10.40w)
10.52	Drew McMaster
10.60	Les Hoyte (10.54w)
10.64	David Jenkins
10.65	Cameron Sharp
10.65	Daley Thompson (10.50w)
10.66	David Baptiste
10.66	David Roberts
10.68	Brian Green (10.58w)
10.70	Trevor Hoyte (10.58w)
10.72	Cecil Moven
10.73	Tim Bonsor
10.75	Graeme Watson (10.72w)

Wind assisted

10.70w	John Stark
10.71w	Earl Tulloch
10.73w	Micky Morris

Note also hand times

10.3	Don Halliday
10.4	Steve Green
10.5	Brian Green
10.5	Trevor Hoyte
10.5	Michael Powell
10.4w	Ivan Loftman
10.4w	David Roberts

200 METRES

20.61	Allan Wells (20.12w)
20.97	Mike McFarlane
21.05	Steve Green
21.15	Trevor Hoyte (20.90w)
21.16	David Jenkins
21.30	Philip Cooke
21.35	Danny Laing (21.34w)
21.36	David Baptiste
21.36	Ernest Obeng (Ghana)
21.36	David Roberts
21.41	Les Hoyte
21.43	Drew McMaster
21.47	Tim Bonsor (20.89w)
21.50	Michael Bond
21.51	Terry Whitehead
21.52	Cameron Sharp

Wind assisted

21.51w	Earl Tulloch

Note also hand times

20.5	Allan Wells
21.0	David Jenkins
21.1	Drew McMaster (21.0w)
21.1	Micky Morris
21.2	Glen Cohen (21.0w)
21.2	Les Hoyte
21.2	Cameron Sharp (21.1w)

400 METRES

45.49	Glen Cohen
45.97	David Jenkins
46.23	Terry Whitehead
46.27	Richard Ashton
46.39	Danny Laing
46.74	Jeff Griffiths
46.92	Mike Delaney
46.93	Roger Jenkins
46.96	Alan Bell
47.05	Carl Hamilton
47.1	Peter Hoffmann
47.2	Steve Scutt
47.3	Walcott Taylor
47.6	Neil Jackson
47.6	Steve Wymark
47.6	Garry Cook
47.6	Dane Joseph
47.7	Andrew Kerr
47.7	Sebastian Coe
47.75	Roderic Milne

800 METRES

1:44.0	Sebastian Coe
1:44.1	Steve Ovett
1:45.8	Garry Cook
1:46.6	Peter Hoffmann
1:47.7	Dane Joseph
1:47.9	Alan Gibson
1:48.0	Paul Forbes
1:48.1	David Warren
1:48.8	Glen Grant
1:48.8	Peter Browne
1:48.9	Colin Szwed
1:49.0	David Moorcroft
1:49.1	Peter Lewis
1:49.1	Julian Spooner
1:49.1	Pat Chimes
1:49.1	Frank Clement
1:49.2	John Robson

1:49.2	Laurie Nicholson
1:49.3	Mel Edwards
1:49.3	Richard Ashton
1:49.4	Terry Young

1500 METRES

3:35.5	David Moorcroft
3:35.6	John Robson
3:35.6	Steve Ovett
3:35.7	Frank Clement
3:37.7	Graham Williamson
3:38.1	Glen Grant
3:39.7	Jim McGuinness
3:40.1	Steve Cram
3:40.6	Tim Hutchings
3:41.9	Alan Gibson
3:43.3	Chris Sly
3:43.3	Ray Smedley
3:43.4	Bob Maplestone
3:43.6	Alan Mottershead
3:43.7	Steve Emson
3:43.8	Nick Rose
3:43.8	Paul Lawther
3:44.1	Malcolm Prince
3:44.3i	Mike Fromant
3:44.4	Neil Black
3:44.4	Kevin Steere

1 MILE

3:52.8	Steve Ovett
3:54.2	Frank Clement
3:54.3	John Robson
3:55.5	David Moorcroft
3:55.8	Graham Williamson
3:57.0	Brendan Foster
3:57.4	Steve Cram
3:57.8	Tim Hutchings
3:58.9	Nick Rose
3:59.4	Paul Lawther
3:59.4	Mike McLeod
4:00.0	Erwin Hartel
4:00.4	Steve Emson
4:00.6	Jim McGuinness
4:00.9	Tony Leonard
4:00.9	Bob Maplestone
4:00.9	Ray Smedley
4:01.2	Walter Wilkinson
4:01.5	Alan Mottershead
4:01.5	Chris Sly

3000 METRES

7:40.4	Nick Rose
7:43.5	David Moorcroft
7:44.3	Steve Ovett (during 8:13.5 2 miles)
7:48.2	Mike McLeod
7:49.1	Paul Lawther
7:49.7	Ray Smedley
7:49.9	David Black
7:51.5	Tony Simmons
7:52.1	Nat Muir

7:53.9	Keith Penny
7:54.1	Lawrie Spence
7:54.2	Dennis Coates
7:54.2	Charles Spedding
7:54.4	Bernard Ford
7:55.0	Peter Standing
7:55.2i	Peter Shaw

5000 METRES

13:25.2	Mike McLeod
13:25.4	Nick Rose
13:25.4	Brendan Foster
13:25.7	Tony Simmons
13:28.7	Charles Spedding
13:31.8	Julian Goater
13:32.6	Bernard Ford
13:34.9	David Black
13:34.9	Nat Muir
13:36.6	Malcolm Prince
13:37.2	Keith Penny
13:37.7	Lawrie Spence
13:38.8	Steve Jones
13:40.5	Peter Standing
13:40.6	Tony Staynings
13:41.6	Allister Hutton
13:43.8	Nick Lees
13:45.5	Andrew Catton
13:46.0	Ray Smedley
13:49.8	Neil Coupland

10,000 METRES

27:30.3	Brendan Foster
27:36.3	David Black
28:04.2	Mike McLeod
28:12.4	Bernard Ford
28:15.0	Tony Simmons
28:16.7	Julian Goater
28:35.1	Steve Kenyon
28:36.4	Jim Brown
28:36.5	Geoff Smith
28:37.1	Allister Hutton
28:38.6	Neil Coupland
28:39.1	Keith Penny
28:44.1	Graham Ellis
28:45.3	Jim Dingwall
28:46.6	Grenville Tuck
28:48.0	Peter Standing
28:49.5	Hugh Jones
28:53.8	Jon Wigley
28:56.3	Jeremy Odlin
28:59.3	Nick Lees

3000 METRES STEEPLECHASE

8:26.0	Dennis Coates
8:26.6	John Davies
8:31.1	Ian Gilmour
8:35.8	Tony Staynings
8:35.8	Micky Morris
8:39.3	John Graham
8:42.2	John Wild

8:46.9	Ron Harris
8:47.6	Roger Hackney
8:48.1	Graham Tuck
8:48.4	Graeme Fell
8:51.1	John Wheway
8:51.8	John Bicourt
8:53.5	Robert McKim
8:53.7	Peter Griffiths
8:54.0	William Sheridan
8:56.3	**Alan Parkinson**
8:57.1	Derek Blakeley
8:57.6	Jim Evans
8:57.8	Andrew Sharp

MARATHON

2:12:32	Trevor Wright
2:12:33	Tony Simmons
2:12:50	Jeff Norman
2:13:29	David Cannon
2:13:49	Ian Thompson
2:13:58	Jim Dingwall
2:14:06	Ian Beauchamp
2:14:45	Stan Curran
2:15:43	John McLaughlin
2:15:47	Colin Taylor
2:15:54	Mike Hurd
2:16:39	Paul Eales
2:16:57	Keith Penny
2:17:16	Mike Critchley
2:17:16	Barry Watson
2:17:21	Mike Rowland
2:17:25	Greg Hannon
2:17:48	Chris Stewart
2:17:48	Roger Brown
2:17:55	**David Clark**

110 METRES HURDLES
(*Fully automatic timing*)

13.74	Berwyn Price (13.70w)
14.01	Mark Holtom
14.40	David Wilson
14.55	Mark Hatton
14.60	Ian Ratcliffe
14.71	Philip Barthropp
14.75	Tony James
14.75	Neil Gerrard
14.85	Daley Thompson
14.86	Alan Drayton
14.87	Trevor Clifton
14.92	Stephen Burke
14.93	Bob Danville
15.06	Malcolm Kindon

Wind assisted

14.90w	Alan Sumner
14.91w	**Nick Alexander**
15.01w	Robin Simpson

Note also hand times

14.4	Mark Hatton
14.4w	Ian Ratcliffe
14.5	Alan Drayton
14.6	Tony James (14.5w)
14.6	Neil Gerrard
14.7	Malcolm Kindon
14.8	Trevor Clifton (14.6w)
14.8	Alan Sumner
14.8	Roger Honey
14.8	Robin Simpson
14.8	Michael Morgan
14.8w	Huw Jones

400 METRES HURDLES

49.63	Alan Pascoe
50.96	Gary Oakes
51.03	Bill Hartley
51.21	Steve James
51.38	David West
51.45	Clive Beattie
51.47	Roger Bell
51.88	Roger Jenkins
52.02	Mike Whittingham
52.4	Chris Preston
52.5	Harry Robinson
52.9	Colin Richardson
53.0	Carson Porteous
53.27	David Anderson
53.42	Wilbert Greaves
53.43	Antoni Tarquini
53.4	Steve Hinchliffe
53.4	Norman Gregor
53.46	Bob Danville
53.6	John Sherwood

20,000 METRES WALK
(*t = track walk*)

1:28:44	Olly Flynn
1:29:19t	Brian Adams
1:30:18	Roger Mills
1:30:27t	Steve Gower
1:30:54t	Amos Seddon
1:32:37	Carl Lawton
1:32:45	Chris Harvey
1:32:56	Graham Morris
1:33:00	Ian Richards
1:33:47	David Cotton
1:33:57	Ken Carter
1:34:15	William Wright
1:34:30	Shaun Lightman
1:34:31	Bob Dobson
1:34:39t	George Nibre
1:34:39	John Warhurst
1:35:13	Mick Greasley
1:35:22	Alan Callow
1:35:25	Eric Taylor
1:35:28	Peter Fawkes

50,000 METRES WALK
(*t = track walk*)

4:08:39	Bob Dobson
4:14:25	David Cotton

4:15:22	Brian Adams
4:18:32	Ian Richards
4:20:24	Adrian James
4:20:25	Peter Ryan
4:21:06	Chris Maddocks
4:23:32	John Lees
4:24:09	Shaun Lightman
4:28:56	Barry Ingarfield
4:29:00	John Warhurst
4:29:04	Graham Young
4:29:17	Roy Thorpe
4:29:40	Mick Greasley
4:31:04t	Peter Hodkinson
4:31:16	Tony Geal
4:33:49	Ron Wallwork
4:37:36	Geoff Hunwicks
4:39:03	Dennis Holly
4:39:20	John Eddershaw

HIGH JUMP

2.20m (7′ 2½″)	Brian Burgess
2.19m (7′ 2¼″)i	Mark Naylor (2.17m)
2.15m (7′ 0½″)i	Trevor Llewelyn
2.14m (7′ 0¼″)	Colin Harris
2.11m (6′ 11″)	George Robertson
2.10m (6′ 10¾″)	Mike Butterfield
2.10m (6′ 10¾″)	Claude Moseley
2.10m (6′ 10¾″)	Milton Palmer
2.10m (6′ 10¾″)	Vincent Clemmens
2.10m (6′ 10¾″)	Tim Foulger
2.08m (6′ 9¾″)	Adrian Ord
2.08m (6′ 9¾″)	Ross Hepburn
2.07m (6′ 9½″)	Alan Breden
2.07m (6′ 9½″)	Daley Thompson
2.06m (6′ 9″)	Colin Boreham
2.06m (6′ 9″)	Alan Dainton
2.06m (6′ 9″)	Rupert Charles
2.05m (6′ 8¾″)	Floyd Redley
2.05m (6′ 8¾″)	Martyn Shorten
2.05m (6′ 8¾″)	Steve Parsons
2.05m (6′ 8¾″)	Robert Gater
2.05m (6′ 8¾″)	Angus McKenzie

POLE VAULT

5.42m (17′ 9¼″)	Brian Hooper
5.25m (17′ 2¾″)	Keith Stock
5.20m (17′ 0¾″)	Jeff Gutteridge
5.18m (17′ 0″)	Steve Chappell
5.10m (16′ 8¾″)	Allan Williams
5.05m (16′ 6¾″)	Mike Bull
4.98m (16′ 4″)	Dick Williamson
4.80m (15′ 9″)	Daley Thompson
4.70m (15′ 5″)i	Andrew Jackson (4.65m)
4.60m (15′ 1″)	Rupert Goodall
4.60m (15′ 1″)	Nick Phipps
4.60m (15′ 1″)	Tim Gardner
4.60m (15′ 1″)	Andrew Jackson
4.55m (14′ 11″)	Adrian Ross
4.45m (14′ 7¼″)	James Johnstone
4.45m (14′ 7¼″)i	Norman Donachie
4.41m (14′ 5½″)	Graham Eggleton
4.40m (14′ 5¼″)	Tim Anstiss
4.40m (14′ 5¼″)	Girish Patel
4.40m (14′ 5¼″)	Panayiotis Zeniou
4.40m (14′ 5¼″)	Alan Drayton
4.40m (14′ 5¼″)	Brian Drayton

LONG JUMP

7.93m (26′ 0¼″)	Daley Thompson (8.11m)(w)
7.88m (25′ 10¼″)	Roy Mitchell (8.06m)(w)
7.75m (25′ 5¼″)	Ken Cocks
7.71m (25′ 3½″)	Billie Kirkpatrick
7.62m (25′ 0″)	Colin Mitchell
7.61m (24′ 11¾″)	Aston Moore
7.51m (24′ 7¾″)	Tony Henry
7.44m (24′ 5″)	Megarry Effiong
7.42m (24′ 4¼″)	Geoff Hignett
7.35m (24′ 1½″)	Graham Hughes
7.34m (24′ 1″)	Gus Udo (7.58m)(w)
7.34m (24′ 1″)	Roy McKenzie (7.35m)(w)
7.33m (24′ 0¾″)	David Johnson
7.33m (24′ 0¾″)	Eddie Starrs (7.40m)(w)
7.33m (24′ 0¾″)	Micky Morris
7.32m (24′ 0¼″)	Richard Smith (7.36m)(w)

Wind assisted

7.56m (24′ 9¾″)w	Peter Brugnani
7.44m (24′ 5″)w	Len Tyson
7.44m (24′ 5″)w	Henry Walters
7.41m (24′ 3¾″)w	John Gloag
7.37m (24′ 2¼″)w	Graeme Watson
7.33m (24′ 0¾″)w	Alan Drayton

TRIPLE JUMP

16.76m (55′ 0″)	Keith Connor (17.21m)(w)
16.69m (54′ 9¼″)	Aston Moore (16.76m)(w)
16.29m (53′ 5½″)i	David Johnson (16.33m(w) and 16.11m)
15.88m (52′ 1¼″)	John Phillips
15.87m (52′ 0¾″)	Chris Colman (16.17m)(w)
15.85m (52′ 0″)i	Frank Attoh (15.87m) (w) and 15.58m)
15.74m (51′ 7¾″)	Megarry Effiong
15.59m (51′ 1¾″)	Eric McCalla
15.35m (50′ 4½″)	Donovan Perkins
15.25m (50′ 0½″)	Roy McKenzie
15.17m (49′ 9¼″)	John Slaney
15.13m (49′ 7¾″)	Richard Philps (15.33m)(w)
15.11m (49′ 7″)	Matt Cannavan
15.10m (49′ 6½″)	Tim Moore
15.08m (49′ 5¾″)	Nick Stoppard (15.55m) (w)
15.06m (49′ 5″)	Albert Earle
15.03m (49′ 3¾″)	Chris Carden
15.02m (49′ 3½″)	Sean Power (Eire) (15.27m)(w)

15.00m (49' 2½") Stephen Metcalfe
(15.28m)(w)
Wind assisted
15.52m (50' 11")w Dennis Greene
15.20m (49' 10½")w Willie Clark
15.08m (49' 5¾")w David Corless

SHOT
20.68m (67' 10¼") Geoff Capes
19.12m (62' 8¾")i Mike Winch (18.64m)
18.46m (60' 6¾") Bob Dale
17.44m (57' 2¾") Hamish Davidson
17.12m (56' 2") Richard Slaney
16.83m (55' 2¾") Simon Rodhouse
16.70m (54' 9½") Paul Rees
16.66m (54' 8") Bill Fuller
16.60m (54' 5½") Tony Satchwell
16.53m (54' 2¾") Ian Lindley
16.49m (54' 1¼") Roger Kennedy
16.20m (53' 1¾") Peter Tancred
16.18m (53' 1") Ian Mowatt
16.16m (53' 0¼") Nick Tabor
16.00m (52' 6") Steve Francis
15.97m (52' 4¾") Neil Griffin
15.94m (52' 3¾") Andrew Vince
15.82m (51' 11") Dennis Roscoe
15.80m (51' 10") Sid Clark
15.47m (50' 9¼") Trevor Walhen

DISCUS
59.84m (196' 4") Colin Sutherland
57.54m (188' 9") Peter Tancred
57.02m (187' 1") Peter Gordon
56.90m (186' 8") Richard Slaney
55.18m (181' 0") Mike Winch
54.84m (179' 11") John Hillier
54.20m (177' 10") Geoff Capes
53.92m (176' 11") Dennis Roscoe
53.38m (175' 1") Neville Thompson
53.16m (174' 5") Guy Dirkin
53.12m (174' 3") Mike Cushion
51.90m (170' 3") Arthur McKenzie
51.74m (169' 9") Geoff Tyler
50.98m (167' 3") John Howell
50.94m (167' 1") Paul Rees
50.88m (166' 11") Neil Griffin
50.22m (164' 9") Tony Satchwell
50.02m (164' 1") Steve Francis
48.86m (160' 4") Ian Mowatt
48.72m (159' 10") Bill Fuller

HAMMER
70.32m (230' 8") Paul Dickenson
70.20m (230' 4") Chris Black
69.00m (226' 4") Jim Whitehead
66.76m (219' 0") Ian Chipchase
65.86m (216' 1") Matthew Mileham
64.60m (211' 11") Eugene Lawlor (Eire)
62.84m (206' 2") Peter Gordon
61.60m (202' 1") Mike Petra

61.52m (201' 10") Martin Girvan
61.34m (201' 3") Ron James
60.76m (199' 4") Andrew Pollock (Aus)
58.26m (191' 2") Malcolm Fenton
57.24m (187' 9") Alan Woods
56.64m (185' 10") Geoff Whaley
56.20m (184' 4") Nick Lia
56.04m (183' 10") Mike Mason
55.72m (182' 10") Sukh-Binder Sandhu
55.12m (180' 10") Karl Lasis
54.70m (179' 5") Peter Stark
53.94m (177' 0") Paul Rees
53.76m (176' 4") Brian Stebbings
53.16m (174' 5") Niall McDonald

JAVELIN
80.90m (265' 5") Peter De Kremer
80.62m (264' 6") Peter Yates
79.20m (259' 10") David Ottley
79.06m (259' 4") Brian Roberts
77.36m (253' 10") Simon Osborne
76.70m (251' 8") Charles Clover
75.32m (247' 1") David Travis
75.28m (247' 0") John Trower
73.94m (242' 7") Gareth Brooks
72.62m (238' 3") Ian Marsh
72.06m (236' 5") Tony Smith
69.76m (228' 10") Ken Taylor
69.76m (228' 10") Simon Pearson
69.16m (226' 11") Chris Harrison
68.44m (224' 6") Daniel Scullion
68.16m (223' 7") Tim Newenham
67.14m (220' 3") Neville Thompson
66.98m (219' 9") Jeff Brooks
66.70m (218' 10") Pawlo Ostapowycz
66.14m (217' 0") Kevin Sheppard

DECATHLON
8467 Daley Thompson
7484 Alan Drayton
7443 Pan Zeniou
7381 Graeme Watson
7287 Nick Phipps
7239 John Howell
7233 Mike Corden
7165 Brad McStravick
7025 Phil Lewis
6990 Kevan Lobb
6856 Pat Bredin
6785 Ray Knox
6742 Mike Bull
6727 Snowy Brooks
6705 Geoff Ward
6613 Bob Thorne
6568 Bill McCarron
6552 Ian Grant
6506 Peter Brugnani
6490 Kevin Maguire

233

WOMEN

100 METRES
(Fully automatic timing)
11.26	Sonia Lannaman (11.24w)
11.32	Andrea Lynch
11.49	Beverley Goddard (11.30w)
11.56	Wendy Clarke (11.38w)
11.60	Heather Hunte
11.62	Sharon Colyear (11.42w)
11.64	Kathy Smallwood (11.61w)
11.68	Margot Wells (11.53w)
11.71	Helen Golden (11.68w)
11.73	Eleanor Thomas (11.50w)
11.75	Barbara Clarke
11.76	Shelley Ratcliffe (11.74w)
11.87	Michelle Probert
11.90	Helen Barnett

Wind assisted
11.74w	Janine MacGregor
11.83w	Shirley Strong
11.84w	Lorna Boothe
11.86w	Pippa Baker

Note also hand times
11.2	Andrea Lynch
11.3	Beverley Goddard
11.3	Heather Hunte
11.4	Wendy Clarke
11.4	Margot Wells
11.5	Sharon Colyear
11.6	Eleanor Thomas
11.6w	Lynda Stewart
11.6w	Pippa Baker

200 METRES
(Fully automatic timing)
22.75	Donna Hartley
22.88	Sonia Lannaman
22.99	Kathy Smallwood (22.73w)
23.11	Beverley Goddard (22.95w)
23.26	Andrea Lynch (23.15w)
23.29	Verona Elder
23.42	Debbie Bunn
23.51	Eleanor Thomas
23.52	Sharon Colyear
23.61	Joslyn Hoyte (23.45w)
23.62	Linda McCurry
23.76	Janine MacGregor (23.54w)
23.83	Helen Golden (23.17w)
23.85	Shelley Ratcliffe (23.71w)
23.92	Wendy Clarke
23.92	Michelle Probert
24.03	Lorna Boothe
24.05	Jane Parry
23.81w	Margot Wells

Note also hand times
23.1w	Linda McCurry

23.2w	Debbie Bunn
23.6	Helen Golden
23.7	Michelle Probert
23.7	Janine MacGregor

400 METRES
51.2	Donna Hartley
51.70	Verona Elder
52.15	Joslyn Hoyte
52.98	Karen Williams
53.4	Ruth Kennedy
53.5	Gladys McCormack
53.59	Janine MacGregor
53.7	Liz Barnes
53.80	Jane Colebrook
53.98	Adrienne Smyth
54.0	Liz Eddy
54.01	Linda McCurry
54.15	Carol Dawkins
54.28	Liz Sutherland
54.3	Ann Harley
54.6	Elizabeth Beton
54.78	Lesley Kiernan
54.80	Linda Burnett
54.8	Susan Smith
55.22	Joylyn Saunders
55.2	Angela Creamer

800 METRES
2:01.2	Christine McMeekin
2:01.6	Jane Colebrook
2:01.7	Liz Barnes
2:02.6	Evelyn McMeekin
2:03.1	Christina Boxer
2:03.1	Janet Prictoe
2:03.2	Paula Newnham
2:03.6	Angela Creamer
2:03.7	Christine Benning
2:03.7	Mary Stewart
2:04.0	Alison Wright (NZ)
2:04.1	Penny Yule
2:04.3i	Verona Elder
2:04.5	Lesley Kiernan
2:05.0	Denise Kiernan
2:05.5	Cherry Hanson
2:06.3	Margaret Coomber
2:06.7	Adrienne Smyth
2:06.8	Janet Marlow
2:06.8	Alice Linton
2:06.9	Gillian Dainty

1500 METRES
4:06.0	Mary Stewart
4:07.5	Christine Benning
4:10.0	Christina Boxer

4:10.3	Penny Yule
4:11.6	Cherry Hanson
4:12.4	Christine McMeekin
4:12.5	Glynis Penny
4:12.7	Hilary Hollick
4:12.9	Alison Wright (NZ)
4:13.4	Wendy Smith
4:14.6	Ruth Smeeth
4:15.6	Sandra Arthurton
4:16.1	Ann Ford
4:16.2i	Jo White
4:16.3	Gillian Dainty
4:16.9	Paula Newnham
4:17.0	Bernadette Madigan
4:17.5	Paula Fudge
4:18.0	Angela Mason
4:18.0	Sharon Harvey

Jo White.   Peter Tempest

3000 METRES

8:48.7	Paula Fudge
8:52.3	Christine Benning
8:53.1	Ann Ford
9:06.4	Glynis Penny
9:08.6	Penny Yule
9:11.2	Joyce Smith
9:13.9	Alison Wright (NZ)
9:15.8	Ruth Smeeth
9:15.9	Kathy Binns
9:18.6	Thelwyn Bateman
9:18.9	Annette Roberts
9:20.3	Jill Clarke
9:20.7	Monica Joyce
9:21.8	Wendy Smith
9:23.0	Carol Gould
9:25.1	Susan Simpkin
9:26.6	Lynne Harvey
9:27.2	Angela Mason
9:28.6	Betty Green
9:29.5	Julie Armstrong

100 METRES HURDLES

13.08	Lorna Boothe (12.98w)
13.23	Sharon Colyear (13.12w)
13.41	Shirley Strong (13.08w)
13.65	Wendy McDonnell
13.77	Yvette Wray
13.81	Blondelle Caines (13.53w)
13.82	Ann Simmonds
13.85	Judy Vernon (13.68w)
13.88	Elaine Davidson (13.76w)
13.99	Judy Livermore
14.11	Violet Douglas (14.04w)
14.17	Sue Mapstone
14.23	Theresa Chipp (14.01w)
14.26	Sue Longden
14.34	Moira Walls (14.27w)

Wind assisted

14.25w	Sue Morley
14.27w	Heather Ross

Note also hand times

13.7	Blondelle Caines
13.8	Elaine Davidson (13.7w)
13.9	Judy Livermore
14.0w	Sheila Drysdale
14.1	Catherine Hardaker
14.1w	Susan Dalgoutté
14.1w	Heather Ross

400 METRES HURDLES

57.0	Christine Warden
57.43	Liz Sutherland
59.02	Susan Smith
59.15	Jannette Roscoe
59.2	Jane Colebrook
59.53	Veronica Langley
59.64	Diane Heath
59.9	Denise Kiernan
60.36	Susan Dalgoutté

60.5	Sue Reed
60.5	Linda Brady
60.6	Frances McCall
60.6	Amanda Stacey
60.69	Wendy Griffiths
60.9	Gillian Mather
61.07	Kim Tuffnell
61.2	Catherine Hardaker
61.3	Fiona Paterson
61.5	Margaret Marshall
61.78	Violet Douglas

HIGH JUMP

1.85m (6′ 0¾″)	Gillian Hitchen
1.83m (6′ 0″)	Val Rutter
1.83m (6′ 0″)	Louise Miller
1.82m (5′ 11½″)	Diane Elliott
1.81m (5′ 11¼″)	Barbara Simmonds
1.80m (5′ 10¾″)	Ros Few
1.80m (5′ 10¾″)	Ann Marie Devally
1.80m (5′ 10¾″)	Judy Livermore
1.79m (5′ 10½″)	Linda Haysman
1.79m (5′ 10½″)	Brenda Gibbs
1.79m (5′ 10½″)	Gillian Howell
1.79m (5′ 10½″)	Carol Mathers
1.79m (5′ 10½″)	Moira Walls
1.78m (5′ 10″)	Kim Hagger
1.78m (5′ 10″)	Heather Spencer
1.78m (5′ 10″)i	Allison Manley
1.77m (5′ 9¾″)	Tonia Philpotts
1.77m (5′ 9¾″)	Valerie Kelly
1.76m (5′ 9¼″)	Joy Crouchley
1.76m (5′ 9¼″)	Veronica Langley
1.76m (5′ 9¼″)	Jackie Pinkerton
1.76m (5′ 9¼″)i	Claire Summerfield

LONG JUMP

6.59m (21′ 7½″)	Susan Reeve (6.64m)(w)
6.40m (21′ 0″)	Susan Hearnshaw (6.59m)(w)
6.33m (20′ 9¼″)	Ruth Howell
6.28m (20′ 7¼″)	Sharon Colyear (6.42m)(w)
6.24m (20′ 5¼″)	Barbara Clarke
6.21m (20′ 4½″)	Janet Frank-Lynch (6.34m)(w)
6.19m (20′ 3¾″)	Jill Davies (6.34m)(w)
6.17m (20′ 3″)	Carol Earlington
6.17m (20′ 3″)	Moira Walls
6.13m (20′ 1½″)i	Sue Longden (6.00m)
6.12m (20′ 1″)	Ann Simmonds (6.27m)(w)
6.06m (19′ 10¾″)	Sue Mapstone
6.05m (19′ 10¼″)i	Gillian Regan
6.04m (19′ 9¾″)	Gillian Howell
6.02m (19′ 9″)	Allison Manley
6.02m (19′ 9″)	Tina Greisen
6.01m (19′ 8¾″)	Val Mullin
5.98m (19′ 7½″)	Sandy French (5.99m)(w)
5.98m (19′ 7½″)	Janet Peacock
5.97m (19′ 7″)	Susan Hay (6.10m)(w)

Wind assisted

6.08m (19′ 11½″)w	Janice Arscott
6.04m (19′ 9¾″)w	Yvette Wray

SHOT

16.74m (54′ 11¼″)i	Judith Oakes (16.14m)
16.40m (53′ 9¾″)	Margaret Ritchie
16.34m (53′ 7½″)	Angela Littlewood
15.72m (51′ 7″)	Brenda Bedford
15.52m (50′ 11″)	Venissa Head
15.27m (50′ 1¼″)	Janis Kerr
15.09m (49′ 6¼″)	Lana Newton
15.03m (49′ 3¾″)	Vanessa Redford
14.81m (48′ 7¼″)	Vivienne Head
14.54m (47′ 8½″)	Janet Thompson
14.27m (46′ 8¼″)	Janet Beese
13.95m (45′ 9¼″)	Susan Tudor
13.82m (45′ 4¼″)	Elizabeth Elliott
13.75m (45′ 1½″)	Suzanne Allday
13.69m (44′ 11″)i	Catherine Hartnell
13.58m (44′ 6¾″)	Helen Clarke
13.58m (44′ 6¾″)i	Nnenna Njoku (Nigeria)
13.18m (43′ 3″)	Caroline Dyer
13.17m (43′ 2½″)	Sue Reeve
13.13m (43′ 1″)	Beverley Wright
13.08m (42′ 11″)	Heather Yule

DISCUS

60.80m (199′ 6″)	Margaret Ritchie
55.06m (180′ 8″)	Janet Thompson
51.04m (167′ 5″)	Lesley Mallin
49.06m (160′ 11″)	Janis Kerr
49.00m (160′ 9″)	Vanessa Redford
48.24m (158′ 3″)	Denise Sturman
48.22m (158′ 2″)	Angela Littlewood
47.64m (156′ 3″)	Fiona Condon
47.40m (155′ 6″)	Vivienne Head
46.44m (152′ 4″)	Nnenna Njoku (Nigeria)
45.76m (150′ 1″)	Jean Robertson
45.72m (150′ 0″)	Janet Beese
45.72m (150′ 0″)	Venissa Head
45.46m (149′ 2″)	Jo Frampton
44.90m (147′ 4″)	Amanda Franks
44.66m (146′ 6″)	Suzanne Allday
44.64m (146′ 5″)	Christine Chalk
44.26m (145′ 2″)	Rosemary Payne
43.58m (143′ 0″)	Judith Oakes
43.40m (142′ 5″)	Susan Tudor
43.36m (142′ 3″)	Diane English

JAVELIN

64.00m (210′ 0″)	Tessa Sanderson
53.88m (176′ 9″)	Fatima Whitbread
53.32m (174′ 11″)	Maxine Jervis
52.16m (171′ 1″)	Sandra O'Toole
52.04m (170′ 9″)	Jackie Zaslona
51.74m (169′ 9″)	Diane Williams
51.20m (168′ 0″)	Jeanette Rose

50.84m (166′ 9″)	Shara Spragg	4119	Sue Longden
50.80m (166′ 8″)	Ann Farquhar	4070	Gillian Howell
50.20m (164′ 8″)	Janeen Williams	4028	Judy Livermore
47.70m (156′ 6″)	Sara Fry	4022	Ruth Howell
47.44m (155′ 8″)	Sue Flack	4013	Val Mullin
47.08m (154′ 5″)	Jean Lintern	3936	Veronica Langley
47.08m (154′ 5″)	Yvonne Fountain	3907	Kim Hagger
47.02m (154′ 3″)	Linda Stratford	3826	Allison Manley
45.56m (149′ 6″)	Val Price	3756	Val Kelly
45.10m (147′ 11″)	Susan James	3702	Rosemarie Hudson
44.96m (147′ 6″)	Nnenna Njoku (Nigeria)	3668	Shirley Dewhirst
44.58m (146′ 3″)	Sandra Williams	3636	Wendy Phillips
43.68m (143′ 4″)	Pamela Brindle	3575	Sarah Bull
43.18m (141′ 8″)	J. Eliot	3544	Margaret Sommerville
		3535	Marcia Marriott
PENTATHLON		3491	Vivienne Weston
4292	Yvette Wray	3483	Barbara Corbett
4222	Sue Mapstone	3466	Janet Manson

Previous page: *Meg Ritchie*   Tony Duffy

238

Major Fixtures for 1979
(May to September)

MAY

13   AAA Marathon Championship, Coventry.
16   Philips Night of Athletics, Crystal Palace.
26–27   Netherlands v UK v Denmark Decathlon and Pentathlon, Roosendaal.
27–28   Inter-Counties Championships, Cwmbran.

JUNE

2–3   European Champion Clubs Trophy, Lisbon.
6   England v Kenya v Canada (Men's Track Events), Gateshead.
9   European Trophy Marathon, Brussels.
10   England v Scotland v Belgium v Norway (Men), Gateshead.
17   Women's AAA Marathon Championship, Sandbach.
23–24   Germany v UK v Poland v Switzerland.
30   UK v France 'B', Cwmbran; European Cup Semi-Final (Women), Sofia.
30–1   European Cup Semi-Finals (Men),
July   Malmo, Geneva and Ludenscheid.

JULY

1   European Cup Semi-Finals (Women), Cwmbran and Sittard.
1–15   Pan-American Games, San Juan (Puerto Rico).
6–7   English Schools Championships, Nottingham.
8   Gateshead Games.
13–14   AAA Championships, Crystal Palace.
14–15   European Cup for Combined Events (Decathlon and Pentathlon) Semi-Finals, Schielleiten, Budapest and Bremen.

21–22   AAA Under-20 Championships, Cleckheaton; World Veterans 10km and 25km Road Championships, Bolton.
24–29   International Spartakiade, Moscow.
27–28   Women's AAA Championships, Crystal Palace.
27–29   International Veterans Meeting, Hannover.
29   Dewhurst Invitation Games.

AUGUST

1   UK v Italy v Canada (Juniors), Wolverhampton.
4–5   European Cup Final, Turin.
11–12   UK Championships, Birmingham; USA v USSR.
16–19   European Junior Championships, Bydgoszcz.
18   Edinburgh Highland Games, Meadowbank.
24–26   World Cup, Montreal.
25–26   Lugano Trophy (Walking) Semi-Finals, Hove, Reus (Spa) and Gdansk.
27   England v Poland v Switzerland (Men's Track Events), Crystal Palace.
31   International Rotary, Crystal Palace.

SEPTEMBER

1   GRE Cup Finals, Crystal Palace; International Team Marathon, Karl-Marx-Stadt.
1–2   European Cup for Combined Events Final, Dresden.
2–13   World Student Games, Mexico City.
8–9   UK v Yugoslavia, Gateshead.
14   IAC/Coca Cola Meeting, Crystal Palace.
22   RRC International Marathon, Milton Keynes.
22–23   UK v USSR, Crystal Palace.
29–30   Lugano Trophy (Walking) Final, Eschborn.

Fancy a quick Steak Sandwich on Lap 18?

It's impossible, of course. But still not quite so ridiculous as it may seem. Whereas starchy foods often provide you with instant bursts of energy, meat turns into energy slowly, and its effects last for several hours. In other words, that juicy piece of steak could give you the energy you need during Lap 18 to break away from the rest of the field. Meat, quite simply, builds stamina. And for the very best in meat, you simply have to come to Dewhurst.

DEWHURST
The Master Butcher